Dating, Intimacy *Relationships* *Love* *Commitment* *and Happiness*

The Eight Stages Women Who Succeed Go Through

(and why so many of us lose our way)

Luis Ipinazar

Request 52 free pages at free52pages@gmail.com or free52pages@outlook.com

Copyright © Luis Ipinazar 2017

All rights reserved. No part of this publication may be reproduced, stored in a retrieval system, or transmitted in any form or by any means, electronic, photocopying, mechanical, recording or otherwise, without prior written permission by the author-publisher.

AUTHOR CONTACT DETAILS
The author-publisher's telephone number and mailing address in Sydney (Australia) are in the last two pages of the "free 52 pages" PDF. Download it by saying "hi" to his no-reply automatic responder at *free52pages@gmail.com* or *free52pages@outlook.com*. Letters to the author-publisher need to include a self addressed stamped envelope and an email address. Business and professional contacts with a company letterhead are welcome. Mail from the general public is welcome too, but may not be replied to unless accompanied by a $5 handling fee, as a cheque payable to Luis Ipinazar.

National Library of Australia.
Cataloging-in-Publication entry.

Ipinazar, Luis, author.

Dating, Intimacy, Relationships, Love, Commitment and Happiness: The Eight Stages Women Who Succeed Go Through *(and why so many of us lose our way).*
/ Luis Ipinazar.

ISBN   978 0 646 96216 0   (paperback)

1 Love. 2 Man-woman relationships. 3 Dating. 4 Emotions. 5 Interpersonal communication. 6 Sex. 7 Self-help techniques.

646.77

Check prices!   There are big price differences between online bookstores, mentioned in the third last page of the "free 52 pages" PDF. For how to download it, see *author contact details* above.

Specifications   Has 140,339 words, 336 pages. Size A5 (8.27 x 5.83 inches or 21 x 14.8 cm). Main text Times New Roman 11. Weight 442 gm.

Acknowledgment

As a now more mature and wiser man, I am grateful to the smart women in my life. By sharing their observations they were teaching me about my feelings and those of others, and that helped me to develop a healthier and sturdier inner balance. I especially thank the countless men and women who sought my advice over the years, because on opening their hearts and discussing their concerns they were educating me too.

And a second reason for this acknowledgment is to remind every man that there is a lot we can learn, by simply listening carefully to the woman we love.

A thought to begin with

Knowledge is less than wisdom, but acquiring sufficient high quality relationship-relevant knowledge can provide a burst of acceleration to the process of improving whatever level of relationship wisdom we already have. This could be enough to tilt the balance towards better outcomes in love, work, friendships, and other situations which require considered thinking and careful management of emotions and actions.

Contents

A SHOULD-READ-FIRST INTRODUCTION 011

    Precautionary comments and three assurances about
the quality of books on sexually intimate relationships 011

    The four deeper issues influencing how established
relationships function: Emotional balance, emotional
intelligence, relationship knowledge and maturity-wisdom 014

    The question of finding true love and keeping it for life ………... 018

STAGE 1 - MANAGING THE BREAKUPS:
Time for healing solitude and helpful reflection 020

    First reactions if our partner has left us 020
    "All men are bastards" talk 021
    Sense of liberation when we have left our partner 022
    Duration of Stage 1 022

STAGE 2 - EXPLORATORY EARLY STEPS:
Cautious tentative risks and hurried retreats ... 023

    Ideologies of independence 023
    Blaming ourselves or others for our mistakes 024

STAGE 3 - THE STARRY-EYED PHASE:
Searching for the man we believe we want 026

    Where we are at when the search begins 026
    The qualities we believe Mr. Right must have 027

STAGE 4 - THE PERFECT MAN MUDDLE:
From collisions with reality to growing unease 029

    I am not looking for a perfect man 029
    Collisions with reality and growing unease 031
    The influence of predominant culture 034
    Recognizing unwanted clutter for what it is 036

Acknowledging facts that make a difference 037
Are we giving men negative messages without realizing it? 039

STAGE 5 - THE NEED TO UNDERSTAND:
Why established relationships suceed or fail 047

The visible and deeper reasons why relationships succeed or fail 048

"First order" and "second order" understandings 051

Intellectual-emotional equipment for second order understanding ... 054

Personality: The six core components 055

Conviction of worthiness: The
foundation of personality and self esteem 055

- Unconscious conviction of lovability:
  The case of eight year old Christine 058
- Unconscious conviction of competence:
  The case of the boy under four 060

Self-other acceptance 063

Self-other awareness 066

Self-other respect 068

Sense of identity and meaning 069

Self confidence 075

Self esteem: An important but misunderstood issue 076

The American controversy about the definition of self esteem 076

What exactly is self esteem? 078

The better and second best varieties
of self esteem: Secure and Contingent 080

The foundation, core and peripheral
components of self esteem and personality 084

Self esteem from best to worst: Where
we fit, how it shows and what underpins it 087

How and why contingent or secure
self esteem begin to develop in childhood 090

Contingent self esteem and the problems it creates 097

| 006 | Secure self esteem and the benefits it brings .... 100 |

How the kind and level of self esteem can
damage or benefit adult intimate relationships 105

The influence of self esteem and personal
development on marital therapy outcomes 111

How to improve self esteem as an adult 113

- The process of "second order" understanding and
  intervention in the case of the excessively jealous wife 115
- A "second order" analysis in the case of the
  excessively jealous wife, and avenues for improvement 119

Communication: Bigger, smaller and sum-total problems ... 123

Bigger problems 123

Smaller problems 125

Sum-total problems 129

Love: What it is and how to improve our skills at it 132

What is love? 132

The art and skills of getting better at loving 135

What can happen when we lack the skills of loving 139

Happiness: What it is and depends on 140

Prevailing views on what influences happiness 140

The four categories of inherent higher needs 142

The role of self esteem in meeting inherent higher needs 146

What is happiness? 149

Putting it all together: The deeper and truer
reasons why established relationships succeed or fail 151

For counselors, teachers and researchers:
A core components theory of personality and self esteem,
integrating couples communication, love and happiness 157

STAGE 6 - SEARCHING COMPETENTLY:
How to recognize Mr. Rights and Mr. Wrongs 161

Four conditions for searching competently, and four critical
issues influencing whether a relationship will succeed or fail ...161

Four major partner compatibility evaluation areas, and
three absolute minimum requirements for a relationship to work 163

The relatively less harmful Mr. Wrongs 165

The not attractive enough 165

Men with personality problems, limitations or difficulties 166

Men who lie up to a point 167

Significantly younger men 168

Men who are much less educated, less intelligent, and/or boring 169

Definitely dangerous men (and women) 171

Potential domestic violence perpetrators 172

- Kinds of victim powerlessness and implications for counselling 175
- Feminism's excesses and disregard about female perpetrators 177

Emotional time bombs 182

Macho men 185

Certifiable bastards 186

More about dangerous men *(and women)* 190

Desirable personality qualities in men (and women) 194

Tempered honesty, fairness, responsibility 195

Self-other awareness, emotional
intelligence, communication skills 198

Flexibility, tolerance, optimism 200

Active kindness: The most important quality 201

Further issues in the search for Mr. Right 202

Do similarities and differences matter? 203

Do significantly older men qualify? 205

Financial security and family responsibilities 208

Selecting a man or settling for one? 209

Problems and potential of Internet dating and hook-up sites 211

Safer sex issues: Information, criminality and irresponsibility 214

STAGE 7 - OUTSMARTING THE TRAP:
Designing and implementing an Action Plan ... 218

Robert and his beloved: A case to motivate us 218

Time Is Short: Life's Turning Points 219

Considerations before designing an Action Plan 223

Rationale and components of the Action Plan 225

Other advantages of implementing the Action Plan 229

The risks and potential of the Action Plan 231

STAGE 8a - ENSURING IT WORKS FOR LIFE:
Some important things to know and to avoid .. 235

Some important things to know 235

Predictable stress periods and pressure points 237

The role of sex in men's non-sexual needs 239

The gradual turnaround in gender relationship power 241

Some important things to avoid 248

Neglect of care and domestic abuse 248

Destructive complaints 251

Marital sadism 253

STAGE 8b - SEX, LOVE AND MONOGAMY:
Needs, wishes, fears, low desire and solutions 256

The three C's women need in order to be happy, or is it four? 256

Bedroom competence begins with knowing who and how we are .. 259

Why a man's personality makes a big difference in the bedroom ... 263

The consequences of childhood sexual abuse 265

Pain during intercourse, genuine, misdiagnosed and fake 267

Dealing with normal differences in sexual desire 269
Other sexual tensions in established couples 272
The six major factors influencing sexual desire and enjoyment 276
Safe and risky sexual fantasies, consequences
of mismanaging them, alternatives to "yes" or "no",
and the importance of understanding and caring 278

- The woman who asked to watch her
  man urinating, and its unexpected bonus 281
- The woman who dared to request
  having her man tied up and blindfolded 284
- Two female fantasies about rape: Tied
  up while having sex, and home intruder 285
- The man who asked his woman how
  she would feel about trying bottom sex 287
- The man who asked his woman to
  consider swinging with safety precautions 292
- The grass is greener elsewhere: The
  most common and dangerous fantasy 294

How to get dearly loved, as well as forgiven for our favorite faults 298
Recapitulation about influences from the relationship
knowledge environment, and barriers to improvement 302

Autobiographical Appendixes

Appx. A - THE DOORS OF HEAVEN:
            Boyhood rites of passage before the days of sex education 304
Appx. B - THE JAPANESE CONNECTION:
            Men's fascination with women's bottoms 310
Appx. C - PRESCRIPTION GLASSES CAN BE SEXY:
            The formation and reshaping of sexual preferences 314

Qualifications and References

Reference 1, NSW University degree with subjects and grades over 5 years ... 316
Reference 2 regarding expertise in relationship therapy and education 318
Reference 3 regarding expertise in relationship therapy and education 320
Reference 4 regarding expertise in relationship therapy and education 322

Reference 5 re. expertise in relationship therapy and education 324
Reference 6 by Editor of the ANZ Journal of Family Therapy 326
Refer. 7 by University of NSW re. Adult Intimate Relationships Course 328
Refer. 8 by NSW Department of Health re. Marital Communication Course 330
Refer. 9 by Leichhardt Women's Health Centre re. voluntary work 332
Refer. 10 by Lucy's Out West Single Women's Refuge re. voluntary work .. 334

Diagrams and Tables

DIAGRAM 1 - Conviction of Worthiness and Self Esteem:
Secure, contingent, higher, lower 083

DIAGRAM 2 - Personality and Self Esteem:
The Core and Peripheral Components 085

DIAGRAM 3 - Normal Distribution Curve for quality and
levels of Self Esteem and Personal Development 088

TABLE A - Comparing feelings, thoughts and behaviors
by location in the Normal Distribution Curve 089

DIAGRAM 4 - The Deeper Motivation Cycle
propelling feelings, thoughts and behaviors 091

DIAGRAM 5 - Perceptual and communication
differences between men and women 127

DIAGRAM 6 - Couple conflict accumulation
by poor communication plus underlying issues 130

TABLE B1 - Core component features in people *low* in
the Diagram 3 normal curve, plus consequences 154

TABLE B2 - Core component features in people *high* in
the Diagram 3 normal curve, plus consequences 155

TABLE C - Typical age gaps between women and the
NUSSC men they tend to get as permanent partners 246

DIAGRAM 7 - Safe and risky sexual fantasies, consequences
of mismanaging them, alternatives to "yes" or "no"
and the importance of understanding and caring 279

DIAGRAM 8 - Influences from the relationship knowledge
environment, and barriers to improvement 302

Jokes

- The fire and brimstone preacher 017
- A sexist joke about men 178
- The bickering couple 197
- Why men are relationship socialists 218
- Why women like wearing high heel shoes 242
- Men's marital bliss fantasy 258

A SHOULD-READ-FIRST INTRODUCTION

Sexually intimate relationships are a part of life where personal development is most needed and most lacking. I have written this book after twenty five years experience as a relationship therapy and education specialist, preceded by a degree with top marks at a reputable university. It provides comprehensive professional quality education on love and relationships for fully grown adults, whether they are looking for a life partner or have one already.

In either case, superior knowledge about relationships will increase the person's capacity to anticipate problems, plan strategy, cope with the pressures, learn from mistakes, strengthen his/her confidence, and become surer about which compromises are and aren't worth making. Doing it all as best as possible requires a clear understanding of the deeper and often obscure issues that really matter, for strengthening a couple's bonds and making it work for life.

Every partner has a unique configuration of personality and circumstances. This determines how they interpret reality and react to it, how they interact and influence each other, and how well they manage the inevitable tensions. Such complexities should never be ignored, or simplified over a limit beyond which any education or advice is bound to be superficial and ineffectual. Readers, adult education students and therapy clients are entitled to be treated with honesty and competence, although quite frequently they are not. How and why this happens is discussed in the next heading.

Because there are so many relevant matters, various sections of the book come with different flavors. For example, parts of this introduction may feel a little academic. Stages 1 to 4 are as easy to read as the average supermarket magazine. Stage 5 will take some effort, not because it is difficult, but due to the large amount of information to be chewed and digested.

The more intricate critical issues are discussed in a manner reasonably easy to understand and remember, without sacrificing the depth or breadth of what needs to be addressed. Presenting the complexities of personality and relationships in relatively simple terms is an intellectual and artistic challenge, and readers will be the ultimate judges of my efforts at doing so.

Precautionary comments and three assurances about the quality of books on sexually intimate relationships

The question of whether any book on intimate love relationships, course or relationship therapist/counselor/clinician is good enough to be trusted deserves careful consideration. There is an overabundance of them making unrealistic claims, without due regard for the difficulties involved. Therefore we need to keep in mind that the level of expertise of all writers, teachers and therapists is open to question, for several reasons.

Very few combinations of a university degree plus subsequent occupation provide a suitable foundation for building up the relevant knowledge, let alone an ideal one. Most practicing therapists have had little or limited experience working with couples, and hardly any of them would have been long term full time specialists. But even if they have, many years doing that (or any other job) is not the same as being good at it.

Therapists or writers could be overestimating their competence, because they are unaware of how much there is that they don't know. In addition some might be exaggerating that overestimation, in ways which involve a degree of self delusion in addition to the dishonesty. Their main motivation may have been to make money and elevate their status, rather than to produce a book or course which can actually help, or to provide effective therapy.

Therefore we need to be careful before relying on advice, especially about something as potentially complicated as the deeper reasons for relationship problems and the personality factors underpinning them. Therapeutic excellence requires (1) superior understanding, (2) many years experience in the field of specialization, plus most importantly (3) a healthy and well developed personality with an inclination for honesty and helping people (as against a proclivity for deceiving or taking advantage of others).

Only the small minority of clinicians who have all three to a high enough level are able to develop the necessary but difficult to master combination of knowledge, intuition and skills which leads to a good reputation among peers, clients and readers. This is the case with every therapist and writer regardless of any postgraduate or fancy named degree, impressive job title, and anything else suggestive of credibility or competence.

All the above **precautionary comments** apply equally to me and this book, to any presentation or course we attend, and to any therapist we consult. There is a possibility or probability of being misinformed or under informed, and that could be costly when an important relationship is at stake. Given the reality of human imperfections, some risk is inevitable. But it can be greatly reduced by the combined effect of **three assurances**.

The <u>first assurance</u> is that qualification documents need to be from a reputable university easily contactable for verification. Apart from the commemorative degree title, such documents are also and always officially issued with grades in all subjects undertaken during every year of the degree, and that constitutes reliable evidence of academic performance.

If that evidence is good, it would be in the interest of writers, educators and therapists to show it. That is because everyone realizes that other things being equal enough, graduates whose marks were distinctions and high distinctions for example, can be expected to have become better therapists than those whose marks were just passes or credits. Therefore, if they are unwilling or allegedly unable to show a university issued qualification document with marks in all their subjects for every year of their degree, they may well have something to hide.

A second assurance involves providing reliable references, because even impressive grades, high qualifications or prestigious job titles cannot guarantee therapeutic excellence. But if there are a number of good references by respected professionals who knew well the writer-therapist and his work, any education or counseling provided by the latter is likely to be trustworthy.

The third assurance is evidence of voluntary work in the field of specialization, because it shows that the person is not too materialistic or status oriented. Again, that makes it more likely that the intention was to produce an honest book, presentation or course to genuinely assist people, rather than a feel-good one intended primarily to maximize popularity and sales.

As a testimonial of professional credibility, I have included References 1 to 10. They are listed in the Table of Contents, and taken as a whole represent **compelling evidence for the three assurances**. They include my degree with all subjects and grades over five years. Then there are five references regarding my level of expertise in relationship therapy and education by highly reputable and experienced clinicians who had known me for years, seen my work with couples live through one-way screens, and/or attended my case presentations.

There are two references on the quality of short relationship education courses created and run by me. One for professional counselors as part of the 1993 Summer Studies Program run jointly by Sydney and NSW Universities, and the other for the general public within the NSW Department of Health. And finally, two references about voluntary work with Leichhardt Women's Health Centre and Lucy's Out West Single Women's Refuge.

Five of the above references are a selection from many more written around 1990 by current and former colleagues, in support of my re-grading and salary increase application. That was based exclusively on the grounds of especial expertise in relationship therapy and education. The application was submitted to my then employer the NSW Department of Health, and granted as per recommendation by an independent Grading Committee.

The ten original references are in A4 size paper, and were written in typewriters or word processors during the first twelve years of my career. Some are a bit faded by now, and one or two are photocopies of the originals which have since been lost. Furthermore, in order to make their photographic copies fit inside the 13 mm. margins of the half-A4 book size pages, they needed to be reduced to about 36% of their original surface area. All that makes some of those copies a bit hard to read.

Therefore, only the key parts of every A4 size reference have been re-typed, to make them easier to read while still fitting them inside the much smaller space available in the half-A4 size book pages. However, if we are to trust information or advice about managing important relationship issues, it is essential to be able to verify all claimed evidence of expertise. To facilitate verifiability, each of the partly re-typed ten references and the reduced size picture of its original are placed next to each other in opposite pages.

The four deeper issues influencing how established relationships function: Emotional balance, emotional intelligence, relationship knowledge and maturity-wisdom

On considering any relationship issues associated with the extent to which someone's personality incorporates the above features, each person-situation configuration is unique and needs to be assessed on its merits. With that kept in mind, some generalizations can still be useful and I list three below:

- All the above four features (and other related ones) are interconnected and influence one another.
- The timely acquisition of relevant knowledge can improve them and make a difference in our life, but there is no complete substitute for life experience.
- Relevant knowledge can help develop associated skills, and these too contribute to those personality features being noticeably better in some people.

One starting point in thinking about the importance to us of emotional balance, emotional intelligence, relationship knowledge and maturity-wisdom is to ask ourselves four questions, and then reflect on issues A to D:

1. Do I know what level of the above features I have?

2. Do I need or want a higher level of them? If I do,
3. Am I wiling to do the work needed to achieve it?
4. Given the levels I am at, is it worth all the effort?

A. To the extent that I lose my temper or become annoyed when I don't get what I want, whether it shows or stays hidden, there may be room for improvement in my current level of *emotional balance*.

B. To the extent that I tend to blame other people for my problems, as against accepting sufficient personal responsibility, there may be room for improvement in my current level of *emotional intelligence*.

C. To the extent that my relationships have been unsuccessful, or that I avoid them for fear of the pain they can cause me, there may be room for improvement in my current level of *relationship knowledge*.

D. To the extent that I am not sure I can figure out correctly enough what is really going on within me and within the person I am having or intending to have a relationship with, there may be room for improvement in the kind of perceptions and insights which would enable me to increase my current level of *maturity-wisdom*.

In Stage 5 during my elaboration on what love is, I mention that "nobody who is reasonably informed and moderately sane has ever claimed that love is easy to understand". This matters, because nearly all of us have had at least one significant relationship which did not work. We may comprehend what happened and why, but only to the depth which our perception and insight are able to reach. Sometimes this may be enough to explain everything, but quite often it isn't, and we are left wondering or uncertain.

That is when we get a gnawing feeling that something deeper is going on, although we can't quite put the finger on precisely what it is. However, understanding the deeper issues influencing how a relationship functions is important. If we don't there is a risk it may fail, as indeed could any subsequent ones, since our actions will not be based on sound knowledge about the reasons which matter most in determining the final outcome.

Those reasons are discussed in Stage 5, which is the longest and most important chapter. It has definitions and extensive elaborations on the core components of personality and self esteem, couples communication, love and happiness. As a whole, these constitute what I have called a core components theory of personality and self esteem.

Like every other theory, this one is nothing more than a group of interconnected ideas. It can help us develop a deeper understanding of the nature and causes of relationship problems, and suggest possible ways of resolving or better managing them. The theory plus a number of related contemporary issues about counseling, education and research are summarized in Stage 5 under the heading *For counselors, teachers and researchers: A core components theory of personality and self esteem, integrating couples communication, love and happiness.*

Stage 5 includes many real life examples of how and why contentment or dissatisfaction in any relationship are greatly affected by personality and self esteem, and the reasons why they may develop the right or the wrong way from early in childhood. The cases discussed may add to parents' appreciation of what to do and avoid in order to help their children develop a personality and self esteem as healthy and resilient as possible.

The above is expanded by issues discussed in Stages 6 and 8, centered around more of the thoughts, feelings and behaviors which influence whether relationships will succeed or fail. The totality of that knowledge, if properly understood, increases the chances we will make better informed decisions about which potential partners are and aren't worth trying. And then, of managing constructively the unavoidable major and minor differences.

If we could see our future as in a film, depicting for us the options we have and the precise consequences of each, we would choose correctly. But the best we can do in order to anticipate the outcome of our choices, is to do the learning and reflection needed to achieve an understanding as accurate as possible of the issues at hand and how to manage them in the best possible way. Doing this is how, overtime, knowledge can help to increase wisdom.

While this book is designed primarily for women searching for a life partner, it can be equally useful for single men and heterosexual or same sex couples. Established partners should read at least this introduction plus Stages 5, 6 and 8, encompassing the over 80% of the book which is most relevant for couples. That can give them a shared knowledge base and terminology, which will help when they have to talk about the delicate issues and tensions which exist in every successful relationship.

Discussion can be encouraged and focused on what matters by each person marking areas of interest on the margins as a reminder, preferably with pencil because it does not stand out too much and can be erased or changed. Again, this can improve intimate communication and generate ideas about how to better manage or resolve problems, before they deteriorate seriously and perhaps irreversibly.

Like every book on the psychology of individuals and relationships, this one may activate a natural propensity to misinterpret things in a manner which suits us, by over-focusing on what we like and ignoring or distorting the points that feel threatening or unfamiliar. Therefore we may fail to pay attention to the very things which could be most important, in terms of helping us advance our personal development.

Probably we have all done this without realizing it, and there is an old joke which illustrates how and why it happens: *During a sermon to his congregation, a fire and brimstone preacher put a worm into a glass of water for ten seconds and then pulled it out still wriggling. Next he put it into a glass of whiskey for another ten seconds and the worm came out dead.*

Leaning down from the pulpit towards the benches where the hard drinking menfolk sat, he lifted his finger to command attention and asked in a stern voice what the lesson was from the dead worm. The local drunk who hadn't realized it was a rhetorical question, struggled to stand up and replied "If you drink plenty of whiskey you never get worms."

Likewise, self serving faulty interpretations or failure to grasp the wider issue are common. Which is why neither this book nor any other can do more than assist readers, in learning about personality and relationships through live experiences with real people. This said, there is no doubt that the contribution which a good and timely book can make towards understanding the deeper layers of ourselves, others and relationships, could be significant enough to tilt our life towards better outcomes.

Such contribution can be helpful for everyone, including those whose personalities were affected by less than ideal family circumstances as children. If they never improve their problem areas, parts of themselves will remain stuck where they were during childhood or adolescence. Their usual quick fix attempts rarely work for long, and their insufficient understanding of themselves and others keeps leaving them bewildered.

This underdeveloped capacity for insight is often accompanied by a propensity for inappropriate or excessive emotional reactions, especially under stress. They may not fully realize the nature of those reactions or comprehend the true reasons behind them, and to that extent they are unable to do anything about it. Consequently they remain disproportionately vulnerable to life pressures, unless luck is temporarily on their side.

A common problem between husbands and wives arises when a widening gap has developed over the years, in self-other awareness and understanding of their marriage and people related issues. That can make it increasingly difficult for them to retain a stimulating meaningful friendship or manage differences through effective communication. It may combine with other stressors in creating significant tensions, causing ongoing unhappiness and an increased likelihood of divorce.

018 Husbands and male partners who get this book as a present may wish to read parts of it for educational purposes, on the grounds that much of it is about women and they are living with one. Furthermore, they couldn't possibly be blamed for the author reminding wives about certain facts of life regarding their responsibilities about sexuality and respect within marriage. They might also like the fact that it is written by a man, who understands the male perspective in addition to the concerns of women.

The question of finding true love and keeping it for life

Choosing a life partner is the biggest gamble and piece of horse trading most of us will ever undertake. In addition to the hard bargaining, the singles jungle is plagued by unrealistic expectations, misunderstandings, half truths, downright lies, stupid mistakes, plus all kinds of hopefully polite direct and indirect rejecting and being rejected. Holding ourselves steady in such an emotionally destabilizing environment is easier when we have self-trust.

First of all trust in our own instinct to differentiate between men who have the potential to love us the way we want to be loved, those who don't, and the ones dishonest enough to lie about the prospects of a relationship in order to keep it while it suits them. And second, trust in the reliability of our mind as a means for understanding what is going wrong when we are not succeeding, for maintaining our feelings reasonably balanced as we deal with disappointments, and for working out how not to repeat the mistakes.

Getting the sense of control and empowerment needed to do all that requires enough of the kind of knowledge which is clear, real and useful, as against obscure, fake or useless. And gradually shedding off the latter as we come to understand and absorb the better alternatives. That may be difficult, because familiar ways of thinking and acting feel easier, while acquiring new knowledge requires effort and implementing it can be stressful.

Some readers may like skimming through the contents to find out which stage they are at, or to read about something specific such as love, happiness or sexual fantasies. All of that is a legitimate part of enjoying the book. But those who seek a deeper knowledge about themselves, others and the complexities of relationships, love and happiness, would do best by reading it once from cover to cover and then re-reading parts of it as needed.

That is because this introduction and earlier material help put into context everything that follows. Being aware of which stage we are at and why can help in preparing ourselves for doing what is needed to move towards our goal. Again, that includes improving our capacity to plan strategy, cope with the pressures, learn from mistakes, strengthen our confidence, and generate a realistic understanding about the compromises needed. All this will help in finding a partner with enough imperfections to want to love us for life, plus the qualities he has to have for us to be able to love him.

Those who already have such partner, still need to keep in mind that every marriage has its own unavoidable difficulties, and that dealing with them in an informed sensible way will reduce the risk of increasing relationship deterioration over the years. Taking care to avoid this danger is important, given three facts of married life in developed western countries, where most men and women have the economic capacity to live independently.

The first fact is that roughly around half of all marriages break up, if we count de-facto ones not appearing in divorce statistics. The second is that out of the surviving couples, many become progressively less happy after the earlier years. In the worst cases partners grudgingly tolerate each other, but do not divorce for fear of facing life alone, disappointing children, becoming poorer, etc. And the third fact is that virtually all those people started with the expectation that it wasn't going to happen to them.

Certain "solutions" will not fix the usual problems. These include pretending that marital tensions don't exist, hoping they will go away by themselves or at least not get worse, and doing more of what hasn't worked in the past. Well intentioned advice is also unlikely to resolve anything permanently, if it comes from people who do not fully and properly comprehend the complexities involved, whether or not they have formal counseling qualifications.

Making the most of what we have in order to achieve a happier life will be easier if we obtain enough relevant knowledge. It is possible for most people to do so, but this requires certain conditions which do not often coexist: (1) Access to such knowledge in a format easy enough to learn. (2) The courage, intelligence, strength and humility required to face uncomfortable realities. (3) The determination and discipline necessary to learn from our mistakes. (4) In some cases, enough consultations with a good therapist.

> **NOTE:** Out of respect for my clients and also for my own peace of mind, case examples from my clinical practice are from over twenty years ago, when I was working for the Department of Health as a salaried therapist. Names and non essential details have been left out or changed, in order to make everyone unrecognizable. No examples from my private practice are included unless mentioned with permission, and they are never publicly discussed or recorded in any file.

STAGE 1

MANAGING THE BREAKUPS:

Time for healing solitude and helpful reflection

First reactions if our partner has left us

Most unattached people learn who might suit them as a life partner largely by trial and error, usually in shorter or limited relationships. For those who have a conscience therefore, being able to try out and then leave without guilt is important. Guilt would only be appropriate when our intention was to exploit, by direct deception or by encouraging expectations we are sure we cannot fulfill. So, for most singles, the issues are fairly straightforward.

But when we have lived with a man we love for long enough, or even if we lived apart but were in an exclusive relationship for years, things can get complicated. It is common for our sense of identity to have fused with his to some extent and thereafter to be made up of two parts. One is the identity we have as an individual, and the other is couple based. If he leaves us unexpectedly or against our wishes, it can feel as if the ground has suddenly been taken from under one foot, leaving us standing precariously on the other.

If too big a part of our identity had become couple based, one immediate and temporary consequence may be a feeling of helplessness, like an abandoned child longing for safety and love. Depending on the kind of personality, that feeling may be covered up by intense anger, which at times becomes irrational. It happens to men too when we leave them. But having usually less understanding of the deeper emotional issues and fewer social supports, they can feel excruciatingly distressed behind a stoic façade.

After the initial shock is over, this first stage is primarily one of retreat in order to lick our wounds and begin to recover. We are just not ready to risk closeness, because we are hurting too much from our sentimental debacle. Each in a unique way we are still bleeding, and all most of us can manage is to just keep breathing while we stick to the comfort and security of the familiar. These are difficult periods to live through.

We may find ourselves alone, isolated and disheartened at home, struggling to cope as best as we can. A recently divorced woman told me how she would sit in her sofa at night, fishing sultanas out of the breakfast cereal packet and worrying about getting fat, while looking without interest at some television program and wondering about the point of life.

Despite the loss and dislocation, a period of solitude at this time can be a healing experience as well as a survival strategy. For some time following the breakup there may be phone calls or other communication with the former partner, which could help discharge pent up emotion. But if such activities are primarily keeping the wound open, it may be better to have a clean break and cut off contact as much as possible. It is only after the numbness of the initial pain subsides that we may be able to begin to digest the blow, engage in productive reflection, and absorb valuable lessons.

"All men are bastards" talk

In cases where it is the man who ended a longish relationship, "all men are bastards" talk of one sort or another is not uncommon among those of us who are hurting and our supportive friends. If we or the girlfriends we are with have an aggressive streak, any passing male who dares to say hello risks being unceremoniously sent away, after having his head bitten off. It may not be because we are bad girls, and we certainly don't want to think we are. We realize that we are not being fair, but just seem unable to help ourselves from scratching any man who places himself within range.

Those of us with more affable tendencies will still need a lot of support in order to simply go out there, but is difficult to put ourselves through it regardless of any amount of help and encouragement from friends. We know we have to sooner or later, for the sake of forgetting and surviving. As against the less demanding alternative of locking ourselves up into the safety we find at home and spending time with family, close friends or at work. But whatever we do, the point is avoidance of emotional risks at any cost, for the very good reason we cannot afford them.

022 Sense of liberation when we have left our partner

For women who have at long last been able to leave there may be a sense of liberation and temporary elation, after years of trying to improve an unsatisfactory relationship or of not wanting to take that final step while the children were young or for other reasons. For them the initial shock may be less, due to the emotional working through resulting from considering the pros and cons over a number of years. Although the struggle to readjust will still be there, it can be mitigated for those who already have or quickly develop a satisfying enough new relationship.

Those who don't but have gone through a number of similar experiences in the past may have a relatively easy glide through the frequent anguish of Stage 1, possibly largely skip the typical Stage 2 of independence for the sake of identity and safety, and perhaps the starry-eyed exploratory illusions of Stage 3. But unless they are uncommonly lucky, they too are likely to find themselves back and unprepared in the perfect man muddle of Stage 4.

Duration of Stage 1

This first stage rarely lasts for more than six months or so, and it can be a lot less. Its duration will be influenced by similar prior experiences, the length and degree of involvement, individual resilience, social supports, and our level of personal and self esteem development. It may be shorter for the partner who decided to leave, or longer if there has been traumatic loss of health or criminal behavior such as domestic violence.

If such violence was ongoing or severe enough to have caused significant damage, the option of having a clean break and cutting off contact as much as possible becomes still more pertinent. That would be in addition to any police or legal interventions which may be warranted. Understanding which men can become violent and why is important, and discussed in Stage 6.

A few people remain in this stage for life and become unable to form intimate and trusting meaningful connections. These are often later middle aged people whose partner has left them after their one very long marriage. Generally it takes longer to recover from a living together relationship than from a living apart one, especially if it was their first marriage or de-facto experience and lasted for a long time. For now suffice to say that there is broad agreement among therapists that reestablishing our identity as a new single can take about two years, as a rough average.

STAGE 2

EXPLORATORY EARLY STEPS:

Cautious tentative risks and hurried retreats

After having recovered enough we may drag ourselves to some singles venue or are taken there by our friends, and before long we are going regularly. "But I just want to dance", we might say determined to protect ourselves if dancing is what they do there, because at least for now we don't want any involvement with men. And we dance till we drop, because it helps to avoid thinking too much and lifts our morale by being near men who we can feel want us. Some people drink to forget while others dance to forget, the second being a much better option.

This stage is characterized by barely daring to approach a risk, or more precisely a relationship with a man, followed by a hasty retreat. The retreat is at least emotional, and very often physical too, into whatever we were doing previously that made us feel safe. It is as if having finally dared to step a toe into the pool, we realize the water is far too cold and retreat with a shiver. We can go to the pool and may even frolic around, but we are not there emotionally because the degree of pain still makes it far too dangerous for us to take the plunge.

Ideologies of independence

Ideologies of independence at any cost are a common coping strategy during this stage. But after some time they are no longer enough to manage the emotional backlash of our self imposed blanket rejection of attentions from men. As our unmet need for intimacy bites harder, we may try to relieve the underlying loneliness by escaping into activities such as family, work, solitude, sisterhood, shopping, fitness, dancing classes, evening courses, walking clubs, overseas holidays, pets, etc.

Involvement in activities is a healthy way of coping at the beginning of this Stage because, again, being busy leaves us with less time to think and helps us forget the painful feelings. It also allows us to avoid the fear of getting hurt by getting into relationships, without destabilizing our emotions further by having to confront that fear too soon or too directly.

Escapism aside, activities are also a perfectly reasonable way of enjoying life, but involvement in them is bound to decrease as the recovery gradually progresses. That is because they can never replace the basic human need for intimacy with an adult companion, and no trick of ours will succeed for long against the forces of evolution which made us as we are.

The longing to love and be loved, to give and receive the very special care which develops within a committed loving relationship is just too strong. There is no way out, and sooner or later we have to admit that if we don't have it our life is and will remain poorer. That if we want to find love we need to go out there, overcoming the discomfort or unease which unsettles us. And learn, in all probability the hard way, which risks to take and which ones to avoid.

When we finally do take the plunge, it may be easier to think of it as an adventure. This helps us believe we can retreat from risk at any time. In other words, it feels like a roundabout form of protection from the fear of getting hurt or of hurting too much the feelings of others. If it happens with a man we really like, it may lead to one of the premature over involvements and subsequent likely disappointments which are more typical of Stage 3.

It is mostly with certain kind of emotionally independent and internally secure men and women that an adventure may evolve into an especially trusting non sexual friendship or occasional sexual friendship. The latter's advantages and disadvantages are discussed further in Stage 4.

A first involvement after a breakup is unlikely to develop into a permanent relationship, but it can happen when we have been lucky to bump into a genuinely nice man who is also imperfect enough to be able to love us truly, especially when circumstances are favorable and there has been quality intimacy all along.

Blaming ourselves or others for our mistakes

We need to accept responsibility for the consequences of our choices without blaming ourselves. Trying to connect with men in a sensible way is not a matter for moral judgment, as long as we have acted honestly. If anything, trying out some relationships and managing the inevitable lacerations to us or to the other person is an indication of a reemerging capacity to risk and willingness to learn.

Managing a relationship reasonably well is a delicate art in the best of circumstances, but it can be a particularly challenging balancing act at this time. That is because we are prone to feeling a tinge of insecurity if he doesn't love us, and so we may encourage him to do so.

But as soon as he begins to do it and our fear of never finding true love goes down, our other fears of losing our hard-won independence, selling ourselves short or causing pain we do not wish to inflict may take over, and we are likely to make a run for it. Or we may do so upon realizing he is using us. Either way, it is important to resist the temptation of blaming men for the mistakes we make during this confusing period.

Blaming men puts us on the role of a victim, thereby wasting time and energy in an unproductive state of mind, and requires us to surrender part of our grip on reality in exchange for short term relief. That is why it is always a better option to acknowledge the hurt or regret, feel the pain, and express it in an appropriate manner. This makes it easier to digest the bulk of it, and then to let go of what is left. Only then can we regain our balance, reflect on what went wrong, and learn the lessons which will reduce the likelihood of repeating the problematic experience.

Despite the inevitable mistakes and consequent disappointments we cause to ourselves and others, the occasional knee jerk blaming, the regrets and the hurried retreats back into safety, we keep slowly moving forward. Eventually these difficulties begin to be overcome to a degree which allows our natural and healthy need to relate intimately with a man to take a better hold, gradually displacing our fear.

By now we have survived the initial shock and have been calmer for sufficiently long to reassess our situation and reestablish enough emotional balance. Some residual tendencies towards unproductive anger or dejection may still arise occasionally, but we can contain them before they become a problem and are no longer consumed by it.

Another six months or so is not an uncommon duration for Stage 2, and the length varies for the same reasons as in Stage 1. We wouldn't know it yet, but are about to enter the overoptimistic search for a perfect man, which is the hallmark of Stage 3.

STAGE 3

THE STARRY-EYED PHASE:

Searching for the man we believe we want

Where we are at when the search begins

By now enough time has elapsed for some healing to have occurred, and our coping strategies can be less restrictive. If it was our partner who left us and we experienced the anguish of feeling abandoned and the struggle of having to start all over again, our initial instinct may well be to look for a man whose love and commitment will be truly secure. If it was us who left our partner, we still have to go through the effort of learning to be single again and honing up our men-relating skills.

Most of us begin to be able to risk closeness, physical at least, without a knee-jerk retreat into safety. But emotional closeness is another matter. We have become very guarded and trusting is difficult. A few of us will still avoid any involvements, and rationalize our fear by telling ourselves it is not worth the hassles unless the man has definite potential.

Some of us may take on a much younger man, too immature for significant emotional involvement, or some other clearly unsuitable one. This helps us feel safe while we recover our strength, and meets our needs for forgetting, being found attractive, filling up time or just enjoying our sexual freedom. The stronger we get the more our initial longing for a very secure commitment eases up, and the more attention we pay to the bigger picture. The point being that if we are going to risk all that pain again, it must be with a man whose qualities are such that the risk is worth it.

The protective withdrawal of Stage 1 has dissipated by now, and the uneasiness and discomfort of Stage 2 are well on the way out. More and more often we find ourselves able to relax, laugh and actually enjoy the pleasure of the moment, rather than just pretend it in an effort to cover up our pain. At times we feel even happy.

We are beginning to re-experience our power over the men who find us attractive, and the fear of getting hurt is fading away. When we are in a dancing floor we let them have a little of what they want while enjoying it ourselves, without making a move either way. We are regaining our poise, and sense the present is getting better and the future looks promising.

The qualities we believe Mr. Right must have

As the earlier residual fears gradually give way to more confident ways of behaving, we begin to cautiously become involved with men and try them out. For example, over a year or two we may have known four men: One who is good for dancing and relaxing with, without being dangerous because we don't find him attractive enough. Another who is kind hearted, loving and better looking, but a bit dull.

One intelligent and attractive enough, but unfortunately too old. Another one who is young and rather handsome, although clearly immature. And from all this it is easy to conclude that the sort of man we need and want is one who combines the good qualities of each of the four men, but without their liabilities. For example someone who is fun to dance and relax with, kind hearted and loving, plus intelligent and attractive without being too old or too young. Through this and similar experiences we develop a growing conviction that we know who could and couldn't be right for us.

We come to believe that we will eventually find him if we look long and hard enough, and so we embark on a determined search. This is how the beliefs and attitudes most characteristic of Stage 3 begin to crystallize in us. Often without knowing and certainly without admitting to it we are searching for Mr. Perfect, although we prefer to think of him as Mr. Right. That sounds less egotistic, without us having to actually compromise on any of the expectations we consider important.

The qualities we think a man should have to be eligible, reflect the belief that there are such men out there who will want us permanently. The more innocent or inexperienced we are, the more we make our list of expectations unrealistically demanding. But we are not fully aware of the unreasonable-ness of it, because our perceptions are not yet accurate and balanced. And therefore the way we feel about it is that we are simply not going to settle for second best, come what may.

We remind ourselves that there is plenty of fish in the sea, especially in the big and ever expanding seas of online dating. With abundant energy fuelled by over optimism, the luckier and more energetic among us may find ourselves checking out several men in the same week. We may ratchet up the search by trying out different singles venues, join courses or activity groups, and even venture into things like "speed dating".

We are unwavering in our determination, and anyone daring to suggest we might be too picky risks being bombarded with what we consider our very sound arguments. In this frame of mind we may get close to a succession of otherwise OK but too young or too handsome men who are unlikely to love us enough for them to ever want a relationship for life.

It is easy to become prematurely overinvolved with such men, and the subsequent breakups will take their toll. Some of them may be attractive enough and long term interested, but have serious though not immediately noticeable personality and other problems or unsuitable circumstances. Others may simply have too many differences or limitations in terms of who we or they are and need to be with, in order to develop a relationship which would be satisfying for both in the longer term.

A proportion of the genuinely nice men we meet will themselves be at a stage where they are simply not ready to commit, whether they are aware of it or not. Some may be ready to do so and have most of the features we seek. But to put it bluntly for the sake of honesty, and just like we do with most men who approach us, they want someone "better".

We are looking for quality intimacy with a man, but at the same time sabotage ourselves by hanging onto unrealistic expectations. They rule out just about all men with enough of the imperfections which would be necessary, to give them the potential to genuinely love us. Again, deep down our hope and belief is that we will eventually find at least one man who is close enough to our dreams and wants us permanently. The American film *As Good As It Gets* could be somewhat of an antidote to this way of thinking and feeling, which might perhaps rebalance things a bit.

By the time we have tried and been left by a number of such men we may have had enough however, especially if we conclude they had been using us. It can take another year or two in this Stage and sometimes longer, before we can recognize a subtle shift in our mood and way of thinking. This is how, almost imperceptibly at first, we begin to slide into Stage 4.

STAGE 4

THE PERFECT MAN MUDDLE:

From collisions with reality to growing unease

I am not looking for a perfect man

The perfect man muddle is the confusing mess we got ourselves into, as a result of searching over many years for our dream man and ending up disappointed again and again. But hang on, we might say, "I am not looking for a perfect man". And then add something such as "All I want is to be loved by a man I can love back", which sounds fair enough.

We all like to think that our expectations are sensible, a bit modest even. The man we seek does not have to be any more than reasonably attractive, reasonably intelligent and reasonably nice in bed. We are not overdoing it by hoping he will be reasonably educated, reasonably affectionate when he does not want sex, reasonably solvent like as in owning his home rather than renting, or at least having a secure job with a reasonable salary.

Naturally, we would prefer if he also liked talking about the relationship, could fix things around the house, and was not too much into drinking or gambling, going out alone with his friends or looking at other women. Of course it would be better if he was sophisticated enough to impress friends and family, but without being too complicated. And, oh yes!, got on with our mother so that we can get her off our back.

On the other hand we know that nobody is perfect, we don't want to be picky, and are prepared to compromise in the non essentials. And here is what wiser heads would say to all that: "Snap out of it!" Any man who ticks reasonable in all of those areas, and probably a few others we forgot to mention, is in fact a pretty solid Mr. Perfect.

A reliable indicator that we are trapped in the perfect man muddle is the realization that we are repeating an unproductive pattern, especially if it has been going on for a number of years. Its major features are:

- Most men interested in us seem unsuitable, from our point of view
- Most of those we would like to consider do not want us permanently
- All attempts at connecting with suitable men seem to come to nothing
- We either don't understand why, or don't know how to break out of it

Life keeps knocking us around time and again, until we gradually come to realize that we might have been looking for a man who is too close to being perfect. And that even finding a more modest Mr. Right may turn out to be more difficult that we thought. But we remind ourselves we knew it was never going to be easy, and continue the search.

As the cumulative effect of repeated disappointments makes itself felt, we are prone to a lot of exaggerated complaining about there not being enough available nice men. Or about it being so difficult to find places which supposedly should be crowded with them, to make life easier for us. We may find ourselves discharging pent up pressure through the usual clichés like "there is nothing out there", and then half-joke that all nice men are taken or have gone gay. Or arguing that the reason it is so difficult to find the right man is that men are commitment phobic, which of course is not our fault.

While conveniently forgetting that for all the married women there had to be an equal number of men who were obviously not commitment phobic, towards them. And that there are about the same number of gay women as men, which means that the proportion of available heterosexual men has to be fairly balanced.

We should never underestimate the power of denial, when our only alternative is uncomfortable self examination. Complaints about commitment phobic men have kept me dealing with women's denial throughout my counseling career. Countless women have told me over the years that their man said he was not ready for commitment, and they kind of partly believed it.

It might have been true, but every time I felt duty bound to remind them that what he could have meant was that he was not ready for commitment *with them*. And that the reason he would be putting it in such general way was to make it less hurtful because he was kind, or perhaps not brave enough to tell it like it was. Or in some cases because he had been a cold blooded calculating user from the start, and did not want to admit to it.

But let's not rush to condemn anyone. There are many fairly decent men and women out there, relationships involve some uncertainty, and unclear feelings need to be tested to see how they evolve. Last but not least, we should not forget that most women seeking a committed relationship do not want it with the men who would offer it, if given a chance.

That is why the myth of commitment phobic men is mostly an example of denial. Including denial about the inconvenient truth that we women are just as commitment phobic when it suits us. We convey this fact towards men who fall short of our expectations by taking the preemptive step of being relationship phobic towards them, and justifying it on grounds that we cannot possibly be expected to go for a man we don't feel attracted to. That sounds totally sensible, but there is more to it than meets the eye.

Collisions with reality and growing unease

In this Stage there are still far too many burn-your-bridges types of unwise and at times even resentful rejections of presumed Mr. Wrongs or Mr. Not Right Enoughs. In the earlier mind frame of Stage 3, our over-optimism allowed us to dismiss and fly over such men without much consequence to us, but our increasing frustration means that we may by now begin to resent them for being as they are. This challenges common sense, but has its own twisted emotional logic.

We resent them for not to being who we had hoped for, as every non-prince coming our way makes us increasingly alarmed and impatient about it. What is actually happening is that whenever another non-prince puts the truth in front of our eyes by smiling at us, the unreality of our Prince Charming fantasy threatens to surface into awareness and flood us with anxiety.

What we experience as his audacity to disturb our illusions may cause us to feel annoyance. "Who does he think he is?", we may retort with our attitude. The less kind and intelligent among us could be rude too, by looking away or worse without a kind word or face saving excuse. And then we dig our heels deeper as an unconscious defense against genuine self awareness, because the prospect of having a hard look at our expectations is still too daunting.

Occasionally we meet men who are close to what we want. And although it doesn't work because they don't want us permanently or turn out to have a problem or limitation, it is enough for our hopes to live on. Despite the left over defiance and sense of entitlement however, we are feeling growing unease because deep down we know we can't afford to dream our life away.

After too many disappointments with supposedly nice men who fitted well enough with our expectations, we could end up anticipating failure in every new relationship. We may fear trying out even those men who clearly have the potential to give us what we need. We hold emotions close to our chest, and sometimes retreat exhausted and disheartened into the safety of avoiding physical or emotional contact typical of Stage 2. Put simply, repeated letdowns have hurt us to the point of not daring to risk the pain which unrequited love can put us through.

But complete avoidance of relationships is also hard to sustain for long, and so we put on a front while swallowing our unease and soldier on. It feels bad because it is bad. Eventually we are forced to drag ourselves kicking and screaming into making what we consider as significant compromises. They are probably little more than tokenistic ones however, because that is the most we can manage for now. The unforgiving reality is that we have not yet suffered enough, to acquire the wisdom to realize we have to change.

As our deprivation of genuine tender loving care accumulates and weights us down, we may end up projecting desperation or emotional instability. This could show even if we don't want it to, and might alarm away some of the better men we meet. We pass opportunities for honest sexual friendships, which could become a useful emotional training ground, as well as provide much of what we need in order to feel better and balance ourselves.

We avoid such friendships because we fear not being able to withstand yet another blow, or because we underestimate the coping capacity of a person who may wish for more than we could give. Therefore, we move away from affection rather than risking the problems, and remain excessively needy. In such run down emotional state, we may fail to recognize those few men who could be truly right for us, on the rare occasion when one crosses our path.

It seems sensible to assume that if a man doesn't have enough crumpled edges, he is probably too good to be real. But in the frame of mind we are in, a few imperfections is all we need to start running. Or we could sense he might be right for us, but are too hesitant to make a move. And by the time we realize our mistake someone faster or smarter is giving him a wonderful time, and poor slow learner us are back in square one.

In time we may lose confidence in our ability to distinguish between men who have potential and those who don't. When our confidence goes down our self esteem might follow, because they influence each other. We wonder whether we are losing our grip. We feel bogged down in a slippery quagmire, and sometimes despair about ever being able to get out. With enormous effort we resume the struggle and continue to search.

The recurring setbacks often become almost too much to bear, but we feel we have no choice. This state of affairs can go on and on, reinforced by acquaintances and friends in the same situation. They may not be ready to give up the prince, and do not want us to get real because if we did they would be left alone and unsupported.

Hanging onto any residual starry eyed expectations becomes increasingly difficult, as our growing apprehension takes hold while time is getting shorter and the smarter among our friends are choosing sanity. The length of this stage varies but it tends to be the longest one, and many of us get stuck there and unfortunately never find the way out.

As the strain of having been trapped in Stage 4 for too long hits us harder and harder, it may set in motion some serious thinking about why we find ourselves in such predicament. These concerns are likely to be superficial and temporary at first because realistic self examination can feel too threatening, and it is still easier to hope it will all go away soon.

But the pressure keeps piling up, until we feel a need to search deeper. Finally we are forced to accept, reluctantly and with some anguish, that it cannot always be the fault of men. In the privacy of our own mind we begin to ponder whether something might not be entirely right with our expectations, feelings or behavior, or with how we go about searching for the right man.

We may begin to contemplate the rather unsettling possibility that something might not be entirely right with who and how we are or come across. But is this the case? And if so, what is it precisely? We realize we need to change, but in what way? And will we be able to? Developing a more accurate understanding of what is happening can be difficult. We know we have to, and it makes us uneasy.

For some, the self examination and questioning of cherished beliefs is just too scary, and therefore they avoid it by hanging onto any excuse they can think of. These are the people who even at this critical juncture, when they know decisive change is needed, will retreat into doing more of the same. That is because they feel safer in familiar territory, although they sense it is unlikely to get them anywhere worth being at.

Only the unforgiving passing of yet more time combined with the benefit of hindsight will eventually persuade them to acknowledge their mistakes, at the very least to themselves. But in some cases that may not happen until well into their fifties, and by then it might be getting a bit late. That is because the few available men who still want to love them may have become too unacceptable, while the ones these women would be prepared to consider only want them for a short time, and sometimes just for one night.

It is when things reach this point, that remaining as they are begins to look like the better option. Gradually it dawns on them that they probably did push the envelope too far, and may end up alone. This could happen to any of us unless we see what is happening, have the courage to learn by facing reality in order to get to the bottom of it, and are sufficiently determined to do whatever it takes to bring about a change in our life.

When Stage 4 remains unresolved for too many years, a demoralizing resignation may begin to develop, especially in those whose self esteem is a bit shaky. It could remain at that or trigger a slow drift towards cynicism, hopelessness and depression. In the worst cases these can become permanent features of personality and reveal themselves through negative attitudes or behavior. And in extreme cases they may show through an unconscious expression of unhappiness, carved over the decades into the lines of their faces.

While in that state of demoralizing resignation we may come to depend on unhealthy props such as overeating, smoking, alcohol, gambling or antidepressants. We could turn to mindless television, ritualistic religion, or psychic predictions as a desperate last ditch hope. We might begin putting increasingly unreasonable demands for company and support on friends or family, and not realize we are being heavy until we notice they are avoiding us. Overreliance on hobbies or companion pets is common, and one of the least damaging ways of coping.

Only a fortunate few enter this stage with a good preexisting level of relationship wisdom. In rare cases it may combine with timely luck and other favorable factors, enabling the person to jump from a milder Stage 4 into the more sensible and productive mind frame of Stage 7. But for the majority who find themselves stuck in the perfect man muddle, being there is a major obstacle to searching competently and forming viable relationships.

Unfortunately, most of us have to put ourselves through the hard slog of Stage 4 in order to become receptive to making the necessary changes. For those who have come across this book and to the extent that it is properly understood, acquiring the knowledge about personality and relationships contained within it could be an eye opener. Before looking at the deeper aspects of that in Stage 5 however, we should consider some of the circumstances which led us astray, beginning with the influence of predominant culture.

The influence of predominant culture

There are times when for all sorts of reasons many of us prefer to escape into pleasant fantasies rather than confront the complexities of real life. This is one of the insidious ways in which some aspects of predominant culture gradually sneak their way into our psyche. A not uncommon such escape is the grossly unrealistic fantasies propagated by cheap romantic novels, which are consumed around the world almost exclusively by women, and are sometimes referred to as "emotional pornography".

Reading them can be damaging even if we know they are unreal, because eventually some of the fantasies begin to influence our perceptions. As required by the international publishers, these short novels have to be written according to a tried and tested commercially successful formula. The first part of that formula requires the hero to be whatever readers might wish for. As a successful Australian writer said candidly on television, "It is all a fantasy, so I might as well go for broke".

It was with the hero that she went for broke, of course, and there is undoubtedly an art in dreaming it all up in a way which facilitates suspension of disbelief. For example, he could be a combination of what follows or the whole lot and more, all at the same time. Tall, dark and handsome, or something different but equally good. He can have hair in the chest if it looks nice, but never in the back according to another successful writer.

He is appreciative of the value of a good personality in the woman he is going to fall in love with. Rich or at least well off, although aware about the limitations of money for achieving happiness. Soft and sensitive with the heroine, while definitely very masculine and as tough as it takes when dealing with nasty people. Likely to have a killer instinct in business, combined with a heart of gold and a penchant for fighting injustice when it comes his way, but without being an activist or anything as political as that.

A hard worker who nevertheless never forgets the importance of quality time with the heroine, during which he likes to talk about their relationship. Spontaneously amusing and lighthearted, although capable of being serious when the situation requires. Occupying a socially prestigious position, yet slightly disdainful about social status. Etc., etc., etc. All of which makes the heroine shine with happiness and reflected glory, as he invariably comes to appreciate her wonderful human qualities and love her truly. And the story ends when they are about to start living happily ever after.

The second part of the formula is that the heroine has to be as ordinary as any reader. She comes to know that she is not only fully accepted, but that her different perspective in life is understood and appreciated. The purpose of course being to make it easier for any reader to slide into the pleasant fantasy that it could really happen. And happen to her too, as her heart throbs in unison with the heroine's during those utterly predictable peak moments.

Never mind that some of the qualities ascribed to the hero and being absorbed into the reader's wish list may be mutually contradictory, and therefore unlikely to coexist in the same person. Most readers eventually realize that it is just not going to happen. But it is a bit like knowing we are not going to win all those millions and still buying that lottery ticket, stubbornly clinging to the faintest hope of resolving our life problems without effort.

Of course, trashy romantic novels are not the only villains, although they are among the most brazen examples. Countless movies cater to the same needs, including that one in which a pretty woman who is a sex worker is going to be truly loved by a man who is handsome, rich, nice and important. There are plenty of such Cinderella fantasies on television serials too, as well as on magazines, the Internet, and the advertising industry.

Quite a few such unhealthy influences may have infiltrated our psyche and established themselves there over many years, through the never ending bombardment of the mass media. Therefore they could unconsciously and perniciously be lingering around, including in those of us who are very down to earth in most other areas of life.

Recognizing unwanted clutter for what it is

Despite the cultural brainwashing, sooner or later we all have to face it: If we haven't found Prince Charming during all these years, we are not likely to get lucky all of a sudden. Our once defiant do or die proclamations become less and less convincing, because deep down we know it is getting more difficult with every extra candle on the birthday cake.

Many of those stuck in Stage 4 may never have the chance to discover how to get out of it. If we do have access to knowledge and are determined enough to acquire it, we still have to start by recognizing and getting off our chest some of the accumulated clutter which has been constricting our mind, and in this way preventing us from learning through experience.

Those of us with a gentler heart could begin by complaining bitterly about the unfairness of life. And then resort to those half deluded sisterly commiserations about all the good men being taken or having gone gay. That they can't be trusted, only want one thing, or prefer younger women because their naivety allows men to feel secure and superior. Therefore it is them who have a problem and not us women, and certainly not me.

If we have more aggressive inclinations, we could indulge to our heart's content by becoming thoroughly inebriated with self righteous indignation and blaming specific men. And then finding fault with the whole male half of humanity too, if our outrage is really biting us. Bitching about shameless tarts who outcompete us by demeaning themselves with various unfair tactics, and then top it off by using all their bullets on a first date. Or about younger women stealing from us men old enough to be their fathers, who ought to be available for women of an appropriate age.

Of course, we could go on and on, and throw into the fray every pet hate and sentimental debacle which takes our fancy. And after all that, and then some more if it still keeps making us feel better or we enjoy spoiling ourselves, let's come back to the real world and move on from such self-pitying unproductive pursuits.

We have a stark choice: To confront and understand reality better in order to become able to change as needed, or to keep doing more of the same. This second option is the easiest in the short term, because it does not require us to have a hard look at ourselves or alter our behavior. And the problem with it is that expecting different outcomes while doing more of the same, is almost a form of insanity.

Adding to the obstacles already discussed, some of us may subscribe to unscientific beliefs about relationships, or to outdated cultural or religious views. If we are ever going to be able to search effectively for a good man, each of us needs to enter our own private maze of crisscrossing beliefs and expectations. We need to disentangle them and question the unproductive ones, because carrying excessive clutter leaves little room for acquiring relevant knowledge, even if we know where to find it.

The more such knowledge we get the more obsolete the old unproductive beliefs become, and we are likely to gradually shed them off as we get hold of better alternatives. But it is very difficult to totally discard unproductive beliefs until we have something better to put in their place, because otherwise we would end up with an identity void. That could leave us feeling uncomfortable at best, and at worst it might lead to considerable distress.

Acknowledging facts that make a difference

When we finally come to accept that doing more of the same is unlikely to produce the desired results, we could follow up by considering certain facts which could make a difference in our search. The first is that in societies with reasonable gender equality, women generally control the gate to sex for the simple reason that in most couples they crave it less than their male partners.

The rules may well be different inside a valued marriage, where women have more to lose because a chronically dissatisfied husband may seek sex elsewhere or ultimately divorce. But with no such worries yet in the hard bargaining world of the mating game, everyone is looking for the best deal we can get.

Therefore we keep opening the sexual gate only to those men who meet or surpass our expectations. "Not me", might be the knee jerk protest. But when we have a choice of several men, many of us will be sorely tempted to go for the one who is more attractive, younger or richer on the hope it will work. We don't want to scare him away by asking too many questions just yet, and therefore he doesn't need to lie if he only wants us for a while.

If we are the kind of woman men find attractive there will be plenty of offers after every disappointment, and the process may be repeated many times. Eventually we will become sufficiently burnt out to begin asking relevant questions early in the relationship, even if we risk losing him. But then we come up against the fact that most men will lie to a woman they want to sleep with, in order to get there. And unless we are good enough at understanding human nature, we may be unable to detect the liars in time.

Not willing to recognize that our unwise choices have been major contributors to the outcomes, we prefer to conclude the problem in the search for love is that men are dishonest, in addition to commitment phobic. Of course many are, and all our friends confirm it by reference to their own experiences. Having similar truths to hide from, they collude in maintaining the delusion that the main problem is the way men are. We focus on this having nothing to do with us, which makes us feel slightly better for a while.

By the time enough men too good to be real have left us, we could have become accustomed to their level of attractiveness. Therefore we may not be quite as able to tolerate the less attractive men we have rejected, and possibly all similar men who might approach us in future. As soon as any such man tries to get physically close we feel like moving away. It becomes visceral and automatic, and therefore rather difficult to overcome.

Sure enough, there may be other factors in the equation. Some of us may be hooked into money or status, younger men, muscle men, tall men, macho men, funny men, dancing men, or whatever turns us on, and are hopefully aware of the consequences of our choices. In any case, for those of us trapped in the perfect man muddle without really understanding why, my own observations still point to unrealistic expectations and automatic visceral rejections as the two major culprits keeping us stuck there.

So, we ended up where we are through a combination of romantic fantasies, innocent expectations, and our very natural but usually denied search for a perfect partner. Through long term exposure to predominant cultural values we absorbed the underlying belief that we would find a man close enough to our ideal, willing to make a lifetime commitment with us. And this belief may have been a major factor preventing us from managing our relationships and our life in the best possible way.

Are we giving men negative messages without realizing it?

The bad news is that we are never going to be as young, attractive, slim, tall, educated, intelligent, sweet, sexy, etc. as some of the competition. The good news is that it may not matter, provided our expectations are realistic. Men know they are imperfect too, and therefore unavoidable imperfections are not necessarily an insurmountable problem for us or for them. But avoidable imperfections are another matter.

We may cause a negative impression very soon, by the way we behave. First impressions tend to stick, and therefore we have to be careful. When boys and girls begin liking one another in High School, their inexperience shows in various ways. There may be insufficient consideration for others, mistreatment of various kinds, pretense, superficiality, and a multitude of games which are normal at that stage of life.

A common such game is to try to raise our own value by playing hard to get. Actually, what research suggests is that men prefer women who are difficult for others but easy for them. But this knowledge should not be used to keep playing games, albeit in a more refined manner, because they are likely to put off most reasonably intelligent men.

When grown up women act like High School girls, they are giving a very negative message to men who can see through it. Even after taking into account the possible insecurities propelling their behavior, what comes across is that they don't seem to act with a degree of maturity commensurate with their age. This could create the impression that they are not very bright.

Some women may arrive late to a meeting with a man, offer no apology, and not bother with a perfunctory explanation either. Apologizing and doing the same next time is just as bad, or worse. It gives the message that we do not care about him, are unreliable and can't be trusted.

040 If we say we are going to do one thing and don't, we lose credibility. If we say we are going to do two things and don't, we may annoy him too. And if we keep making mistakes, we could lose a relationship with potential. A woman in her forties danced and talked on two separate weekends with a man, just before going on a one month holiday. She took his phone and email but did not give hers, and agreed to email him before going and call when she came back. However, she did neither.

Sometime after her return they saw each other again in the same venue, and she did not approach him. When the man finally came to her, she said she hadn't made contact because she lost his number and email, and had not approached first because she wasn't sure it was him.

They danced and talked for a third time and she agreed to meet for dinner. However, she refused the invitation to have it in his home, even after he suggested it a second time on the grounds they would be able to talk in a quieter and more comfortable setting, and assured her she would be totally safe.

Given all that had happened, the potential for a relationship was probably in intensive care by the time they finally met in a restaurant. Although they spent two hours there and seemed to like each other, she kept making yet more mistakes. The first one was to say she had refused dinner in his home because it was against a safety dating rule. She though this was making her look appropriately cautious, but was it?

Rules may be OK for women up to around their mid twenties or so, when few are wise enough to properly evaluate danger. But relying on rules in our forties after having repeatedly danced and talked with a man who doesn't seem dangerous, gives four negative messages: We don't trust him. We don't have the self confidence to assess him on his merits. We are treating him just like any other man, rather than as someone especial we might come to love. We don't understand why being "managed by rules" could displease him.

A more sensible option would have been to rely on her intuition plus what she already knew about him. Accepting dinner in his home, especially after he asked a second time and reassured her, would have created a much better impression. If we are over thirty and still cannot trust our judgment, we may benefit from personal development as discussed in Stage 5. The same applies if we believe we are doing the right things, but have been for years in a repeating pattern of unsuccessful relationships.

Over dinner he offered to send her an email with something short he had written about something or other. She declined in a manner which might have been experienced by him as unnecessarily adamant. Having forced him to meet in a restaurant instead of accepting the invitation for dinner in his home, the smart and sensible thing would have been to put her money on the table and insist on sharing the bill. Instead she put him on the spot by asking whether he would like her to pay half.

Her offer was genuine, but again, made without having realized the effect it could have. He might have interpreted it as she not understanding the implications (and therefore doubt her intelligence), as checking his willingness to spend money on her, or as using manipulation for financial advantage. In any case, that seems to have been the straw that broke the camel's back. He accepted her offer politely, but quite unexpectedly did so in a manner suggesting he had decided their budding trial was not going to continue.

He added that her not calling him upon her return plus earlier not emailing as agreed had prompted him to start a relationship with another woman, which had just become sexual. If he was a decent man, he could well have felt bad about being put in the position of having to reject that woman, and make her disappointment all the worse by doing so at that point.

It probably would have turned out differently if her actions had not depleted his tolerance beforehand. There was a good chance he was already somewhat annoyed, her further mistakes over dinner must have made it worse, and therefore it seems that he overreacted. But men's mistakes are their responsibility, and we can only do something about ours.

Behind her nonchalant reaction she was taken aback and bewildered. The hurt prompted her to ignore two messages he sent later, thus never learning what went wrong through subsequent chats, and preempting a second chance with a man who could have been right for her. In such highly charged situations both men and women make mistakes, and they become costlier as we get older. More about sensible rejection management in Stage 7, under *The risks and potential of the Action Plan.*

Many employed or financially solvent women exploit any man interested in them by not paying their way. Some do it blatantly, as if it was their unquestionable entitlement. A few will go as far as arguing that if he doesn't go along with it he is not "a real man". However, this is not a matter of manliness or tradition anymore. In fact it is often an abuse of power, and can make a woman look as if she wants to be paid for granting a favor.

On the other hand no self respecting employed man would agree to a woman paying half of their dinner if, as an extreme example, she is a single mother on social security living in private rental accommodation. But unless there is a legitimate reason, employed women on reasonable earnings who expect egalitarian relationships and claim to respect men and themselves would want to walk their talk, on the grounds that it is the proper thing to do.

There will be times when a woman puts her money on the table and insists on paying half, and he steadfastly refuses to accept. One way out provided we still want to see him, is to agree on condition that we meet again and this time he will accept our invitation for dinner, which we will pay for or provide. This would convey the messages that we are independent, fair minded, owe him nothing, and expect men to respect us as we respect them.

Of course a first drink or diner date is neither here nor there, to some extent we have to play it by ear, and there are always circumstances, manners and subtleties to be considered. Whatever happens, a better quality man is likely to say nothing but take note. If he happens to be looking for a potential wife, those critically important first impressions will be one more factor influencing his perception of us. This is also why paying our way from the start is to our own benefit, although that is not the honorable reason for doing it.

Men who remain interested in women who disregard or pretend to be unaware of their financial responsibilities include those who are less intelligent, have some significant limitations, are less sane as in having as yet undetected personality problems, or possibly want them only for a while. Such men will also be more inclined to lie in order to use a woman sexually, and may feel justified in doing so because they know she is using them financially.

If a relationship develops between two exploitative people it is less likely to work. Both partners have personality problems, which aren't going to go away just because they "love" each other. But in fact most such people don't actually have much capacity to care for anyone. In all probability they don't understand love or human nature very well either. If we wanted to be unkind, we could say that they deserve each other.

If an exploitative woman develops a relationship with a better quality man, he is likely to eventually drop her. If on being asked he says why and she promises to change, it could be too late because her true nature has already been revealed by her attempt at getting away with it while she could.

Regardless of any self serving beliefs we might subscribe to, men want to be treated fairly at the very least, just like we do. And in the absence of that, not even good sex is going to be enough after a while. Exploitative women are in stark contrast with a friend I have always respected for her intelligence and integrity. Her incisive sense of humor makes me smile every time she says "I am a feminist when it suits me".

After paying for their first dinner together, a smooth talking youngish lawyer drove his date home. On getting there he asked if she would invite him in for a cup of coffee. She politely refused and he left without obvious sign of anger. But shortly after he phoned and abused her in a rude way, feeling he had been cheated out of what he saw as his reasonable expectations. Paying her half of the bill would have given him the message he needed to hear, in time.

A woman who had been consulting me met a new man in an unusual way. He stopped his car next to her as she was walking home, and after a very brief conversation persuaded her to give him her number. He called and suggested meeting for dinner. She had accepted, and asked me what I thought about it. The essence of my comments was as follows:

All you know about him is that he is attractive, was driving an expensive car, was daring or atypical enough to stop by your side as you walked, and talked barely enough to ask for your number. I suggest you insist on a restaurant in your suburb and share the cost of dinner. Go there and return home walking or in your car, and don't give him your address. Don't go inside his car for a chat, and if you do, don't go anywhere. If you go somewhere don't go near his home, and if you do, don't go there for a drink.

She told me what happened in the next interview. He insisted in paying, so she accepted. Then she went in his car to a nice coffee shop next to the beach in the suburb where he lived. After coffee she went for a drink to his home, which was nearby. While sitting in the sofa he began caressing her breasts. He did not stop at that, and soon things were getting out of hand.

She asked him to stop but he didn't, and he was much bigger and stronger. The vast majority of men would not behave like that, but they do exist and can be dangerous. "In the end I became quite frightened", she told me. And then added, "I had to masturbate him until he came, because it looked like if I didn't he was going to rape me".

"If he had raped you it would have been almost impossible to prove" I said, mindful that an "I told you so" wouldn't have been helpful. By the time it was all over he knew he had gone too far, as indeed he must have known well before then, and the expression he saw in her face confirmed it. "You are not going to have another date with me, are you?" he asked. She didn't.

A small minority of women suffer from below average emotional intelligence, and that leaves them unable to understand how obvious and potentially dangerous certain manipulations or misbehaviors can be. If these are serious, and depending on the kind of man they are dealing with, they unwittingly put themselves at risk of being exposed or much worse, as in the two examples next. If that were to happen, it could have significant social and mental health repercussions for them, with all the resulting negative consequences for any children they might have to care for, then or in future.

044 A woman in a newish relationship with a man went through his drawers when he left her alone in his home to bring a take-away, and discovered a stash of pornographic magazines. Later that evening she mentioned it, thinking it might lead to something especially sexy. Instead he probably felt emotionally exposed and violated, because he never called her after that day. And when she did, he ended their friendship.

Two professional women were in a relationship, in which the lesbian partner was inflicting verbal and physical violence on the bisexual one, who aside from that wanted to have a child. The latter hatched a plan to ambush a nice man with a pregnancy, on the grounds that he would probably be a good father and pay regular maintenance. This was made even more despicable by the fact that he had helped her quite a lot in her work, out of kindness.

Ashamed of her bisexuality, she used their brief relationship to pretend to her family and others that she wasn't. At times she boasted obliquely about her cleverness, unable to see how pitifully transparent she was. Unaware of his vasectomy, she attempted to lure him into sex when he had no access to condoms, believing he was using them only for contraception. As the lesbian partner began to suspect that the bisexual actually liked the man, her violence escalated.

Although still not knowing about the intended entrapment, the man could sense that something wasn't right whenever he was with the closet bisexual. Eventually he found out exactly what had been going on, when he next had a relationship with the bisexual's heterosexual "best friend", who knew the story from A to Z and couldn't wait to spill the beans.

Whether male or female, educated or not, emotionally unintelligent people may be treacherous and cause huge irreparable damage. Being kind, the man decided not to retaliate or even expose her. But concluded this had probably been a mistake two years later, when he saw her pushing a pram, and realized that the thoroughly deserved suffering he could have inflicted might have saved a less fortunate man from having to pay a lifelong price.

People's age and money are private matters. If we ask an impertinent question we should not be surprised to get an evasive or diplomatic answer. If we ignore the message and continue to ask, he may come up with a straight lie and we would surely deserve it. If he refuses to tell because of a preference for honesty, he may see us as responsible for having created an unnecessary awkward situation, and perhaps wonder whether we are smart enough.

He might also conclude that we are the kind of woman willing to misuse the power which his feelings give us. That, in order to force him to disclose something he would prefer not to, instead of respecting his right to privacy.

If he is the type of man unwilling to be pressured or manipulated, his decision before long could quite easily be to retain his integrity by dropping us, hopefully in a considerate and respectful manner.

Rather than risk pushing him towards that reaction or a less extreme but still negative one, we could try to figure out his age by how he looks. We can always improve our guess by asking friends to check him out and then averaging the estimates. We may also get a lot of information the safe way, by just giving it time and letting conversation flow naturally.

Trying to find out how much money he has or earns by the car he drives, the home he lives in or how much he is prepared to spend on us could be a problem too. The message the man may get is that the woman is too materialistic, and that would probably be correct. Without being aware of it, many women lay bare the problems or limitations in their personality through the questions they ask or the manner in which they behave.

Such attempts can be very obvious, and a good example is what a lawyer did with me many years ago during what became a fascinating dinner date. By then I had read or browsed piles of material about relationships and personality. That included many bad or mediocre books intended for the general public, which I looked at in order to get an overview of what gets published and readers consume.

There was one such bad book in my shelf, with a wildly overoptimistic title implying it contained a set of sure fire instructions for marrying the man of our choice. From memory and among other things, it recommended not wasting time by beating around the bush, and having instead a list of questions in the back of our mind ready to be put to any man being evaluated.

It had been written about ten years earlier by some female lawyer, which could have been one reason why my lawyer date found it so convincing. She followed the advice to the letter, by asking a long string of questions one after another. It seemed almost like she was cross examining a witness in court, and she obviously had no idea about the impression she was giving. That was telling me loud and clear that she was not emotionally intelligent, despite being a grown up woman and practicing lawyer.

I kept recognizing her line of questioning and even specific questions from the book she had read and was unaware I had too, but it didn't seem proper to embarrass her by saying so. Although disappointed by the unexpected turn of events, I was also making the most of a bad situation by enjoying it all behind my very straight face. The kind of questions she was asking plus her manner of doing so and the fact that she thought they were relevant, were an open window into her personality.

That wasn't a pretty picture and I would never have considered her as a potential life partner, although she could have been a therapeutically interesting case to work with. But she was very far back from having a modicum of self-other awareness, which is usually a precondition for wanting any kind of meaningful personal development.

The above example conveys a valuable lesson: How we come across matters far more than getting premature information about facts, most of which may have little relevance to whether a relationship will be successful in terms of meeting our deeper needs. That is because better quality men are like better quality women, who try to make men feel relaxed and comfortable while unconsciously or intentionally evaluating us in ways we may not realize.

If we are in a singles venue and treat badly those less appealing men who aren't drunk, dirty or obnoxious, we are giving ourselves a reputation as having a personality problem. Nice men with potential could be discreetly watching although they may not have approached us yet, or they might get to hear about it.

There are some men and women who suffer from halitosis and are usually unaware of it. They can't smell it themselves, and friends or family may feel uncomfortable about telling them. The problem is aggravated by a dry mouth, which may be caused by a blocked nose due to a cold, or by foods which encourage the growth of bacteria. We can find out if we have a problem by asking our doctor or someone we can absolutely trust. If we have this problem it can be managed, but brushing and flossing alone is usually not enough.

It is important to scrape the tongue as far back as possible. This can be done with a tongue scraper (although a spoon will do too), in order to physically remove most of the microorganisms which cause bad breath. And then use an alcohol based mouthwash as per instructions in order to kill whatever is left. After doing that it will help if we avoid food or sugary drinks, as they contribute to bacteria being reintroduced and multiplying.

Heartburn aggravates halitosis, because stomach acid in the lower esophagus produces gas which then mixes with the air we exhale. If heartburn happens regularly we should consult our doctor because it is probably curable, or at least can be managed better than by taking ordinary antacid tablets.

In contrast to the mistakes discussed, there are certain things likely to make a difference to a better quality man, _if_ he happens to find us attractive enough to be considering the possibility of a permanent relationship. We want him to appreciate with his mind and feel in his heart that we are reliable enough to be trusted, intelligent enough to be tactful, respectful and responsible enough to be financially fair rather than exploitative, and naturally kind.

STAGE 5

THE NEED TO UNDERSTAND:

Why established relationships succeed or fail

Established relationships are greatly affected by both partners' personality and self esteem. These have consequences for their capacity to communicate well, understand love and happiness, and avoid gradual deterioration especially after the first years. Professionals in the field agree that human interaction mediated by circumstances during early childhood is a major determinant of how personality and self esteem will turn out.

However, both of these can be improved in adulthood through relevant personal development. This is likely to result in a burst of acceleration to the usually slow process of increasing whatever level of relationship wisdom we have. And that could be enough to tilt the balance towards better outcomes in love, work, friendships, and other situations which require considered thinking and careful management of our emotions and actions.

But personality and self esteem are complex entities, and other factors play a part too. For example, normal brain chemistry variations in serotonin and dopamine act over and above everything else, in causing us to feel relaxed or happy as against stressed or unhappy. Substance abuse impinges on how we feel and think, and may sometimes cause irreversible personality damage.

Science keeps discovering ways in which the tens of trillions of microorganisms living inside us and reacting to our diet can alter the workings of the mind, as well as of the body. The operation of the genes which influence intelligence, personality, health, etc. may be modified by environmental conditions. In laboratory mice some of these changes are then inherited by subsequent generations, and that could well be happening in humans too.

Together with other causes, hormonal variations between and within men and women play a role in predispositions such as aggressiveness, spatial abilities, emotional responsiveness, and the perceptual and relating skills needed to detect, understand and articulate subtler feelings.

The visible and deeper reasons why relationships succeed or fail

When Stage 4 drags on for too long, repeated sentimental disappointments become sufficiently painful to trigger some serious questioning of our beliefs and expectations. And with it the need and desire to understand ourselves and others better, due to the fact that mindlessly doing more of the same has become too hard to bear. By this stage therefore, it is increasingly important to get a good grip on the deeper reasons why relationships succeed or fail.

Doing so is not only a question of psychological knowledge, but has to include the values and morality which are part of our philosophy of life. That is because the latter play a part in achieving a healthy personality and self esteem, good communication, true love and genuine happiness. However, few of us are entirely clear about what exactly all these are and what makes them work. And as long as that remains so, we can never understand how the issues underpinning them can be utilized for improving on what we have.

Relationships succeed or fail fall for what can be broadly categorized as "visible" and "deeper" reasons. Both kinds operate simultaneously, and are supported by conscious and unconscious thoughts, feelings and behaviors which may be quite entrenched and hard to shift. However, because visible reasons are fully conscious and we understand them well, the degree of importance we give them and the reactions they trigger may be easier to change if we become convinced it is in our interest to do so.

Many relationships we desire fail to start or break up due to common visible reasons. Available potential partners may not meet each other's minimum requirements for permanent suitability, such as attractiveness, height, age, education or financial solvency, and it makes no difference whether these requirements are realistic or not as long as we operate by them.

A potential partner's personality also has to seem free from obvious serious deficiencies or obnoxious features. If everything looks fine and two people may be suitable, they still have to want the same thing at the same time. If a relationship does start, the sexual side has to be good enough or become so within a reasonable time. Financial expectations, major life goals and other circumstances have to be compatible.

There are also less common visible reasons. For example, the ex-husband of a woman who consulted me had began living with a man as his new partner some years after the divorce, having finally accepted that he was more attracted to men. Despite the initial inevitable shock and distress in his wife, both knew that each in his/her own way had been victims of prevailing homophobia. Therefore there was no hostility or resentment, and they supported each other as friends and joint parents.

Some of the above and other visible reasons for unsuitability have been covered in previous Stages. Understanding them is easy and they need no further elaboration. But when they are not enough to explain what is happening, and especially if we recognize a repeating pattern of sentimental disappointments, there are likely to be deeper reasons operating under the surface. These are usually unknown or not clearly understood, function largely on automatic, and are correspondingly more difficult to change.

Deeper reasons involve personality features which are harder to detect, describe and improve, and will be discussed at length under the headings for personality and self esteem. Furthermore, confronting and examining how we are can feel threatening, and the psychology of sexually intimate relationships is always intricate. Therefore a proper attempt at understanding it all has to begin with developing awareness and knowledge about the core components of personality, and how life circumstances affect its development.

Such complexity makes this chapter the most challenging part of the book, but those who persevere are bound to benefit from the knowledge they will acquire. The kind of learning discussed here does not happen in a linear way, by for example first obtaining a body of knowledge, then applying it, and next seeing our relationships get better. It is in fact a much more convoluted matter, only part of which is based on learning by direct study.

But also and most importantly by paying constant attention to a multitude of clear or subtle feedback loops, which keep coming our way as we experience relationships and life. These loops embody a two-way process of sharing information about how we come across, how others react to us, we react to their reactions, they react to our reactions, and so on. Many women notice this intuitively, most men would benefit from improving their skills at it.

However, for both men and women good self-other awareness takes time to develop. And it matters, because looking for a well suited life partner without enough of it is like trying to hit a target by shooting into the night. It becomes mostly a matter of luck, and we are no more likely to get it right than if we paid a passing gipsy to foretell our future by consulting her crystal ball. But sorry, I forgot. There are no longer gypsy fortune tellers travelling around in horse driven carts, and crystal balls are out of fashion.

Although if I may divert for a moment, crystal balls still have their uses. When I was a salaried therapist with the Department of Health, the secretaries had a divination-size crystal ball on the front desk, with the top covered by a very tiny beautifully embroidered cotton hankie. And pinned onto it was a note in a small piece of paper obviously intended for us the counselors, and anyone else who stepped on their turf.

I first noticed it one of those times when I needed to get out of my office and would drop onto an armchair in theirs, just to let the world pass by while I tried to unwind and gather my thoughts after an emotionally exhausting interview. And the note pinned to the hankie said: "If you have a really stupid question you can ask the crystal ball". I had to laugh at their creative use of humor to fix up over-intellectual absent-minded university types.

Coming back to the issue of understanding relationships, dishonest and/or deluded operators call themselves clairvoyants, psychics, astrologists, etc. Professional matchmakers, dating sites' spokespersons and their customers would all improve their knowledge about the deeper and truer reasons why relationships succeed or fail by reading this book, to everyone's benefit. More on this under the heading *Problems and potential of Internet dating and hook-up sites* (page 211).

A few genuinely good matchmakers have common sense and life experience. Their partly informed guesses about who might be suited plus a proportion of success-by-luck matches, together with self interest and wishful thinking, are enough for them to convince themselves about their skills being better than they are. The better dating sites' formulas for matching people have only limited value, and they too succeed by chance sometimes.

Believing in signs of the Zodiac is based partly on the need to understand plus the fact that they are better than nothing, for those who have not yet developed a more convincing way of understanding human nature and behavior. Lists of personality features like those ascribed to Aries or Taurus for example have no predictive value, although they may help somehow.

That is because such lists encourage readers to consider whether or not they apply to them, thereby triggering some thinking about the sort of person they are or aren't. Doing so might occasionally add some clarity and accuracy to how they see themselves, and in this way help with self understanding. This could in turn assist in alleviating existing deficits in their sense of identity which, if excessive, could aggravate anxieties and uncertainties.

As will become clear through the discussion in this Stage 5, the need to rely on some of the above is due to most people's insufficient understanding of what actually makes relationships work, and suggests their personality would benefit from further development. Until that is done, the individual's capacity to find reality-based answers to the complexities of love and relationships will stay impaired. Identity limitations and other personality vulnerabilities will remain partly misunderstood and unresolved, contributing to causing avoidable anxiety and poorer life decisions.

"First order" and "second order" understandings

> First and second order understandings are about having or developing the ability to recognize perceptions of reality which are incomplete or incorrect, and replacing them with more comprehensive, sophisticated and accurate insights into whatever is happening.

There are two types of self-serving distorted perceptions common in adult relationships. The first is wishful thinking about who we are in terms of the nobility, reasonableness or effects of our actions and reactions, and of how we come across from others' point of view. The second is insufficient and/or inaccurate appreciation of the way others are and the reasons for their behavior. If certain such perceptions are challenged or even just not accepted, it may in some people trigger self-protection through anger, blame, and/or emotional distancing.

For clarity' sake, I begin to illustrate first and second order understandings with a non-relationship example. Until about a thousand years ago ordinary people believed the Earth was flat because everyone could see it, and because if it had been round those on the underside would have fallen off. They also believed the Earth was not moving, except during earthquakes. And because the Sun went down on the West every evening and rose from the East every morning, it was obvious to them that it had been circling the Earth.

Such conclusions were based on good intelligence and common sense observation. These combined with the limited knowledge of the time, resulting in what we may call a "first order" understanding of how the universe works. When additional knowledge was added to exactly the same good intelligence and common sense, it led to a "second order" understanding.

It revealed the Earth was actually round, moved around the Sun, and that we do not fall away just because we are living down under. Something comparable applies to psychology, in that whenever we are faced with a difficult situation and need a better understanding of what is happening, we typically first try to do it with good intelligence and common sense plus the existing limited and limiting knowledge available to us at the time.

Doing so addresses our immediate concerns in a manner we are familiar and comfortable with. That feels better than the uncertainty of digging deeper into our mind and heart, which would involve the time and effort of having to learn new things and think harder, the courage of self confrontation, and the stress of enduring it for the sake of personal development.

So, the quicker and apparently sensible and easier and way of looking at relationship problems involves another form of first order understanding. It is based on reflecting about concerns which are clearly visible and easy to appreciate, without sufficient knowledge about the deeper issues involved.

For example, about one third of divorcing couples say it was due to financial pressures, and believe it on the grounds that they had frequent arguments about money. This interpretation often comes about because, not being willing to face or able to comprehend the deeper factors at play, some divorcees opt for relatively face saving explanations from within the boundaries of what they understand and may be reasonably easily explained to others.

Money problems cannot be the real cause of many such divorces however, because if it was all couples with money problems would argue about it. But many don't. Instead they cooperate to make ends meet, and their relationships grow stronger as a result. In most cases therefore, something else has to be going on in couples who say they divorced because of financial issues.

When couples try to fix their problems on the basis of their first order understandings and things don't turn out as they had hoped, they may get a sense that there is something more going on further down. But they don't really know quite what that is, let alone how to fix it. In addition and given their situation, they could feel uneasy or threatened about their imperfections and the possibility of having them exposed if they looked too close. Therefore they prefer not to, and even admitting to this fact would be unsettling.

Any change intended to improve a relationship which has been negotiated and implemented on the basis of first order understandings, is known in psychological terminology as a *first order change*. There is general acceptance by specialized therapists that this is likely to be ineffectual, as expressed by the motto *the more things change the more they remain the same*. It means that the problematic ways of relating invariably re-impose themselves before long, because neither the deeper and stronger forces propelling the partners' personalities nor their circumstances were ever meaningfully altered.

As an example of how first order changes apply to the search for a suitable man, we have probably tried a number of different men during Stages 3 and

4, after repeatedly tweaking this or that in an attempt to avoid previous mistakes. But it never worked as we hoped. And all our attempts at creating satisfying permanent relationships kept producing the same bad results, because nothing of significance had changed within us, which would usually be the only thing big enough to actually make a difference.

The pulls and levers which propel people's real motivations, thoughts and feelings from under the surface can be complex. The roots can go as far back as their early childhood, and beyond it through the experiences which shaped their parents' personalities. This is why thinking about what lays deeper under the surface may be too obscure to be easily appreciated, but that is precisely the essence of second order understanding.

Some people can sense it intuitively because they have naturally occurring good emotional intelligence, although they may not be able to describe the ins and outs of it. Others have enhanced that and other kinds of intelligence later in life, through relevant education and personal development leading to better observation skills. All this is discussed at some length under each individual heading for the six core components of personality and self esteem, listed from the next page and elaborated thereafter.

But for now I will use an example to illustrate the differences between first and second order understandings, without clouding the issue by going too deep into the reasoning behind it or the details of the work involved. A couple came for a consultation after the wife had told the husband that if they didn't she was leaving him, and he knew she meant it. The wife said he was an alcoholic, and that was the reason for her lack of desire for sex, their poor communication and all their marital arguments.

The husband replied that he worked very hard and liked to relax with a few drinks after work and in weekends, but it had never been a problem and he could stop drinking whenever he wanted. He added the reason they had an unhappy marriage, which is what pushed him to drink too much sometimes, was that she "never" wanted to have sex and he was constantly frustrated. She then related a number of drinking episodes happening regularly and frequently month after month and over the years, which he did not dispute.

That left me in no doubt his behavior met the criteria for alcoholism and that he was protecting his self image by denying he had a drinking problem, which alcoholics usually do. This was a fight against reality he could never win. But he had kept it up because until his wife had been driven to the point where she was ready to divorce him, the consequences of his self deception had been the less frightening option. The alternative was having to seek out and confront the deeper unhappiness within himself and the marriage.

There was no doubt they had a sexual problem too, which she would have to accept rather than just focus on his drinking. Both had legitimate dissatisfactions and all attempts at resolving their problems had failed, partly because they were based on first order understandings. These had enabled both of them to keep avoiding the kind of awareness which would generate anxiety in each, preferring instead to look at just one side of the surface manifestation of their problems, as the "easier" option.

That consisted of each insisting he/she was right and that the other ought to accept their "correct" interpretation of events and change accordingly. This would of course spare the "winner" from ever having to look inwards. And by avoiding it, from having to change after confronting the anxiety and discomfort of doing so and enduring the stresses involved. The outcome was ongoing arguments which never resolved anything, and the accumulation of frozen resentment which had been gradually poisoning the relationship.

Intellectual-emotional equipment for second order understanding

Much of what maturation and acquisition of wisdom are about involves a lifelong gradual process of improvement in second order understandings. That is why facilitating a burst of acceleration in that process is a central objective of this Stage 5, of this book as a whole, and indeed of all the relationship and personal development therapy and education I have ever done.

Getting the (a) *motivation* for seeking such acceleration may require a major change in our circumstances. Then we would need to acquire (b) *sufficient relevant knowledge*, plus a (c) *storage-and-retrieval framework* to avoid forgetting it. Such framework consists of various classifications and diagrams, the latter being especially important, as each easily remembered image reminds us in a flash of all the ideas it embodies. This matters whenever management of a delicate situation can be improved by remembering and applying knowledge which is clear, real and useful, as against obscure, fake or useless.

Because second order understandings are so critical, I want to discuss at length the intellectual-emotional equipment which is involved and can improve them. This equipment is what I consider as the forever evolving and interacting six central aspects of personality, which I call its "core components":

1. Conviction of worthiness
2. Self-other acceptance
3. Self-other awareness
4. Self-other respect

5. Self confidence
6. Sense of identity and meaning

The same components also make up the critically important multifaceted entity of self esteem. That means self esteem is not just one more aspect or trait of personality, as it is often thought of, but an outcome and manifestation of what is at the heart of it. This is a new and original way of looking at personality and self esteem. It evolved out of necessity as I struggled together with countless clients over the years, in their efforts to improve their relationships and their lives through better self-other understanding.

Each component is discussed next, and the point of doing so will become clearer once they are seen in the totality of the picture. This is presented under the main heading of *Self esteem: An important but misunderstood issue* plus its subheadings and diagrams. Diagram 2 includes what I have called "peripheral components" of personality and self esteem, which are nowhere near as relevant as "core" ones to the substance of either.

PERSONALITY: The six core components

Personality is the total interacting conglomerate of thoughts, feelings, behaviors and the patterns in which they are expressed, which make the intellectual-emotional essence unique to each individual. It can be understood and analyzed through the core components listed above and elaborated below, each under its own heading.

Conviction of worthiness: The foundation of personality and self esteem

Conviction of worthiness is an automatic and sometimes unconscious positive self evaluation, reflecting an inherent human need to feel valuable. It begins very early in life as an immensely beneficial natural phenomenon nurtured mostly within the family, which I refer to as "unconscious convictions of lovability and competence".

Conviction of worthiness is the center and foundation for the other five core components of personality. While it is less urgent that food and less noticeable than the sexual instinct, the need for conviction of worthiness (and self esteem) can be relentless when not adequately satisfied.

That is because we are social animals, with a mind which allows everyone to recognize the fact and the feeling that being worthy facilitates wellbeing. This would have been especially so within the small groups in which humans have lived throughout most of their existence, when the issue would have been not only wellbeing but survival itself. Therefore the need for conviction of worthiness and self esteem became an evolutionary imperative imprinted in our genes, just like nest building is in the genes of birds.

In a family with emotionally healthy significant others, our conviction of worthiness begins to be gradually built into the structure of our personality probably from not long after we are born, as a result of the consistent love and attention we receive. There is some anecdotal evidence that abandoned babies adopted into loving families before the age of six months do not seem to develop more personality problems than average, while those adopted later and especially a lot later are much more likely to do so.

The above suggests that the unconscious conviction of lovability component of worthiness begins to set in from at least as early as around six months. In most cases, much of the level and quality of it is well established by adolescence. The stresses of this period may unbalance it temporarily. But by then the essential groundwork has already been done, and those fortunate children who got it right are likely to reap the benefits for life.

An example of how unconscious convictions of lovability and competence can help in managing the stresses of adolescence is included as Appendix A, an autobiographical narrative by me entitled *The doors of Heaven: Boyhood rites of passage before the days of sex education*. It explores the impact of peer pressures on the sexual milestones in adolescent boys, and incorporates character formation and socio-political awareness.

During the early period of a child's life, it is usually mothers who as the primary care givers deliver most of the attention and affection which will be absorbed as an unconscious conviction of lovability. Most grandmothers are excellent at it, but can only do so to the extent that children have access to them.

All that care and attention is enriched by women's genetically influenced skills at doing it very well. That makes them pivotal in creating the natural and highly beneficial kind of brainwashing which unconscious conviction of lovability is really about, and permanently improves the hardwiring of the child's brain.

Most men are not as good as most women at conveying lovability. Grandfathers tend to do it better than fathers, probably to some extent because a much longer life experience plus age related hormonal changes have mellowed them. And on doing so, un-suppressed aspects of their nurturing side, thereby enabling them to develop whatever potential capacities they had but were previously less able to put into practice.

An emotionally nurturing environment also leads to the development of an unconscious conviction of competence, which comprises the second half of what will become adult conviction of worthiness. Both lovability and competence are integral and inseparable precursors of adult conviction of worthiness. That is because it would be very difficult to feel lovable if we felt incompetent, or competent if we feel unlovable.

The unconscious feeling of competence begins as soon as babies succeed in getting attention by crying and sense the connection, and keeps developing as they overcome the never ending trials of growing up. By and large however, conviction of competence begins to emerge a bit later than that of lovability, and if it is to develop properly has to extend over a much longer number of years. Most fathers play a very important role in its encouragement and development, and indeed so do an increasing number of mothers who are used to fighting it out in a competitive workforce.

While this is based only on my own observations, I believe that just as there is a genetic predisposition making most women better at conveying lovability, there is a parallel predisposition making most men better at conveying competence. This often happens through play when children are younger and through guidance or other forms of support as they get older, especially from middle childhood and well into early adulthood.

As children progress towards adolescence they become more self aware, and this gradually solidifies the childhood unconscious convictions of lovability and competence into a more conscious conviction of worthiness. Like its two components it ranges from very high to very low, and is the foundation of personality and self esteem upon which all subsequent components are built and evolve through life.

When the process of developing unconscious convictions of lovability and competence does not go well, it often (but not always) contributes to creating personalities ranging from less than good enough to very problematic. Many examples are discussed in Stage 6, under the headings *The relatively less harmful Mr. Wrongs* and *Definitely dangerous men (and women)*.

Those who were less fortunate as children in the sense of not getting quite all the quality love which would have been desirable, are not condemned to a lesser conviction of worthiness if they happened to end up that way. It can be increased by expanding our second order understandings, beginning as one possible method by attempting to develop all the intellectual-emotional equipment components discussed in this Stage 5.

Various psychological theories as well as cultural, religious or philosophical traditions may advocate methods other than the ones in this book for trying to achieve better second order understandings. But one way or another and regardless of the terminology or sociocultural context, they all revolve around attempts at developing interacting configurations of knowledge, emotional balance and wisdom. With these come the tolerance, humility and capacity for compassion they engender, plus whatever personal, social or religious practices are believed to underpin their development.

Improving second order understandings leads to the ongoing development of all core components, and these will in turn contribute to strengthening our conviction of worthiness throughout life. This process will be elaborated later, under the heading *The foundation, core and peripheral components of self esteem and personality*. Next I give two examples of how worthiness keeps evolving from early childhood, the first illustrating primarily the development of lovability and the second that of competence, although in practice they happen simultaneously from an early age and influence each other.

Unconscious conviction of lovability: The case of eight year old Christine

Christine (not her real name) was the first and only child born into a household where mum, dad and the paternal grandparents lived together. The parents separated when Christine was around six and since then she has been living with mum, not far from the maternal grandparents, her uncle and cousin just one or two years younger, who they visit regularly.

During the time when mum was discussing relationship issues with me, Christine was sent alone on a long trip overseas. This was for a one month holiday with a paternal uncle and cousins of similar age she had never met in person, under special care arrangements with the airline company. That was when mum told me about her telephone communication with Christine.

She allowed me to hear her voice messages and read Christine's SMS replies, and gave me permission to quote the material below without identifying details. Mum was understandably a bit worried as well as finding it difficult to be separated from her child for the first time, and had been calling Christine's mobile every day for her first week overseas. Christine sent mum an SMS shortly after her last call:

SMS by Christine:	"Don't actually call me every day. It's very …"
Mum's message:	"I call you because I am missing you so much, I will keep calling you"
SMS by Christine:	"I won't reply then, bye"
Mum's message:	"Whatever you do, I love you"
SMS by Christine:	"Disgusting!!!"
Mum's message:	"Whatever you say I still love you"
Christine didn't reply	

Christine has always been getting that kind of unconditional love and attention from all the family adults around her, especially mum, and doesn't know how lucky she is. Her unconscious convictions of lovability and competence are so well established that she has become very independent for her age, to a point which enables her to challenge mum.

Not only is she daring enough to feel sufficiently secure travelling alone in a very long plane journey, which not all children of that age would despite the best arrangements. But once overseas, she is relaxed enough to enjoy the fun and adventure without needing the reassurance of mum's presence or voice. Being with supportive relatives helps of course, but these are after all people she had never met in person before.

The combination of unconscious convictions of lovability and competence facilitate the development of social-emotional intelligence. Even by age eight Christine is already instinctively savvy and diplomatic enough to say "Don't actually call me every day. It's very …" and leave it at that, rather than risk hurting mum's feelings further by being too heavy on her.

Being only eight she does not yet have a vocabulary extensive enough to express the finer subtleties of how she feels about mum calling every day, but she is already perfectly able to deliver the message. It is mostly mum's fault of course, for having been such a good mother. And the fault of dad and the grandparents too, for apparently having done rather well what was undoubtedly their pleasant duty of unconditional love.

Emotionally healthy and independent children who don't need us as much or as often as we might prefer, is the price we pay for good parenting. High unconscious convictions of lovability and competence in childhood facilitate the development of a healthy personality, unhindered by undue burdens.

When these burdens exist they are most often due to self-doubt about being lovable, which crept gradually into the structure of the child's personality. That can happen despite parent's considerable efforts and best intentions.

It may be due to unfavorable circumstances or personality limitations, and lead to love and attention which too often are insufficient, inconsistent or conditional on doing what parents wanted.

For example, if mum had reacted to Christine's challenge by saying something which carried the message of withdrawal of love as punishment, then her love becomes conditional on Christine behaving as mum wants. As another example, insisting on homework or enough orderliness in their room can be totally different from withdrawing love, in that the child feels always sure about his/her lovability despite being admonished.

If parenting practices making their expressions of love conditional upon the child behaving in ways approved by them apply too often, the child can never feel totally secure about being loved. That is because the withdrawal of it is always one mistake away, or even one instance of self assertion. When this happens it is rarely the fault of parents or other family, who mean to do the best they can and do it as well as they are able to.

But they may have more than their fair share of stress in their life such as significant poverty, limited knowledge, personality limitations, discrimination, poor health. etc. Regardless of the causes however, lesser quality love and attention can reduce the development of unconscious convictions of lovability and competence. When these are towards the lower end of the continuum, they become a major hindrance to an otherwise natural progression towards a higher level conviction of worthiness throughout life.

Better emotional balance and intelligence, financial comfort, education and other favorable circumstances in the parents may facilitate the process. But in a majority of cases these would be secondary to what really matters, which is sufficient, consistent and unconditional love and attention received throughout the growing years. This kind of love and attention is more important the younger the children are, because their still relatively blank psyche is absorbing it all into the budding foundation of their personality.

Unconscious conviction of competence: The case of the boy under four

This example is self-explanatory, and presented in the form of a long quote from an autobiographical narrative. When compared to psychology style writing which is tighter and more economical, a literary narrative has the advantage of taking its time to put the reader into the context of what is happening. And therefore when the point is finally made it comes across clearly and precisely, in a way which stands out and has a stronger emotional impact. The example is quoted next:

.../... "Life wasn't meant to be easy", said the late Australian Prime Minister Malcom Fraser. And when he went to America and lost his trousers, he found out that life can get tricky too. Of course, I had known all that since I was three and a half. It was then, one evening before we sat down for dinner, that my mother decided I should learn to wash my hands all by myself. Probably because I was going to need it, after the village nuns had agreed to make an exception and accept me six months earlier into their "kind of preschool".

Anything my mother could earn while the nuns looked after me during the day was going to be desperately needed, because the meager earnings of my oldest brother were about to disappear with his oncoming conscription into the army. My grandfather who lived with us had died recently, three years after my father's death from a legacy of injuries sustained during the civil war, some years after returning from exile following a general amnesty. It must have been hard on her. But not for the first time, feeding her family was the imperative she had to attend to.

As in most houses of the village poor there was a big kitchen with an artificial stone sink which was huge by today's standards, located in front of a window in the center of the front wall. In it women did the dishes, gutted and cleaned the occasional casualty from the chicken or rabbit coop, washed the family's clothes, and bathed their children and themselves. When hot water was needed it came from the wood and coal stove, which during the cold winters was kept going throughout the day. It was built into the chimney with bricks, mortar and a blackened cast iron top and front, right next to the sink.

I remember standing at the edge of the sink, on the one foot stool where I liked to sit after dinner at my favorite spot, near the warm stove. By outstretching my arms as far as I could, I was just able to reach the water tap. About one foot to the right hung a chicken wire basket with the single piece of soap which was used for clothes, dishes and every personal use. The soap when new was about the size of a quarter of a brick, and most of the time it was just as dry.

As I stood there wandering what to do next I looked at my mother, who was sitting to my left, to see how I was going to wash my hands. "First you wet your hands, and then you rub the soap", she told me. And so, I stretched myself as my tiny hands struggled to reach for the water tap.

But as I was getting there, one of my grown up brothers who were also watching the big occasion from my right, had his say. "No, you don't do it like that", he told me with a smile, "First you rub the soap and then you wet your hands". Having straightened myself back onto the stool while absorbing this new piece of information, I began to stretch myself again, trying this time to reach the soap in the wire basket.

"No darling", said my mother from the left. I stopped and listened. "First you wet your hands and then you rub the soap", she explained lovingly. And so, with the matter finally cleared, I began again to stretch towards the water tap. But it was not to be. Both my brothers came in this time, insisting the proper way to do it was to rub the soap first and wet my hands after.

I stood there for a few moments, feeling rather confused, repeatedly turning my head from them to my mother. Until one of my brothers asked me. "Well, who are you going to believe?"

There was this one thing I remembered most clearly, whenever my mind drifted back to the incident as I was growing older. And that was the overwhelming feeling of being trapped, and searching furiously for an escape.

I knew who I believed, but certainly did not want to get off side with these two very big brothers. The seconds felt like hours as I stood there unsure about what to do, turning from them to my mother and then back again, my poor little brain struggling for a way out.

The resourcefulness which is bred out of desperation produced a strategy intended to gain time, while I tried to figure out how to wriggle myself out of trouble. Realizing I couldn't stretch it any longer and had to answer the question, I looked straight to the wall between them and said: "I'll believe whoever is right". I've never remembered what happened next, except that suddenly all three burst into laughter. And I sensed immediately that, somehow, I had gotten myself off the hook. .../...

This boy had also been growing up as the only child in a household of four adults, with another household just upstairs made of a childless uncle and aunt plus other extended family nearby within the village. Just like Christine in the previous example he would have been the center of attention and affection, but he had other advantages too.

The most important were that his mum was a very experienced mother, in addition to a mature woman with common sense. Furthermore, with her being a recent widow and his brothers close to twenty, she was always there for him and he never experienced the distress of a marital argument or dethronement by a new baby.

Although the hand washing episode became a bit of a challenge, he managed it well enough, probably because of his by then budding unconscious convictions of lovability and competence. And the positive reaction of the adults following his unexpected precocious attempt at a diplomatic escape, must have reinforced both.

All children experience countless trials in the process of growing up, and are likely to manage them well enough if they live with consistent unconditional love. This is without a doubt the most precious gift a child can be given, and it is a solid foundation for subsequent healthy personality and self esteem development throughout life.

Self-other acceptance

> Self-other acceptance is a desire and capacity to acknowledge and be comfortable with the fact that whoever we and others are and whatever is happening or anyone is doing, this is the reality at the moment. It is unconditional in the sense that it does not involve judging ourselves or others as being more or less worthy, and it is open to the possibility of everyone and everything evolving and changing, currently and in future.

Acceptance is a component of personality built over the foundation of conviction of worthiness and with its assistance. How this assistance works may be better understood if we consider it in the context of the opposites of acceptance, which are "denial" of reality and its milder version of "avoidance". Denial and avoidance are natural and normal mechanisms of emotional defense. They activate automatically and usually for a limited time, in order to protect us from significant fear or anxiety.

However, they may also be used in a more or less ongoing way, which can range all the way from unconscious to deliberate. When ongoing, they become very damaging to personality and relationships, through the perceptual distortion of those realities experienced as uncomfortable. The fear and anxiety which denial and avoidance are used to protect us from, are most often generated by possible realistic or unrealistic negative judgments about us by ourselves or others. But denial or avoidance can also be triggered by events which may be too distressing to be absorbed and accepted immediately.

For example, we may behave as if the seriousness of an unexpected terminal illness diagnosis or the proximity of death do not exist somehow, until such time as we have survived the initial shock and are better able to manage the anguish of our new reality. Some of us will be overtaken by death still in denial of its impending approach. And because dying is probably the most distressing process we will ever face, we are all entitled to cope in whatever way we can without judgment or undue interference.

Deliberate denial and avoidance are close to lying to ourselves. But it may not always quite get there because they usually contain a component of self-delusion, and the likely proximity of our own death is not the only situation where it happens. A recently widowed elderly woman made a dummy which she sat on a chair and dressed in her late husband's clothes and hat. The community nurses assisting with her personal care reported to the Adult Mental Health Team I was a member of, that she talked to it as if it was her husband when he was alive.

They believed she had gone mad, and something should perhaps be done about it. I insisted that it was just a form of temporary conscious denial, by which she was trying to cope with her unbearable grief and loneliness. And that she should be left in peace to keep talking to the dummy for as long as she wanted. Heartbreakingly sad, but given her extreme predicament it was the best way she could manage her tragedy for the time being.

The problem with denial and avoidance under more normal circumstances is that when we surrender to it regularly for the sake of short term relief of fear or anxiety, it is as if we put an automatic filter between us and reality. The purpose is to do away with unpleasant information, preferably before it enters awareness, because our conviction of worthiness is not strong enough to cope with it. For example if someone points out something negative but real and truthful about us, we may feel threatened and react defensively.

We may then fight our way out of it by "winning" any ensuing discussion. This makes us feel better, but can ultimately result in a perception of reality which is plagued by blind spots. A person who does this as a norm ends up failing to see certain things which are strikingly obvious to others. This not only hinders development of self-other acceptance, but it is in fact the direct opposite of it. Consequently it will also obstruct self-other awareness, for which the critical requirement is precisely the self-other acceptance necessary to observe and absorb all the information we can gather.

Because some aspects of self acceptance can feel so threatening for people with low conviction of worthiness, improving it will require from them greater determination and courage than what is needed by those who do not suffer from this problem. In contrast, higher conviction of worthiness enables a person to consider all the information which comes in with relative ease, and to seek additional "threatening" information if considered useful.

Such a person does not feel unduly unsettled by any of it, because whatever happens he/she retains an unshakable conviction of being worthy. In other words, those with a high conviction of worthiness are better able to accept critical feedback and consider it with equanimity, even if it presents them in a negative light or is noticeably intended to be destructive. This is how self acceptance becomes the second core component of personality, assisted in its formation by a good level of preexisting conviction of worthiness.

When self acceptance is poor, that insufficiency hinders the development of subsequent core components of personality. This makes it virtually impossible for the person to progress properly into developing self esteem of the better "secure" variety. The better and second best varieties of self esteem will be discussed at length under their own subheadings.

The bigger the fear or anxiety we are trying to protect ourselves from, the stronger the denial and avoidance may become. If interpretations of reality based on ignoring or distorting those parts of it which trigger anxiety about inadequacy or shame are challenged by anyone, the deniers or avoiders may defend them strenuously and react resentfully, angrily or aggressively.

Some forms of denial are so widely accepted that they form an integral part of cultures and civilizations. From the point of view of non religious people for example, a prime example of denial is caused by the fear of death. For them, denial of death is manifested by the belief common to all religions that when our body dies, we retain a spirit or soul which remains immortal. Whether the hope for an afterlife is or isn't a form of escape, it seems to make the fear of death more bearable for many of those who truly believe.

Regardless of religious belief, improving our self acceptance requires the courage to stand up to and confront any distressing anxiety or sense of threat, rather than to escape from it. And to understand and live with it, for the sake of developing a healthier personality. When we can fully accept the unpleasant facts and tragedies of life, plus ourselves with our strengths and limitations, it is easy and natural to also see and accept others as they really are irrespective of whether we like them or not.

People with good self-other acceptance do not feel inferior to anyone or need to believe they are superior, because they know everyone has qualities and flaws. And that how fortunate or otherwise people end up being, has a lot to do with circumstances and luck in addition to personal effort. They are also more likely to develop secure self esteem, and thereby become less impressionable by impressive titles, honors, wealth, power, fame, etc.

Acceptance is unconditional and in that sense different from liking or not liking ourselves or others, which is always conditional. I would argue that the minimum condition for liking ourselves is self respect, to be discussed further below under its own heading. And we can only decide with enough certainty on whether or not we deserve that self respect, if we have an at least reasonably accurate understanding about ourselves, others and the situations we are in.

Without such understanding and the grounding on reality it provides, we may just be deluding ourselves, which in extreme cases could take us worryingly close to a form of insanity. A reasonably accurate understanding requires in turn and as a minimum a good enough level of self-other awareness. The latter will in turn be significantly influenced by the level of self-other acceptance we have built, superimposed on our preexisting conviction of worthiness.

I conclude this subheading by repeating two important points: The first is that children who have been lucky to grow with naturally occurring high convictions of lovability and competence are much more likely to develop a better conviction of worthiness, self-other acceptance and self-other awareness. These will in turn facilitate the development of the three subsequent core components of personality, and in a best case scenario the process culminates in lifelong "secure high" self esteem.

And the second point is that people who were less fortunate as children are not condemned to live with underdeveloped core components of personality. It will take them more effort to lift their "contingent" self esteem towards the "secure" variety, and in some of them a lot more effort (all this is elaborated in the subheadings about self esteem). But if brave and determined enough they are likely to overcome the damaging consequences of the disadvantages they suffered as children, by improving their core components during adulthood through genuine personal development.

Self-other awareness

> Self-other awareness is the capacity to notice and understand the deeper intellectual-emotional issues and functioning in ourselves and others. It includes not only our current perceptions, but also a propensity and desire to continually improve on them. When properly developed it goes much further than "empathy", which is part of it but refers only to being aware of how others feel and experience their reality.

The previous discussion on self-other acceptance incorporated the reasons why it is a prerequisite for the development of a higher level of self-other awareness. But this is so important for understanding our own and other people's motivations and behaviors, that it is worth recapitulating.

Self acceptance allows us to not be excessively afraid of taking on board and considering all the information we can gather, and the one about ourselves is particularly helpful. Our intake of it can be increased by seeking feedback on whatever we think might be useful, especially on mistakes we make, until we figure out what went wrong and how to avoid it in future.

We also improve our self-other awareness by becoming attentive observers of people's qualities and imperfections, and noticing how they understand themselves, others and reality. We need to be alert about their comments and behavior, particularly when we sense that they are better observers than us, because it is from such people that we can learn the most.

During my first year university tutorials, I began noticing that some female students were making comments about people related issues which I recognized immediately as being correct and sensible. That led me to consider why I hadn't thought of them myself.

It wasn't long before I realized that some of these women were more emotionally aware than I was on certain things, and in that respect I could learn from them. Thereafter, every time one of them made a comment I considered valuable I made a mental note and tried to remember it, so as to absorb their perceptual skills in order to enhance my own.

Other people's comments and behavior manifest the human nature we all share. By noticing them we are observing and learning about ourselves, because they are like a mirror on which we see our own reflections. That means we can learn even from people whose awareness is less developed than ours, because, aside from showing us how their personalities function, they too can make observations which had escaped our perception.

When we behave with less than our usual awareness, we may not be able to grasp the full extent of it due to being partly blinded by our own feelings. But when we see the same thing in others it is easier to recognize, because having less or no emotional involvement can enable us to appreciate the subtleties of a situation with more clarity and accuracy.

The more we learn about ourselves from observing others and reflecting on what we see and hear, the better able we become to use that self awareness in order to develop awareness of others. This is how the learning process involved in increasing our self-other awareness happens. That is, not so much in a one way linear progression, but primarily as a never ending series of feedback loops through interaction with others.

These feedback loops with enough people are essential, and it bears repeating that the most valuable ones are with those whose level of self-other awareness is higher than ours. Without such feedback from others we would be excessively reliant on our own interpretations of reality. That would be fine if we were entirely correct, but we may not be. And what if we are totally wrong and don't realize it?

People who believe they are always right are in fact likely to be wrong about quite a few things, and it is common for them to be unaware of how much there is that they don't know. For example, some people think of themselves as morally upright, intelligent, respected, etc. But if several people who are generally recognized as being well balanced and know them sufficiently think differently, there would be grounds for considering whether "blind spots" might be involved.

In other words, it is possible that the belief in our self-other awareness could be based on illusion or delusion. And therefore we need to make sure that its accuracy and validity are based on tried and tested reality, preferably including corroboration from reliable others. This does not disregard the primacy of our own thinking and conviction, or the possibility that some of the feedback we receive may be inaccurate or malicious. It merely emphasizes that enough external sources are needed to keep tabs on ourselves, as a way of validating the reliability of our self-other awareness.

Again, it is best if the above can be done by somehow checking whether our observations and conclusions are shared by reputable people who have considered the issues at hand. However, not all our self-other awareness learning happens through live interaction. We can also learn indirectly in other ways, through for example good literature, books such as this one, watching good films, and many other sources.

Indeed the teacher could be anything or anyone such as the cleaner at work, a psychologist, next door neighbor, friend, someone who hates us or is not very bright, an overheard comment, Shakespeare's plays or The Simpsons. How far we are able to develop our self-other awareness depends always and primarily on our ability and eagerness to observe, reflect, and seek feedback if possible. And only secondarily on the skills or intentions of whoever or whatever happens to be a potential teacher.

Self-other respect

> Self-other respect is a central value, indicative of a healthy personality and expressed mostly by behaving according to our principles within the reality of what is possible. It includes a supportive orientation towards others, especially the vulnerable, and an acceptance of the right of people to be as they are provided this does not interfere with the rights of others.

Our level of self-other respect is one of the factors determining whether we will end up becoming opportunistic users seeking our advantage at any cost, at one extreme, as against being fairly decent people who consider and care for the needs of others. Without the supportive orientation side of it, we could be proud of our skills at legalized robbery for example, or at being able to exploit and abuse people in immoral or criminal ways.

While good to bad hearts come in many forms and shades of gray, most people's values would not allow them to consider high skills at economic exploitation, legalized robbery or criminality as realistic grounds for self respect. That would be regardless of the fact that run of the mill small and big psychopaths as well as some philosophically minded thieves with pretensions of respectability might discreetly disagree.

The latter often rely on cleverly rationalized conscious denial of the lying kind to prop up their fake self image, for the purpose of stealthily trying to let themselves off the immorality or criminality hook in the eyes of others. But we should never forget that in addition to a desire for economic justice, a supportive orientation has to include respecting other peoples' differences, their freedom, and especially their dignity.

Unless both aspects of respect are present, a supportive orientation is likely to become paternalistic, counterproductive and ultimately destructive. Well known historical examples include the treatment of aboriginal nations and different races or cultures in Australia and the United States.

Current examples of general disrespect include negative attitudes to cultural and racial minorities, or towards those with atypical victimless sexual orientations. Individual examples of disrespect by ordinary male or female bullies are something most of us are familiar with. And my understanding of human nature as well as my personal values, tell me that it is not possible to have a realistic claim to self respect while being disrespectful to others

Sense of identity and meaning

Identity and meaning are distinct but closely related entities, in the sense that as the latter develops it becomes part of the former and reinforces it.

> Sense of identity is a feeling and conviction that we know who and how we are, plus an understanding of the way we fit in the immediate and broader contexts in which we live.

Knowing who and how we are means being well acquainted with how we think, feel and behave as we do and why. This includes having a clear awareness and acceptance of our likes and dislikes, wishes and fears, values, needs, aspirations, strengths, weaknesses, limitations, personal history, future plans plus everything else that makes us who and what we are.

Understanding well the way we fit into our immediate and broader contexts requires an awareness of what those contexts are, how they operate and why. They include among innumerable others the personalities of people in general, the functioning of our sexually intimate relationship, family, friendships, neighborhood, work, socioeconomic and political systems, country, the world, as well as the visible and hidden forces which impinge on it all.

Sense of identity interacts with all the other core components of personality and many peripheral ones. This makes it an all-inclusive entity, with underpinnings and ramifications extending in every direction. That is why it is constantly evolving, ranges from very high to very low, and is strongly influenced by factors such as formal or informal education, life experience, emotional intelligence and degrees of personal development.

> Sense of meaning is our understanding of the reasons for existence, if there are any, in a way which addresses the issues generated by the four major concerns emanating from the human condition.

It usually starts later than sense of identity, in an attenuated and often not seriously thought-through form at first. Its development adds to our sense of identity, and both can change and expand as we are exposed to additional experiences.

Our sense of meaning as defined above is embodied in our answer to the question "What is the purpose of life?", or something along those lines which represents the same concern. The actual manifestations of a growing need for a clearer sense of meaning may begin with feelings of emptiness, a sense of alienation and detachment, preoccupations about whether life is worthwhile, or what all our struggles are ultimately for.

Sometimes a stronger need for a sense of meaning may come suddenly, for example due to an unexpected serious illness or accident, family tragedy, a traumatic divorce or retirement from work. It is at these junctures that people may find themselves a bit lost and not knowing what to do or where to turn. But for most of us, issues about meaning only begin to gather force from midlife onwards, after earlier imperatives like economic security and bringing up the next generation are largely out of the way.

Because issues of meaning emanate from fundamental realities of the human condition and have to do with the reasons or purposes of our existence, the concerns people feel about them are often referred to as "existential". To the extent that these concerns are felt but remain unresolved, they generate existential anxieties. There are four major such anxieties which affect most people at various points in the second half of life, maintained by ongoing although often not clearly delineated or understood concerns about:

- The inevitability and distress of death
- The possibility that life has no purpose
- The risk of intimate and social isolation
- Taking responsibility for how to live life

There are good reasons why religion may facilitate wellbeing, by among other things helping with these anxieties. Believers include highly intelligent, educated and emotionally sophisticated people, who each for their individual reasons choose some kind and degree of religious faith. Even if they have other means for addressing existential concerns, genuine religious belief can still mitigate any residual existential anxieties they might have.

The point of commenting on religion is not to defend or undermine it. But simply to point out that it is one of the most common ways of adding solidity to many people's sense of identity and meaning, while simultaneously soothing their major existential and other anxieties.

By far the biggest existential concern is **the inevitability and distress of death**, which is frightening for most of us to varying degrees as it gets closer and we have to face it. All religions try to alleviate this fear, by asserting as a fundamental tenet that we have a soul or spirit which continues to live after our body dies. And the more we fear death the more comforted we are by believing that we have an immortal soul, regardless of the manner in which different religions claim that it continues to exist.

The possibility that life has no purpose but simply exists, can also create anxiety in many of us. As life pressures increase through declining health and in other ways, the never ending struggle for wellbeing may begin to drag our morale down, unless we can find some higher purpose for our efforts or suffering. Given the desire for understanding created by the inborn capacities of our brain, we begin to ask ourselves questions such as "Why do we exist?" and "What is the point of it all?".

Such answers are not easy to find however, and many people opt for accepting religion as a source of truth and guidance. Those who feel left out or otherwise disappointed by established religions may turn to cults or alternative belief systems. Without some such beliefs, our efforts at finding meaning come up against the lack of evidence that life has a predetermined purpose. And therefore, that if we want one we have to create it ourselves and keep backing it up with actions which confirm and support it.

People who do not rely on religion (even if they have one), may seek and find their own answers through psychology and philosophy, or just through the wisdom of everyday common sense. But given the uncertainties and complexities of life, it can be difficult for most people to create their own sense of purpose in life. Therefore again, it is simpler and easier for many to accept the ready made one plus promised rewards offered by religion.

Although the underlying workings of each individual's personality and circumstances are unique, a valid generalization can still be made: In most cases, the less psychologically resourceful people are the more appealing religious guidance or some other external source of wisdom is likely to be, for addressing anxieties about the meaning and purpose of life.

Evolution has made us into social animals, and that is why most people need to be and feel part of at least one group in order to feel secure and experience wellbeing. Therefore **the risk of intimate and social isolation** can generate anxiety, and a consequent need for belonging. The more of this anxiety we have the more likely we are to experience aloneness as loneliness, although they are very different, especially for introverts.

Most of us defend against isolation by striving to form and maintain connections with people who accept us. The smallest example is a permanent sexually intimate relationship. Then there is our family, and next our circle of friends, work colleagues, a multitude of community associations, country, race, culture, etc. But religious affiliation is one of the most common.

That is because religion is already established and sanctioned by tradition, easily available, and does not exclude most other options of seeking further ways of belonging. Depending on the individual's personality and its level of development, the fear of isolation ranges from very high to very low. And the greater that fear, the more we seek to minimize it by secure and multiple affiliations.

Taking responsibility for how to live life can also generate anxiety, because creating a comprehensive plan for living is not easy. In addition to helping us deal with the present, any such plan needs to be credibly able to anticipate major future events, suggest ways of managing them, and be adaptable enough for us to feel reasonably secure. But the never ending changes, complexities and uncertainties of life have the potential to make creating and maintaining this plan anywhere from difficult to daunting.

People whose personality has reached a higher level of development can face the task with more equanimity and confidence. Those who have such plan still have to implement it by personal action, see whether it works, and then adjust it and keep trying while they live with all the associated stresses. Compared to what would be for many all that ongoing hard work and uncertainty, religion tells us not only how we should live life, but tops it off by promising eternal happiness if we follow its rules.

We all prefer things the easy way, so the temptation to rely on religion can be strong. This is encouraged in all sorts of direct and subtle ways by those who want us to believe for various reasons. Genuine believers may sincerely think their religion is the only true one, and that we would be better and happier if we believed. For some people, another reason could be to make themselves feel better by our belief adding credibility to theirs, thereby helping to reduce any residual uncertainties about the existence of an afterlife.

Ruling elites benefit from the population being religious, because as long as people keep hoping for eventual everlasting happiness in their next life, they are less likely to resist or rebel against economic disadvantage or exploitation. That is why throughout history, religion has been distorted and misused by the powerful to protect their interests.

However, it is important to recognize that religion can also be a force for individual and social good. And to acknowledge the personal merit of the good deeds aimed at improving the lives of the less fortunate, by countess religious humanitarians who see one aspect of doing it as part of their religious convictions and duties.

There is nothing wrong with having power or making a lot of money. But those whose focus in life has become to accumulate and secure it, are bound to come across many opportunities to do it in morally objectionable or criminal ways. They may be tempted to hide their true nature behind religion, precisely because it is associated with so many socially laudable goals and aspirations and so many genuinely good people.

We should never forget that greed manifested by corruption and a desire for exploitation or legal robbery, is the real motivation of many people who use religion to prop up their position on the social ladder. And that as people ascend through it, hypocrisy and viciousness wear a thicker mask.

Jesus Christ himself must have been well aware of this, when he said that it is easier for a camel to pass through the eye of a needle than for a rich man to enter the Kingdom of Heaven (In Christ's time, a "needle" referred to a low narrow arch designed for people to walk under, but not big enough for a camel to pass through without a very great deal of difficulty).

Christ's truths challenged the status and self image of some among the powerful, who retaliated by claiming he was worse than Barabbas, the most notorious criminal at the time. The accepted Christian narrative is that they contributed to getting Christ crucified using lies and political manipulations, although allegedly the Roman Governor was willing to let him off after a brutal flogging.

We may believe that Christ was God, one of his prophets (as Muslims do), or just an ordinary mortal. But during his time as a human being he is generally considered to have been uncommonly intelligent, brave and kind, and an example for all who want a better world. This is a shared belief among the many variants of Christianity, despite the fact that that many who consider themselves Christians envy, hate, and directly or indirectly exploit and otherwise abuse others, justifying it with all sorts rationalizations.

Having a sense of meaning irrespective of what it is or how it is arrived at, is mentally and emotionally a healthier option than the uncertainty of the alternatives. That is because for example, not having a sense of meaning or lacking enough clarity about it at a time in life when we need it, would leave a gnawing void in our psyche. This could contribute to creating or aggravating all sorts of anxieties, and might become a significant factor in creating mental health problems or worsening preexisting ones.

Anxiety and depression can be reduced by medication such as antidepressants, but they involve damaging side effects. Furthermore, they are not always appropriate, and can never compensate for not having a good enough level of development in sense of meaning and all the other core components.

So, for genuine believers and those without better alternatives, religion may reduce distressing anxieties including the four major existential ones. That must have been part of what Karl Marx had in mind when he said that religion is the opium of the masses, at a time when opium was seen as a helpful curative substance which only the rich could afford.

But there is a major problem with having a sense of identity and meaning too dependent on religious belief: Relying on any source of presumed truth which requires an unquestioned acceptance of other people's interpretations of reality, discourages people from doing the thinking and actions needed to develop their own knowledge and confidence.

That creates a disadvantage for them, by making it more difficult to reach the wonderfully fulfilling and liberating experience of achieving a higher level of personal development, and the "secure" or "secure high" self esteem which it may ultimately bring about. And missing on that or even having less of it, is certainly a significant loss.

Self confidence

> Self confidence is a conviction that our intellectual-emotional abilities are adequate for understanding and managing the situations we face competently enough, after allowances for our limitations and other unfavorable circumstances. Genuine self confidence is imbued with humility and capacity for compassion, which distinguish it from arrogance, boasting or self-delusion. It is also a subtle but definitely noticeable manifestation of healthy development in all the other core components, which it depends on and reflects.

Our childhood unconscious conviction of competence was the precursor of self confidence. How good it becomes depends on and reflects the quality of all other core components, and that plus its importance is represented by "self confidence" being on top and in bigger bolder letters at Diagram 2 (page 85).

The quality of all core components combines to produce accurate assessments about the realities at hand, and it is this accuracy that clearly sets genuine self confidence well above any unrealistic-to-delusional pretense of it. Confidence can also be influenced by *peripheral* components like education, income, family or work, because all components interact with one another.

Genuine self confidence is imbued with humility, which comes from an appreciation that what people become has much to do with favorable or unfavorable circumstances in terms of natural intelligence, country of upbringing, access to education, social and work connections, inherited wealth, parental personalities, etc., all of which include an element of luck. This acknowledgement does not diminish the fact that determination and hard work very often play a crucial part too, for which the individual deserves due credit.

Humility also distinguishes self confidence from arrogance or boasting, which involve a defense against usually denied underlying fears of inadequacy. But denial never works perfectly, which is why arrogant people have such compulsive need to overcompensate by boasting about their presumed superiority in all sorts of direct and oblique ways. Underpinning this need is the fact that although they try to bury as deep as possible their real or imagined "secret" inadequacies, they retain a gnawing worry about being found out.

Their most common way of overcompensating is by trying to become as wealthy as possible in order to increase their status through material ostentation. Other times arrogance comes out as a propensity to bully the vulnerable. Such people can also be subtly pretentious regarding all sorts of things. The same underlying need for self protection makes them prone to envy or resentment, especially towards those who in the past were seen as similar but who are currently perceived as being above them somehow, because that reality makes them feel unnervingly inferior by comparison.

The insecurities underpinning arrogance often predispose some such people to racist, sexist or homophobic views as a desperate last-ditch attempt at propping themselves up by putting others down. In contrast, genuinely self confident people will take a lot of care not to do any of that, and instead treat everyone with respect.

The internal appraisal component of self confidence can only be arrived at through our best efforts at reflection and good judgment. But this will always be fallible, which is why external appraisals of one sort or another are needed to complement and confirm ours, or to challenge it and in so doing force us to reconsider our self assessment.

External appraisals about our self confidence may be difficult to obtain by asking direct questions, because that would immediately result in those asked getting on guard and having to weigh the consequences of telling the truth, especially if they know us intimately or socially. But one way or another, enough reliable external feedback has to be there to ensure our self confidence is warranted rather than imaginary.

Probably the best way to ensure the availability of this external feedback is to always be alert for it, because it may come in subtle or unexpected roundabout ways. To ensure its accuracy we need to get it from a variety of sources, preferably indirectly, and also from people who don't care about us or dislike us. This feedback process is similar to the one described earlier for the gradual development of self-other awareness.

SELF ESTEEM: An important but misunderstood issue

The American controversy about the definition of self esteem

Before going into an in depth discussion of "self esteem", it seems appropriate to consider why the controversy about the precise meaning of the term remains unresolved. This has contributed to bringing self esteem advocacy into some disrepute in the United States and elsewhere, and the complexity of the issue is just one of the reasons why therapist-writers, scholars and the public at large have different views on precisely what it refers to.

Another reason is the attempts by some American academics to enhance and protect their professional prestige. Incomes, access to scarce research funds, job security and ultimately careers depend on it. That is connected to the inevitable but often unacknowledged or denied political games, over competition for high status university jobs. As I see it, these factors operate more or less as elaborated next.

Prestigious academics need to protect their jobs from current or future competitors. To survive in their "publish or perish" world they need to maintain their reputation by publishing research, based on methods which they obviously must defend as being valid. The complexities of self esteem would make it difficult and expensive to research it properly, but most of that difficulty and expense can be bypassed by adopting a simple definition such as "feeling good about oneself" or "feeling worthy".

That would be presumably on the basis that this is how most ordinary people understand the meaning of the term. But many would argue that such definitions are simplistic, and research findings based on them are somewhere between unreliable to worse than useless. My own view is that people whose research is based on this kind of definitions are swimming against the current of existing knowledge. And also that they are not fully aligning themselves with a central purpose of psychology, which is to develop an ever deepening understanding of behavior and its motivations.

One good thing about oversimplified definitions is that they have excellent "psychometric" qualities. The relevant part of what that means in the context of this discussion is that self esteem research based on these definitions can be done cheaply, by easily measurable methods such as self evaluation questionnaires. However, they have serious inherent problems.

The first is that while positive self evaluations may reflect objective and verifiable reality, they may also be based on something ranging from wishful thinking to delusional one. Many people generally considered as having nasty, difficult or limited personalities tend to be unaware they have them or are unwilling to accept the extent of it, and therefore will not lower their self evaluations accordingly. A parallel problem is that others may evaluate themselves less positively than they deserve.

An assumption of such research methods is that all kinds of people who feel good about themselves have a legitimate claim to high self esteem. That could include successful criminals, conceited snobs, those with delusions of grandeur resulting from social adulation or ostentation of wealth, others whose self concept is artificially inflated by drugs, or with personality disorders which they would deny but are obvious to impartial observers.

Even more implausibly, claims by such people are taken as equal in credibility to self evaluations by persons generally considered as intelligent and emotionally balanced. Presumably, on the grounds that those filling the questionnaires have ticked the same self evaluation boxes about how worthy they are or how good they feel about themselves.

Most informed reasonable people would not agree with those conclusions, and the validity of such research is highly questionable to say the least. However it does enable easy publication without too much expense or hard work, which as mentioned earlier is essential for securing the researchers' careers. Consequently, the politics and high stakes mean that for some "experts", their definition of self esteem is and will always remain impervious to challenge by common sense or reasoned argument.

Sparks fly from time to time and the need to shield vulnerable egos adds fuel to the fire. This would always be denied by those who feel the heat, and in polite academic debate the whole foul smelling mess is sanitized by being referred to as "theoretical differences". Unlike most researchers, real life therapists are involved in the daily grind of helping clients improve their lives. And the good ones know full well that there is more to self esteem than what *some* researchers claim, irrespective of their academic rank.

That is why the controversy over the definition of self esteem has two sides: On one is the minority who benefit from a simplistic definition, some being academic researchers with limited or no counseling experience. On the other side down to earth researchers, writers and therapists who want to get to the bottom of what self esteem is, in order to enhance their competence and retain their professional integrity.

As an independent Australian therapist and educator with no connection to American squabbles and no university position or research funding to protect, my aim is to be clear and truthful about the complexities of self esteem for the purpose of assisting my readers with their self education. I make additional comments about self esteem knowledge, teaching and research in page 157, under the heading *For counselors, teachers and researchers*.

What exactly is self esteem?

Most people understand the common usage meaning of self esteem to be about matters such as considering themselves to be good at various things, able to cope with most problems, feeling worthy, good or proud about themselves or some accomplishment, and generally liking oneself. They assume that when good things are happening in their life those feelings go up and constitute better self esteem, and when things are bad they go down and represent poorer self esteem.

Much of that may be true or partly true but it is definitely not the whole truth. Widespread ignorance about the complexities involved has led to the superficiality of how adult self esteem is understood. But when we dig deeper into what self esteem involves, we find that it has intricate underpinnings and ramifications. In order to get to them we need to move away from the idea that self esteem is just one feature or trait of personality out of many, which is how most people think about it.

Instead and as mentioned earlier, my long and hard thought-through view is that both personality and self esteem have the same six core components. From this perspective therefore, self esteem is the one byproduct of personality which embodies its essence better than any other. That in turn makes self esteem of the "secure high" variety (pages 80-89) the peak achievement of a healthy personality. And as a consequence, the nature of personality has to be understood in order to appreciate what self esteem actually is and involves.

Given the importance of self esteem in every area of life, including committed intimate relationships, a clearly outlined and agreed upon understanding of its meaning is critical. Without it we could be talking about something which means different things to different people although they all call it self esteem, which considerably reduces its usefulness.

That is because when the issue is not clearly delineated in a person's mind, self esteem is likely to be experienced as something amorphous, obscure and confusing. This makes it difficult to even begin to comprehend what it is other than superficially, and consequently what would need to be done in order to address problems related to it.

But if we recognize self esteem and personality as being made of clearly defined and discussed individual components, then, the task of disentangling and expanding each one as needed becomes much more manageable. This can be a productive way of thinking about how the quality of self esteem in adults can be made better.

My way of helping couples and individuals to better manage relationship issues *may* include direct or indirect education about the core and peripheral components of personality and self esteem, in order to expand and strengthen what they already know and have. The extent to which people succeed will be influenced by factors such as preexisting capacity for insight, plus levels of defensiveness and resourcefulness. But most important of all, by their courage and determination to do whatever it takes to achieve improvements.

Every self esteem writer is tempted to produce an elegant single sentence definition of it and many already exist, some much better than others. But none can do justice to its complexity unless preceded and/or followed by a substantial elaboration, and not having it reduces its clarity and value. This is why I began to describe self esteem by defining and discussing its interacting ever-evolving core components in their own subheadings, under the previous main heading of *Personality: The six core components*.

That is followed below by comprehensive discussions under several subheadings. They incorporate a number of diagrams, in order to facilitate a better understanding of the underpinnings of self esteem and their impact on our relationships and lives. With all the above in mind I propose that,

> Self esteem is an evaluation of our personal worth which embodies the essence of personality and can be "contingent" or "secure". In the secure variety that sense of personal worth is stable, and determined mostly internally by its core components. However, enough confirmation by sufficient reliable external sources is needed to ensure it is warranted, rather than based on defensive self deceptions such as wishful thinking, denial or delusion. In the contingent variety, that sense of personal worth is unstable and dependent on external approval or its internalized forms, and on its peripheral components.

The better and second best varieties of self esteem: Secure and Contingent

While this is largely unknown by the public and most mental health professionals, it is now generally accepted in specialized circles that there are two kinds of self esteem. One is beneficial to wellbeing and relationships and the other much less so. Because self esteem and the conviction of worthiness on which it is based are an inherent and imperative human need (see pages 55-56), those who have never been able to develop the better variety are driven by anxiety into seeking and securing the second best. And by that plus insufficient knowledge, into believing it is the only one there is.

I refer to the two types as "secure" and "contingent" because these terms incorporate a reasonable balance between two legitimate but competing objectives. The first is to be accurately descriptive about their most defining feature. The second is to select a name for both types which minimizes the risk of either being experienced as a putdown, by the around three quarters of the population who in my opinion have the less beneficial variety. However, regardless of any amount of care in selecting the best possible labels, examining our psychological underwear is likely to cause a degree of unease in some people and probably in most of us.

Contingent self esteem refers to an unstable sense of personal worth. It is based primarily on external approval or internalized versions of it by way of real or imagined favorable comparisons with others, and on its peripheral components. Because it is dependent on external factors, this sense of personal worth can increase when good things are happening in the person's life.

But it may also decrease suddenly if a job or business is lost, a relationship or marriage breaks up, there is a serious unexpected loss of health, etc. It can decrease gradually too and usually does as people become older, less attractive or healthy, poorer, or those with whom the person was comparing rise in socioeconomic status. These possibilities, probabilities and certainties mean that contingent self esteem is always at risk, because it depends on factors over which no one has permanent control.

Secure self esteem is a stable sense of personal worth, based primarily on internal self assessment by the individual. Again, that needs enough confirmation by sufficient reliable external sources in order to make sure it is level headed and warranted, rather than unduly influenced by defensive self deceptions such as wishful thinking, avoidance, denial or outright delusion.

The extent to which the thoughts and feelings responsible for this kind of sense of personal worth reflect reality accurately, depends on the level of development of the individual's ever evolving interacting totality of self esteem's core components. This largely internally based nature of secure self esteem results in it being quite stable over time, because it is very substantially under the control of the person.

External approval is pleasant to people with secure self esteem, but unimportant when compared to the internal approval based on the robustness and sophistication of their core components. Material ostentation is unnecessary, and what matters is the adequate satisfaction of their inherent higher needs for relationships, security, autonomy and competence. These will be discussed further below in the subheading *The four categories of inherent higher needs*, under the main heading *Happiness: What it is and depends on*.

Self esteem is a bit like food, in the sense that if it has always been reliably at hand to be used as needed, the person doesn't think much about it because its availability is taken for granted. That is why self esteem is not a preoccupation for those who have the secure variety, but is usually an ever present concern for those with the contingent one. Most people have predominantly one type or the other, and each can be higher or lower.

One way of visualizing how self esteem starts to evolve as secure or contingent is in Diagram 1. It shows how conviction of worthiness begins in childhood like the two sides of the same coin, one being lovability and the other competence, laying a foundation which will strongly influence the kind of self esteem we are likely to develop. As we grow towards adulthood, this conviction of worthiness becomes progressively more conscious, despite operating partly on automatic.

It seems reasonable to speculate that roughly three quarters of the population have contingent conviction of worthiness and self esteem and about one quarter the secure variety, although this may well be overoptimistic. That is based on my own observations of people, and I am not aware of any credible theory or research suggesting otherwise. The 12.5% at the top represents the highest conviction of worthiness and most secure self esteem, and the bottom 12.5% the lowest and most contingent.

The tendency towards the secure or contingent kinds of self esteem begins to be generated when childhood unconscious convictions of lovability and competence move above or below a "tilting point". This is represented in the diagram as the crossing point of the thick double-arrowed lines showing those dimensions. Every adult's conviction of worthiness and self esteem can be thought of as being represented by one dot.

All dots are somewhere within the big square, and their location is at the crossing point of a perpendicular line from the position the person occupies on the lovability axis, with another from the competence one. Three examples in the diagram are represented by the dots at the end of six thin dashed arrowed lines. Although all three are at a similar level of self esteem, the dot within the secure quarter represents the more stable variety because both dimensions are above the tilting point level.

When contingent self esteem is caused by lower childhood unconscious conviction of lovability, as in the middle left quarter, it is more difficult to improve through personal development by the individual alone or with the assistance of a good therapist. That is because lovability is a highly beneficial kind of natural brainwashing, which was implanted from quite early on. It is reinforced throughout childhood and substantially established by the onset of adolescence, although it can be improved throughout life.

By comparison, unconscious conviction of competence begins a bit later and its development lasts a lot longer. That makes it more amenable to being increased during adulthood, by for example the person becoming increasingly competent in various areas of life. That is why in cases where their self

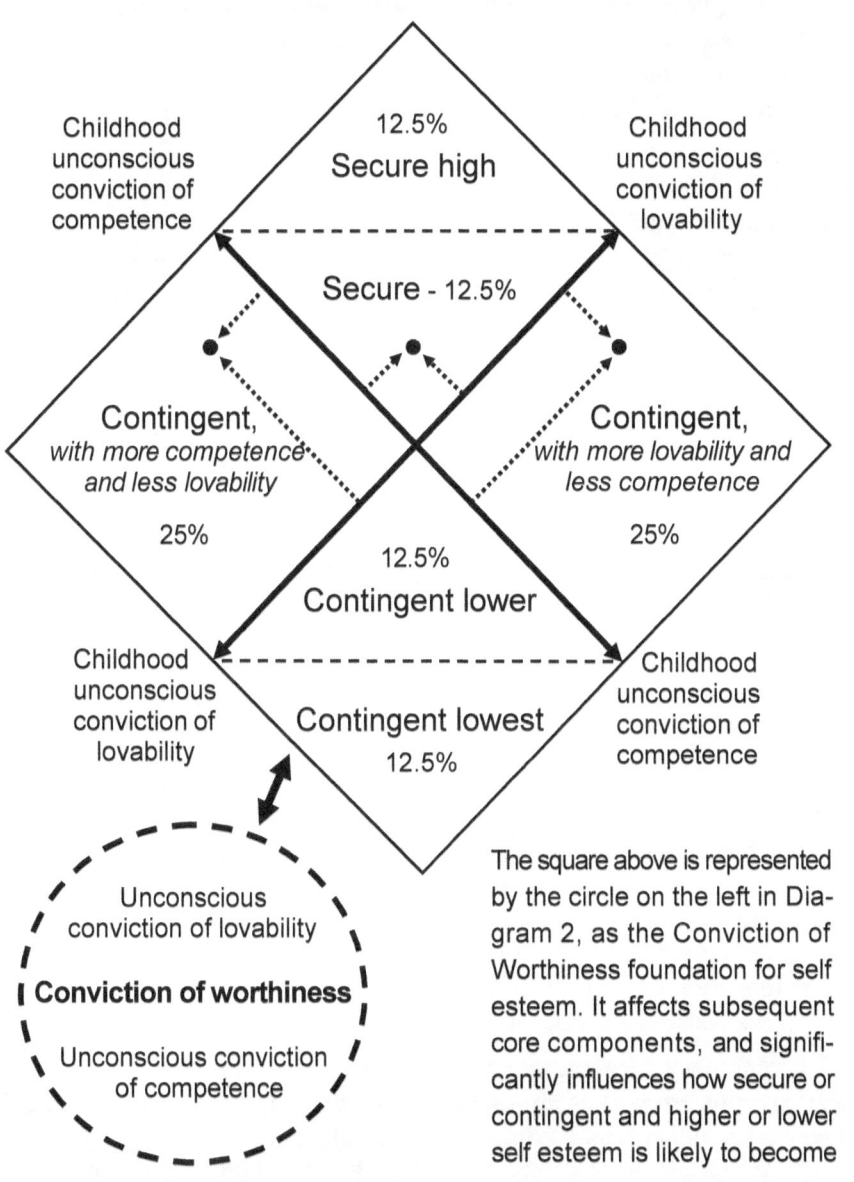

esteem is of a similar level, a person with higher lovability and lower competence (middle right quarter) has an easier potential for self esteem improvement than one with lower lovability and higher competence.

Our unconscious convictions of lovability and competence evolve as we emerge from childhood and become more self aware, into a similar level of fully or partly conscious conviction of worthiness. This is not the only factor in determining the kind and level of self esteem we will develop later in life, but it is the first and most important one, and therefore the center and foundation on which all subsequent core components are being built.

In other words, whether our conviction of worthiness ends up being secure or contingent will significantly influence whether self esteem itself will become likewise, and both kinds are discussed more extensively later under their own headings. Contingent self esteem can be shifted towards the secure variety during adulthood, but it is not easy. It can be done however, and the specifics of how to go about it are discussed further below under a number of headings, including *How to improve self esteem as an adult* (page 113).

The fact that some people with contingent self esteem may have it at a higher level than others with secure one does not alter the former's instability, and regardless of its level it remains more likely to deteriorate or collapse when under significant strain. Evidence for this is sometimes in the news, when socially known "successful" people succumb to alcoholism, drug abuse or depression after personal stresses or business failures, perpetrate domestic violence, and in extreme cases attempt or commit suicide or murder.

The foundation, core and peripheral components of self esteem and personality

Diagram 2 shows Conviction of Worthiness as the center and foundation of the other five core components built upon it. The definition of these core components and how the foundation influences them have already been discussed within their own subheadings, under the main heading of *Personality: The six core components*. Peripheral components are positioned outside the circles. Some are more important to most people, and this is symbolized by they occupying more peripheral space, and by their name being in bigger font.

All components can interact with one another, outwards, inwards or sideways, and this property is represented in the diagram by the circles and lines being dashed rather than continuous. For example, the lovability part of conviction of worthiness may have been less than ideal on entering adulthood.

Diagram 2

PERSONALITY and SELF ESTEEM:
The Core and Peripheral Components

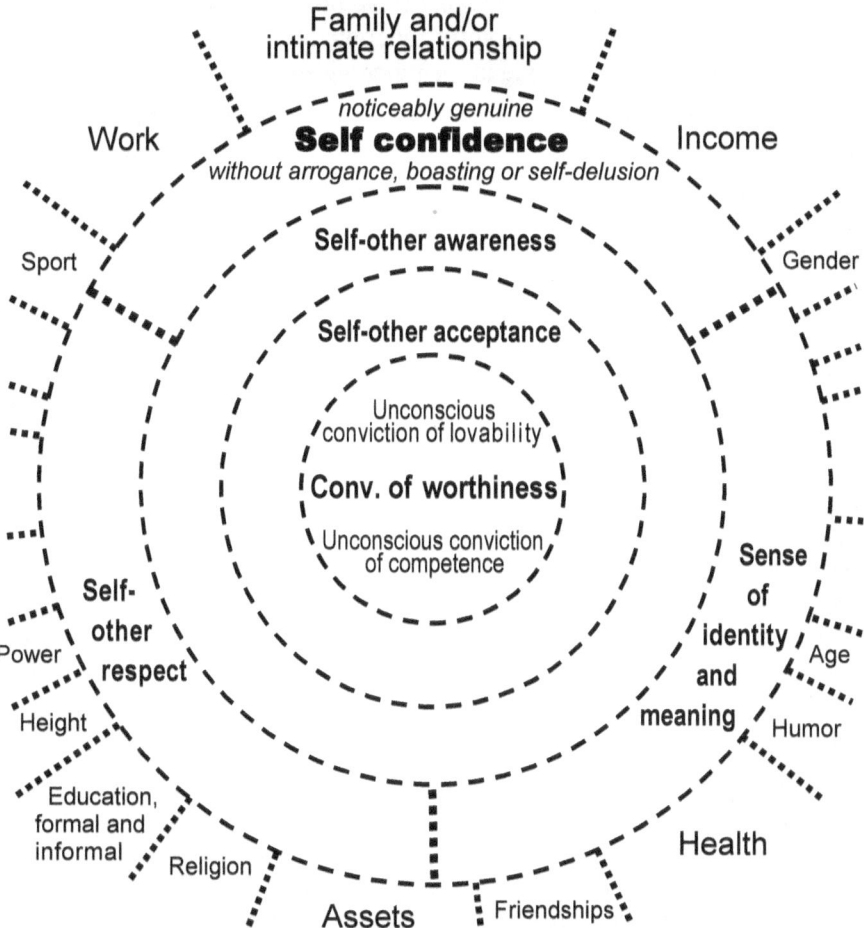

The Worthiness foundation made of Lovability and Competence significantly influences the other core components of Acceptance, Awareness, Confidence, Respect and Identity-Meaning, and with them the kind of self esteem we are likely to develop as adults. Peripheral components and their value may be different for each person. They do not matter as much in creating, maintaining or improving secure self esteem, but are important in the contingent variety

But if the individual develops subsequent core components to a high level through personal development later in life, then their influence is likely to filter inwards all the way and improve the foundation itself.

That may not create the best possible outcome, as when the foundation's underlying unconscious convictions of lovability and competence evolved naturally to a high level. It is more like if we break a bone in one leg and it heals completely, it will become fully functional again. But it is unlikely to ever be as good as the same bone in the other leg which was never broken.

Although predominantly people have secure or contingent self esteem, there can be a mixture of both due to the complexity and interactivity of their components. In terms of the inwards influence of some peripheral components for example, success or failure in work may affect self confidence and sense of identity, education can lead to a better defined sense of meaning, and culturally diverse friendships to expanded self-other acceptance.

There is an outwards influence too, for example in people whose core components are strong. For them, a potentially offensive joke involving their race or gender is unlikely to threaten their sense of identity, and therefore trigger laughter if it is funny, rather than necessarily feelings of indignation and anger. Similarly, these people are likely to feel comfortable relating to others whose race, culture, religious beliefs, sexual orientation, education, work and so on are very different, or whose income and assets are significantly bigger or smaller.

An example of sideways influence within core components is the way in which self confidence, sense of identity and meaning and self-other respect support and strengthen one another. How education, work or income influence friendships, intimate relationships or health, are examples of sideways interactions among peripheral components.

In people whose self esteem is secure, the secure components are the core ones. Although some of their peripheral components may be tenuous, they can never undermine the essential solidity of secure self esteem. In contrast, contingent self esteem is likely to have instability and fragility in several or all of its core components, as well as in some or many peripheral ones.

The number and importance of peripheral components is different for each person, and they encompass domain skills, physical attributes, personality features and circumstances. Domain skills include those related to work, housekeeping, sport, etc. Physical attributes can be health, age, height, and so on. Personality features refer to issues such as calmness versus excitability, gregariousness versus introspectiveness, or styles of humor. Nationality, wealth, education, family, etc. fit into the category of circumstances.

To the extent that core components are less developed and understood and therefore remain obscure or undetected, peripheral ones will be thought to be more important in defining sense of identity and generating self esteem, with many individual variations. For example, financial success may matter most to a business person, a good and secure job to an employee, sport skills and fitness to a professional footballer, money or power to internally insecure people addicted to ostentation or bullying.

Core components of self esteem are covert and complex, while peripheral ones are highly visible and easy to understand. Therefore again, it is not surprising that most people believe peripheral components are what matters most for creating and maintaining self esteem, and even happiness.

Self esteem from best to worst: Where we fit, how it shows and what underpins it

In many aspects of life and certainly when it comes to relationships, our interpretations of reality and responses to specific events can be significantly influenced by the type and level of self esteem and personal development we have. That type and level is represented by people's position relative to others in the "normal distribution curve" continuum, as illustrated in Diagram 3 (next page). Their location in the curve may rise steadily due to personal development, and often shift up or down when self esteem is contingent.

Lifting ourselves from contingent towards secure self esteem begins with understanding in depth the issues involved. The whole process can take sustained effort in addition to courage and determination, and would be very difficult for some people. It may be facilitated by favourable life circumstances such as finding the right kind of knowledge and having the time and capacity to be able to acquire it, partner support, or money for quality therapy.

The various ways in which people along the curve feel, think and behave about specific concerns or situations can be appreciated by comparing them side by side, as in the columns of Table A (page after next). Its two columns have fourteen examples showing how such differences may manifest themselves. For the sake of clarity and contrast, the comparison is between those at the top and bottom 12.5% ends of the continuum in Diagram 3.

Not all the generalizations given as examples would apply to every person, and many more would be applicable to most people. Furthermore, generalizations should never be used to define anyone, because everyone and his/her circumstances are unique and should be evaluated individually.

Diagram 3

Normal Distribution Curve for QUALITY and LEVELS of SELF ESTEEM and PERSONAL DEVELOPMENT

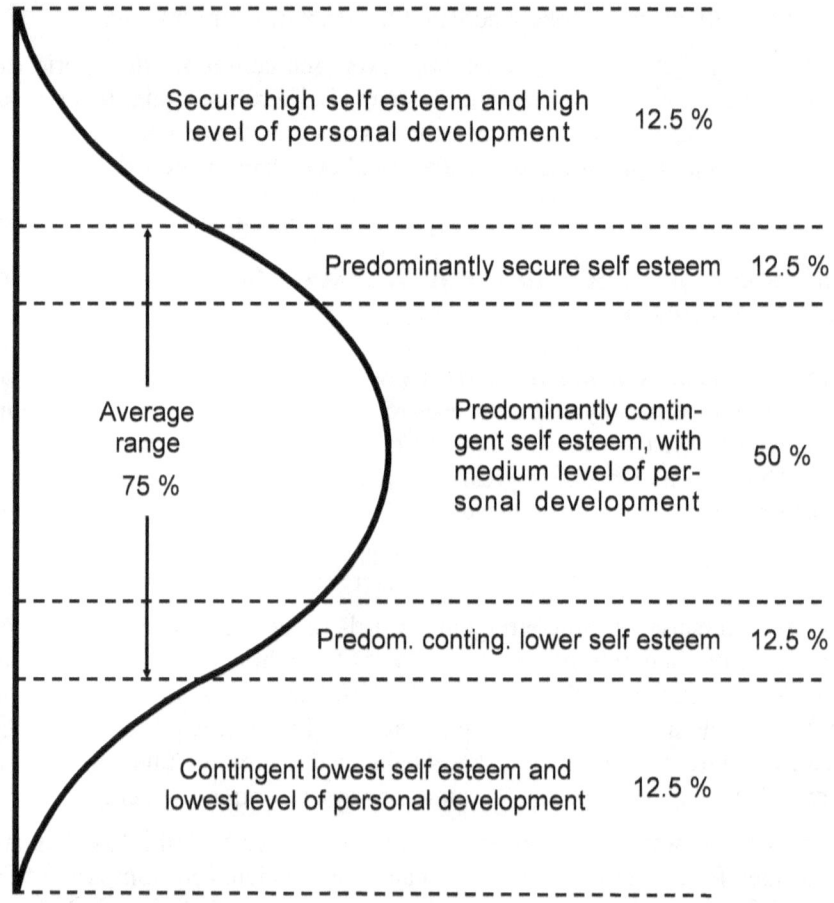

Secure high self esteem and high level of personal development — 12.5 %

Predominantly secure self esteem — 12.5 %

Average range 75 %

Predominantly contingent self esteem, with medium level of personal development — 50 %

Predom. conting. lower self esteem — 12.5 %

Contingent lowest self esteem and lowest level of personal development — 12.5 %

Where people stand in the curve depends on their levels of personal development and the quality of their self esteem. These influence our interpretations of reality, attitudes to everything in life and also responses to specific events. Lifting ourselves towards secure self esteem has to begin with understanding the issues involved. It may take sustained effort, courage and determination, plus at times assistance by a competent therapist. It is easier with favorable life circumstances such as time for study, education, money and partner support

Table A

COMPARING Feelings, Thoughts and Behaviors by location in the Normal Distribution Curve

Bottom 12.5% of the curve Contingent lowest self esteem and personal development	Top 12.5% of the curve Secure high self esteem and personal development
• Worry excessively about the opinions or comments of others	• Aware of how others think and feel, but not unduly concerned
• Constantly aware about how they compare in all areas of life	• Not into comparison or competition games, enjoy what they do
• Blind spots or distortions about any "threatening" imperfections	• Aware, accepting and relaxed regarding most imperfections
• Like status symbols, ostentation and feeling superior to others	• Feel no need for status symbols, ostentation or feeling superior
• Will disregard any alleged principles if self interest is at stake	• Behave according to their principles, even if at a personal cost
• Willing to deceive or exploit others, will rationalize it somehow	• Will often help others out of kindness, especially the vulnerable
• Rely frequently on "authoritative" opinions, parroted explanations	• Have curiosity and desire to seek the truth, trust own judgment
• Admire and envy the rich, often look down on those "below" them	• Treat all with respect, know everyone has qualities and flaws
• Secretly dislike many things about self, do not trust others	• Like a lot of things about self, trust those seen as deserving it
• Dishonest with self, internally unbalanced by having to pretend	• Have self honesty, internally at peace, treat others honestly too
• Express envy or hate disguised as virtuous "moral indignation"	• Virtually immune to envy, rarely hate anyone and never for long
• Blame others or "society" for their unhappiness or problems	• Accept responsibility for their problems, seek to remedy them
• When stressed may experience irrational anger, lack of control	• Seldom feel anger, expression of it is controlled and purposeful
• Believe their race, culture or subgroup is somehow superior	• Evaluate every person by the content of his or her character

© Luis Ipinazar 2016

090   What filters clearly through the bottom 12.5% of the curve on Diagram 3 as represented in the left column of Table A, are the typically unacknowledged anxieties which are a manifestation of contingent lower self esteem, some consequent common self-protection strategies, and the barriers to personal development which the use of such strategies brings about.

The feelings, thoughts and behaviors represented in Table A have underpinning motivations, made of a combination of the wishes and fears emanating from the person's needs. This process is illustrated as the Deeper Motivation Cycle in Diagram 4, which is largely self explanatory.

In it, the centrality of needs manifested as wishes and fears is represented by those three words being in big bold letters. Those who have too much faith in the reliability of intellect may wish to ask themselves this question: Why do equally intelligent people experience emotions and reach conclusions which are very different, when exposed to the same circumstances, reasoned argument and fairly objective facts?

Part of the answer is that while knowledge and intellect are important, so are the person's needs felt as emotions in the form of wishes and fears. Furthermore, strong emotions can often overcome rational thinking, because we humans are hardwired for this predisposition. The issue of needs is essential for understanding happiness, and will be elaborated further below under the heading *The four categories of inherent higher human needs*.

How and why contingent or secure self esteem begin to develop in childhood

Although this issue has already been discussed at various points, it is so important that a recapitulation is in order even at the cost of some repetition. The purpose here is to view the uncluttered totality of the picture more clearly, now that finer details mentioned elsewhere can be left out of the way.

Embryonic self esteem starts early in life, as unconscious convictions of lovability and competence begin to fill in the infant's blank psyche. In this way, they become the foundation upon which the rest of the personality will be built. As we grow older and more self-aware, that unified dual foundation gradually transforms itself into a more or less conscious conviction of worthiness. This can be secure or contingent and higher or lower, and its level and quality is largely a reflection of the child's unconscious convictions of lovability and competence.

The examples of Christine and the boy under four illustrated how the de-

Diagram 4

The DEEPER MOTIVATION CYCLE
propelling Feelings, Thoughts and Behaviors

FEELINGS, THOUGHTS and BEHAVIORS
by location in the normal distribution curve

↓

with Underlying Motivation propelled by

↓

NEEDS → WISHES and FEARS

(Different for SECURE or CONTINGENT self esteem)

SECURE self esteem needs are about Relationships, Security, Autonomy and Competence. Their satisfaction enables true fulfilment because they are an intrinsic and central part of human nature

CONTINGENT self esteem needs are about external approval and favourable comparisons, to avoid fear of inadequacy and shame amplified by reaction patterns developed in childhood

Wishes & Fears can be:

1. **Acknowledged** (the person is insightful, articulate, relaxed)
2. **Denied/avoided** (the person fears being judged but denies it)
3. or **Unconscious** (the person functions in automatic, no insight)

velopment of those unconscious convictions keeps progressing in early childhood, which in a best case scenario will ultimately lead to naturally occurring secure high self esteem. This is more likely to happen when healthy parental personalities and other favorable childhood conditions are followed in adolescence and earlier adulthood by various circumstances conducive to further healthy growth of the core components.

But personalities and circumstances can be less than ideal, and to that degree the budding self esteem of children could begin to tilt the wrong way. In the case of Christine for instance, mum's own self esteem might have been sufficiently contingent for her to have felt bad about being asked not to call every day. In such eventuality she could have reacted by expressing some form of disapproval, and if that had not been done carefully it could have been experienced by Christine as withholding love to some extent.

If such attitude were to have been a regular pattern, Christine's self esteem would probably have been developing towards the contingent variety. That is because her being loved would have been conditional upon doing what made mum feel best about herself, which would have eroded Christine's progression towards independence. And when we learn to think of ourselves as lovable or unlovable depending on whether or not we do what parents want, the seeds have been planted to make our adult self esteem excessively dependent on all sorts of external approval.

Instead and instinctively without even thinking about it, mum made very clear that her love was unconditional, not once but twice. With innumerable variations over all sorts of issues, Christine has been getting the message that she is unconditionally loved all her life. Hers is not yet fully fledged naturally occurring secure high self esteem, which can only come in adulthood. But her sturdy unconscious conviction of lovability (and probably competence too) provide an excellent foundation for it to become so.

Of course children need to be shown clear limits and sometimes scolded for inappropriate behavior, but this needs to be done in a way which does not undermine the reassurance that they are deeply loved. Any scolding should be about their behavior and never about their lovability, and most parents do this automatically because they love their children very dearly. As long as that pattern is well established it doesn't matter much that they make the occasional mistake, because children are resilient.

Different but comparable patterns to Christine's assurances of being loved were probably operating in the example about the boy under four. Although unplanned and spontaneously brought about just for fun by his much older brothers, the "Who are you going to believe?" challenge in the hand washing incident turned out to have been accidentally finely calibrated, to still just allow the little boy to overcome it.

With hindsight it was perhaps a bit too risky, because it might have been more than he could withstand. But that risk was mitigated by the reassuring presence of mum, the fact that very young children can already be quite smart, and his probably already strong unconscious convictions of lovability and competence. Both would have been reinforced, no doubt, by the successful resolution and the positive reaction of the adults.

Mum' sensible judgment in letting the boy figure his own way out is another illustration of why a healthy and emotionally balanced personality in the child's primary care giver is so important. Because if instead of being a very experienced mother and mature woman with a healthy personality she had been an overanxious person, less emotionally intelligent, too young, or chronically overstressed due to marriage problems, lack of family support or other unfavorable circumstances, she probably would have been a less reassuring figure throughout the short life of the little boy.

In such eventuality the challenge could have become more than he could bear, as indeed might have many other challenges, and ultimately his unconscious convictions of lovability and competence could have tilted towards the contingent variety. In this and countless similar ways, the benefits of a healthy personality in the primary care giver and significant others, or alternatively the problems inherent in their less than healthy personalities, are likely to be transferred to the next generation.

The example of the boy under four points to the second important condition conducive to secure self esteem in children, which is encouraging age appropriate challenges. There is experimental evidence that it is best for children's motivation if challenges are celebrated in terms of their effort at managing them as best as possible, rather than just in terms of success.

That makes sense because if parents over-focus on success, the child is more likely to be discouraged after the inevitable failures or only partial successes. Failing partly or completely can still be celebrated as a source of accomplishment, by having learned valuable experience through genuine effort, calculated risk taking, and sensible management of the outcome.

Countless challenges with potential to foster competence happen throughout childhood in various ways. In most families their importance is acknowledged and celebrated, and a child's effort plus eventual success at toilet training is a common example. An uncommon one is that on reaching certain age children are expected to deliver a prepared speech to the whole assembled family, during some special occasion with everyone dressed up.

Preparing and giving the speech about oncoming plans for schooling or whatever, is obviously a stressful event. Of course the child gets enough help and encouragement to enable him or her to succeed, and that is naturally followed by positive comments or reactions by everyone. The point is to provide another winnable and in this case planned and structured age-appropriate challenge, in order to foster a sense of competence and accomplishment though determined work.

With less fortunate children, the starting point for poor child rearing may be an unsatisfactory parental marriage plus its underlying causes, which makes it difficult for partners to work cooperatively. They could instead compete for the affection of their children, or give too much of their attention to a favorite child. Consequently and instead of becoming allies against a united parental team, the children too may begin competing among themselves.

When a favorite child gets especial treatment by being more "loved" in all sorts of obvious or subtle ways, the other child or children can become anguished or enraged by the injustice and may feel envy or hostility. There may be lifelong consequences for the disadvantaged child in the form of contingent lower self esteem, often manifested by all sorts of insecurities. The exaggerations in TV comedies such as Everybody Loves Raymond make good fun of it, although in real life this can be a troublesome matter.

The favorite child may also grow into an adult with significant personality distortions. A good example is in what was a very popular Australian sitcom called "Mother And Son", written by Geoffrey Atherdam and produced by the ABC, which started in the mid 1980's. In it, the discriminated child who is now a middle aged man has a propensity for excessive and inappropriate guilt, and is forever trying to please his manipulative memory-challenged elderly mother in order to gain her approval. While his older brother and favorite child is still playing up her predilection for him, while using and exploiting everyone he can with no sense of guilt whatsoever.

As long as the physical and mental health in the child are more or less within the normal range, a healthy personality in the primary care giver is by far the most important childhood circumstance for the development of secure conviction of worthiness and subsequent self esteem. Another favorable circumstance is stability in as many areas of life as possible, because it contributes significantly to the child feeling safe. These two factors create what we might call "a secure emotional base", from which the child is better able to take on all sorts of challenges with an interested and positive attitude.

In a case I remember well, the now adult woman had been dad's favorite child. Due to an unsatisfactory marriage mum associated her with him, and the anger generated probably by her own personality problems but blamed on her husband was discharged onto that child. Her younger sister became mum's favorite who could do no wrong, while daddy's beautiful girl was an easy target for the ongoing frustrations she could not throw with impunity at a powerful husband. Such situations are not uncommon, and I have worked with a number of comparable cases.

A typical way of coping with the resulting distress by such defenseless children, is trying not to notice and not to feel the pain of neglect or abuse by the primary care giver. As these children keep growing, they have to suppress their anguish at the unfairness of being discriminated in relation to siblings. This is the best survival strategy available to a distressed child, and therefore very appropriate at that age. Many of these children overcome this disadvantage, and function well (or well enough) as adults.

But for others, the defensive patterns of distorting reality for the sake of self protection become deeply ingrained overtime, and remain active after most of the actual events have long been forgotten. When these unlucky children become adults, they retain a propensity for feeling excessive fear of inadequacy, rejection and abandonment. They may continue to defend themselves by distorting, ignoring or avoiding threatening aspects of reality, and in various other ways invariably detrimental to their intimate relationships.

When parental personalities and circumstances are bad enough, they can cause far more damage than just predisposing their children to develop contingent self esteem, with its problematic behavior patterns at a moderate level plus resulting life difficulties. As they move through the stresses of growing into adulthood those patterns may become more entrenched, and crystallize into "personality disorders" significant enough to be diagnosable. In extreme cases their sense of self has been damaged so severely, that it merits being described in the professional literature as "fragmented" or even "shattered".

Seriously affected individuals are very poorly suited for sexually intimate relationships. Their attempts to have them generally fail, and often become quite distressing. In the worst cases they can bring about serious danger for themselves and anyone close to them, and several examples are discussed in Stage 6 under the main heading *Definitely dangerous men (and women)*.

Sometimes parents' concern is unnecessary however, as children use every trick in the book to get their way, and girls especially can be quite smart. An adolescent girl in a family I worked with had become very adept at softening up her parents, after getting the hang of it by trial and error. She would hit them straight in the heart by referring to her older sister as "your favorite daughter". This often got them worried enough to dismantle their opposition to whatever she wanted, and by the time they came to see me it had become a regular ploy.

A family therapist I trained with told me how her adolescent daughter had began complaining that she must have been adopted, which was allegedly why mum didn't love her enough to let her come home later than stipulated on Saturday nights. It was becoming a habit and eventually mum had to prepare an effective reply, which she told me with a good laugh: "If I had wanted to adopt a daughter, what makes you think I would have adopted someone as ugly as you?" A bit tough I thought, but it worked.

Bringing up children is invariably a delicate balancing act, which is never easy. This is why it is often heard that by the time parents learn their job they are likely to be unemployed. But that may not be so, because younger or older, educated or not, rich or poor, parents with healthy personalities tend to be naturally good at parenting. Bearing in mind that nobody can do a perfect job, even if there could be agreement on exactly what that was, in each of the countless thousands of infinitely varied situations which require immediate and spontaneous interaction between parents and children.

However, it may help parents produce more of the best possible responses if in addition to love and instinct they have a clear understanding of how lovability and competence emerge, develop, and will influence their children' self esteem. And also of how genetic predispositions tend to make most women better at instilling lovability, and many men rather good at encouraging competence. Advancing such understanding is one of the objectives of this chapter, and that is helped along by the broad goal of this book about promoting quality relationships between parenting adults.

In conclusion, there are three essential ingredients for helping children develop well built unconscious convictions of lovability and competence, and the foundation they represent for leading into better quality self esteem as they move towards adulthood and later in life. They are (1) abundant consistent unconditional love, (2) age appropriate challenges with celebration of the child's effort at taking them on and learning to manage them as well as possible, and (3) an emotionally stable home and family environment.

This combination makes it more likely that subsequent conviction of worthiness and self esteem will be of the better and more resilient secure variety. In contrast, if unconditional love, challenges or stability are insufficient or otherwise less than adequate, they may tilt the budding conviction of worthiness and subsequent self esteem towards the second best contingent variety.

A sturdy conviction of worthiness facilitates self-other acceptance, which is essential in expanding self-other awareness. Worthiness, acceptance and awareness make up the three layered foundation for the subsequent components of self-other respect, sense of identity-meaning, and self confidence.

When the six core components of personality and self esteem are well developed, they become effective mental-emotional tools for interpreting reality and managing it. The understandings they generate are deeper and more accurate. This makes it easier for people to experience and express appropriate emotions, enabling them to make wiser decisions about relationships as well as all sorts of other issues in life.

Contingent self esteem and the problems it creates

The need for self esteem is a genetically imprinted evolutionary imperative, but people are limited by being the way they are unless and until they evolve. These two realities mean that for those who do not have secure self esteem, contingent self esteem is a rational and unavoidable protective "solution", which enables the management of anxieties in the best way available to them.

Such anxieties are about being found out to be not good enough, and thereafter being ashamed, ridiculed, ignored, abandoned or otherwise disadvantaged. While this would be unpleasant for anyone, it can feel very stressful for those in whom such consequences would be amplified by negative emotional reaction patterns established from childhood.

Although they can rarely acknowledge it because doing so would be distressing, they suffer from "self esteem anxiety". That is, they are excessively concerned about whether they are worthy. This ongoing worry and insecurity propels people with contingent self esteem to over-focus on it, leaving them with less head or heart space to consider or care for anyone else's needs.

Some with contingent lower self esteem opt for trying to be or be seen as worthy by being helpful, competent, etc. Regardless of that, they tend to be more self centered than those with secure self esteem, because they use up so much of their energy in trying to feel worthy. They do not see themselves as self centered however, and believe they are "normal" because they have always been like that and believe this is how people are and how life is.

Their nagging self doubts make any awareness development in themselves or others rather unnerving, since they believe that what is to be seen will not be liked. This is because the feared real or imagined negative aspects of themselves, which await to be discovered under the façade they strive to project, would undermine further their already fragile self esteem.

Therefore they have something to gain by others staying unchanged and something to lose by them getting smarter, and possibly as a result demanding fairer treatment. Such changes in others' thoughts and behavior could take some of the focus away from the self interest of the person with contingent lower self esteem, who as a result would feel he/she is losing out or being hard done by.

That may not be how it is or turns out, but very much how they see it and what they fear. Any loving partner who is better balanced will eventually realize the real cause of their problems, probably leave the marriage or relationship, and thereafter avoid any potential partners with this type of personality. While a tendency for defensiveness and self centeredness exists in most of us, the difference in people whose self esteem is both contingent and lower, is the noticeably greater intensity of it.

Due to their underdeveloped conviction of worthiness, being like everyone else is never quite enough for those with very contingent self esteem to feel adequate and secure. This can make them extremely motivated to do whatever it takes to become wealthy or noteworthy, and may contribute to a propensity for depression when things don't work as they had hoped.

Depending on circumstances and various aspects of their personality, their attempts to become wealthy or noteworthy could be morally defensible, or done with little or no consideration for any damage they inflict. In any case, appearing to conform to socially valued standards in order to be approved of, becomes far more important than being true to themselves or fair in their dealings with others. Whatever the means, their ultimate goal is to bury as deeply as possible those vulnerabilities they experience as shameful.

They need to do so because their "secret" self doubts threaten to rise to the surface and flood them with anxiety every time they feel a serious challenge, which given the way they are happens frequently. Whenever they anticipate such challenge and feel that fear, the truth and any alleged principles are likely to be thrown overboard in the interest of self protection. This keeps them engaged in an ongoing unwinnable fight against reality.

Their priority is not to achieve a clear view of it, but to filter out anything threatening through avoidance, denial, wishful thinking, pretense, anger, or any barely credible strategy they can lay their hands on. This is why they can only feel safe when they believe their worthiness is beyond doubt and beyond challenge, by way of those around them accepting as real the façade they believe makes them look best.

This comparison-dependent contingent self esteem combines with their self doubts to make them prone to envy. And if they have power, that may lead to behaviors which could be very damaging for the envied. Envy can never be admitted to however, because doing so would reduce their worthiness in their own opinion, and certainly in that of others. Such mostly unconscious denial leads to envy usually being experienced and discharged as virtuous "moral indignation", over some real or alleged negative aspect of the behavior or personality of the envied. Thereby indirectly making it easier to believe, imply or claim that they are morally superior.

Their inability to control their own shaky feelings of self worth leaves them with little tolerance for insecurity. As a result they may develop a tendency to overcompensate by attempting to somehow manipulate and influence the people around them, in order to obtain and maintain the inner sense of safety which has always eluded them.

For his purpose they may deliberately although not necessarily with full awareness of their underlying motivations, go to great lengths to control their family and others through persuasion, dispensing favors, generating guilt, or through some direct or implied bribe or threat. They may also try to attract into their orbit people over whom they have some kind of advantage, or who need their help perhaps due to having less education, attractiveness, social or work connections, intelligence, money, power, language skills, etc.

When some or all of the above strategies are not possible or not enough to make them feel secure, they are likely to adopt ideologies of superiority on the basis of race, religion, nationality, sexual orientation, etc., in an effort to feel good about themselves by believing they are better than others. Perhaps the biggest misfortune for these people, especially those towards the lower end of the contingent continuum, is that their intractable self esteem anxiety and defensiveness diminishes their capacity to relax and enjoy life.

Most people with serious damage to their childhood unconscious conviction of lovability never get to develop properly their correspondingly underdeveloped core components of personality and self esteem, although it is possible to do so. This may be due to insufficient awareness or knowledge about their condition and how to remedy it, limited capacity for study and reflection, not enough money to hire a competent therapist for long enough, not being able to find one, etc.

Some cannot do it simply because they have a degree of damage which makes the option of personal development too threatening, even if it is possible and accessible. That is unfortunate, as it is precisely the changes they would have most difficulty in making, which would allow them to grow and evolve into healthier and happier versions of themselves.

It is all rather sad, because they and those close to them have to live with the consequences. Worst of all and as mentioned in the previous heading, they can transmit to their children their personality twists or vulnerabilities. These include overdependence on external social approval or internalized equivalents, which is what contingent self esteem feeds on. That happens in many ways, but especially through the dysfunctional interaction patterns which tend to become a norm in their family.

Adolescents and young adults may also be influenced directly by the culture, into accepting the same values. These put a lot of emphasis on conspicuous material things and the financial ostentation which money can buy. For the same underlying reasons they may also want to be as "better than others" as they can rather than as good as they can, in other visible ways such as prestigious sounding titles, physical attractiveness, etc.

One problem with relying on the material success pursued by people with contingent self esteem, is that their fragility stays unresolved and they remain vulnerable. In the 1980's (from memory), the Government introduced a new tax on imported cars. I remember the TV news that when the owner of an imported car dealership realized that it was going to tilt his faltering business into bankruptcy, he went to Sydney's most notorious seashore cliff suicide spot known as The Gap and jumped to his death.

It seems reasonable to speculate he became convinced that his status as a successful business owner was about to be irretrievably lost. Without what he presumably considered as an essential support for what must have been his very contingent self esteem, it collapsed with the result that he became severely depressed. He would have still probably ended financially better off than his employees, but that wasn't the issue and made no difference to how he felt.

Apart from a reduced capacity to enjoy life in general, people with contingent lower self esteem tend to have chronic problems in managing the intense emotions of intimacy. They can be serious enough to eventually cause the breakup of otherwise viable relationships, and in bad cases this becomes an emotionally costly repeating pattern in their life.

It can sap their morale to a point where they find very difficult to trust, and effectively withdraw from attempting intimate relationships. These kind of problems are discussed further under the heading *How the kind and level of self esteem can damage or benefit adult intimate relationships*, and illustrated with an extended example.

Secure self esteem and the benefits it brings

In contrast to the contingent variety, secure self esteem is a sense of worth based primarily on the person's positive feelings and reflection about the self. This internal evaluation focus is supported and reinforced by the healthy development of all core components of personality. It does not inflate with success or deflate with failure, because the underlying strong conviction of worthiness is an integral and deep rooted part of their personality. These features make secure self esteem quite stable, and enable people who have them to become more daring in most areas of life.

Because failure does not diminish their self esteem, it can be experienced as a valuable lesson rather than as something personal evidencing their inadequacy. Making mistakes and learning in the process makes it easier for them to get better at meeting their important human needs, as well as all sorts of challenges. Their relatively fearless disposition helps them to behave with more authenticity and integrity too, including in situations when doing so may be disadvantageous in interpersonal, financial or other ways.

People with secure self esteem are more likely to be emotionally intelligent and balanced, because their personality core components are better developed. Once secure self esteem has reached a sufficiently high level of development, it becomes resilient to the point of being almost indestructible, even under severe stress. We can often sense we are with someone whose self esteem is *secure high* when we interact with them, although it is not always easy to put the finger on precisely what it is that conveys the message.

They tend to be aware and accepting about human limitations and imperfections, confident without either being boastful or exhibiting false modesty about their skills or qualities. They are virtually immune to envy, respectful to everyone, rarely aggressive, soft-spoken and calm rather than loud or agitated, helpful and fair rather than exploitative. But regardless of what gives it away, good observers of human nature can soon feel the caliber of the person.

Developing secure self esteem does not require formal education or uncommon intellectual intelligence, although these may help raise it to a higher level. Their relative fearlessness about the possibility of failure does not make these people reckless, but simply better able to take calculated risks if the potential outcome seems worthwhile. That can make a big difference for people who grow up poor and uneducated in environments with few options.

One example is the central character in the American film *The Pursuit of Happiness*, who was able to virtually pull himself up by his own bootstraps. Another example I know particularly well is the case discussed earlier under the heading *Conviction of worthiness*, about the boy under four learning to wash his hands. The additional elaboration which follows illustrates in some

| 102 | detail how naturally occurring secure self esteem can help in overcoming life's obstacles.

During his early adolescence his family sent him to additional classes with great sacrifice, to help him continue studying. His seventeen years older brother, who had taken the role of de-facto father, used to pay the teacher in person. But after the first two years the teacher, who knew the family's circumstances, told him: "The boy doesn't have the capacity to study, and I don't want to steal your money". He ploughed on for a while. But all things considered, shortly after turning fifteen he began working full time as a child laborer, as was common among the poor in such villages at the time.

However, within about a year and following some mistakes at work, his boss fired him. Allegedly on the probably compassionately attributed grounds that he did not have enough "strength" for the job. This was a little bit credible because he was not a physically strong boy, as well as being a late developer who looked younger than his age.

Being told that he had neither the intelligence to study nor the physical strength to be much good at working, could have been a serious blow to his morale and put him on a downwards slide for life. But that little boy's unconscious convictions of lovability and competence plus the self confidence they had fostered were to come in handy and allow him to prevail over his presumed personal limitations, as well as the very real ones resulting from his background and circumstances.

Still at fifteen he taught himself to cut his own hair, which he has been doing ever since, and that was a sign of things to come. The cultural impact of pop groups like The Beatles had played an interestingly convoluted part in motivating him to learn it, but that is another story.

At sixteen he began training himself as a boilermaker, after buying a book for self study and learning by observing and asking tradesmen in the factory where he worked. On turning eighteen he persuaded the factory manager to employ him as a boilermaker, arguing that he knew the trade well and was a hard worker. And that if the manager didn't, he was going to apply for a job in another company which he knew had a vacancy for such tradesmen.

Conscripted at twenty for fifteen months of compulsory military service and after the initial three months of general training had been completed, he requested an appointment and asked his Commander to let him work in the office. This, after promising he would teach himself to type within the three months left before the senior soldier he would be replacing was due to leave the army, and on the grounds that this new skill would allow him to improve his job prospects and life.

The Commander reacted by saying he was pleasantly surprised to discover he had at least one soldier who wanted to learn something while in the army. And for the same reason some months later, he agreed to let him have three free afternoons per week so that he could attend a language school to study English. Although in actual fact he ended up going there only one afternoon per week.

He succeeded in finding a job as a boilermaker behind the army's back for two afternoons per week, knowing that if discovered he would have been severely punished. He managed to find such unusually limited part time job by personally walking into several small workshops he came across, while walking for that purpose through an industrial area and asking for it. Eventually an employer said he was impressed by him trying to work while putting up with the pressures of being a soldier, and gave him that very small illegal part time job.

Two months after being released from military service he left the village with the money he had saved over the previous years, and went to London despite speaking only a few words of English and knowing nobody there. He was using an international student card obtained for him by a resourceful army friend from an educated family, which was needed to get a three month work permit picking up strawberries in England.

However, having innocently bought a one way airfare, he was arrested at the airport after naively admitting when questioned that he might stay a bit longer in order to study English. And after a rather stressful night locked up in a cell, the next morning he was taken by the police into the first available plane and deported back to his country.

Undaunted he bought another airfare to Dublin for a fortnight later, after finding out that they also spoke English in that place. As the uneducated village boy he was, he hadn't realized the plane would go via London while in transit to Ireland, and was arrested again at the airport when it made a stopover and they saw their own rejection stamp in his passport.

But having learned from the previous experience, he had taken the precaution of buying a return airfare, with the idea of cancelling later the return part of it for a refund. And after a few hours in detention he was allowed to fly on to Dublin, where there were no checks for passengers flying from London.

Within a month however, the Irish police found him working illegally as a kitchen hand. He was questioned, and then given two weeks to leave the country. After urgently contacting his Embassy and showing he had enough money in traveler's checks to live without working, they persuaded the police to relent, and he was allowed to stay for three months on condition he would not work. But he actually needed the money, and managed to work illegally in two jobs.

His full time job was cleaning staircases and toilets for a subcontractor at Donnybrook Hospital. And he also taught conversation in his own language at the homes of people who had replied to his newspaper ad, written with the help of a kind post office employee at Dublin's GPO in O'Connell Street. In a frantic search for a way of stabilizing his situation, he discovered how he might be able to travel back to London in a semi legal way.

He got his brother to obtain a certificate from a village pub owner stating he had the required five years experience as a professional waiter, and then paid a London employment agency to use it in order to organize a temporary work contract in a big hotel. Once in London however, the headwaiter realized within the first day that he had no idea about the job, and the second day told him he was going to be fired.

But was eventually persuaded to let him stay, on the promise he would work very hard delivering breakfast trays to hotel rooms in the early morning shift. After a succession of hairbreadth escapes he finally had an employment permit, even if precarious and limited. However, the search for security and a way to improve his life was still on. And within six months of being in London, where he attended English classes after work in the evenings, he had applied for and was in due course accepted for migration to Australia.

Once there he studied French and Italian during his work hours as a boilermaker, using a hidden pocket tape recorder and earphone. And at night High School by correspondence, in order to improve his written English. After saving for three years, he stopped working to prepare for High School exams in the one year full time Day Matriculation Curse at his local Technical College. Subsequently he completed a university degree with top marks, while always working during the end of the year "holidays".

At those times he moonlighted with a second full time job as a waiter in the John Cadman dance-till-late floating restaurant, which cruised its diners around Sydney Harbor. Every time he was asked "Didn't you get enough sleep last night?" which happened frequently despite his attempts at hiding it, he would tell some lie to avoid the risk of being fired. He needed the extra money in order to keep paying the mortgage for the cheap apartment he had invested his savings into, just before starting university, convinced that housing stability would help him focus on his studies.

And the reason I know so much about his life is that I was the little boy learning to wash his hands. When now as a mature man I remember the determined adolescent and young man he became, I am still amazed at what he was able to go through, and feel like giving him a pat on the back. I have no doubt that the solid foundation for self esteem created mostly by my mother's unconditional love plus her own healthy personality, was essential in enabling me to persevere in seeking and managing big challenges and arduous struggles, especially during my twenties.

For those who weren't lucky enough to get that effortless quality foundation as children, is important to know that it is possible to make self esteem more secure as an adult. Depending on the circumstances and potential of each person, it can take from serious determination to a considerable struggle. It will take time too and success is never guaranteed, although even limited improvements can have substantial benefits.

But there is no doubt that many will transform themselves through their own effort, from individuals who began adulthood with contingent self esteem, into people with secure and in some cases secure high self esteem. And enjoy for the rest of their lives all the advantages this will bring about, for themselves and those around them.

How the kind and level of self esteem can damage or benefit adult intimate relationships

Having worked with countless couples over decades, I can say with certainty that when contingent self esteem is towards the lower end of the continuum in at least one partner, that is usually the main cause of often intractable relationship problems. When contingent self esteem is roughly around average in both partners, it is often a significant factor in creating many of the problems which can be improved or resolved.

In other words, adult intimate relationships can benefit or be damaged by the quality of the partners' self esteem, and a good way of appreciating how it happens is by looking in some depth at an extended case example comparing two extremes. That is, what a jealous wife referred to as a "contingent lower" actually did, as compared to what she would probably have done if very good self esteem had made her into a "secure higher". This case is discussed within this heading after some general comments, and it will continue to be elaborated in some detail over several headings.

As mentioned elsewhere, contingent lowers have many negative beliefs about themselves, some of which may be correct and others partly or totally unrealistic. That leaves them in a state of more or less constant self esteem anxiety, always excessively concerned about what others might think, feel or say about them, and punctuated by sharp increases in that anxiety whenever they feel threatened. This ongoing anxiety makes them more self absorbed than the average person, and therefore less focused on considering and meeting the needs of their partner.

Most of their negative self beliefs are hidden or denied because acknowledging them would only increase the anxiety and shame generated by their fears of inadequacy. But hiding or denial does not make a self conviction or its consequences any less real. Those beliefs can be as entrenched and intractable as the ones in sufferers of anorexia, who are convinced they are fat even when emaciated to the point of risking death by starvation.

They think their partners see through into their frighteningly hidden poor self image, and consequently secretly believe that they don't compare well with potential competitors. Therefore and in the privacy of their own mind, they consider their partners as being better than themselves. As a result it is difficult for them to accept they can be truly loved, and cannot help living in fear that they will ultimately be rejected.

This keeps them always vigilant for clues about how their partners feel about them, and prone to negatively misinterpreting their comments or behavior. Such misinterpretations make them feel hurt and rejected because after all, *their feeling* goes, how could their partner be truly committed to someone with as many shortcomings and defects as they have? And I said "their feeling" advisedly, because as every real or imaginary clue comes along and before the thought is ever articulated, the negative emotion has already automatically taken over and impacted on them.

For example, their partner could be stressed about something unrelated to the couple, and therefore less attentive or reassuring. If it happens repeatedly, contingent lowers could quite easily misinterpret it as the other's doubts about the value of the relationship, and therefore about his/her commitment to it. Those beliefs often predispose them to developing hostile feelings and behaviors as a usually unconscious defend-by-attacking maneuver, whenever realistically or not they sense a whiff of rejection, and eventually such reactions tend to become a regular defensive pattern.

By attacking the character or actions of their partner they are protesting against the hurt and discharging it, which is what makes such hostility into a form of self protection. That creates emotional distance, thereby temporarily reducing their dependence on a person experienced as an unreliable source of support. But such support remains important, and having less of it through their own actions increases their vulnerability.

They may also initiate conflicts over disappointments or resentments from way back, in an attempt to persuade their partner to accept interpretations of reality which fit best with their need for reassurance and self protection. Despite the often seriousness of these conflicts however, contingent lowers rarely initiate divorce even if they have repeatedly threatened to leave. That is because they would experience the breakup as extremely distressing, in addition to a deeply wounding failure.

The extended example alluded to earlier, involves a chronic propensity for excessive jealousy in a woman. She was regularly picked up by her husband from her workplace, on his way home from his. He described an occasion when he was waiting for her while parked in a busy city location. As soon as he saw her coming out he began reversing in order to drive out of the narrow cul-de-sac he was in, to save her the walking.

But on entering the car she immediately accused him of looking at another woman, who she said had been walking on the pavement as she came out. He explained that he never noticed this other woman and could hardly have been looking at anyone while reversing the car, which required his full attention. But she remained unconvinced, and after a brief argument remained silently angry and hostile for the rest of the day. He knew from experience, he said, that any attempts at further discussion would have been fruitless.

This incident damaged their capacity for affection and intimacy for several days, and he felt unjustly treated and uncared for. All this undermined further their already diminished feelings for each other, and created yet another residue of unresolved anger and frustration. This was one of several comparable incidents the husband complained about, in which neither disputed the facts despite their different interpretations.

As far as I could see, the husband's personality was roughly within the normal range in all relevant respects. All things considered I soon became convinced that a major cause of their problems was excessive jealousy in the wife, which was largely created and maintained by her contingent lower self esteem. One reason for this couple's inability to manage their problems well enough was that neither of them had a full and proper understanding of what was going on at a deeper level.

They had tried very hard to deal with the situation from the standpoint of their first order understandings. That was essentially about each emphasizing their interpretation of events and insisting the partner accepts it and modifies their behavior accordingly. But that had only caused more arguments and never resolved anything. By the time they came to see me they were exhausted and disheartened, and divorce was a very real possibility.

Those of us with partners who refuse to see the obvious and whose behavior has repeatedly irritated us can feel increasingly fed up. We may be tempted to smash their defenses, by blasting through their blind spots and forcing them to see themselves as they really are, utterly naked and defenseless in the floodlight of our expose. However, that is a side of themselves they are trying hard to cover up or ignore, because acknowledging it would make them feel stupid, unworthy and despicable.

So, would we really wish to do that to someone we love and whose love we want to have? If we do it, their defensive structure could break down. In other words, the combination of unconscious psychological defense mechanisms and conscious defensive strategies which enable them to cope with the stresses of life as they experience them, could stop functioning. And if the glue that holds them together comes undone, they could collapse into a heap of unbearable shame and humiliation.

If any of that was to happen to our partner, would we have resolved anything? Or would we have solved nothing plus created an additional problem? And if in view of the results we regretted our actions and wanted to remedy them, would we be able to? Would the damage to our partner's feelings for us and to the viability of the relationship be reparable, or irreparable?

The personality issues underpinning this kind of problem are difficult to overcome. When it affects certain kinds of contingent lower men (and women), they may develop a pattern of resisting what they feel as threats to their defensive structure by becoming "uncontrollably" angry, with disastrous effects on their intimate relationships. It can lead to threats, assaults, minor or major injuries, and in extreme cases to killing. Several examples are discussed in Stage 6, including under the heading *Emotional time bombs*.

Other contingent lowers can react to their collapsing defensive structure by becoming severely depressed, occasionally to the point of opting for the ultimate escape. This was probably what happened in 2013 to the British nurse who was hoodwinked into believing her caller was the Queen, enquiring about her granddaughter-in-law who was in hospital at the time, being treated for pregnancy sickness.

That nurse simply could not cope with what, *for her*, must have been the shame and humiliation caused and rubbed on by everyone having fun about the incident. Those who initiated the whole thing from Australia had no idea of the serious damage which such actions can have on a contingent lower. And obviously neither did Prince Charles when he too joked about it before her suicide, as I saw him doing on television.

When people seek therapy, it has to start where they are at and proceed at a speed they can manage. And that, only after having created a context of sufficient acceptance and support. In our example of the excessively jealous woman, one of the early things to be done would be to understand the limited unconscious conviction of lovability which she almost certainly experienced as a child. And its consequences, after explaining to them why and how that is behind some of her reactions and behaviors.

This would allow them to see that she does not deserve any blame for having become as she is, although she is fully responsible for acknowledging her problem and managing it well enough. They could use that knowledge as a motivator for working on any underdeveloped core components of personality and self esteem. That would have to be done for their marriage to improve, and they are the only ones who can do it. This side of the case will be discussed at length further below by continuing with the same example, under the heading *How to improve self esteem as an adult* and its subheadings.

Still continuing with the example of the jealous wife, we can now consider what probably would have happened at various points during the car reversing incident if her self esteem had been secure high instead of contingent lower. First of all, as a result of being much surer about her own worth, she would have been far more certain about her husband's commitment to her and their relationship. Therefore she might have been less vigilant and in all probability not even notice the other woman in the manner she did.

But if she had noticed and doubted, his assurances would probably have been enough to reassure her. If she had known for sure that her husband had actually looked at the other woman, she would have given it no more attention than it deserved. Her better self-other acceptance would have enabled her to keep in mind that the male eye was designed by nature to be always on duty, and that would have been a mitigating factor in an already very minor "offence".

Therefore she probably would not have taken it so personally if her husband's discreetly roving eye had momentarily landed on the other woman and appreciated her attractiveness. If he had done so but denied it she would have most likely assumed, probably correctly, that his denial was primarily intended to spare her from any bad feelings because he cared about her.

She would have understood in her mind and felt in her heart that there was no real threat to her husband's love from any attractive woman walking next to her, just as there is no threat from those erotic pictures men's eyes are irresistibly drawn to. Consequently there would have been no accusation, no voice rising, no attack on his character, no passive hostility, and no unavailability during several days for emotional comfort, intimacy and sex.

Most important of all, none of those love eroding behaviors would have been going on for years and undermining the pleasure, stability and security of their relationship. Of course, jealousy is not the only aspect of contingent lowers which causes problems in their relationships.

This same couple had once been seating in a public gathering, when a woman of some social standing who had once briefly met them came close by to talk to someone else. This woman moved away shortly after, having either failed to notice or chosen to ignore them. The husband described how he had noticed his wife's facial expression of humiliation and anger at feeling ignored, and tried to make her feel better.

He pointed out that this woman might not have noticed them, and that even if she had deliberately ignored them it was not important because they did not know each other much at all. When that did not work he reminded her that they themselves often chose to have little to do with various people who would have liked to be their friends. Therefore there was no reason to feel bad because sometimes they were doing the same thing to others, and so did everyone else.

But it still made no difference, and she remained in a bad mood for the rest of the evening. He felt he had done nothing to deserve having to be in the company of someone looking and acting so miserable, and the episode detracted from their enjoyment of the evening and stretched into avoidance of emotional and sexual intimacy at night.

There had been too many comparable incidents, and he had been unhappy about them for a long time. Equally unpleasant situations occurred every year around Christmas, he added with a mixture of annoyance and disappointment, as she became overstressed for no obvious reason and he had to keep walking on eggshells. That was to try to avoid her mood getting from bad to worse and all the way into an emotional crisis. But his efforts never worked, he was tired of it all, and had been for years.

To summarize the essentials of the above, secure high self esteem and the healthier personality which it is an expression of, increase the chances of positive or tolerant interpretations. These give the benefit of the doubt and foster forgiveness about human imperfections, whenever we feel a bit neglected by our spouse. In other words, it tends to produce reactions which benefit the relationship. Secure highers are usually happier with themselves and life too, and that also contributes to making them nicer and more caring companions.

In contrast, the emotional overreactions of contingent lowers often trigger self protective accusations, blaming and retaliatory responses towards their partner, leading to progressive relationship deterioration via the accumulation of disillusionment and unresolved resentment in one or both. This in turn decreases commitment to the relationship by the partner with a healthier personality. In this way, the ongoing "secret" negative self evaluations and anxieties about rejection and abandonment in contingent lowers often become a self fulfilling prophecy.

When these fears ultimately come to pass they confirm their negative self beliefs, whether realistic or not, and entrench their problematic reaction patterns. Then they take all of those plus the extra emotional baggage from their failed relationship to the next one. And not long after the honeymoon phase, they again begin to build up an increasingly heavier burden on it.

If that new relationship fails again, their insufficient understanding may lead to lamentations such as they always ending up with the same type of man or woman. What they mean by this is that they have been unlucky, in that there was something not right with all their partners. That may actually be true, especially if their choices were based primarily on physical attraction, which is often combined with wishful thinking about imaginary qualities in their new partner's personality.

While there may or may not have been something wrong with those partners, such comments are just another self protective device based on a form of denial or avoidance. More precisely, on choosing to ignore the crucial fact that what each of their failed relationships had in common is that they involved the same one person, namely themselves.

As their confidence drops and hopelessness increases, some contingent lower men and women try unproductive ways of protecting themselves from distressing awareness about their own shortcomings or about responsibility for their bad choices. For example, they may develop fear, disdain, anger or hatred towards the opposite sex. And in the case of some women, the excesses of feminism have tended to aggravate this problem.

Such views are often justified on questionable or untrue alleged facts about there being something wrong with men or women, that is, with half of humanity. If their underlying "hidden" distress is less intense, it is more likely to be expressed in a milder and face saving way such as avoidance, through feigned indifference towards the opposite sex. But their true feelings often reveal themselves through spontaneous negative attitudes or comments.

The influence of self esteem and personal development on marital therapy outcomes

As illustrated in the above example, people's level of self esteem and personal development have a major influence on wellbeing, including happiness or unhappiness in their intimate relationships. Couples in which both partners are above the average range in the Diagram 3 "normal distribution curve" (page 88) rarely seek therapy, and tend to manage their differences well enough by themselves. If they do seek therapy it is more likely to be primarily due to stressful circumstances rather than personality issues, and they are more likely to use it productively.

In couples where one partner has personality and self esteem above the average range and the other is average or below, that gap will probably increase over time because the more we know the more we learn and vice versa. If the higher up partner decides to leave the marriage, it is more likely to be for sensible reasons. He or she may also be better able to steer the process towards a reasonably amicable ending to the extent that it is possible, keeping in mind that a divorce brings about big stresses even in the best of cases.

When both partners are below the average range, it is likely that there will be substantial personality issues as well as stressful circumstances, and therefore the chances of improvement are reduced. For the majority of couples with both partners within the average range, the chances of successful therapy would depend on factors such as whether their personality and self esteem are towards the upper or lower side of that range, the severity of their circumstances, and most importantly on their determination to learn to manage their problems more effectively plus their commitment to the marriage.

But in addition, a high level of expertise in the therapist is likely to be a significant factor in increasing the probability of an at least good enough outcome. During my years as a salaried therapist with the Department of Health I had to work with all cases which came in, and give everyone a fair go. In couples where I considered both partners were genuinely committed to work towards improving the marriage, roughly around three quarters achieved improvements they were at least reasonably satisfied with.

By comparison private practice is expensive, clients are preselected by their capacity to pay, and are therefore less likely to have severe financial pressures. This reduces their total stress load, and therefore more of their energy may be able to be directed towards the therapeutic effort. They also tend to have a higher education level, which means they are more accustomed to acquiring knowledge from others and from written material.

For all those reasons the percentage of good outcomes for couples in private practice is higher than for Public Health ones, again of course, provided that both partners are truthful about their desire to improve their marriage and prepared to work on it. Therapeutic success does not depend primarily on the personality of either partner having to change in a major way, which would be rather difficult to achieve even if it was aimed for.

Instead, good therapy is largely cognitive-behavioral. That is, focused on improving cognitions and changing behavior. The motivation comes from second order understandings, aimed at removing the obstacles preventing couples from implementing solutions. In other words, the therapist's job involves instilling the all-important realistic belief that change is possible and they can do it, while simultaneously providing guidance, emotional support and case-tailored education about the combined inner workings of the mind and heart. I elaborate in the two subheadings (*in italics*), after the heading below.

How to improve self esteem as an adult

For the roughly three quarters of the population who I consider have the contingent variety of self esteem, its quality can be improved but it is not a short or easy process and the usual ways of attempting it don't work well. The most common is making a lot of money and showing it off, or by being successful or noteworthy in some other way.

The problem is that these may only lift self esteem within the parameters of the contingent variety, but cannot change it into the much better and safer secure one. Other common methods not involving financial or social striving may include telling ourselves or being told that we are unique, innately valuable, loved by God, somehow better than others, or just better off.

These too are unlikely to improve our self esteem in a meaningful way, no matter how true they are or how many times such statements are made or by whom. They might be somewhat helpful for those who are at rock bottom with nowhere to go. But they don't work for most people, and counselors who use such methods do so largely out of well intentioned ignorance.

There is nothing special about being unique, since everyone is. Being innately valuable or loved by God does not stop bad things from happening. And believing we are better or better off than others aggravates the fragility of contingent self esteem by drawing us further into comparison games.

Although such questionable methods may cause a minor temporary wobbly lift in the level of contingent self esteem in some people, their effects can also be worse than useless. That is because they take valuable time and energy which could be used more productively. And the inevitable ultimate lack of success, undermines further the morale of those who are already in need of all the encouragement and support they can muster.

Earlier in this chapter I mentioned that first of all and most importantly, self esteem is an outcome and manifestation of deeper personality issues and therefore inseparable from them. And that consequently such issues must be understood in order to appreciate what self esteem actually is and involves, and to attempt to improve it if warranted. So, we have to start with developing our understanding of personality.

By improving this understanding, we achieve greater awareness of our inner functioning. More of what self esteem is about becomes fully conscious, facilitating the articulation of problematic issues with more clarity, certainty and sophistication. That clearer knowledge makes us better able to improve each individual core component of self esteem, as the need arises in the process of managing the ongoing stresses of living.

The way knowledge can enable us to improve our core components works more or less as follows. If awareness of our counterproductive propensities is in the forefront of our mind, we will be more alert. Before we began to change for example, if someone had said or done something we experienced as negative or inappropriate towards us, we would have reacted automatically with our usual sense of injustice. Often followed by contained hostility, resentment or distancing, and sometimes by voice rising or passive aggression.

Then if questioned, we would have probably denied we ourselves had acted inappropriately, and possibly argue about it if challenged. But as we increase our self-other acceptance and awareness, more and more often we come to realize we may have made a mistake in our negative ascriptions about the motivation or intention of the other person. And consequently, begin to take more responsibility for our subsequent feelings and behavior.

Because we are paying more attention, our ongoing vigilance enables us to catch ourselves doing the wrong thing almost as soon as we have overreacted. With further practice we begin to realize what we were about to do, just in time, and stop ourselves. As we keep getting better at it, we make mistakes less and less often until it rarely happens.

This is how the process of getting better at managing our reactions about people related stresses, has similarities to how we learn the grammar of a foreign language. Initially we make lots of mistakes. With further awareness and practice we recognize the mistakes almost as soon as we make them. Eventually we notice just beforehand and avoid them. In the end we make very few mistakes until they almost disappear, and that is when we have finally mastered that once unfamiliar foreign grammar.

Understanding the individual core components is important in this process, because it is a lot easier to deal with smaller and more manageable specific parts than with the much bigger totality of self esteem, especially when such complex totality is obscure and poorly understood. As these smaller improvements happen and accumulate, they keep increasing the overall quality and stability of each core component throughout life. This is how self esteem which was contingent to begin with, can overtime be gradually shifted towards the secure end of the continuum.

To the extent that self esteem was already of the secure variety or close to it, the process will be easier. These people may end up developing self esteem which is high as well as secure, and represents the uppermost achievement of a healthy personality. What can help us most in changing ourselves for the better, is the kind of knowledge that self-other acceptance and awareness bring about and allow to be absorbed and acted on.

Considering and reflecting on the issues discussed in this book is one way of expanding the knowledge readers already have. Doing so to a level which will make a difference in their life takes time, alertness and practice. As mentioned earlier, it can be assisted by favorable circumstances such as personal courage and determination, preexisting general education because it facilitates learning, support from a loving partner, stability in other areas of life, financial capacity to enable the purchase of time with a good therapist, etc.

One way of continuing the process of knowledge acquisition within this book is through the example of the excessively jealous wife, discussed earlier under the heading *How the kind and level of self esteem can damage or benefit intimate relationships*. I continue with it by discussing the therapeutic intervention in her case under two subheadings. The first one is next and focuses on the process of what needs to happen, and the second on an analysis of the facts plus avenues for improvement.

The process of "second order" understanding and intervention in the case of the excessively jealous wife

Due to the jealous wife's limited level of self understanding, a bigger part of her conviction of worthiness and its underlying lovability and competence have remained unconscious, in addition to underdeveloped. As indeed have other components of her self esteem, although they all keep automatically influencing her feelings, thoughts and behaviors. In other words, her perceptions and reactions continue to be involuntarily and excessively swayed by her unwarranted uncontrolled emotions.

As long as the nature and causes of those emotions are not well understood, she will remain incapable of responding to situations she experiences as distressing on the basis of a more objective consideration of the facts. Her husband has attempted countless times to reassure her by explaining that there is no reason for her jealousy, all to no avail. He has learned the hard way that if he insists it will lead into an unproductive argument, and does not try anymore.

In order to work out what is happening, we need to look at these situations from the perspective of a second order understanding, which neither partner had. The wife reacted to the perception that her husband had been looking at another woman with an angry, retaliatory, and probably unfounded accusation. Underneath that was her deep hurt, which would have been excessive even if her husband had actually had a passing look at the other woman.

The reason for that excessiveness is that the incident resonates all the way back to her childhood, and is magnified out of proportion because it reactivates residual psychological injuries about not feeling sufficiently lovable and loved. She has forgotten about nearly all of those injuries, because most of them happened when she was a very young child. But the bruises and distortions they left etched into her personality keep revealing themselves, by the pattern of unjustified and excessive emotional reactivity to certain kinds of perceived threats to her shaky conviction of worthiness.

Apart from her over-reactivity, there are other reasons why the above is a realistic assessment. She still remembers some instances of being neglected as a young child. Her mother was very poor and had to work outside the home as much as possible. She had six children too, and was therefore unable to give enough attention to all. Other unfavorable circumstances included her mother's troubled personality and consequent marital problems.

In addition, three of her siblings were younger, and her mother had to divert attention away from her to care for the new babies. And so her childhood unconscious conviction of lovability was never developed properly, which ultimately led to a contingent lower self esteem. As a result she lives excessively concerned with whether she is worthy, and remains oversensitive to real or imagined fears of rejection and abandonment.

One way of improving the contingent lower self esteem underpinning her marital problems, is by refocusing attention away from whatever they argue about and looking instead at what lurks under the surface in terms of **three kinds of issues**. The **first** is what is happening without being acknowledged, with the emphasis on what she does and doesn't do and why.

The **second** issue involves putting her feelings and behavior into the wider perspective of her parents' personality and economic conditions during the time of her upbringing, which affected their capacity to give her sufficient unconditional love. That exempts her from deserving blame for the way in which at times her emotional reactions override common sense. Bearing in mind again, that deserving blame is totally different from the responsibility which she does have, for managing her behavior well enough in order to do away with its damaging consequences.

The **third** issue is about seeing the conflict in terms of developmental level in core components of personality in both partners, in order to work out viable solutions and stabilize improvements. All three kinds of issues are discussed further below.

Therapy has to begin by instilling realistic hope that change is possible in order to motivate the couple. So that as a result of their better understanding, both of them want that change for their own benefit. But in order to become able to absorb and cope with the uncomfortable issues involved, each spouse has to feel that he/she is genuinely and securely accepted, respected and supported by both the partner and the therapist.

That would be essential in order to stop the usual defensive pattern of accusatory blaming and counter blaming from taking over every discussion, as it has habitually happened. They also need to be convinced that the therapist understands their problem, has the competence to guide them, and can be trusted to stop things from getting out of hand.

Developing and maintaining all those supports and restraints while simultaneously listening, responding and planning ahead is not easy to do, and constitutes what I referred to in the *Should-read-first introduction* as a "difficult to master combination of knowledge, intuition and skills", which is necessary for achieving therapeutic excellence. There are so many intricacies, delicate issues, subtleties and fleeting possibilities to consider and act upon with little time to reflect, that the ability to do it all simultaneously and well enough is justifiably referred to as the "art" of therapy.

This involves a superior mastery of the craft, which requires not only extensive knowledge and experience, but also and most importantly a high level of development in the personality of the therapist. That is why it is considered a truism that no therapist can help clients develop their personality above the level of his or her own. The dictum "know thyself" is relevant here because, except for brief and unusual revelatory moments, it is very difficult to understand others above and beyond the limits of our own self understanding.

Given the extent and complexities of the job, less than ideal therapeutic interventions and downright mistakes are inevitable, particularly by less skilled therapists. They could quite easily make a bad situation worse, while remaining oblivious to what is happening or how they are contributing to it. That is why live supervision of therapists through a one-way screen is so important during training, preferably by several people at the same time and including at least one senior therapist. Live supervision is a tough but effective way of learning. It can feel threatening to trainees and experienced therapists alike because it leaves them with nowhere to hide, as their mistakes are undeniably exposed and commented on by others.

I was fortunate to have a lot of such supervision during my formal training, and continued organizing it extensively for myself during the earlier stages of my career. For this purpose I used experienced colleagues, with two examples mentioned in References 2 and 8 (pages 318-319 and 330-331). I also did further postgraduate informal training with the Editor of the ANZ Journal of Family Therapy, Marriage Guidance Council of NSW, and others.

To achieve meaningful long lasting change couples have to be involved with both their intellect and emotions. For the acquisition of knowledge to happen and to stick, both partners may need emotional support in order to counteract the effects of possible intense anxiety, which would often be denied if asked about. Such denial may be helping the person to cope, and therefore it should in principle not be challenged without a good reason.

That anxiety is usually about excessive fear of being judged, which in contingent lowers can at times become overwhelming. Therefore, indirect but clear expressions of support with the respect and acceptance they convey, are in most cases a sensible or essential starting point which has to be taken care of. It needs to be done properly and reinforced as necessary for as long as it takes. This support is an important part of the therapeutic process, and is referred to in psychological terminology as "unconditional positive regard".

Indirect expressions of support are more likely to bypass automatic mechanisms which may filter credibility out of anything positive which is said directly, because it contradicts the possible underlying but denied negative aspects of the person' self image. Such expressions can be made in various ways, as for example, by the natural but respectful and positive manner of receiving, speaking or listening to the person.

The beneficial effect can be added to by the therapist making sideways admissions in a factual self accepting manner about his or her own imperfections, which can be credibly true because everyone is imperfect. Therefore it involves no lying or undermining of respect for the client, while normalizing everyone's imperfections and thereby encouraging self-other acceptance. It is only after defensiveness has been reduced to a manageable level plus enough trust established, that therapy can proceed to the next level.

The first goal is a therapeutic alliance between partners and therapist, with each contributing tentative interpretations of what is happening as ideas for consideration. In the current case example, working to resolve the problem needs to be done at a speed determined by the wife's capacity to cope, plus her requirements for support as it is being done. Any unproductive self righteousness by the husband or regressions by the couple towards their blame and counter blame pattern, would need to be contained and discouraged.

Getting all that going can take more than one session, with all three participants having agreed to accept joint responsibility for failures and joint credit for successes. If therapy goes well, the couple will develop a blame-free good enough second order understanding of what is happening, without necessarily labeling it so. As the level of threat this process brings about comes gradually down, they are likely to regain hope for their future together, and that alone can begin to make the situation better.

Improving the self esteem of the excessively jealous wife would be simultaneously a means for improving their relationship and a byproduct of it. However, talking about working on their marriage is better and much less threatening at the beginning, than addressing her self esteem issues. That is because both partners need to be involved, and because self acceptance is a very big challenge for a person with contingent lower self esteem.

Nevertheless, self-other acceptance is an essential prerequisite for developing the all important self-other awareness. Although in this case it is the wife who has to make most of the changes, focusing on improving the marriage is a also a more acceptable goal because it gives due attention to addressing the problems as the couple sees them. It is also better balanced, because it considers both partners' need to improve their education on the deeper issues affecting their relationship.

A "second order" analysis in the case of the excessively jealous wife, and avenues for improvement

Next I summarize a ten point second order analysis of possible matters to be considered during therapy when the opportunities arise, spontaneously or as created by the therapist, and underline the critical issues which the couple have never explicitly acknowledged. These second order interpretations belong to the category of the **first** kind of issues mentioned earlier about what the wife may be feeling and doing without it being acknowledged. The second and third kind of issues will be discussed afterwards.

1. The strength and frequency of her jealousy is consistent with she having a possibly unacknowledged <u>excessive fear of rejection and abandonment</u>. She reacts as she does in an effort to safeguard a marriage she values.

2. She thinks his "misbehavior" has happened too many times. Therefore she carries a lot of unresolved resentment, and inflicts what she considers as justified and deserved <u>retaliation and punishment</u> with an angry accusation and attack on his character.

3. This retaliation and punishment incorporate a form of <u>self protection</u>, because by increasing distance through conflict she reduces her reliance on a partner who she experiences as an unreliable source of care.

4. However, because her self esteem is contingent lower, it depends significantly on her husband' commitment. Therefore as she distances herself from that support, her contingent lower self esteem becomes even more fragile and therefore she <u>makes herself more vulnerable</u>.

5. All these emotional pain and unmet needs cause her to feel and act in an <u>excessively self absorbed</u> manner. This results in chronic insufficient care towards her partner, and his correspondingly growing perception that she is uncaring and selfish.

6. The interdependence of living together gives her power over her husband. Her behavior amounts to an <u>abuse of power</u> by disrespectfully making an unproven angry accusation, and by subsequent passive hostility made worse by it being extended over several days.

7. Wanting to be loved by the target of her abuse means <u>she puts herself in a fight against common sense</u>. It reminds me of a satirical comment about the Public Service in big bold letters, which I once read in a notice board. It said: "The management wishes to inform that daily floggings will continue until morale improves".

8. There is <u>poor communication</u> because the real issues are avoided by her sulking and their limited knowledge. These issues are experienced as too threatening, and therefore they have become unable to talk about them without generating further conflict.

9. Her self-absorption and/or passive hostility lead to her <u>unavailability for emotional and sexual intimacy</u> for days at a time. This damages her partner and the relationship, and it may or may not involve sadistic satisfaction at his deprivation.

10. All of the above amount to a <u>significant breach of the implied relationship "contract"</u>, which includes expectations of mutual care and support. Ongoing breaches may increase her husband's dissatisfaction to a point where he decides to divorce.

The **second** kind of issues which are not being properly acknowledged or discussed are about putting her *feelings* and behavior into the wider perspective of her family history. For example, her fear of ultimate rejection is due to the belief that her husband's commitment is uncertain, despite his many reassurances to the contrary. As mentioned earlier, this fear is probably partly created and magnified by the poor intimate relating style she experienced as a child from one or both parents and between them.

Her unconscious feeling at that time may have been that she could never be fully secure about being lovable and loved, probably because expressions of it were infrequent, unconvincing, or conditional on doing what pleased the parents. In such case, the strength of her childhood unconscious conviction of lovability would have been significantly eroded. The consequent limitations were carved into her psyche in a hard to erase way, and this is affecting her capacity to trust even the man who loves her.

Again, this happened through no fault of her own, but she and her man are left to deal with the consequences. Parents cannot be blamed either, because nearly all of them do the best they can for their children. Their capacity for good enough parenting could well have been reduced due to anyone or several out of a large number of possible circumstances for which they were in all probability not responsible or not fully responsible.

For example there could have been insufficient unconditional love from their own parents, which left them emotionally handicapped. Serious poverty forced them to work very long hours. They could have suffered from poor physical or mental health, had limited education or intelligence, lack of family support, substance addictions, or other detrimental personal circumstances.

There might also have been bigger sources of disadvantage affecting whole communities, such as unequal economic opportunity, military occupation or dictatorships, severe racial, cultural or gender discrimination, famine, corruption, etc. And also much broader issues like international economic crises, war, exploitation of weaker countries by stronger ones, etc. The point of all this is to remind ourselves that we have to be very well informed as well as very careful, before apportioning blame to anyone.

The **third** kind of issues mentioned earlier, is about seeing the conflict in terms of developmental level in core components of personality in both partners. She cannot change her past, but understanding it will add to the motivation she needs in order to develop those aspects of her personality which are contributing to poor management of relationship problems.

If we were unlucky in terms of the quality of parenting we got as children, we have to face the fact that its legacy probably (although not necessarily) left us with a degree of disadvantage. Those who suffer from it would have to make a greater effort in order to raise their self esteem from the contingent towards the secure end of the continuum, and this is certainly the case with the jealous wife.

Some of the challenges involved were elaborated during the discussion about the individual core components of personality. The second to sixth components can be developed through reflection and feedback about day to day and bigger life experiences, and through study or therapy. Doing it well enough to make a difference, will require ongoing effort and determination.

As that happens, the improvements in those components filter inwards towards the conviction of worthiness foundation through the porous borders represented by the dashed circles in Diagram 2, and make it stronger. To facilitate that, the unique personality and circumstances configuration of each individual or couple needs to be considered and catered to. And it is the nature of that configuration which will primarily determine how easy or difficult the process will be, provided the therapist is good enough.

Something I said before is so critical in the personal development process within therapy that it bears repeating: Issues like the ten points listed above should only be brought up at a rate which avoids creating counterproductive levels of anxiety. Furthermore, such bringing up should only begin after a therapeutic alliance has been established and the person feels sufficiently supported. Again, in the case of the jealous wife, she would need to feel that support from both her husband and the therapist.

Therapy is a way of combining education with benign interference in naturally occurring but problematic psychological defensive structures, for the purpose of improving the person's life. Just like surgery it carries some risks, and should only be attempted at the request of the person and by a skilled practitioner. There is a fine line between wanting to be helpful and saying things in a way which could be experienced as unhelpful or even insulting, thereby achieving the opposite of what may have been intended.

Partners' discussion of disagreements and friction points is normal and desirable, as long as it is done with care and respect. For example, saying "When you do or say X I feel Y" is generally fairly safe, if we leave it at that and then wait for a reply. But if we are in the habit of accusing, abusing or telling our partner what he/she should or shouldn't do or feel, that is likely to aggravate tensions and ultimately endanger the relationship.

COMMUNICATION: Bigger, smaller and sum-total problems

> One way of defining relationship communication would be as an interacting conglomerate of thoughts, feelings and behaviors, through which people deliberately disclose or unintentionally reveal their understanding of the realities at hand and their reactions to it.

We could begin to analyze communication tensions by classifying them into bigger, smaller and sum-total problems, in order to consider how its different parts add up to the whole experience. This can help us look at the many components impinging on it, and suggest better ways of addressing the relationship pressure points manifested through poor communication.

Bigger problems

Understanding a problem is usually a first step in managing it effectively, and if a couple could talk about it without arguing they might well be able to work out a better way of dealing with it. That is not as simple as it sounds however, because the real issue is never just about what is happening. But also and most importantly, about the two sets of personalities-circumstances through which the facts plus communication about them are being interpreted and reacted to.

This is why when couples discuss something they feel strongly about, uncontrolled emotions can escalate what should be a caring conversation into a disrespectful argument. Contrary to what some might wish to believe, arguments do not clear the air. They pollute it, rarely address the deeper causes of friction, and always create further problems.

Following the marketing success of a certain book about interplanetary relationships quite some years ago, many readers with limited life experience came to believe that most relationship problems are caused by differences between men and women and the communication difficulties this creates. That cannot be right however. Because if it were, the same problems should not exist among same sex couples, but they do. And they would exist in all heterosexual couples, but they don't.

So, male-female differences are not the real issue, and neither is poor communication even if it is the loudest and angriest. The latter is usually the visible manifestation of underlying problems and not their primary cause, although it can be a secondary one by adding fuel to the fire, as mentioned under *Smaller problems*. Therefore, something else has to be involved in creating the relationship difficulties manifested through poor communication.

As the discussion in this chapter has made clear, the biggest obstacle to quality communication is underdevelopment in core components of personality in one or both partners. When couples describe problems in terms of their "first order" understandings (see pages 51-53), they often suspect there is something deeper going on but can't quite figure it out. And sometimes they might feel uneasy about what would show up if they did.

That is why in a not insignificant proportion of the couples who consulted me over the years, what one partner actually wanted was for me to agree with his/her first order interpretations. And then hopefully give the other a good talking to, in exchange for which he/she was prepared to make token concessions. This would have resulted in the "winner" not having to change his/her preferred and most comforting way of seeing and doing things, and all responsibility for change would have been on the other.

Such course of action would also have meant that critical core components like self-other acceptance and awareness could not improve, especially in the "winner". This is rarely appropriate, although it is quite common for one partner to carry a greater share of responsibility for both the creation and nonresolution of marital problems. Keeping in mind, as always, that being responsible is different from being to blame.

Both men and women need to have a good grasp of the real issues creating marital tensions, if they are ever to discuss and manage them effectively. The quality and depth of couple communication is always limited by the level of development in core components of personality and self esteem in the partner who has less of it. For negotiated changes to have a good chance of lasting, that partner will need to somehow develop those components, irrespective of whether the process is acknowledged or understood.

Partners can reduce the risk of accumulating relationship damage by acquiring a shared knowledge and terminology. This would make it easier for them to practice non-injurious communication in the safer context of education, thereby facilitating the management of those potentially troublesome tensions which arise sooner or later in all couples.

As suggested in the Introduction, they could expand their existing shared knowledge by reading and understanding Stages 5, 6 and 8, and marking in pencil on the margins whatever each thinks is important. They could then use those reminders as starting points for discussing issues that matter to them, which might by itself improve their relationship and strengthen their commitment.

Personality and self esteem are the really big issues in communication. When these are insufficiently developed they create the kind of problems which are hardest to resolve, especially when trying to do something effective about it is left until a lot of damage has been done. In managing the risk of relationship deterioration, prevention is better and safer than cure.

Smaller problems

When both partners have well developed core components of personality and self esteem, they don't usually have serious communication difficulties. But most people have an average level of development, and this contributes to widespread marital tensions. Although that tends to be the main cause of friction, this is likely to be aggravated by certain perceptual and communication skills differences between men and women, which exist in every culture because they are the result of natural selection through human evolution.

Such differences account for, among other things, more men than women having problems reading feelings and more women than men having problems reading maps. This reminds me that sometimes I get lost in big downtown shopping centers, and then have to ask some kind woman for the way out. In that state of emotional exhaustion and orienteering confusion, I am not sure I would be in the mood for looking at a map even if I had one.

Until the problem was solved by GPS directory assistance in cars and mobile phones, that might well have been how *some* women felt when driving in an unknown part of the city and trying to find their way by looking at a street directory. It is a bit like that for us men, when our partner wants to talk about subtler feelings. Or a bit like trying to talk about in-between colors. We know about black, white, red, blue, etc. But if the conversation drifts into burgundy, cyan, aqua, magenta and whatever else they are called, most of us men are soon out of our depth.

While most women feel at ease, having been forever buying and combining colorful clothes and talking about it with shop assistants and friends. The more complex the maps or the feelings, the greater the effect of gender based skill differences becomes and the more it can add to preexisting problems. For years early in my career I struggled trying to explain such differences to men, in terms of paying attention to feelings rather than facts, and in a way which would get through and they would not forget.

Eventually I hit upon the idea of two identical faces with different size ears, as in Diagram 5. Hand drawing it in front of couples and explaining it, resulted in men never forgetting about the bigger and smaller ear. And with it, that unlike at work where facts are usually what matters most, what is for them the less comfortable language of feelings is the one they have to pay attention to in their intimate relationship.

The gender-based differences which predispose men to focus on facts can aggravate relationship problems, because they cause many of them to have a capacity for empathy which is less developed than in most women. A less frequent consequence of those differences is that they result in some women not fully appreciating the very real value of their men's non emotional contributions to the viability and stability of the relationship.

Empathy is the capacity to put ourselves in other people' shoes. That is, to understand how they think, feel and experience reality. As against the way we ourselves do and might wish they would, or perhaps believe they ought to. Given the nature of intimacy, empathy is an absolutely essential skill to develop and improve on, especially for men who often do not have enough of it to relate well with their woman. If a man is not sure whether he is sufficiently good at it or wants to improve on what he has, the best and easiest way of doing it is to request assistance from his partner.

There is a useful training exercise which I have taught countless times to couples during therapy. I would then give it as homework before the next interview, always on a subject to be chosen by the woman who is going to help. It consists of the man listening carefully and without interruption until his partner has finished saying what she wants. She should do it in one small chunk at a time, so that it will be easier to remember.

Then the man attempts to repeat in his own words both *the facts* his partner stated, and then *the feelings* she expressed as she was saying it. For most men the facts will be a lot easier than the feelings. After having a go at it and before adding anything else, he has to ask if he understood correctly both the facts and the feelings.

If she has to correct him, as is most likely especially the first times, they start again from the beginning with him listening particularly for the feelings. And then repeat the procedure as many times as necessary until she confirms

Perceptual and communication DIFFERENCES between men and women

There are perceptual and communication style differences between men and women in every culture. These differences would have improved survivability during human evolution, and therefore became genetically based through natural selection. Supressing feelings made it easier for men to kill prey and fight predators or enemies in brutal ways. Better perception and communication of feelings made women more responsive to children's needs, thereby helping them become more confident and resourceful adults, who by being so were more likely to survive and outbreed others he got it right. My usual recommendation is to practice the exercise every other day for the first week, twice in the second week, and then just once a week. It should be done when everything else is out of the way possibly just before going to sleep, because although it may seem easy to a woman, it can in fact be emotionally exhausting for a man.

For the same reason it should last only for a short agreed amount of time, perhaps eight or ten minutes to begin with. And then extended gradually by mutual agreement, if necessary and as tolerated, to a maximum of around fifteen or twenty minutes. I cannot emphasize enough that in this exercise it is essential for the man to resist the temptation of adding explanations or justifications, if he believes or is sure she misunderstood what he said or did.

Whether she misunderstood is not the point, because the sole purpose of the exercise is for the man to improve his skills at listening accurately for the *feelings* being expressed. This remains so even if anything he is supposed to have said, done or intended is incorrect. That will be hard but it is most important, because the real issue is about him resisting his propensity to over focus on facts as he sees them, by learning to detect and describe feelings.

Empathy is a skill men should want to get better at because, among other things, it enhances the emotional warmth and intimacy most women like and need in order to feel ready for and enjoy physical intimacy. But more importantly, men should make an effort to get good at empathy because they love their woman, want to do their part to make her happy, and doing so is one of their marital responsibilities.

When men get better at it, empathic responses and the deeper understanding and caring expressed through them become an increasingly natural part of their communication style. As that keeps happening, eventually it comes to be done fairly automatically and effortlessly. Empathy is and always has been an emotional intelligence component of what it takes for a man to be a good lover, as well as to become his wife's most trusted friend.

A minority of women have problems with empathy too, usually due to significant blind spots often originating from unfavorable childhood circumstances. But few women need to do this exercise for their own sake, because they tend to be naturally good at it. A man who is smart, loving and determined to improve his empathy skills is likely to be able to persuade his woman to help. It is in her interest to be willing too, because she knows that to the extent they succeed this will enhance their feelings for each other and benefit the relationship.

Most of us men are insufficiently skilled *intimate* communicators. It is to be expected that we will not have at the beginning a vocabulary big enough for expressing the many subtleties of feelings, just as we don't generally know the names for most in-between colors. Nothing wrong with asking our partner for help, on the grounds that women are generally savvier and more articulate than us men about emotional issues.

After all, genetically or hormonally influenced gender advantages and disadvantages are not a reflection of a person's good will or overall intelligence, whether they are about reading maps or reading feelings. We men need not feel uncomfortable or defensive about accepting women's frequent superiority in this one particular aspect of emotional intelligence. Namely once more, that when it comes to the finer perceptual skills about subtler feelings and the ability to be articulate about them, women tend to be better than us. This means we can learn from them, and they can help us do so.

Sum-total problems

To recapitulate, the bigger communication problems are caused by underdeveloped core components of personality and self esteem in at least one partner, and can be aggravated by smaller problems. The latter are usually the result of gender differences, often through the effect of men's generally less developed empathy skills. Both add up into a sum-total of communication problems, which is most often a reflection of underlying relationship difficulties rather than their real cause.

Such difficulties tend to exist about a number of different issues affecting the partners, which as a whole create the overall relationship crisis they find themselves in by the time they seek therapy or begin heading for divorce. Couples who argue a lot regarding ordinary pressure points such as money, sex, children, housework or leisure often believe these "things" are their real problems and have unhappy marriages, although other couples with the same pressure points but better balanced personalities have good ones.

What accounts for this difference are the issues underlying communication. Again, the main one is about the extent to which partners' core components of personality and self esteem are well or poorly developed. Perceptual and communication style differences between men and women are generally a secondary issue, provided the main one is good enough.

The process by which a couple's sum-total communication problems grow is illustrated in Diagram 6 (next page). It represents the development year by year of one single problem, out of any number a couple may have. If we forward this process to its tenth year, we can see that by then 90% of the total

Diagram 6

Couple CONFLICT ACCUMULATION by poor communication plus underlying issues

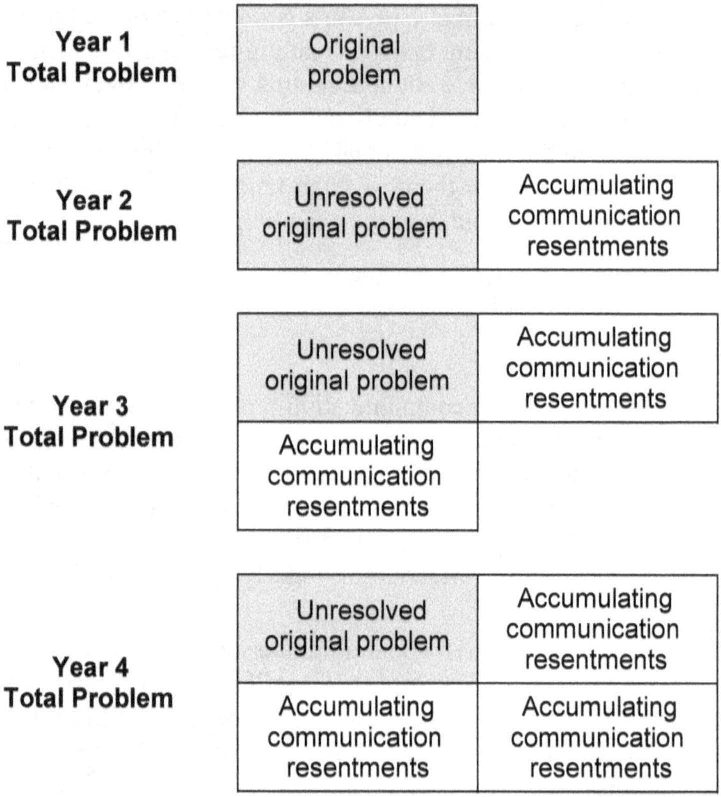

Year 1 Total Problem	Original problem	

Year 2 Total Problem	Unresolved original problem	Accumulating communication resentments

Year 3 Total Problem	Unresolved original problem	Accumulating communication resentments
	Accumulating communication resentments	

Year 4 Total Problem	Unresolved original problem	Accumulating communication resentments
	Accumulating communication resentments	Accumulating communication resentments

By the tenth year, 90% of the total problem may be due to accumulating communication resentments, and merely 10% to the original problems. Couples who argue a lot about money, sex, children, housework, etc. may think they are their only real problems. They have unhappy marriages, although other couples who manage such matters better have good enough ones. What makes a difference is the issues underlying couple communication. The main one is about the extent to which partners' core components of personality and self esteem are well or poorly developed. Perceptual and communication skill differences between men and women are a secondary issue, when the main one functions properly.

problem would be caused by accumulating communication resentments, and only 10% may be due to the unresolved original problem. This is not to be taken literally, but only as a memory aid representation for the process by which serious marital problems tend to keep growing as big as they eventually become. Often however, it is exactly how it happens.

When it does, couples might have a big argument and by the end of it feel rather confused regarding what the argument was actually about. The reason is often that what triggered it was a minor spark, and most of the argument was in fact fuelled up by the need to release overflowing accumulated resentment. The way the accumulation process works is that every time a couple attempt to resolve a problem and fail, that failure leaves a sediment of hurt or anger which does not dissolve away.

Instead, that sediment settles and keeps piling up, as was the case with both spouses in the example of the jealous wife. As the problem persists and continues to bother at least one of the partners, there will be further attempts at finding a solution, but they continue to fail. Probably because those attempts are based on first order understandings underpinned by underdeveloped core components of personality and self esteem, plus possibly aggravated by insufficient empathy often in one partner and sometimes in both.

If there are several friction areas operating simultaneously, for example over money, sex, child management, in-laws, gambling or substance abuse, the partners' sum-total problems can become serious enough to tilt them towards a breakup. They tend to argue repetitively over a number of things without ever resolving their differences. That is because the issues underlying what they are arguing about involve aspects of themselves they don't really understand, and feel perhaps uneasy about daring to understand.

What usually happens in fully grown adults, is that the partner with a healthier personality eventually concludes that the other has a significant and unresolvable personality problem. As a result he/she may stop arguing or feeling angry, and begins seriously considering getting out and how to do it. This is when the point of no return is getting very close or has finally been reached, and improving the relationship from then on becomes quite difficult.

Many unhappy older couples who reach crisis point still remain together out of not wanting to face life alone, become poorer, lose social standing, disappoint their children, etc. If the crisis settles down they may again become able to give each other enough friendship, support and even some genuine caring. In the better cases the relationship is recalibrated, with both doing more of what they like in aspects of life important to them. In bad cases they barely and grudgingly tolerate each other.

The very worst cases happen when both partners have significant personality problems. They may become weary wranglers who argue themselves into exhaustion quite frequently, but are too frightened to divorce or perhaps too worried about being seen to have failed. They may end up hating each other, while living together miserably amidst ongoing bitterness, and in extreme cases one partner may wish the other would die. The joke about the bickering couple in page 197 is an example of such situations.

LOVE: What it is and how to improve our skills at it

What is love?

Lifelong love is not easy to find, or its quality easy to keep. Songs can be good at expressing the general longing for it and the desire to understand better its deeper aspects, but their lyrics are definitely not the best way to learn about it. Neither are trashy romantic novels nor popular TV sitcoms such as *Sex and the City*, which in its day triggered a lot of interesting discussions among women who yearned for a deeper knowledge about love and relationships, in addition to enjoying the comedy.

Information about love from academic psychology is often overcomplicated and confusing. Most popular psychology books and anything in the Internet can be simplistic, unreliable and not infrequently plain wrong. Many people end up half believing cleverly crafted unscientific information as in the signs of the Zodiac, or in feel-good predictions sold by clairvoyants, numerologists and other smooth operators for as much as they can get away with.

Because love has a major impact on our lives and its more profound aspects are so intriguing, many people expect that a definition of it capable of unraveling its mysteries would be not only revealing and meaningful, but even inspiring. Against that, is the fact that love can be understood by considering its manifestations in the form of thoughts, feelings and behaviors, plus whatever underpins them from deeper within the personality. Therefore those are the factors we need to look at in the search for answers.

Most of us would agree that a big part of what true love involves, is caring for another person's contentment and security as much as we do for ours. This means it has to be more than the pleasant thoughts and feelings it engenders, and incorporate what we are *doing* in order to contribute to the person we love feeling contented and secure. That balances our natural tendency towards self interest by redirecting attention towards what the loved person feels and needs, but without forgetting that our own feelings and needs are equally important.

Furthermore, contentment and security are dependent on people's needs as expressed through their wishes and fears, which are in turn significantly influenced by personality, self esteem and circumstances. Needs, wishes and fears can vary for different people, from moment to moment or day to day, and are also influenced by the stage of life we are at. All these are issues of the highest importance in influencing *The art and skills of getting better at loving*, discussed next under that heading.

Needs, wishes and fears have already been commented on under the heading *Self esteem from best to worst: Where we fit, how it shows and what underpins it*, and are illustrated in Diagram 4 (page 91). The issue of needs is critical for understanding happiness, and they are discussed at some length further below under the main heading *Happiness: What it is and depends on*, within the subheading *The four categories of inherent higher human needs*.

To complicate matters further, there are different ways of loving. The purest love is probably that of a mother for her child, although this too may involve some expectations of current and future benefits. In well functioning sexually intimate relationships, families and genuine friendships, people love each other in many ways.

Non religious humanitarians love people because it satisfies an innate desire for kindness, and because they are convinced that it enhances individual wellbeing and social good. In addition to that, religious humanitarians interpret their love for others as an expression of their love of God. And the practice of love in the form of caring for the less fortunate even if we don't know them or they live in other countries, is consistent with the teachings of all major religions about treating others the way we want to be treated.

We are no saints however, and if love within a committed sexually intimate relationship is to function properly and last for life, both partners need to feel that it meets their needs adequately. Or if one partner has become incapacitated for some reason and can contribute less, little or nothing, at the very least he/she needs to be seen as deserving to be loved and cared for.

But under normal circumstances, if the relationship has become unbalanced beyond what is acceptable and a solution is not found, a partner would begin to feel increasingly frustrated or resentful. Consequently he/she may become less giving, in turn affecting the other's perception of imbalance, and a vicious cycle may be set in motion which could ultimately destroy love.

134 Furthermore and as hinted earlier, a precondition for understanding love is the appreciation that it can be passive or active. Passive love is made of mostly pleasant thoughts and feelings, which often exist because we have something given to us by someone else in order to care for us.

That is, we do not actively love anyone, someone else is doing it and we are the beneficiaries. This is usually what happens to us when we are children. At that time it is natural, immensely beneficial to personality health, and influences us positively for life.

But when most of what we "give" as adults is passive love, we do not care much about anyone, other than perhaps ourselves. And even that would be arguable, considering that passivity stultifies our own initiative and personal development. Therefore love can only be real when it is active. Again, this means it has to include the things we do for the purpose of benefiting another person, which of course includes *not* doing certain negative things.

Moreover, there are clear differences between mature and immature love, although both are very real. The most common example of the immature variety is the romantic love of our youth. Its overwhelming feelings are largely triggered by physical attraction plus fantasy, and therefore easy to understand although unsustainable in the longer term. An example is included as Appendix B, an autobiographical narrative by me titled *The Japanese connection: Men's fascination with women's bottoms*.

In contrast to the heightened feelings of immature love, mature love has come down to a more natural intensity, after emotional rebalancing through repeated exposure. The psychological and ethical issues underpinning it involve harder realities related to the strength or fragility of self esteem, and deeper still to the level of personality development. All these complexities can make mature love not easy to maintain at a quality level in the long term, and result in the finer points of it being difficult to comprehend.

Not surprisingly, many sensible adults conclude that a limited understanding will have to do. They leave the rest to strange people like philosophers and serious writers on the subject, who seem to enjoy squeezing their heads by thinking long and hard about it. However, a reasonably good understanding of love is important in the quest for happiness, which we all want.

For all the reasons mentioned so far, explaining what love is requires a substantial elaboration, which I have already partly done and will be continuing over the next two headings. The whole issue involves directly or indirectly most of what is discussed in this Stage 5, and indeed in the whole book. If that sounds too hard, we need to remember that nobody who is reasonably informed and moderately sane has ever claimed that love is easy to understand. With all the above in mind I propose that:

> Love is a combination of mostly pleasant thoughts and feelings plus everything we do as a way of giving for the purpose of caring, which in sexually intimate relationships includes an expectation of reciprocity under normal circumstances.

The art and skills of getting better at loving

I have mentioned elsewhere that if we include the de-facto ones not counted in the statistics, roughly around half of all marriages in Australia and the United Kingdom break up, with the rate thought to be higher in the United States. Exact figures would be arguable, but don't alter the fact that for many people there has to be something difficult about monogamous love.

Despite this overwhelming evidence to the contrary, most people believe that loving is easy, and the main difficulty resides in finding the right person to love. In an ideal world such person would fit with us in the four most important compatibility areas, namely appearance, personality, circumstances and lifestyle preferences. These can make things easier by facilitating mutual acceptance and communication, while minimizing stress and conflict.

Although finding a person who is right enough is indeed not easy, it is nowhere near as difficult as developing a "capacity to love" for those who did not get enough of it effortlessly through a lucky upbringing, as part of their personality and self esteem development. *Capacity to love* is all about being able to give others what they need in order to care for them, and it is essential if we aspire to become good at the art and skills of loving.

That necessitates well developed core components of personality and self esteem, in order to understand what has to be done plus have the surplus of inner security and happiness required to generate the desire and ability to do so. When people have all of that, they are inclined to be kind to everybody. And without enough of it, they would not have what it takes to be able to love anybody.

As suggested by the discussion in this Stage 5 so far, the capacity to get better at the art and skills of loving will depend largely on how well developed the core components of our personality and self esteem are. And the problem is that around three quarters of the population have the less developed variety of core components, pertaining to contingent self esteem.

Furthermore, out of the roughly one quarter of the population with secure self esteem, only around half have the *secure high* variety, and only a few of those are at the very top. This is why nearly all of us would benefit by developing our personality and self esteem, and by doing so, improve our level in the art and skills of getting better at loving.

There are many ways of doing that. Some would argue that quality literature can help us improve considerably our understanding of ourselves and people in general. Indeed, one thing all good writers have in common is an above average and often very deep understanding of human nature, and some of it is bound to rub on as we read them.

Others believe that the best way of developing their personality is through religious-ethical traditions such as Christianity, Islam or Buddhism, and that may be all they are prepared to consider. Indeed life itself bit by bit and blow by blow may also help us develop our personalities, provided we are willing and able to learn. But all these processes are slow and incorporate many biases or limitations.

Perhaps partly in an attempt to fast-track their way towards wisdom, some try the academic road by doing psychology or related degrees, and that may help to varying extents. But contrary to what might be expected, doing them is no indication that those who complete them have achieved secure self esteem, let alone a guarantee of it. Or even that they have improved their personalities by much, if their self esteem was contingent to begin with.

As an insider, I know for a fact that there are many professional counselors of every level and discipline who have significant personality problems. One example is the experienced psychiatrist mentioned under the next heading, who although only a character in a film represents a perfectly plausible case. Two real life examples are a professional counselor with a postgraduate degree and a local community worker, both mentioned in Stage 6 under the heading *Feminism's excesses and disregard about female perpetrators*.

So, considering all the above, what can we do to get better at loving? A good place to start is by improving our awareness of what is going on at a deeper level. Some of this has been made clear through the discussions about core components of personality and self esteem, and is also further elaborated in Stage 8, but can be illustrated now by a few simple observations.

For example, when insufficient childhood unconscious conviction of lovability has caused us to never develop good enough self esteem, our conviction of worthiness is likely to be poor and we will have little to give because our heart is too empty. A worst case scenario is that we reach adulthood as a bottomless barrel of need, with a corresponding level of incapacity to care for others, unless we anticipate that doing so will benefit us.

This kind of neediness is so imperative that it can make us self centered and over demanding, but it can never be satisfied no matter how much love our partner puts in. That is because someone's love can never provide the self esteem we are lacking, although it may help us to forget the void for a while. In addition, being so dependent on another person' support is risky, because one day it might not be there.

A poor conviction of worthiness also obstructs us from developing genuine awareness and liking of who and how we are without arrogance or conceit. Having enough of this conviction is what persuades us that we are deserving of being loved. It also makes it easier to struggle productively in our search for love, recognize the potential for it when we meet a suitable person, and grab the opportunity before it goes away.

Furthermore, an underdeveloped conviction of worthiness cascades down creating subsequent deficits in all the other core components of self esteem for which it is a foundation, and the ultimate result is contingent self esteem at varying levels of severity. This is then reinforced and made harder to grow out of by our prevailing materialistic culture and, as elaborated earlier, can contribute to all sorts of relationship problems.

When our self-other acceptance is underdeveloped, we will find it difficult to face and tolerate imperfections in ourselves and our partner with equanimity and compassion. If our self-other awareness is limited, we will lack an accurate understanding of the two personalities which make up the relationship. Our relative ignorance may prevent us from doing the right things even if we mean to, and instead lead us into doing the wrong things, sometimes despite genuinely good intentions.

As the gap in self-other awareness between partners widens beyond a certain point, due to each developing differently through life, it may become unbridgeable. This can make it increasingly difficult for them to share a genuinely stimulating friendship and may contribute to a breakup, especially if other aspects of the marriage are also unsatisfactory.

If worthiness, acceptance and awareness are underdeveloped, the remaining three core components which grow out of them will be correspondingly deficient. If we don't have enough self confidence we may not know or feel certain about what needs to be done, and our capacity to act may be obstructed or paralyzed by doubt and insecurity. If we don't have enough self-other respect we can easily make matters worse than they have to be by offending, thereby increasing the risk of defensive counter offending by our partner.

To the extent that our sense of identity is not properly developed we will be less able to step outside the heat of relationship tensions while we are immersed in them, so as to get a bird's eye view of what is happening. Being able to do so requires the ability to function alone without undue anxiety, leading to a more detached, objective and sharper appreciation of the issues at hand. This in turn makes it easier for us to remain true to ourselves even when we are being pressured by a partner we love, and to manage everyone's feelings and reactions as constructively as possible.

In the above and many other ways, the six interacting core components of personality and self esteem are critical in determining how good or bad we are as judges of character, and at assessing rapidly and accurately the essence of any issue or situation. People with well developed core components tend to become tolerant, kind, honest, good observers and quick thinkers. And it is these ingredients which, with practice, create the conditions for developing and improving the art and skills of getting better at loving.

When practicing love, or therapy, there may be many factors to consider in the immediacy of the moment and with little time to reflect. Being good at loving gets easier with the acquisition of relevant knowledge plus ongoing practice and reflection. When we persevere in all of that, we eventually learn to do it skillfully enough instinctively and without thinking. That is the point at which we are doing well at the art of loving, or the art of therapy as the case may be. Although occasional mistakes will happen they are bound to occur less and less, with attentive ongoing practice.

If and when we reach that stage, the combination of it plus a wisely chosen partner makes it likely that the relationship will function within a virtuous cycle. As this happens, sharing love becomes a fairly effortless byproduct of mutual giving. Many such virtuous cycles occur spontaneously in partners who are emotionally well balanced, although they may not have the sophistication of understanding to articulate how and why they succeeded.

I saw a charming example of the above in a very ordinary elderly couple. The wife said her husband was most contented when playing with his hobbies, and she was obviously happy for him. She also commented repeatedly that whenever she asked him to do some job around the house he always did something wrong. And what caught my attention and I found rather touching, was that each of the several times she referred to the various things he did wrong, she ended every complaint with the words "but he is very nice".

Her love without resentment or resignation could be read between the lines of her comments. Like all of us he was seen by his intimate partner as having differences to be tolerated and imperfections to be forgiven for. And the point is that he was being *lovingly* tolerated and forgiven, because in some unspecified way inside her heart he was earning it and deserved to be loved.

What can happen when we lack the skills of loving

No long established marriage retains the shine of imaginary near-perfection common during the infatuation stage, or the sexual urgency of earlier years. But a virtuous cycle marriage is blissful when compared to the vicious cycle of distressed marriages heading for divorce, where love is rarely given but often felt as an entitlement to be aggressively demanded.

A graphic example is in the rather good Australian low budget film *Phobia* about the last day of a marriage, written and directed by John Dingwall. The husband is a psychiatrist with significant personality problems. He wants to be loved by his wife, who has become increasingly agoraphobic years after they married.

He shouts at her about all he has provided and the sacrifices he makes to accommodate to her, and then asks angrily what she has ever given him. She replies she gave him her feelings. After he attempts to physically stop her from leaving and there is a violent incident which could have ended tragically, his wife finally leaves him by literally walking onto the street, clutching her cat for security in an effort to contain her agoraphobia.

The enormity of his loss crashes down on him soon after, while watching despondently a video of their happier times. The overpowering pain of his new reality forces him to face that she had indeed given him her feelings, that they made him happy, and that feelings are what makes or breaks a marriage. Because although financial comfort can help, happiness is not primarily about having things, but about something we feel.

That applies to everyone including people like him, who believed that the material wellbeing he had provided should have brought him happiness, or at least bought it. As their relationship deteriorated, his "love" had become demanding and resentful. Perhaps their problems were due in part to whatever she was doing or not doing, and this was not fair on him.

But if so, he would then have been failing to accept responsibility for what was his own mistake in choosing a partner who was not compatible enough. Instead he had been overbearing and inconsiderate about her vulnerabilities, rather than accepting of who she was and respecting her right to be so.

He expresses his dissatisfaction through anger and blame, and tries to push his "psychiatric help" in a patronizing and unethical way. He does what anyone with well developed core components of personality and self esteem would have been very careful not to do. And the point is made more cogent by the fact that he is an experienced psychiatrist, who should therefore supposedly know better.

HAPPINESS: What it is and depends on

Research on marital happiness around the world has consistently shown that couples are happier before children arrive and after they leave home. This is partly because together with all the love and joy they generate, bringing up children takes a lot of time, effort and money. That comes on top of mortgages, work stress, marital tensions, unexpected crises, etc. It all adds up to what partners must bear, and some of these issues are elaborated further in Stage 8a under the heading *Predictable stress periods and pressure points*.

The extent to which we can get a grip on what happiness is and how to get and keep it, depends on our understanding of the many underlying factors involved, in addition to more superficial ones plus the above usual life stresses. In other words, happiness is the hoped for ultimate outcome of various steps, components and understandings which precede it, and are prerequisites for its ongoing existence. These are discussed next, ending with a definition under the last subheading *What is happiness?*

Prevailing views on what influences happiness

Happiness is something everyone wants, which is why the pursuit of it was enshrined as an inalienable right in the United States Declaration of Independence. Long term marital happiness is at its best when each partner is happy enough independently of their relationship. And because happiness means different things to different people, there can never be an easy consensus applicable to all about what it is and depends upon.

However, there are prevailing views among specialists in the field on the major issues which influence happiness within any individual person, centered on a consideration of three factors. They are the physiology of the brain, the nature of the mind and the level of material wellbeing, with the latter traditionally thought to determine only around 10% of happiness.

In later years there has been growing awareness of a stronger association between material wellbeing and happiness, particularly in cases of serious poverty. And especially so when it is accompanied by big social inequalities, with all the resulting inequities and disadvantages. Their combined effect can be hugely detrimental in people' lives, including their intimate relationships. Socioeconomic and political issues are critical for understanding and correcting inequality, but beyond the scope of what can be addressed in this book.

The physiology of the brain is believed to account for around 50%, and the nature of the mind for the remainder 40%. Precise percentages about each factor would be arguable, especially when applied to individuals and as understood by them, and anyone interested can find out more by looking it up in the Internet.

It feels counterintuitive that only a relatively small part of happiness would depend on material conditions. We can all appreciate the benefits of money, and most of us would choose to have more if it came easy. On the other hand, it is equally true that there are many poor people who say they are happy and seem to be, while others are obviously not happy despite their wealth and the expensive or ostentatious material things they have.

Except in those suffering from significant poverty and inequality, the main reason why additional happiness from more money may not last is that humans adapt to what they have, and once the initial euphoria settles down they are likely to revert back to their usual happiness baseline. For most people, decisions about striving for more money would be influenced by whether they feel comfortable enough with what they have, and by what additional effort would be needed in order to get more of it.

For a majority of those who could make more money if they wanted, this might entail working for long hours and perhaps in jobs they don't like. For some it would involve sacrificing self respect by discarding any moral principles in order to exploit everyone they can. Those who were never bothered by a conscience still risk going to jail if caught out in something illegal, which usually involves abusing others in a variety of ways.

When it comes to the contribution of our brain, the broad consensus is that about half of our happiness depends on it. That is because the brain is a chemical factory with a natural variability in producing more or less of the substances which make us feel contented and relaxed as against depressed or stressed. It is certainly true that many people report feeling reasonably happy, even when dealing with many life difficulties.

Epigenetic research suggests that some of the genes responsible for this variability may have been activated or deactivated by social conditions, a common major one being the quality of parenting during early childhood. But whatever the reasons for the propensity we end up with, favorable brain chemistry provides a form of genetically based psychological strength and resilience. This operates over and above the effect of current events or life pressures, thereby facilitating the experience of happiness.

In other words and to compare extremes for the sake of clarity, people with a favorable brain chemistry can feel fairly happy even when they have a lot of difficulties in life. Furthermore, they are more likely to cope better with their problems, and carry on doing whatever needs to be done without being defeated by adversity.

In contrast, people with unluckier brain chemistry may feel unhappy as soon as something doesn't go the way they want, especially if their self esteem is of the contingent variety. They may also collapse into depression and inability to function, far more easily that someone with a healthier brain physiology plus secure self esteem.

The third important factor for happiness is the nature of the mind. This is greatly influenced by the individual's level of personality and self esteem development, which is critical in generating emotional strength and resilience. That is a very good reason to focus on the around 40% of happiness potential which is thought can be influenced with our mind. It is here that the core components of personality and self esteem come into their own, and this will be discussed in the heading after next *The role of self esteem in meeting inherent higher needs*.

The four categories of inherent higher needs

The minimum *survival needs* are food, water, clothing and shelter. One step above are *basic necessities* such as health care, education and sanitation. Next up are *inherent higher needs*, discussed from the next page. By comparison, the latest mobile phone, fancy car, exotic holiday or chic dress are not essential to wellbeing. These luxuries can give us temporary good feelings, but we know that having them does not constitute happiness.

Whatever we come to conclude that happiness is, there is also no doubt it is different and more meaningful than pleasure, because it involves our heart and mind in a much deeper and longer lasting way than the simpler short term experiences of our senses. If our self esteem is of the contingent variety, impressive status symbols could make us feel somehow superior to others. But deep down everyone knows that this is not real happiness either.

We can start looking at happiness and how to get it by distinguishing ongoing stable contentment from temporary pleasure or being "better" than others, and the role personality plays in achieving it. In developed countries where survival needs and basic necessities are available for nearly everyone, most people's feelings of contentment are based largely on having what they consider as important needs met predictably and securely. These change from person to person, at different times and at various stages of life.

Despite those disparities there are inherent higher needs which are common to us all, because they involve our genetic realities as determined by evolution. That is, those needs cannot be removed or replaced by something else, because they are woven into the building blocks of the human condition. I have organized what I consider as the major inherent higher needs into four interconnected overlapping categories in order of importance, which I call *relationships, security, autonomy and competence*.

Relationships needs were produced by evolution in the process of making humans into social animals. With many individual variations, these needs include diverse forms of intimacy, family, friendships, and other affiliations, and they are obviously vital in securing the survival of the species. If we are short of whatever relationships we happen to need, we feel the internal pressure to seek them out. However, circumstances and especially personality account for how many and what kind we want.

For example introverts can feel satisfied with less relationships than extraverts, because their brains are hardwired differently. Introverts have a higher level of reactivity to external stimulation, and therefore less of it is enough for them to reach the level of internal stimulation which represents an optimal inner subjective experience of it. In contrast to them, extraverts have a lower level of reactivity, and therefore need more external stimulation to reach exactly the same level of optimal inner subjective experience.

Both extraversion and introversion are normal, each has advantages and disadvantages, and being one or the other is unrelated to level of happiness. Extraverts are friendlier, outgoing, louder and popular. The process of relating is rewarding to them even if it happens at a superficial level, and therefore they like having a lot of friends and being surrounded by people.

On the advantages side they can be socially useful, because their being as they are lubricates the cogs of team work and social interaction. This, their popularity and the fact that some people mistakenly ascribe negative connotations to the word "introvert", could be why more people describe themselves as extraverts and prefer to be seen as being so. Estimates of the proportion of people who belong in either category range from a simplistic 75% for extraverts and 25% for introverts, to a more realistic 50% of each, with countless variations as in the normal distribution curve at Diagram 3 in page 88.

By comparison, introverts would consider most such "friends" as acquaintances, and superficial social relating can soon feel boring to them. They prefer to have fewer but more meaningful relationships, where they can hear what is really going on in the hearts and minds of those involved or talked about, and express their own deeper thoughts and feelings.

Many original ideas or inventions come from introverts, because they like to think things through. Their personality predisposes them to intricate analytical thinking out of limited external input, and they tend to be well suited for any creative work requiring concentration. They are also more comfortable with aloneness and almost never bored, because their mind can all by itself provide much of what it takes to keep them stimulated.

On the disadvantages side and compared to introverts, extraverts can easily feel lonely and bored when they are alone or there is "nothing" to do, and have correspondingly little tolerance for it. While introverts may not operate smoothly as part of a team, except when doing so still allows them to be as creative and true to themselves as they want to be.

That can be a real problem for them, because fitting in and accommodating to others is a requirement for most jobs. However, many talented introverts manage to have their cake and eat it too. They could be working in any field, and I listen to some of them in ABC Radio and TV.

For clarity of discussion, **security needs** can also be subdivided into four interconnected and overlapping categories of inner, relationship, health and economic. *Inner security* is closely related to self confidence, and through it, to all our core components. If we don't have enough of it nothing else can fill that void, although many things might help to temporarily forget, dilute or disguise the discomfort.

Relationship security is very influenced by three factors: (1) A solid lovability component of conviction of worthiness, which reduces vulnerability to jealousy and the need to control our partner. (2) Having or developing better personality core components, because they have many features beneficial to relationships. (3) The luck or wisdom in choosing, of both partners having a combination of qualities and imperfections which meets each other's needs.

Reasonable *health security* is absolutely critical for everyone, because nature has designed humans to want to live and avoid pain and death. We cannot do much about the genes we got. But what most of us can do is to become better informed about how to take good care of ourselves, and then do so in order to stay as healthy as possible for as long as we can.

Economic security is a subjective feeling of having sufficient reliable financial resources, as against being deprived or burdened by poverty. How much is enough depends mostly on our material needs, what we are accustomed to, and whether our self esteem is secure or contingent. Crucial to economic security are political policies which affect the distribution of economic resources, because their effect is to increase or decrease public access to services such as health care, education, housing, a salubrious sustainable environment, etc.

The adequate satisfaction of security needs is extremely important for everyone, because on producing the kind of brain we have, evolution has enabled us to anticipate what may happen in future. This has the potential to trigger anxiety because bad things could occur at any time, and some are inevitable.

We can cope better with such anxieties if we have some capacity to control the situations that cause them, to the extent that it is possible. Research on people' sense of control has consistently shown that the more they feel they have the happier and healthier they seem to be. This applies, I believe, regardless of their kind of personality or its level of development.

For people with a contingent personality, the most valuable thing greater control would give them is more security, by feeling safer about their relationships, finances, health, work, etc., or by believing they are superior to others. For those with a secure personality and a consequently better inbuilt sense of security, greater control would give them more freedom. This is a higher level need than security, and having it makes them better able to do what they like or want in work, leisure and other aspects of life.

Autonomy needs are about having sufficient intellectual, emotional and economic independence, all of which are compatible with the inevitable, beneficial and voluntary interdependencies of satisfying relationships. The need for autonomy propels us to leave the parental home in order to make our own way in life. And with it into thinking about and taking actions relevant for getting and managing relationships, achieving inner and economic security, and hopefully wellbeing and happiness.

But different individuals have different needs for autonomy. At one end of the intellectual continuum, the ancient Greek philosopher Socrates said "the unexamined life is not worth living". Part of what he meant was that the capacity for independent thinking plus freedom of expression, which he saw as the hallmark of autonomy, are extremely important. That is certainly the case for those whose nature and circumstances have given them the curiosity and desire to understand people, life or anything else they are interested in.

Towards the opposite end of the spectrum, individuals with limited ability or desire to develop such aspects of autonomy may live contentedly with their lives decided and directed by others. Or by what they consider as the higher power or wisdom of God, the Government, family values, traditional cultural rules, the need for social order, etc. Both kinds of attitudes to autonomy are normal and useful, and just like with extraversion and introversion each has advantages and disadvantages.

Competence needs result in developing adequate skills in whatever we do for work or other aspects of living. They are satisfying because in addition to making our lives easier, they fulfill the natural tendencies of our mind. It is only after people feel at least competent enough, that they may develop the additional abilities to carry out their work or other activity in a creative way, to the extent that its nature permits. The artistic instinct can be thought of as just another expression of creativity.

Competence and its creative side are part of human nature because the instinct for survival and wellbeing requires the capacity to adapt, so as to do what needs to be done in the most efficient way. We can be creative in any activity by for example trying to do it in our own original way for the purpose of maximizing pleasure, productivity, quality results, a higher income, or for minimizing the effort we have to put in to get the job done.

The deeper psychological side of competence needs involves self confidence. That is, confidence in our ability to keep meeting the challenges of life as they arise, in a good enough way given our limitations and circumstances. It facilitates the fulfillment and management of all four categories of inherent higher needs. And again, it is one of the core components of personality and self esteem which interacts with all the rest.

Like the other inherent higher needs, competence ones vary for different people. If unable to satisfy them, those with a natural inclination to think, understand and be honest, creative or artistic would have to suppress those needs. That is why for them, work which is repetitive or in other ways precludes creativity or self honesty can be extremely unpleasant. While such work might be better suited for those with a naturally more placid personality, and they can be reasonably contented doing it.

The role of self esteem in meeting inherent higher needs

Diagram 4 in page 91 illustrated how our needs plus the resulting wishes and fears vary depending on whether our self esteem is secure or contingent. Secure self esteem focuses on the seeking and fulfillment of inherent higher needs about relationships, security, autonomy and competence.

In contrast, contingent self esteem needs are primarily about protection from underlying fears of inadequacy, and the resulting shame or other expected negative consequences if the person was seen to not measure up. The satisfaction of such needs relies on external validation or the internalized version of it, by way of real or imagined favorable comparisons with others. The intense craving for security in order to counteract ingrained degrees of underlying self doubt makes contingent self esteem needs imperative, which is why so many people strive to meet them.

And the problem is that the more they are pursued, the more they undermine the person's capacity to meet inherent higher needs, which are the ones best suited to generating a real and stable level of happiness. That is partly because pursuing the set of needs with greater priority consumes most of the person's time and energy, leaving less of it for the other needs.

Furthermore the two sets of needs contain contradictory elements, which means that both cannot be met at the same time. For example, we may not be able to be true to ourselves if we are excessively concerned with what others might think of us. In practice, that could mean having to fake liking something we don't or disliking something we like, in order to be approved of by people with such preferences or prejudices. This carries a psychological cost, which if ongoing becomes an emotional burden detracting from happiness.

It is clear from the earlier discussions about contingent self esteem, that among other things it undermines the quality of satisfying relationships. First and most important is the damage to the person's relationship with his/her sexual intimate, and relationships with family are rarely as good as they could be. Friendships are easier to do without if anything goes wrong, and less personal affiliations don't matter much. Relationship needs are so important for happiness, that it is worth recapitulating on the major issues involved.

People with contingent lower self esteem do not damage just their primary relationship. Sooner or later the more intelligent among family and friends will sense the intensity of the underlying anxieties, plus the inability to genuinely care for others or great difficulty in doing so as a result of these preoccupations. They realize the contingent lower is likely to lie, treat unkindly or betray them if that came to be seen as convenient.

Regardless of any denial or pretense, those who are like that know it only too well. This undermines their self honesty and self respect. And with it what is by far the longest and most important relationship we can ever have, which is the one with ourselves. The quality of this relationship is dependent on the level of development of core components of personality and self esteem. This facilitates better self understanding and that of others, relationships, and all sorts of things in life.

This understanding is part of a process which improves self confidence and inner security, and with them a sense of control and therefore of predictability in our lives. That can only be achieved to its higher levels when we know we can trust our mind and heart as tools of cognition, and this trust has been reality tested overtime rather than being based on wishful thinking.

When the above is good enough we have predominantly secure self esteem, which increases the likelihood we will be able to create and maintain a virtuous cycle within our primary intimate relationship, for several reasons. It gives us the capacity to be alone without fear, which in turn enables us to love without clutching. This allows us to give our partner all the room they want, within reason, including when their choices might not be what we prefer.

We can love without undue jealousy too, because we are confident about being lovable. When we occasionally have doubts as to whether we are truly loved, we are able to manage most of that anxiety within ourselves, thereby avoiding damaging overreactions. The emotional balance which confidence helps bring about makes it easier to appreciate and accept our partner without judging, criticizing or feeling resentful or threatened by differences.

Well developed personality and self esteem give us the capacity to be actively kind, because we are internally OK and therefore can afford to spare some caring. They also facilitate expressing dissatisfactions and requesting changes assertively but respectfully, without anger or blame, and within a context of reassurance of love when that is warranted.

If we think our partner may benefit from our help, we will take great care to offer any suggestions without insulting. And will not unduly insist if our offer is not taken, because we accept our partner's right to decide. Regardless of level of dissatisfaction and even if we believe our partner is mostly or solely responsible for relationship problems, we would not inflict abuse or retaliation by verbal, emotional, financial, sexual, physical or other means, because that would violate our self-other respect.

From the perspective of my own values, such behavior ought to be maintained whether we or our partner have decided to leave the relationship and regardless of the reasons or our partner's conduct. That is because genuine self respect is not negotiable, and therefore not dependent on what anyone else does or doesn't do.

After a career dealing directly or indirectly with people's happiness and unhappiness and the reasons behind it, I am convinced that it is very difficult for people with contingent lower self esteem to create the kind of happiness likely to survive in the longer term.

Those whose self esteem fragility is less severe can still be happy, but their happiness will be at far greater risk than in people with secure self esteem. That is because their capacity to cope can be easily degraded, leading towards feelings and behaviors conducive to relationship deterioration.

The solution can never come by just blaming a partner or ex partner and starting a search for someone else, because comparable problems are likely to reappear sooner or later. Their safest way out of a pattern of repeated relationship failures has to be based on developing personality and self esteem by strengthening their core components, however this is labeled. That is what can make all of us better at searching for, recognizing, getting and keeping a partner who would be good for us in the longer term.

The self confidence which is part of self esteem is one of the core components which would enable us to judge accurately enough who could be right for us. In any case, for a man to have quality permanent relationship potential he needs two features as the bare minimum: The first is a personality and self esteem healthy enough to have or be able to develop a *capacity to love*. The second is the kind of *imperfections* which would enable him to keep loving us, despite our faults and the risk of temptation from other women.

In that regard and given the way men's attraction proclivities have been designed by evolution, it seems sensible to think that being sufficiently older than us may be one of their important imperfections in terms of making us adorable to them. The problems and possibilities with younger and older men are discussed under their own headings in Stage 6. The choices in terms of men's age which actually happen and work for women starting new relationships, from their twenties to their fifties, are further discussed in Stage 8 under the heading *The gradual turnaround in gender relationship power.*

So much for our all-important relationship needs. When it comes to the needs for security, autonomy and competence, most people in the higher up self esteem continuum probably already have a good enough built-in level of emotional security. This plus their relationships skills and other capacities makes it more likely that they will be able to satisfy those three other categories of needs too, at a level they feel comfortable with. In contrast and as discussed at various points, the lower the contingent self esteem the more likely it is to create difficulties in meeting all our inherent higher needs.

If self esteem is significantly contingent therefore, it is worth investing whatever effort might be needed to lift it towards the secure end of the continuum, because it will facilitate everything in life. In the final analysis, what is most relevant for increasing our chances of happiness by adequately satisfying inherent higher needs, is the kind of person we ourselves are and have the potential to become. The next most important thing is recognizing men who may be right or wrong for us, and that is discussed at length in Stage 6.

What is happiness?

Happiness is always going to mean different things to different people, due each person's unique configuration of needs, wishes and fears. Furthermore, it remains perfectly possible that those who achieve their aims may not feel happy for long, probably due to their incorrect understandings regarding what their true needs are. And consequently, about what real happiness would be for them and how to get and keep it.

It is relatively easy to decide what happiness is when it refers to anyone individual or couple at a point in time. But here as in any general discussion, an explanation of what happiness is has to be applicable to most adults, and take into account variations among them and changes in their needs over time and at different stages of life. This creates a challenge when trying to work out a broadly acceptable definition of happiness.

A sensible way to organize our thinking about what happiness is for each one of us as the unique person we are, is by bringing together some issues which have already been discussed or are easy to agree on. One is that genuine ongoing happiness is different from, and much deeper than feeling superior to others or the temporary experience of pleasure.

We cannot change by much the brain physiology we got, and therefore have to work around it in our search for happiness. Seeking it through a relationship with a "better" partner by improving our physical attractiveness has its limits, beyond a certain point. The plastic surgery option is expensive, and risky too especially if done by a less experienced surgeon.

Furthermore, it is clearly obvious that removing unnecessary or unwanted tissue would be a lot safer than putting inside our body something which is not part of it. For example, I understand breast augmentation patients have to sign a document stating they are aware that implants may have to be removed in future. The horror stories about breast implants and facial fillers in news and documentaries are just the tip of the iceberg.

All of us would feel good if we got more money without effort, but getting it may not be easy. And unless we feel very poor, there is no guarantee this would make us happier in the longer term. Therefore again, seeking happiness by making more money may not be worth it, if our material wellbeing is already reasonably adequate and secure. But if it isn't, getting it could well be a priority because financial security removes the very real anxieties, deprivations and disadvantages caused by financial insecurity.

Given everything discussed so far in Stage 5 and the book as a whole, there is one way which stands out as the most sensible and productive to pursue for a majority of those seeking to increase and secure a greater level of happiness. And that is to develop our personality and self esteem in order to become better able to meet our inherent higher needs for relationships, security, autonomy and competence.

Unless we are meeting those needs well enough, social status or the ostentation and things money can buy are unlikely to give us true and stable happiness. But if inherent higher needs are reasonably satisfied, we can be happy even if we are poorer than average. Or if we are fairly alone, as in having just one or two people we can really trust and be close to, bearing in mind that aloneness is different from loneliness. From this broad perspective and willing to reconsider if a more convincing definition comes along, I propose that,

> For most adults in developed countries, happiness is a deep and stable feeling of contentment based on the ongoing adequate satisfaction of inherent higher needs for relationships, security, autonomy and competence.

Putting it altogether: The deeper and truer reasons why established relationships succeed or fail

The purpose of summarizing here everything said in this chapter is to present an uncluttered totality of what is undoubtedly a complex picture. This will make it easier to remember and absorb the essentials, now that important explanations and examples discussed elsewhere can be left out of the way. They elucidated the intricacies of personality and self esteem, plus how they influence our knowledge, thoughts, feelings and behaviors.

The deeper and truer reasons why established relationships succeed or fail involve an ongoing balancing act between mutual attraction plus the extent of partners' similarities on the one hand, and on the other their capacity for effective management of the inevitable differences. The major factors impinging on that capacity are each partner's level of personality and self esteem development, plus the gap between those levels. Underpinning it all is a multiplicity of obscure interconnected pulls and levers operating below the surface. These may be difficult to understand and also to control, especially while we are being influenced by strong emotions.

When the conviction of worthiness which is the foundation for subsequent personality and self esteem growth was less than good enough, it will obstruct the healthy progression of all subsequent five core components. Acceptance, awareness, respect, identity-meaning and confidence will be underdeveloped to varying degrees. One serious consequence when that impairment is significant, is a capacity for empathy below the average for the person's gender. That is, less ability to realize how others feel.

Another major consequence, including in those who are past the normal inexperience and insecurities of early adulthood, is that they have a less comprehensive awareness of the realities at hand. The most important of such realities involves self knowledge which depends on self acceptance, followed by our understanding of others, relationships, and all sorts of situations we encounter in life. This influences the depth and accuracy of our ability to appreciate the facts that matter.

Unless we are lucky, reduced self-other awareness could lead to considering or choosing unsuitable people as potential or actual partners, even after reaching full maturity in the mid thirties and beyond. And then once again, to unrealistic expectations about what an intimate partner or relationship can and should provide for us, manifested by an excessive sense of entitlement. This is bound to cause subsequent disappointments, typically followed by open or hidden blaming of a potential or actual partner.

That is frequently how the first seeds of dissatisfaction in various areas of a new relationship begin to be planted. Unless such dissatisfactions are resolved, things will probably get worse and eventually begin the process of conflict accumulation illustrated in Diagram 6 (p. 130). Furthermore, good management or resolution of differences is unlikely due to first order understandings caused by underdevelopment of core components in at least one partner, and the resulting attempts at first order "solutions".

Worthiness, self-other acceptance and self-other awareness form the three-layered foundation which enables a proper development of self-other respect, sense of identity-meaning and self confidence. The outcome of underdevelopment in all or most of the six core components is contingent self esteem at varying levels of severity, with all the life disadvantages it entails.

When such levels are significant, they can result in a recurrent and in some cases quite frequent or almost ongoing state of low level self esteem anxiety. This is manifested by excessive self consciousness about whether the person is worthy, and punctuated by frequent increases which can range all the way from mild to very high.

The triggers could be anyone or anything the person experiences as a challenge to their vulnerable conviction of worthiness, which given the way they are happens frequently. When self esteem is very contingent, the person may use up a lot of time and energy in activities ultimately largely intended to provide reassurances of self worth. The usual coping mechanisms often include making as much money as possible and showing it off, striving for work promotion, seeking ostentatious titles, etc.

As a result, less time and energy is available for considering and meeting the needs of their partner, who will begin to feel increasingly neglected and develop a growing perception the other is too selfish. If the partner who feels neglected attempts a conversation intended to understand the problem and seek remedies, this can create a lot of unease in the uncaring partner.

That is because any increase in awareness by the neglected partner may lead him/her to conclude that the other is indeed too self centered. Apart from feeling threatening to the latter because it would undermine his/her already unsteady conviction of worthiness, it may lead to demands for fairer treatment by the neglected partner. Therefore, any awareness rising is likely to be resisted in all sorts of direct and subtle ways.

The intensity of emotions triggered by increases in self esteem anxiety reduce further the person's existing capacity to assess reality accurately, since strong feelings tend to overrun common sense. This happens because humans are hardwired for this predisposition, which is not easy to overcome. Consequently, the resulting behavioral reactions to what the uncaring partner may perceive as unfair can range all the way from excessive to extreme, when compared to those by people with secure or less contingent self esteem.

Such intense reactions often take the form of expressed or contained anger, usually manifested by the person behaving or speaking in an offensive or accusatory manner, thereby increasing the risk of defensive counter offending. This can easily lead to a growing spiral of negative feelings and perceptions in both and the development of vicious cycles of relationship deterioration, which can keep feeding on themselves and reignite whenever there is stress in either partner.

When such vicious cycles have developed over the years in relation to a number of problem areas and remain unresolved, commitment is at serious risk. Unexpected stresses may trigger escalations, which can over the years begin to get out of control and tilt the conflict towards the point of no return. Once that has been reached it becomes very difficult to retrieve the relationship from the edge of the precipice, and the longer the problems have existed the greater the likelihood of it tumbling down towards a breakup.

The core component differences discussed so far may be easier to appreciate and remember, if we compare how they are at the two extremes of the continuum. This comparison is illustrated in Tables B-1 versus B-2, in the next two pages, which include also a brief summary of the likely short and longer term consequences for partners in most established relationships.

Table B-1

CORE CONPONENT FEATURES in people LOW in the Diagram 3 normal curve, plus consequences

1. Underdeveloped *Conviction of Worthiness*, cascading down to cause limitations in all subsequent core components. It can ultimately result in excessive "self esteem anxiety", which increases with challenges.
2. Underdeveloped *Self-Other Acceptance*, due to protective strategies such as denial, avoidance, anger, blame, etc. These help to cope with ever-present fears about their imperfections being exposed, which could destabilize further an already wobbly conviction of worthiness.
3. Underdeveloped *Self-Other Awareness*, because the above strategies block off information which would aggravate self esteem anxiety. It leads to a more limited and less accurate appreciation of reality. Does this amount to lesser emotional and/or intellectual intelligence?
4. Underdeveloped *Self-Other Respect*, because when protection of a shaky self image is at stake, the truth about self or others is likely to be thrown overboard and replaced with self-serving rationalizations.
5. Underdeveloped *Sense of Identity and Meaning*, due to reduced self-other awareness. That makes it difficult for people to see objectively who and how they are, plus the interpersonal and wider contexts in which they exist. This therefore decreases their own internally-based understanding about the reasons for and purposes of their existence.
6. Underdeveloped *Self Confidence*, because its creation and maintenance is dependent on the quality of all the other core components.

SHORT and LONGER TERM CONSEQUENCES

Table A (page 89) has examples of outcomes of the above in terms of feelings, thoughts and behaviors. They reflect greater sensitivity to rejection, unwarranted or excessive emotional reactions, and reduced capacity to tolerate differences, love and forgive. More proneness to unrealistic expectations, sense of entitlement, jealousy, neediness, envy, wish to control, self-centeredness, manipulation, anger, blame, aggression, etc. This negative emotional climate combines with couples' ongoing need to negotiate over all kinds of issues, and triggers repeating vicious cycles plus gradual resentment accumulation (Diagram 6, page 130), aggravating the effects of existing differences. Over the years any partner with a healthier personality may run out of patience, eventually out of hope and finally out of love, with divorce being the likely outcome.

Table B-2

CORE COMPONENT FEATURES in people HIGH in the Diagram 3 normal curve, plus consequences

1. Good or superior *Conviction of Worthiness* increases the likelihood of above average development in subsequent core components, leading to significant and resilient immunity against "self esteem anxiety".

2. Good or superior *Self-Other Acceptance*, because the person's conviction of worthiness is so secure that it is never at risk. Therefore all feedback about oneself can be accepted and even sought if seen as useful, including that which would feel threatening to most people.

3. Good or superior *Self-Other Awareness*, due to more information being observed, analyzed and incorporated, making it retrievable. It results in a more comprehensive and accurate appreciation of reality. Does this amount to better emotional and/or intellectual intelligence?

4. Good or superior *Self-Other Respect*, because the person is better able to behave according to his/her principles, even when doing so is going to be disadvantageous in financial, personal or other ways.

5. Good or superior *Sense of Identity and Meaning*, due to better self-other awareness. That makes it easier for people to see objectively who and how they are, plus the interpersonal and wider contexts in which they exist. This therefore increases their own internally-based understanding about the reasons for and purposes of their existence.

6. Good or superior *Self Confidence*, assisted in its formation and development by an above average level in all other core components.

SHORT and LONGER TERM CONSEQUENCES

Table A (page 89) has examples of outcomes of the above in terms of feelings, thoughts and behaviors. People with such features are less sensitive to rejection, and experience more balanced and appropriate emotional reactions. They have a greater capacity to tolerate differences, love, give and forgive. They are also less prone to neediness, envy, jealousy, wish to control, self-centeredness, manipulation, anger, blame, aggression, etc. Realistic expectations plus awareness that love has to be earned facilitates the couples' ongoing need to negotiate over all kinds of issues. Successful management or resolution of differences helps create virtuous cycles and the experience of loving, feeling loved, and of the relationship being stable. Their inner sense of security and contentment makes it easier for them to be kind and supportive to everyone.

Tables B-1 and B-2 summarized how and why lower development in core components of personality and self esteem can lead to relationships becoming progressively less happy, and eventually failing. It is therefore important to increase the development of core components for everyone, but especially for partners trying to better manage significant problems, so as to become happier and thereby reduce the risk of gradual deterioration.

The specifics of the deeper issues operating under the surface and how to deal with resulting tensions have been elaborated on earlier in this chapter and illustrated with a number of brief and extended examples. Additional and common potential problem areas with further examples will be discussed in Stages 6 and 8. The recapitulation below is intended as a way of remembering the total picture of what is needed in order to steer a relationship towards success.

Differences are inevitable, even in couples who are very similar in background, personality, major goals and lifestyle preferences. Most are not that similar however, and this can only increase the number of potential friction areas. Such tensions can sometimes be completely resolved, but that is rare. The common and quite acceptable outcome for couples, is that they are able to manage issues or disagreements well enough to stop them from becoming problems.

Achieving outcomes acceptable to both partners requires negotiation and compromise, and it is in this arena that the level of development in each partner's core components of personality and self esteem can make a big difference. This was illustrated with the extended example of the jealous wife in pages 105-111 and 115-122, by among other things comparing what actually happened due to her personality and self esteem being contingent lower, as against the likely turn of events if they had been secure high.

Relationship problems can generate very strong emotions, but if we are able to peer through the haze and look objectively at most situations, what makes a difference tends to be the number and intensity of friction areas plus the couple' skills at managing them in the best possible way. And when it comes to doing the latter, the crucial limiting factor is usually the level of personality and self esteem development in the partner who has less of it.

I finish by emphasizing a critically important point: Achieving the kind of long-lasting improvements which can change for the better a person's relationships and life, has to begin with understanding what needs to be done. Most of the material in this book is relevant for developing such understanding, and the process of how improvements gradually take place was summarized under the heading *How to improve self esteem as an adult*, in pages 114-115.

For counselors, teachers and researchers:
A core components theory of personality and self esteem, integrating couples communication, love and happiness

Laypersons who read this section will find out things which certain people would not want them to know. While I use plain English as much as possible, these four pages have to include some specialized technical language in order to facilitate communication of complex issues with other professionals, because it makes meanings more precise while requiring far less words.

The theory summarized in this subheading refers to adults rather than children or adolescents, with whom other major factors are involved. It adds to current understandings about the deeper reasons why established relationships succeed or fail, and revolves around the manner in which the six core components of personality and self esteem affect communication, love and happiness. Its concepts involve ethics and values, in addition to psychology. Most important of all, they are based on my down to earth accumulated experience of working as a relationship therapist for over twenty five years.

In addition to their explanatory capacity, these concepts suggest openings for therapeutic interventions and other forms of personal development, for the purpose of better managing or resolving the usual relationship problems. The concepts presented include my own original ideas and diagrams, and to that extent they represent an addition to existing knowledge.

Theories about behavior and its motivations come and go as part of the evolution of psychology, but what seems to remain constant are the time honored central concepts of the three major categories of theories, namely dynamic, behavioral and systems. Assessments need to take into account the *thoughts/beliefs*, *feelings* and *behaviors* of everyone involved, or otherwise analyses will be incomplete and subsequent interventions less effective.

The central concept from dynamic theories is the defensive structure. It focuses on levels of anxiety or stress and coping strategies, both of which can be justified, counterproductive or unrealistic. They range from unconscious to conscious, and if the latter, they can be acknowledged, avoided or denied.

Behavioral theory is based on the concept of reinforcement, and its major sub-concepts include operant conditioning, classical conditioning, and intermittent reinforcement. All three can contribute to a better understanding of many issues affecting individual functioning and established relationships, such as satisfying or unsatisfying companionship, trust and sexuality, negotiation of differences, domestic violence, all sorts of addictions, etc.

The main contribution of systems theory has been to bring attention to how a multiplicity of "systems", including sociocultural, economic, political and circumstantial rather than just psychological, can affect any situation. This could be over and above the issues raised by dynamic and behavioral theories, or in combination with them.

Relationship therapy and related personal development requires input from all three categories of theories, due to the complexity and interactivity of the many factors involved. A multi theoretical approach facilitates a broader and deeper understanding, thereby maximizing options for helping clients in better managing or resolving their problems. The core components theory of personality and self esteem expounded in this chapter incorporates and combines insights and practices from all three major theoretical approaches.

But in reality most highly skilled therapists do the same, irrespective of the theory or terminology with which they explain what they do. They know how to work from an exclusively dynamic, behavioral or systemic perspective, when appropriate. Consequently they can also use them effectively in combination, according to the needs of the moment and as a matter of common sense. Put simply, they are genuinely and efficiently eclectic.

If asked, less skilled counselors may claim to be eclectic and sometimes resort to vague answers, in order to hide the limitations of their knowledge from laypeople or less well informed professionals. Or perhaps advocate something innocuous like "cognitive theory". This is essentially just a sexier label for unpretentious common sense education, which if done properly has to include a combination of dynamic-behavioral-systemic concepts such as "second order" analyses and interventions.

As an experienced insider and in terms of the absolutely critical issue of self esteem, I know for a fact that the level of understanding by the vast majority of counselors is nowhere near as good as it ought to be. This is regardless of whether they are psychologists, social workers or psychiatrists, have a postgraduate or fancy named degree, or a job title suggestive of importance and superior expertise. That is why if asked, most would have difficulty in answering two very relevant and reasonable questions:

- What is self esteem?, including what it is made of and depends on.
- How can it be improved?, plus how and why doing so would work.

If they muddle and struggle with the answer, their comprehension is poor. If their answer is not convincing, they could be asked to elaborate so as to get a clearer sense of how well they actually understand the subject. If they knew or have read and absorbed the material in this Stage, their explanations should be understandable and make sense. That however still does not guarantee they are good therapists, for reasons elaborated in the Introduction. Most of the better qualified counselors have degrees in psychology, social work or psychiatry, and this raises some educational issues.

It is an unmemorable reflection on those courses, that students graduate with a very limited understanding of self esteem, which is unlikely to get better later as a result of work experience or postgraduate study not specialized on the subject. This is lamentable, because helping individuals develop personality and self esteem by remedying deficits in their core components (regardless of how we label them or the process), is often the biggest part of what it takes for people to evolve in positive ways.

The uncomfortable truth is that most professional counselors and even university staff who are supposed to teach about it, do not have a good grasp of the complexities of self esteem. Additional knowledge is constantly being developed, but it takes time for it to filter through to those in universities who are in charge of courses and make decisions about what is to be taught. The conceptualization of personality and self esteem in this Stage 5 is intended to fill a knowledge gap for counselors, teachers and ordinary readers alike.

A good grasp of what personality and self esteem involve is important for understanding what lays under the surface of communication. This helps in getting better at the art of loving, and it is generally agreed that experiencing love in one form or another is a big part of what it takes to be happy. Achieving and maintaining happiness produces a surplus of good feelings, which is then felt by those around the person who has them and benefits everyone.

As mentioned earlier and contrary to common belief, the safest and most fulfilling way towards relationship happiness may not be just to find the right person to love. A couple will function best when both partners were already reasonably good at meeting their inherent higher needs. When in addition to it such people find love, they are much better able to practice "active" loving (elaborated in page 134). If that capacity exists in both partners it will facilitate the creation and maintenance of ongoing virtuous cycles, increasing further their surplus of good feelings.

From the perspective of my own values, some of that surplus can then be channeled towards helping people who need assistance, in ways compatible with our personality, circumstances and preferences. Contributing to creating a better world is a goal and motivation of all humanitarians. That was always a predominant rationale for my choice of occupation and for the not inconsiderable amount of voluntary work I have done, mostly regarding relationship issues but also in other areas of community welfare.

Understanding personality and self esteem as discussed in this core components theory has research implications. People's level of core components development could in principle be estimated on the basis of factors illustrated in Diagrams 1, 2 and 4, plus possible associated feelings, thoughts/beliefs, and behaviors such as those illustrated in Table A.

The outcome could be plotted in a normal distribution curve as in Diagram 3, representing the underlying level of development in core components, plus their nature and likely consequences as outlined in Tables B-1 and B-2. Assessing the position of a person in the curve would be a complex matter, and the outcome only approximate. Creating a systematic reliable way of doing so would require a way of calculating scores for each component.

However, because this theory incorporates some new and original ways of understanding personality and self esteem, no suitable scoring system exists. My opinion regarding how the numbers are distributed in the population as a whole is based on my own anecdotal observation of people over the years, and I know of no research suggesting otherwise. This is represented in Diagrams 1 and 3, indicating that about one quarter have the secure variety of personality and self esteem, and three quarters the contingent one.

Developing a core components scoring system and verifying its validity could be an interesting project for a Doctoral program. More weight would have to be given to the foundation, second and third components in that order, because each is a prerequisite for the proper development of the next level, and all three as a whole represent an integrated foundation for the remaining three core components.

The total score would place a person somewhere along the curve continuum, representing simultaneously the type and level of self esteem and personal development. The challenge of creating a suitable scoring system could make such research more difficult and its validity opened to question. This may well be inconvenient, but it is just a fact of life that multifaceted interacting aspects of personality and self esteem do not lend themselves well to simplistic research methods.

Attempting to make self esteem research easier by oversimplifying its definition involves in my opinion questionable ethics. This is bound to be denied by those who do so, presumably on allegedly defensible grounds. And arguably (but more likely, I think) because their jobs, incomes, reputation, and careers depend on it. Furthermore, it comes at the expense of diverting funds from more deserving research. And also, inevitably, of undermining whatever social good would come about through a better understanding of self esteem within the helping professions and by the public at large.

STAGE 6

SEARCHING COMPETENTLY:

How to recognize Mr. Rights and Mr. Wrongs

Four conditions for searching competently, and four critical issues influencing whether a relationship will succeed or fail

For the sake of honesty I have to emphasize that nothing said in this book or any other is likely to resolve difficulties in some relationships. For example if one or both spouses' personalities are within the categories described further below under the heading *Definitely dangerous men (and women)*, or if there are initially hidden or unacknowledged but unresolved major issues with alcoholism, gambling, drugs, or certain other limitations.

That is because no partner with a reasonably healthy personality is likely to put up with these problems indefinitely. And because for they to be overcome, those having them would need an uncommon confluence of qualities and circumstances which do not often coexist. These include the desire and courage to handle the truth plus a capacity for learning and reflection, resulting in a potential to develop all core components of personality.

If the personality underdevelopment underpinning existing difficulties is significant, what would also be needed in the individual seeking improvement is an almost bloody minded determination to achieve it. Even if all other conditions are present, that kind of determination is unlikely unless something serious enough has happened which has shaken the person to the core.

The above combination of favorable qualities and circumstances including an extreme event is very rare and therefore such people almost never change, although they are more likely to do so if they can afford enough quality therapy. But even if his personality or ours is not as bad as that of dangerous men, it could still be problematic. And our biggest risk continues to be repeating the mistake of choosing on the basis of physical attraction, without due regard for the critical importance of personality.

While attractive women do have more options, they make mistakes like everyone else. Because beauty gave them an advantage when they were younger, the search for love will eventually feel harder for them as they get older and their beauty fades. All this underscores the importance of being aware enough to choose wisely while there is still time, especially if we have already made one or more major mistakes. We can take a step in the right direction by considering the four conditions for searching competently.

The *first* is to be able to detect Mr. Wrongs early enough, in order to avoid wasting time with men who aren't worth it. The *second* is being able to recognize potential Mr. Rights. Neither is easy because some Mr. Wrongs could be handsome or impressive, while some Mr. Rights may look like everyone else or even less appealing at first sight.

Knowing how to distinguish both kinds of men as fast as possible is especially important for those of us who are no longer young. By this time there are far too many Mr. Wrongs everywhere, who keep re-circulating after being dropped by all the sensible women who tried them out. In contrast genuine Mr. Rights have become scarce, as the lucky women who find them realize their value and make an effort to keep them as happy as possible, and therefore less vulnerable to being enticed by the competition.

The *third* condition is about developing the capacity to deal with mistakes constructively by retaining our level headedness when things don't go as we would have wished, rather than avoiding relationships due to hopelessness, exhaustion or hurt. This takes not just the capacity to understand what happened and why. But most importantly, the learn-as-you-do skills to manage it all without making matters worse by overreacting through anger, blame or distancing, and instead reconsidering and modifying our strategies as needed.

These skills will help us sail through the headaches and heartaches of trying but not getting what we wanted with a number of potential Mr. Rights, in between the disheartening sifting through of countless Mr. Wrongs. Unless we are very lucky, that is what it will take to find a worthwhile man who has the capacity to love plus enough flaws to want to be with us for life despite our imperfections. It sounds difficult, but true love is rarely easy. And making the effort of finding and keeping it is much better than the alternative of giving up and living our life without it.

We are more likely to develop the skills for achieving the previous three conditions by motivating ourselves through knowledge. This is the *fourth* condition, which involves improving our understanding through the issues discussed in this book. Because if we are not fully and accurately aware of what is happening and why, we are never going to appreciate realistically our qualities and liabilities or those of others, and that will undoubtedly make more difficult for us to make the best possible decisions.

If our choice of man has been wise and both personalities are within the normal range or above, good quality *caring, friendship* and *sexuality* are likely to create and maintain *commitment*. These have always been the four critical issues influencing whether a relationship will succeed or fail. They are discussed at various points in Stages 8a and 8b, and more directly under the heading *The three C's women need in order to be happy, or is it four?*

Getting all four to run smoothly takes emotional balance, emotional intelligence, relationship knowledge and maturity-wisdom. These were mentioned in the Introduction, and involve most things discussed through Stage 5 and the book as a whole. Joint children or property will not prevent relationship breakup, if the above four issues are not right and attempts to fix them have failed. Much of everything else including money, is in fact ultimately not as important in maintaining relationship happiness and stability in the long run.

Four major partner compatibility evaluation areas, and three absolute minimum requirements for a relationship to work

Just like Stage 5, this chapter attempts to provide a framework for organizing knowledge in a more easily retrievable way, so that we can keep it in mind when important choices have to be made. That is done through a classification and elaboration on various categories of problematic men, the good qualities in men and women which actually make a difference, and other related matters. This has implications when it comes to knowing which men are worth exploring and for improving our chances of getting the odd good one who crosses our path, before a luckier, smarter or faster competitor nabs him away.

Apart from facilitating more realistic evaluations, the development of greater knowledge plus a memory organization-and-retrieval framework encourages informed reflection. Both increase the likelihood of searching competently and deciding wisely about who to try, how, and why. As mentioned in page 135 under *The art and skills of getting better at loving*, the four major partner compatibility evaluation areas are about appearance, personality, circumstances and lifestyle preferences, and all four are reflected in the headings and content of this chapter.

Regarding the above and apart form the inevitable differences between partners, every man with the potential to love us permanently is bound to have a permissible quota of imperfections. Only the woman who is going to live with them is entitled to decide whether to take it or leave it. Hopefully after a correct estimation of the qualities in a man which would best fit with her deeper needs, as well as about the imperfections she can live with.

In addition to the four critical issues in determining whether a relationship will succeed or fail in the longer term, there are three absolute minimum requirements for relationships to work well enough in the short and longer term. They are respect, consideration and not being taken for granted.

Partners must treat each other with respect, even if they are annoyed and have valid reasons to be. This means that raising the voice in anger, direct or subtle insults or derogatory gestures are totally unacceptable, especially if they are becoming a pattern. Common sense and self respect demand that the matter be remedied or ending the relationship be contemplated.

Consideration means that what each partner feels, thinks and believes matters, whether the other agrees with it or not. Whatever is important to either must be taken into account, and significant differences clarified and sorted out in a spirit of care and egalitarianism. The manner of ending a relationship no longer wanted may show vividly whether or not the person was truly considerate, behind the image he/she was trying to present.

A woman in a newish relationship had been waiting for her man in a dancing venue. After a brief greeting following his arrival and without saying why, he left her and kept dancing with other women. Obviously he had decided to create distance, which either partner ends up doing in the majority of relationships, and there is nothing intrinsically improper about it. But what shows a problem with consideration, especially after having shared sexual intimacy, is to move away without an explanation leaving the other person wondering what is happening.

Inappropriate behaviors are common in these emotionally charged situations, and some women behave just as badly. They may turn up later than agreed without prior advice or apology, and exploit a man financially by not paying their way, thus abusing the power which being found attractive gives them. Or instead of asking a man not to call, SMS or email after explaining why, they just ignore him.

Sexual exploitation reliant on indirectly encouraging unfounded illusions is just as bad, and often inflicted on women who open the gate to sex only to men who are attractive or rich. Inconsiderate partners are unlikely to improve overtime and will probably get worse. If the issue of consideration is causing friction it needs to be discussed and resolved. And if a potential partner can't or doesn't want to, we are better off without him.

Nobody should ever be taken for granted, as made abundantly clear by the rate of divorce. Human imperfections plus the stresses of life may propel us towards becoming complacent about appearance, behavior or our partner's needs. These things can creep in gradually, and by the time we finally accept what has been happening it may be difficult to lose all that excess weight or regain the affection or respect of our partner. The resulting negative feelings would make it more difficult to make the major but necessary effort, which by this time would be required in order to properly manage these problems.

The relatively less harmful Mr. Wrongs

The not attractive enough

We may feel bad about having to reject the nice ones among these men, because we find the physical appearance gap too wide for us to ever be able to love them. At the same time and although we resist admitting it, we wish those men we feel attracted to would act differently from us. We would like them to be more appreciative of our wonderful human qualities and not so picky about youth or attractiveness, especially ours.

Accepting that appearance counts is not in conflict with another fact which is equally true. Namely, that it is not all that matters, and usually not the most important thing especially in the longer term. With the benefit of years or decades of hindsight and unless we have been lucky or smart enough to have achieved a satisfying permanent relationship, we will probably come to the realization that we should have seriously considered some of the men we rejected primarily because of how they looked.

But we may in fact be still one step behind reality. As for example, when we have not learned yet that the age difference compromises which would have been sufficient to find permanent love twenty or ten years ago may by now no longer be enough. Therefore we keep making outdated compromises, and getting surprised and anguished when they don't work, as elaborated in Stage 8 under *The gradual turnaround in gender relationship power*.

Men with personality problems, limitations or difficulties

The first thing to keep in mind is that whether in men or women, peculiarities are not problems, but features of personality likely to cause only minor friction. They are relatively easy to adapt to or work around, such as different preferred amounts of social contact and all sorts of likes or dislikes.

By comparison, personality problems are often serious enough to ruin a relationship with potential. If we don't give them due attention when choosing a man, it may take years for us to realize why the relationship hasn't worked and never could have. Even if getting out is no longer painful, it is still costly given the wasted effort and lost opportunities. When there are joint children involved it can be complicated too, we may never get out completely, and the best we could aim for is a respectful and collaborative connection.

After the divorce is over and the dust has settled, we may conclude it was really nobody's fault. Hormones were overactive, wisdom underdeveloped, luck not on our side, and perhaps we were uneasy about a ticking reproduction clock. The initial hurt may have made it more difficult to admit he was not particularly nasty, but just one of the relatively less harmful Mr. Wrongs. On calmer reflection we may be able to accept responsibility for having failed to see the clues, or perhaps chosen to ignore them on the hope that love would make things better.

We should be careful not to blame people, who might have unrecognized impairments. For example, childhood lead exposure can damage brain development. In our drinking culture, "fetal alcohol spectrum disorders" (FASD) are estimated to affect 2-5% of the population in North America, Western Europe and Australia. Some could have "attention deficit hyperactivity disorders" (ADHD), high-functioning or subclinical forms of autism, or various other disabilities none of which may be immediately obvious.

The above and many other disadvantages would aggravate one another, the effects of milder-to-diagnosable "personality disorders" (discussed in pages 190-191), and all sorts of other mental health problems or personality difficulties. Again therefore, we should be respectful to everyone, and consider ourselves lucky if life has handed us a better deal.

Whether or not the above conditions play a part in it, some men are excessively jealous, possessive, controlling, overemotional and aggressive. Others are too self-centered to care for anyone, although capable of exchanging "love" while it suits them. There are emotionally sensible closet bisexuals, influenced by prevailing homophobia into wanting to be "normal", but who may eventually develop a sturdier personality and leave us for a man.

Some high achievers are ruthless exploiters, behind a cultivated facade. There are men with weird or foolish beliefs. Those who seem right but are liable to get off the rails if they stop taking medication for their undisclosed mental illnesses. Perfectionists, workaholics, alcoholics, drug addicts, gamblers, depressives, mummy's boys, eternal adolescents.

There are still more, like the obsessive, the obnoxious, the unemployable, slightly to significantly inadequate, financially irresponsible, plain silly, and many other unclassifiable varieties. And to make matters worse, any of the above could be handsome and therefore tempting.

It is not uncommon for some such features to coexist in one person, and indeed it makes sense that they would. For example, a deluded over optimist I came to know about had a big pile of motivational books of the kind which offer advice on how to get rich quick and retire young. He had become totally obsessed with doing whatever it took to set himself up as the head of a chain of overseas originated franchises, which he said was planning to establish in Australia. Many who join pyramid schemes on the hope of becoming wealthy have comparable obsessions.

No such men (or women) chose their parents, intelligence or personality health. Blaming them reveals something alarming about us: We are capable of being cheap and nasty in order to feel superior, while by implication denying personal responsibility for our disrespect. Treating them properly is one thing, but considering living with such a person is a different matter. If we are, we should think very carefully about whether we can live with the consequences, especially in the longer term.

Men who lie up to a point

In addition to men who are simply incompatible due to personality problems, but still within this relatively less harmful category, are those who lie about being single and play games with women searching for a life partner. They do so especially in dating websites, as a relatively easy underhand way of coping with an unsatisfactory marriage or a boring life.

Other men who are actually available may subtly encourage or allow women to believe they could have a future together, in order to enjoy them for a while or until they find someone "better". Some of the men who lie up to a point could be caught up in that confusing gray area of half truths mixed with hope, and at times with a degree of despair. They have a modicum of conscience, and if questioned respectfully they are unlikely to lie in blatant disregard of the damage they would cause.

That is, these men are fairly average and not very different from most women on the question of lying. If we suspect a serious lie about commitment we should not be coy about asking relevant questions in a proper manner, because it is always better to find out sooner rather than later. Men and women who lie habitually and blatantly because they have no conscience and lack the capacity to feel appropriate guilt belong to a different category, discussed later under the subheading *Certifiable bastards*.

Significantly younger men

Most men who like older women do so because they look sexy or may be "easy", and not because they want a permanent relationship with them. After a while and in terms of their need for mature conversation, most women find significantly younger men somewhere from not stimulating to downright boring. Trying out some younger men sounds harmless enough, but we can become addicted to their standard of attractiveness. And consequently develop a visceral intolerance for the lesser physical appeal of older men.

This danger is particularly relevant for mature women, because they rob themselves of time when they can least afford it. This is unfortunate, as older men are probably the only ones willing and able to love them permanently. Women who are more attractive plus less aware, are at greater their risk of developing a taste for younger men because they get many offers. And also because when there is no suitable candidate in the horizon it is easier to give in to temptation, and imperceptibly become a little bit more addicted with every younger man they try.

Many end up half hoping and half believing that sooner or later they will find one such man who will love them permanently, and may only finally realize their mistake when it is probably too late. A woman in her mid fifties saw me after her latest relationship disaster. "Unfortunately I like younger men", she told me. For decades she had been in denial of the likely consequences of her preference for younger men, and the wisdom she now had wasn't there when she had most needed it. Her underlying sense of loss and loneliness were palpable, despite her strength of character.

Some younger men like older women because repeated experiences have taught them that those around their age or younger will not put up with them. Such men may love them enough to marry, but often have significant personality problems. I have come across many such couples, typically because after the first five years or so the wives were fed up of living with a partner who kept behaving like an overgrown problem adolescent. And by the time they came to see me they were on the brink of divorce, despite having had children together.

A man came for a consultation because he could never hold relationships for long. His latest ex lover was a woman quite a bit older than him who worked in a different floor within the same building. Like many public servants around the late 1980's, they had a one hour lunch break and could stretch it if wanted by using their accumulated "time-in-lieu". Every week they would sneak out once or twice to a nearby motel during lunchtime. He thought it was going OK. But three months later she ended it after telling him, he said, "You are only good for one thing".

Many women who choose younger men fail to learn the lessons and repeat the mistake several times. The unluckiest never learn, and keep making the wrong choices over and over. Many cannot handle the truth, and prefer to think that their failures are due to bad men or bad luck, while others genuinely do not understand it. "I don't believe in men" one such burnt out woman told me. She was still thinking the issue was about men rather than about her, and felt realistically pessimistic about ever achieving permanent love.

Last but not least, in the few cases when significantly younger but otherwise reasonably OK husbands grow out of their naivety or other difficulties, they usually leave their wives for a much younger woman. That is only to be expected. What chance does a wife in her fifties have against competitors who want her husband and may be, for example, ten years younger than him and fifteen years younger than her?

And what chance does she have of finding another partner, when the only ones willing to consider her seriously may be fifteen or twenty years older than her previous husband? Even in the best of cases, searching for a partner from this age onwards is likely to be more difficult than it ever was, and more so if we are recovering from the trauma of a divorce we did not want.

Men who are much less educated, less intelligent, and/or boring

When a well educated woman forms a relationship with a much less educated or intelligent man of any age, this will add to the cost of maintaining the relationship if it becomes ongoing. Most women have an intuitive understanding of emotions which is generally better than that of most men, and disparities in education or intelligence can only add to the gap.

Put simply, such woman may be too far above her partner emotionally, intellectually and financially. All in all, the clash with traditional roles can be substantial. While her physical attraction towards the man may temporarily defuse the effect of these disparities, they are likely to begin weighing the relationship down before long.

A woman who had been living with a much less educated man for five years related how she had been observing him at home one day, while he was unaware. And suddenly it dawned on her, she said, that "there was nothing in that head, other than what I had imagined". What she had imagined had been heavily influenced by her wishful thinking, about how stimulating he was and his potential to improve and become a true companion.

The cost of her self deception had been getting gradually heavier, and after all those years she had to leave him, because she could not stand the boredom and loneliness anymore. These became inevitable due to his inability to communicate in a way which was meaningful and satisfying for her, as neither his intellectual nor emotional intelligence were remotely comparable to hers. "What a costly way to learn", she remarked later.

Of course there are exceptions to the rule, and relationships with less stimulating men can work well enough sometimes. The critical issue is whether the woman has made the decision on the basis of an accurate assessment of reality, as against wishful thinking, lust, neediness or a ticking reproduction clock. A poorly educated man in a low-skilled occupation had a three year old daughter he adored. He didn't strike me as particularly interesting and didn't talk much, but at some point he told me: "Every day at work I am waiting for the time to go home, to be with my little angel".

His wife had a well paid job and was articulate and educated, but knew than most men did not find her attractive. Obviously she had wanted a child, plus a husband and father who would also **not** have the appearance or qualities which would have prevented him from being able to love her. My impression was that she had been well aware of the costs and benefits of marrying her husband, and seemed satisfied enough with the outcome.

She would certainly have had to contend with negative comments about her partner and her decision to marry him. But she was sufficiently independent and internally secure not to care about what others might think or say. I respected her, because only the woman who is going to live with the consequences has the right to decide who is or isn't right for her.

Her strength was in contrast with the vulnerability of another woman who consulted me. She too was educated but unattractive, and very much liked the much less intelligent man she had known for years who wanted to marry her. She found him very attractive and enjoyed her time with him despite his limitations. But, she told me, "How could I introduce such a man to my family?" Her contingent self esteem made her excessively dependent on other people's approval, and she was paying a high price.

A mature woman who saw me about her marital problems was well educated and had a good job. Her de-facto husband of some years had an unskilled job and they had no children. She found him quite attractive, although not particularly stimulating in terms of conversation. But this did not bother her, she said, because she had that from her work and friends. Her complaint was that he was financially irresponsible, and could not be trusted to pay the household bills even after she had given him the money.

He would then lie about having paid them, and she would only find out when the unpaid notices began arriving. She seemed happy with all other major areas of the relationship. When asked, she said he had never been violent or threatened to be, was respectful towards her, nice in bed, and not into chasing other women.

Given her previous experiences with men, she acknowledged that any man who wanted her permanently was going to be imperfect, and only she could decide which particular set of imperfections would best meet her needs. My opinion was that his financial irresponsibility would never be "cured", and that any serious attempt to do so could create significant strain in their relationship.

Eventually we agreed that the best solution was to stop resenting or trying to change him, and to keep enjoying his nice qualities while they were both alive and healthy. She could resolve the one problem which really bothered her by paying all the bills herself. This would amount to no more than a minor extra effort, since she was already providing the money for it anyway.

Despite the occasional limited successes, most boring men tend to become a substantial burden after a while. So, why do so many of us disregard the clues and allow ourselves to fall for such men? I think it is largely because the desire for their attractiveness overrides our better judgment, and we don't want to look at the longer term costs. In any case and speaking about relatively less harmful Mr. Wrongs in general, between the time we meet them and the point by when we realize there is a significant problem, these relationships can use up valuable years and cause us to miss other opportunities.

Definitely dangerous men (and women)

I have classified these men into the categories of *potential domestic violence perpetrators*, *emotional time bombs*, *macho men* and *certifiable bastards*. Knowing how to recognize them early enough may spare some women from being attracted into their orbit, and having to find out their true nature the hard way. If they are already involved, this knowledge can facilitate making a better informed decision about whether to stay or leave.

Potential domestic violence perpetrators

Domestic violence is any form of abuse committed by an adult against a sexual or family intimate, or anyone else living in the household. It is a widespread crime, which involves the often addictive and sometimes sadistic satisfaction of control by intimidation. In the vast majority of *serious* cases that include occasional or frequent one sided physical violence with its concomitant threats, shouting and insults, it is committed by male criminals.

By comparison, labelling such perpetrators as "men" just because they are and leaving it at that, overemphasizes their gender while underemphasizing the criminality. It suggests the labeler has not reflected enough on the implications, or alternatively might be a bit simple-minded and/or have anti-male proclivities. And it is arguably as counterproductive to social good as saying that women are "overemotional", because they do most of the crying.

That is because both labels undermine the goal of improving community attitudes towards violence and sexism, since everyone dislikes their unfair label, as well as the other one being foisted on family members. The point to keep in mind is that most men and women are not violent, but a criminal's criminality should be dealt with. Regardless of the perpetrator's gender, inflicting domestic violence is an example of cowardice for three reasons:

- The crime is typically committed against a person who is physically weaker, emotionally vulnerable, or otherwise powerless.
- It is nearly always committed when there are no witnesses able to testify, so that the perpetrator may get away with denying that it happened or claiming it was less severe than alleged.
- For any number of reasons, the victim cannot escape with safety when the violence is about to happen. And usually feels unable to defend against the perpetrator's greater physical strength or other kind of power, by using the police and the legal system.

Domestic violence can also be sexual, economic, and occur in a variety of subtler forms. It can have severe and lifelong consequences for the victims, as well as significant financial costs to society. It deserves a substantial elaboration, which in this book is primarily aimed at reducing the risk of any woman falling for an otherwise alluring potential perpetrator, or of continuing with such relationship if she is already in it.

In addition to the frequent ineffectiveness of laws against it, two other major factors turning some people into ongoing perpetrators are their personality flaws and the victim's powerlessness. It is important to recognize those flaws, because the consequences of not doing so can be dire. I discuss perpetrators flaws next, and victim powerlessness further below.

There are seven personality flaws we need to watch out for in a potential partner, although noticing one or two may indicate they are all there, even if still undetected. They reflect underdeveloped personality and self esteem at the very least, and are often part of mental health problems known as *personality disorders* (see page 190). Such flaws would typically be "denied", but reveal themselves by the feelings, thoughts and behaviors below.

1. Excessive obsessive jealousy despite reassurances
2. Excessive possessiveness, attempts to control partner
3. Excessive vulnerability to any real or imagined criticisms
4. Propensity for strong emotional reactions when under stress
5. Capacity for empathy well below the average for their gender
6. Assaults, threats or disrespect towards anyone for any reason
7. Unwillingness and inability to forgive or forget real or imagined misbehaviors by others, and to accept responsibility for theirs

All seven can occur irrespective of education, intelligence, occupation or status. A by then divorced woman related on TV how after disclosing the verbal and physical violence by her ordained churchman husband, she was ostracized from their religious congregation while he got off virtually unscathed. In another case which made to the TV news, an older husband took an Apprehended Violence Order (also known as a Protective or Restraining Order) against his wife, who was a well known practicing Magistrate.

It is generally accepted among therapists that while genetics or unrecognized brain impairments may play a part in generating the flawed personalities which underpin the perpetration of ongoing domestic violence, in most cases the main reasons are rooted in childhood, especially in early childhood. And often have a lot to do with not having received consistent sufficient unconditional love from the primary care givers, for a variety of reasons.

However, the parents of a domestic violence perpetrator should never be blamed, because most did the best they could for their children. But this may not have been easy due to any number of unfavorable circumstances, and I will repeat below what I mentioned in page 121 regarding the family background in the case of the excessively jealous wife. If a man with her kind of personality happened to be living with a vulnerable woman, the likelihood of ongoing domestic violence would have been high.

As was the case in her family, many parents have to work for very long hours to avoid serious poverty. Other times it is for meeting contingent self esteem needs through material ostentation, to finance addictions to gambling or drugs, or for other reasons. There might also have been physical or mental impairment, ill health or injury in the child or parents. They could have suffered from serious racial, cultural or gender discrimination, the premature death of one parent, alcoholism, sexual or physical abuse, etc.

In any case the final outcome was that parents weren't able to give their children enough of the love, time and attention they needed. So, perpetrators themselves may have been victims, and they don't necessarily want to feel or behave as they do. It is not uncommon for some to feel remorseful especially after their wife has left, and ask for forgiveness in what seems a deeply felt and sincere way. But when they regain access to their partner, the so-called "domestic violence cycle" usually restarts after a while.

Perpetrators are once again swayed by the hurricanes of their own emotions plus their addiction to control by intimidation. Like runaway alcoholics, most of them can't or won't help themselves, and they keep committing the crime until their relationship finally disintegrates. Many former long term perpetrators claim to have reformed and want to restart the relationship, but if their former victim has strengthen her personality and become independent, she probably won't need or want them back.

If we see indications that a new man could become a domestic violence perpetrator, waiting for it to go away or trying to sweet talk him out of it are likely to fail and can be dangerous. If we do not feel safe we may wish to say goodbye by SMS or email, and if his behavior becomes threatening consider the registered letter option discussed in page 194. Domestic violence advice can be obtained in Australia by calling "1800 respect" (1800 737 732).

The flawed personality in potential perpetrators is not by itself generally enough to lead to repeating violence unless there was already enough predisposition to powerlessness or actual powerlessness in the potential victim. If this had not been there already, most potential victims would move away from the perpetrator early enough and avoid becoming ongoing victims.

Kinds of victim powerlessness and implications for counselling

I made an original conceptualization of powerlessness in adult victims of domestic violence in a 1993 article for professionals, commented on by the editor of the ANZ Journal of Family Therapy in Reference 6 (pages 326-7). It was titled *N.S.W. Domestic Violence Core Training Package: An Independent Analysis and Conceptual Elaboration,* and was an attempt to add to the effectiveness of the 1991 *N.S.W. Domestic Violence Core Training Package,* by Wendy Styles and Heather McGregor. Their otherwise commendable effort suffered from the limitations of excessive adherence to feminist theory, and the consequent non-inclusion of absolutely critical alternative insights.

It was being used for the compulsory training of many NSW Department of Health employees, including me, and in other settings such as Women's Refuges and Women's Health Centers. Among other things, my feedback article proposed that in addition to the views expressed in the *Package*, there was usually a component of victims' powerlessness which was additional to the one generated by the violence, and a secondary factor in its occurrence.

On that basis I argued that the complexities of such powerlessness would be easier to understand and manage by both counselors and clients if classified into five types. I named them *intra-psychic, interpersonal, socio-cultural, economic* and *circumstantial*. This book is not the right place for a full elaboration on the above types, but a simplified explanation is still appropriate.

While all five types of powerlessness are interrelated in the sense that each influences the others, such classification can be used to make each of the various components of powerlessness easier to understand for victims and their counselors. And therefore, easier to overcome by developing remedies specifically tailored to manage each type of powerlessness, after considering the unique personality and circumstances of each current or former victim.

Intra-psychic powerlessness is a profound feeling of personal impotence, usually supported by a conglomerate of unproductive beliefs about oneself, others, society and/or life. In addition to the sociocultural and economic disadvantages suffered by women, any significant underdevelopment in core components of personality and self esteem (however this is labeled) will contribute, without doubt, to creating a predisposition for powerlessness.

This predisposition then becomes real powerlessness through the chronic fear and intimidation which the violence engenders, plus the deliberate relentless undermining of the victim' self esteem. And these are two major reasons why victims gradually lose their capacity to leave the perpetrator.

An important step for a victim who wishes assistance is to remove access to her by the perpetrator, using police and the law if necessary. After imperative security needs for her and any children are taken care of, the next stage is likely to be one of just surviving the massive shock and change in her life. Eventually though, it is important for the former victim to restart developing her personality in order to make it stronger.

The length of the initial stage of shock and readjustment varies. But once it is over, the relief from fear and stress which personal development can bring about is as important as economic independence. A sturdier personality makes it more likely that the former victim will never again become incapacitated to defend herself. If it can be implemented, personal development aimed at removing powerlessness may be the best way towards self confidence and a capacity to feel sufficiently in control of her life.

Self confidence stands directly opposite to intra-psychic powerlessness, and therefore improving it is at the core of what it takes to reduce and remove that powerlessness. This view is not in conflict with acknowledging that personal development may not be suitable for some victims, or that there are things in life over which nobody has control.

Personal development can be a gradual and sometimes arduous process for anyone, including a former victim. But at times a happy and exhilarating one too, as she experiences often for the first time in many years how it feels to no longer be afraid. Instead she will feel adequately in control of her personal safety, life and destiny. And most important of all, capable of standing up to any future would be perpetrator if the need ever arose, despite some residual distress being reactivated.

It is important to emphasize that without sufficient personal development to back up situational improvements, these are likely to be fragile. The former domestic violence sufferer will remain at risk of becoming a victim again if unfavorable circumstances were to arise, even if she has achieved economic independence.

Overcoming intra-psychic powerlessness to a significant degree is a first step and prerequisite for removing permanently any propensity towards *interpersonal powerlessness*. The latter is the inability to have a fair amount of influence within a sexually intimate relationship, and it is caused and maintained by violence and fear in combination with underlying intra-psychic plus all other forms of powerlessness.

Socio-cultural powerlessness is a combination of discriminatory social practices plus internalized negative cultural beliefs about the personalities, roles and status of women. *Economic powerlessness* is the inability to obtain a fair share of economic resources. *Circumstantial powerlessness* is the sum total of any other additional power eroding characteristics, such as responsibilities to young children plus whatever degree of financial dependence and reduced free time and energy they entail, limited education or social supports, poor physical or mental health, substance addictions, etc.

A graphic example of typical domestic violence is in a commercial film called "Te Doy Mis Ojos", directed by Iciar Bollain and co-written by her and Alicia Luna. Its quality and unforgiving realism merited six Goya awards in Spain where it was produced. It was premiered in the United States in 2004 with the title "Take My Eyes", has been shown repeatedly in Australia by SBS TV with English subtitles, and may be downloaded free at *SBS-on-demand.*

The two hour Australian documentary "Hitting Home" by Sarah Ferguson, produced by ABC TV and shown on 24-25 November 2015, includes interviews with victims, perpetrators, police and helpers. It looks at the warning signs of domestic violence, what is being done to address this form of criminality, and how such relationships can escalate into violence and even murder.

Feminism's excesses and disregard about female perpetrators

Feminism as a social movement and those who support its gender equality and social justice goals deserve much of the credit for today's greater awareness about the criminality of domestic violence and the efforts to reduce it. At the same time it is important to acknowledge that like me and all of us, feminists are imperfect human beings who have made and keep making their share of mistakes.

By around twenty five years ago their growing influence had led to some of them becoming advisors to government, thereby finding themselves in a position to define what domestic violence was and wasn't. On doing so, some inconvenient truths were ignored or distorted in order to fit not only with laudable social goals, but also with feminist theory and ideology plus what might be interpreted as the individual neuroses of some activists and supporters.

The combination of those factors resulted in a subtle legitimization of thinly disguised hostility against the male half of humanity by *some* women who considered themselves feminists, thereby aggravating their mental health problems. That indiscriminate hostility towards men went on for many years and revealed itself in unintended oblique ways, even among women who should have known better. The following two examples show how intellectual ability or a counseling role are no guarantee of emotional balance.

A divorced counselor with a postgraduate degree had commented she didn't need men, and lived with two cats she adored. She insisted to the point of arguing repeatedly and quite seriously that there was, she said, "something wrong with men". On the grounds, she added among other things, that "all serial killers are men". Although factually incorrect, those beliefs were undoubtedly making her feel less bad about her failed relationships and apparent fear of attempting new ones, as well as providing an excuse for not facing up to how her personality was contributing to her problems.

Within some years after her divorce, she accused at least two respected male colleagues in two separate employment settings of not doing their job properly. She also interfered with their work through various manipulations, with consequences serious enough to warrant official intervention by management in both cases. Most alarming of all, for a time she took it upon herself to do counseling with women in a state of crisis due to being on the verge of a marital breakup. That had disastrous consequences in at least one case I knew the details of, and probably in others too.

Two female colleagues who run our domestic violence groups told me about a local community worker. She had used Council funds to set up a support group exclusively for mums who were also lesbian, on the highly questionable grounds that it was needed because there was no such group for such women. We joked that she must have been looking for an easy way to get a string of girlfriends, and they added with a grin: "She is a man hater".

I asked what the evidence was, for such a drastic statement. "You'll see if you meet her" was the cryptic reply, which they gave me with a smile. Two or three weeks later I did meet her by chance, on a presentation about local needs and resources. It was she who approached me about something or other. And within the first minute of our very short conversation, out of the blue and for no apparent reason she told me: "I am not a man hater". I was left wondering why she had needed to tell me that.

Later I saw her leaving a bundle of keys on a table. It had a very large key tag with something written on it, and I looked out of curiosity. It said: *"What is the useless bit of skin hanging off a man's penis? Answer: A man"*. After a good laugh I had to agree that she was a man hater after all. Her key tag joke plus unwarranted denial suggested she was emotionally unbalanced, possibly along the lines of those who resent men for "undeservedly" winning the affections of those feminine women who lesbians find so irresistibly attractive.

Anti male hostility eventually lost all credibility, but residual problems linger on even now. Roughly around seven to nine years ago from memory, a member of the audience in the Australian forum "Insight" on SBS TV, hosted by Jenny Brockie, stated that "domestic violence is violence committed by men against women", and her comment was left unchallenged. Such definition implies that exactly the same abhorrent behavior is not domestic violence, when the perpetrator is a woman.

If we accept that sexism is prejudice based on gender, the above definition is clearly inappropriate. From the publication and implementation of the 1991 *N.S.W. Domestic Violence Core Training Package* and for very many years thereafter, that exact definition was promoted by the feminist movement in Australia. As a result, it lost support from men and women who disliked what they saw as blatant sexism, regardless of any alleged justifications.

The less known reality is that some women commit domestic violence too. Schoolgirls who bully vulnerable classmates do not always change later in life. Some women hit, verbally abuse and in other ways damage their female sexual intimates, and the incidence is probably not very different from that in heterosexual couples.

Some feminist writers still ignore female domestic violence or claim it is not significant, on the grounds that violence by women is not as serious, not as frequent, or not well documented and therefore not ascertainable. Much of that is true in many cases, but certainly not in all. I suspect another reason for brushing it aside, is that it undermines the cherished delusion that women are not the kind of people who perpetrate domestic violence.

We need to know in our mind and feel in our heart that the above is incorrect, in order to discourage irrational anti male sexism and promote egalitarianism and harmony between genders. The respected ABC TV program "The Drum" on 28 September 2015 included in its panel Rosie Batty, Australian of the Year and its best known and most loved domestic violence activist. Another panelist (Nick Cater) said that 30% of domestic violence incidents are perpetrated by women, and nobody disputed it. I give specific examples next, to correct misperceptions and promote further awareness of the problem.

Domestic violence arises and is maintained due to a combination of causes which include the perpetrators' flawed personalities, insufficient community awareness and education, the economic dependence of mothers with young children, and perpetrators' power without accountability due to the limited effectiveness of laws against it. The latter is even worse when the perpetrator is female, and sexual harassment tendencies in a lesbian are something to watch out for by any woman searching for a female partner.

That is because any form of lesbian harassment towards women who appear defenseless or unlikely to want to cause a problem, increases the likelihood that such abuser will attempt to inflict domestic violence on any future female partner. Over the years a number of heterosexual women have told me in detail and with emotions consistent with the events, about the sexual harassment they suffered from lesbians socially and in the workplace, in a manner so gross and blatant that it defies belief.

One former resident of "The Women's Factory" in the Sydney suburb of Parramatta during the second half of the 20th century, recounted on TV in 2014 how she had been raped with a brush handle by another girl while two others forcibly held her down. From then on, what she feared most was further sexual harassment and assault by other females. There had been other victims too, and she added that those in charge of the institution were complicit by having known and done nothing to stop it.

A now mature woman who as a child had lived in an institution run by Catholic nuns, related on TV how they were regularly abused and lived in constant fear. Her visible emotions as she described what happened, gave me the impression that one of the nuns was not just a domestic violence perpetrator, but a sadistic one too. This is no reflection on nuns as a whole, most of whom are admirable people who work helping the less fortunate.

Many maids get regularly abused and even beaten by their female employers. One only needs to hear a few distressing stories by former expatriate Filipino maids, to appreciate the extent of the female perpetrated domestic violence they endured. As reported in international TV news in February 2015 with alarming graphic details, a Hong Kong woman was convicted for physical and emotional domestic violence against her Indonesian maid.

Comparable violence is also inflicted on trafficked or vulnerable sex workers by brothel "madams", who are able to abuse and exploit them because they are illegal migrants with poor education and language skills, and often threatened with retaliation against family in their countries of origin.

These later examples would not classify as *family violence*, which is now a common way of referring to such crime. But they are domestic violence because all involved were sharing the household, with perpetrators having a lot of power and victims being largely or totally powerless.

Some women shake their babies in frustration, risking or causing permanent brain damage in addition to inflicting distress. Feeling frustrated is not a valid excuse, anymore than it would be for a man who hits or abuses his female partner, child or baby for allegedly the same reason. Of course caring for a challenging baby by a mother who is inexperienced, unsupported and may have personality problems can be difficult and might be an extenuating circumstance. But on the other hand nobody is more defenseless than a baby, and that aggravates the criminality of it.

On rare occasions women abuse their children sexually in various ways. In one case I came to know about from an absolutely reliable source, a newly employed nanny was about to bathe the three year old boy of a business woman who lived alone with her child. Out of the blue, he asked the nanny in a most natural way: "Do you want me to suck you?"

The nanny realized what had been happening and resigned the next day, claiming a sudden family crisis. Because as she said, if he repeated it in the preschool he was about to begin, everyone would have believed the mother and blamed the nanny. Her reputation and livelihood as a nanny would have been ruined. It is hard to stomach, but what else could the nanny do?

The following six examples were reported in Australian TV, and include women who had killed their own children. In one case there was video evidence suggesting a mother had put her baby in the water, where it drown. She then sent police in the opposite direction, after telling them that someone had taken it from her pram. According to the TV news, she did not have a mental illness or a disadvantaged family background, enjoyed partying and having fun, and a baby would have been an obstacle to her lifestyle.

In December 2014 a mother with stab wounds to her chest was taken to hospital, after her seven children and a niece were found stabbed to death in her home. She was charged with eight murders, but ordered to be assessed for mental illness. In July 2015 a six week old baby was found dead with knife injuries, and its mother was charged with murder. As another real life horror, in June 2015 a thirty year old woman was taken to hospital with stab injuries, including to her genitals and breasts. Her female sexual intimate was charged with rape, and "assault intended to maim, disfigure or disable".

In April 2015 a forty five year old woman was charged with a double murder. After her much older lover ended their relationship, she entered his house and tied and gagged him. She then waited for hours until his wife came home and stabbed her to death. That, after having killed their four year old grandson, who happened to be in their house at the time. In January 2017 a woman pleaded guilty to having killed her three children by deliberately driving the family car into a deep pond, where they drowned.

A man who had been hit and verbally abused by his wife for years was too afraid to tell anyone other than the counselor he was seeing for "depression". Because if he did tell, he said, "everyone will say I am a fuckwit". These men are doubly trapped into silence. First because their male upbringing dictates that their "weakness" would mark them as unmanly and inadequate. And second by the certainty of being ridiculed, if they were to disclose the verbal-emotional violence and especially the physical one.

No wonder there is so little publicly or easily available evidence about this kind of domestic violence. Physical domestic violence by wives is rare however, given the generally greater physical strength of men and consequent likelihood of effective defense if assaulted.

However, some elderly men suffer various forms of domestic violence perpetrated by younger and stronger wives who seem to hate them. Many frail elderly, especially among those with dementia, are being abused in nursing homes because some female (and male) managers and owners attempt to maximize profits by operating with inadequate staff-patient ratios. And by employing insufficiently trained workers, without good enough screening and supervision to detect personalities unsuitable for the job.

Many women have better developed emotional intelligence and are more articulate than men regarding relationship issues. When domineering women with psychopathic tendencies have an emotionally vulnerable husband, those superior skills combined with the power which granting or refusing sex gives them, make verbal-emotional abuse the weapon of choice for inflicting domestic violence on their men. They were sometimes referred to as "castrating women", until the term became politically incorrect.

The label has gone but the reality remains, and it happens in more than just a figurative sense. As shown in TV in 2013 referring to a country in South East Asia, enough men there have had their penises cut off by wives while sleeping, to result in some surgeons becoming specialized in reattaching penises. Perhaps a cause of celebration for the most mentally disturbed man haters, but unquestionably an act of premeditated and brutal domestic violence and mutilation perpetrated by female <u>criminals</u>.

For the reasons mentioned earlier, I reiterate my view that labelling domestic violence perpetrators as men or women instead of "criminals" is careless, unfair and socially counterproductive. And in the case of some labelers, an indication of simple-mindedness and/or personality problems.

Emotional time bombs

"We are not interested in them", we might say with complete conviction, and argue if anyone disagrees. But then again, some of them can be so handsome, romantic and soft-spoken that we feel all our Sundays have come at once. Perhaps that uneasy feeling we noticed at the beginning was a mistake, we think, and then tell ourselves that nobody is perfect. We feel in Heaven and throw caution to the winds. There may be flowers, cards, the attentiveness, the declarations of love and honorable intentions, the sweet little nothings, his obviously heartfelt emotions ...

We can hardly believe our luck. But these men are like those wonderful investment opportunities which seem too good to be true. It makes sense that if he looks far out of our league but isn't, something might be wrong with him. As soon as emotional time bombs gain a foothold, their true colors begin to show. They are jealous, possessive and controlling. But because we like them and don't know them well enough yet, we tend to re-label such features in some positive way and believe it for as long as we can.

Their most dangerous characteristic is an extreme sensitivity to rejection, which makes them emotionally over reactive, unstable and unpredictable. They tend to have a history of being left by the women they had relationships with, and those endings were usually rather unpleasant at best. These are the men who will not leave us alone after we have told them it is over. Any remaining involvement can be physically and psychologically dangerous, and the risk may remain for quite some time after we have finally refused to see or even talk with them anymore, personally or by phone.

A tall attractive physically strong youngish man came to see me with his de-facto. They had lived together and separated several times. Her parents were dead against the relationship but she loved him, she said. Every time I made the slightest move towards encouraging him to consider whether his behavior might be contributing to their problems, he became agitated. And probably unaware of it, he leaned forward in his chair with an expression and demeanor which forced me to consider my own safety.

After three consultations during which I failed to achieve any progress, I felt morally obliged to tell them that I thought I would not be able to help. As I was in the middle of suggesting they might wish to seek help with someone else, in which case I would be willing to make a suggestion, the woman interrupted visibly distressed. She told him I was the third counselor who had said that to him and she had had enough. As I left the building after work that day I kept a wary eye for trouble, but fortunately he wasn't there.

Sometime around the early-mid 1980's if my memory is correct, a Sydney man entered a real estate office and stabbed his former girlfriend seventeen times. Being obviously far more than needed to kill her, this immediately suggests that there was something seriously wrong with his personality. By one of those coincidences of life, a woman who later became my friend had met him in person at a party around two years before the murder, and after the TV news she followed the newspaper stories about the case.

What she remembered about him was that he came across as polite and educated. He must have been intelligent too, because he dismissed his lawyer and undertook his own defense in the murder trial. He based it largely on what he had felt, which he obviously had an intense need to express. Later while serving his sentence in Long Bay Jail, his social skills made him rather well liked by both prisoners and guards, and he managed to get a cushy job in the prison library.

No doubt, some of his fellow inmates would have sympathized with his anguish at being "deceived" by "his" woman and being unable to cope with the suffering and distress caused by her rejection and disregard for his "love". Another comparable example which is illuminating because it is related from the viewpoint of the killer, is in the lyrics of the 1960's hit song "Delilah" by British singer Tom Jones, available in the Internet. And most of us have heard on TV the story about South African Oscar Pistorius' killing of his partner.

These kind of personalities exist equally in women. A man consulting me commented how when living with his ex-wife, he had to lock himself in a bedroom to sleep at night and block the door from the inside with a heavy piece of furniture. That was a necessary precaution to ensure she could not get in without waking him up, after she had threatened to knife him while asleep. This was a dangerous threat, he said, made when she became angry while they were both eating in the kitchen table. That had happened many times, he added, and she had repeatedly and deliberately swept the tip of a sharp knife close to his eyes with an angry menacing expression.

Another man told me he couldn't "get rid of" his ex-girlfriend no matter what he tried. He even moved to a new address but she tracked him down through his "customers", and kept making a racket on his door at night. Not wanting the police involved for his own reasons, he had to let her in. I asked whether he thought it might be worth coming to the next appointment with her, so that she would have an introduction to discussing her concerns with me, or the option of referral to another counselor if she wanted. That was my well meaning but very bad idea, as I discovered when they came.

Within less than five minutes and for no reason which would cause such reaction in a normal person, she unexpectedly got up from her sofa chair visibly disturbed and left my office without saying a word, leaving the door wide opened. To prevent the possibility of her returning to overhear from behind the door, I deliberately did not get up to close it for the time being. But about two minutes later she rushed back in all of a sudden. Immediately and without saying a word or looking at me at all, she began punching him violently in the face with all the force she could muster.

She looked and was insanely angry and totally out of control. I instinctively got up from the low lying sofa chair and sat on my desk, so that my face would be higher up and harder to reach if she attacked me next. While all the man had time to do was lift his arms in an effort to protect his face. But after a few seconds of the frenzied attack she left just as suddenly, again not having said a word. A drug and alcohol counselor who saw them in the corridor told me later he was a small time drug dealer, and that she always carried a knife under her car seat.

And I remember feeling certain that if she had been wielding that knife as she came back, the man could quite easily had been seriously injured or killed. A while after the interview was over I left my office, and saw them through a window walking embraced away from the building. I have no doubt she would have been diagnosable with *borderline personality disorder* (definition and elaboration available in the Internet), and clearly fitted into the category of emotional time bombs.

When we see clues that a man could be dangerous, it is important not to ignore the possibility of a worst case scenario. Domestic violence perpetrators tend to inflict a more measured and calculated violence, which gives them control by intimidation through an ongoing grinding process of psychological destruction. In contrast, emotional time bombs can act suddenly, unexpectedly and dramatically. They have the potential to kill, although only a tiny minority would go to that extreme.

Male and female emotional time bombs are obsessive, revengeful, and may vandalize property and do whatever they can to harm us or any new partner we meet. Harassment by them may continue in one form or another until the next love of their life comes along. Thereby mercifully helping us fade away from the forefront of their consciousness, after being dishonorably discharged into the much safer backstage of their indignant oblivion.

Macho men

Macho men also involve a physical as well as a psychological risk, in the form of an above average potential for domestic violence and other forms of criminality. They have some common defining features, which would hopefully alert women to recognize that there is a serious problem and stay clear. Most obvious is their view of themselves as tougher than other men, often as more intelligent, and sometimes as morally superior too.

Due to their need to show off, they have an above average propensity to disregard other people's rights in order to abuse them if they complain, with the pretext that they felt offended or provoked. But "coincidentally" they would claim if asked, to hide their underlying cowardice, this never happens with anyone who has the obvious capacity to beat them up. Especially if the other man looks like he might be easily tempted to do so.

The deficits and limitations of their personalities make it difficult for them to access many of the healthier life enjoyment alternatives available to most people. They are forever trying to compensate for the hidden angst arising from grinding loneliness, frustrations and insecurities. These can never be admitted to however, and any questioning of their justificatory interpretations about their behavior could trigger serious hostility or aggression.

They derive distress relief plus sadistic enjoyment from the harm they cause and the ostentation of physical strength or some kind of power. These are the main reasons why insulting, threatening and assaulting have for them become an addictive activity. Another reason is that their "secret" fears of inferiority are pushed further down from consciousness, by propping themselves up through inflicting aggravation on whoever they can with the lamest excuse, as long as they believe they can get away with it.

Underneath the image they like to project, most macho men are opportunistic bullies whose behavior rarely changes while they are able to keep it up. This type of personality is not exclusive to men. Some school girls abuse vulnerable peers for the same reasons, and as mentioned earlier they don't necessarily grow out of it when they become women. Quite often instead, those tendencies become more underhand and sophisticated.

Most of us have witnessed on TV the way macho men behave, and have an image of them as being involved in threats or brawls. However, it is important not to judge on appearance. Most big strong men do not go around abusing women or anyone else, while some meek-looking men and women can be quite sadistic towards anyone over whom they have power.

A macho man is problematic and dangerous for any unfortunate woman lured to him, perhaps because her own personality limitations cause her to be naively impressed by his aggressive-abusive version of masculinity. But the way a macho man treats others is likely to be how he will sooner or later end up treating her too, because that is how he really is.

Certifiable bastards

Among people I admire most are religious and non religious humanitarians who dedicate a substantial part of their energies and lives to helping the less fortunate, especially when they take personal risks by doing so. The vast majority are the countless "do-gooders" of society, as some cynics like to call them, and most do their work without seeking fame and unnoticed by society at large. Some are threatened by the powerful for protecting the vulnerable, and occasionally jailed or killed. A few exceptional individuals such as Nelson Mandela and Mother Theresa reach iconic status.

Certifiable bastards are at the opposite end of the spectrum. They invariably take advantage of others to a strikingly greater extent than the average person, and this is what makes them financially and psychologically dangerous. Whether male or female, in their most extreme form they are the hidden no-axe-murdering psychopaths of everyday life. Their defining characteristic is a lack of conscience, with a consequent incapacity to feel appropriate guilt for the damage they inflict.

Their personal interaction style is based on lying. Apart from any material benefits this might bring about, it helps them to believe they are more intelligent that those they deceive. That is made more credible for them by their limited capacity to understand how other people feel, which also makes it more difficult for them to realize how very transparent their "clever" manipulations can be. The way they understand, explain and justify themselves is based on "denial" of inconvenient truths.

The critical point about certifiable bastards' denial is that it is excessive. Some time-limited denial is a normal component of most people's psychological defensive structure. Or to put in plain English just one aspect of what that means, most of us need a few rationalizations to get through the day, especially if it has been a stressful one. Which help us feel better, by reinterpreting our behavior and motivations through the heart soothing rosier colored glasses of alleged noble intentions or common sense reasoning.

Some certifiable bastards may be successful in very visible ways. We can all think of work environments where having no conscience and feeling no guilt, would increase the probabilities of occupational and financial success. In this regard, it has been claimed by some researchers that psychopathic features (which are the norm in certifiable bastards) are four times more common among top company executives than in the general population.

Indeed there have always been successful psychopaths who are seen as pillars of society, and whose true nature only becomes widely known on the rare occasion when one of them is caught out and exposed. But even garden variety certifiable bastards can be intelligent and calculating enough to deceive and exploit us in every way they can, until we realize what is going on and get rid of them, or until they find a more profitable victim.

Some of them can be attractive, educated, smooth talkers, and very well practiced at creating the impression that they are honest. Those are of course, ideal qualifications for successful con men or women. When we become involved with a certifiable bastard who looks good and presents well, it is easy to fall for him/her. But inevitably sooner or later, we are bound to pay a high price for our mistake.

An attractive man had lived with this woman for about three years in the apartment she owned. During that time he was mostly unemployed, while she worked permanently on a good salary and paid for nearly all their living expenses. After he left for a younger and more attractive woman he sued his former de-facto for part of her property, as he was entitled under Australian law, and she only found out about it when she received the legal notice.

I am happy to report that he was laughed out of court, but the mere fact that he attempted legal robbery should alert any man or woman who owns their home to consider a "financially binding agreement", also known as a prenuptial agreement. This is a sensible precaution, in order to protect our assets from a former partner who might turn out to be unprincipled.

A man who had recently left a longish de-facto relationship came for a consultation. He wanted my opinion about the distribution of joint assets, which I told him immediately was outside the boundaries of my work duties or expertise. They had bought an apartment together, with her paying 90% of the cost. The value of the apartment had increased considerably in the years they were together.

He wanted his original 10% plus 50% of the revaluation money. Because as he put it and wanted to believe, "without my 10% she would not have been able to buy the apartment". Two more examples of certifiable bastardry are discussed at the end of this Stage under the heading *Safer sex issues: Information, criminality and irresponsibility*.

So, it is important for any woman looking for a life partner to keep in mind that totally unscrupulous people do exist and are more numerous than we might think. And to be alert for the signals which would indicate the possibility of such hidden personality features. The best indicator is the way our man treats others who, unlike us, have nothing he wants.

Especially, we need to watch out for any tendency to be disrespectful or exploitative to those over whom he has some kind of power, which makes the latter unable to defend themselves. For example subordinate employees, those in low-ranking jobs serving the public and therefore vulnerable to a complaint, and indeed anyone who looks like they could be abused, exploited or threatened without negative consequences for the abuser.

A clue which often leaks out of certifiable bastards without their awareness, is their view of themselves as very astute plus the need to boast about it in some way. Again, their poor capacity for empathy prevents them from realizing that the ulterior motive of proving their "superiority" may be glaringly visible to wiser observers, as an attempt to bolster an unsteady self image by presenting a successful external façade.

When such people have nobody to feel superior to, they will often resort to self delusion. As mentioned earlier referring to other problematic personality types, their most easily available delusions of superiority are manifested as vilification and hostility towards those of a different race, culture or sexual orientation. This, as a desperate last-ditch attempt to prop themselves up by believing that others are below them in some way, in order to keep at bay the anxieties generated by their gnawing fear of inferiority.

Financially successful certifiable bastards may unintentionally reveal their vulnerability through a compulsive ostentation of wealth. This is obvious to observers but will be rationalized if brought to their attention, and may be fiercely defended if their interpretation is challenged. The degree of defensiveness will be directly proportional to their underlying fears, which feel too threatening to ever be acknowledged. In this respect they are no different from domestic violence perpetrators, emotional time bombs or macho men.

The demarcation line between certifiable bastards and those who may be so inclined but don't perhaps quite make the grade is not always clear. A man left his wife and two young twins and went to America, where he remarried and did well financially. When his sons graduated from High School, he sent them a return plane ticket for a holiday with him.

While there he persuaded them to stay and become American citizens. His former wife, who had brought them up alone in Australia with a lot of sacrifices, felt he had stolen her children and future grandchildren. As she told her story, I could see she was utterly devastated and knew there was no way out of her predicament.

A woman who was no longer young had been in a relationship with a man she loved for six years, while he studied a university degree and postgraduate. Shortly after he completed it he dropped her. "I have wasted six years" she told me. Or rather, it overflowed out of her heart in a tidal wave of dejection and regret she could no longer contain. She had learned a valuable lesson the hard way, and made a much wiser choice the next time around.

As a final point, it is important not to fall into the comforting temptation of labeling a man as a certifiable bastard, simply because he could not love us enough to make the relationship permanent. It might have been an honest try, men and women have only a limited capacity to choose who to love or how much, and sometimes people feel ambivalent or unclear. Some men may not be ready for commitment whether they know it or not, and we reject them as often as they reject us.

We may be hurting badly, but retaining reasonable equanimity and a good grip on reality is a matter of sanity. It is also a matter of self respect and respect for the man, which also leaves the door open for reconciliation if that was to become a future possibility.

More about dangerous men *(and women)*

The majority of mental illness sufferers are not dangerous, and those with the real potential to physically abuse or kill their sexual intimate usually have a "personality disorder". Unless we have some knowledge about the nature of this condition, we are unlikely to ever understand personality health fully and properly. The more intricate clinical issues involved are complex enough to generate debate and disagreement among mental health professionals, and therefore would be far too lengthy to explain in sufficient detail here.

What matters to most readers of this book is that even when the condition is below diagnosable level, it tends to cause serious problems in intimate relationships. Most such people have well above average fear of shame, rejection and abandonment. Obsessive delusions about their partner being unfaithful or unfair are common. In the case of *emotional time bombs* their behavior can be self centered, unpredictable and impulsive, with rapid mood changes, intense aggressive anger, and poor or no capacity for empathy.

Their problems with anger management and all sorts of inappropriate behaviors arise not only because they have poorer control than average people over the same amount of emotion, but also because they are predisposed to experiencing much more of it. That is, the same incident which would be managed sensibly by an average person may cause in them an intensity of stress, anxiety or anger which is out of proportion with the event. It overwhelms them triggering their typically unwarranted, excessive, obnoxious, unexpected, and sometimes dangerous reactions.

They never seek help voluntarily because they are adamantly convinced that all their problems are someone else's fault, and because any meaningful self examination feels extremely threatening to such fragile personalities. They usually remain undiagnosed, unless caught out in an offence of such nature that they are legally forced to present for a mental health assessment.

Personality disorders are not mental illnesses, although a person could have both. For example, in the case of the illness known as "paranoid schizophrenia", it is likely the sufferer already had a paranoid disorder which then added to the subsequent schizophrenia, giving it the paranoid flavor. Individuals whose personality disorders have antisocial or aggressive features are dangerous, more so if that is combined with a paranoid and/or sadistic streak, and even more if they have schizophrenia on top of it.

When those with personality disorders relate their troubles, the intense emotions they express can be seen and felt to be genuine. In the absence of sufficient knowledge about the condition, that genuineness and intensity could quite easily convince a perfectly intelligent layperson who hasn't heard the other side of the story, that this poor man/woman has been badly treated by those complained about.

People with significant personality disorders are impervious to reasoning and virtually "incurable". These disorders occur equally in both sexes, but the behavioral manifestations vary due to differences in gender roles, hormones and physical strength. Some types are more common in one gender than the other, for example *narcissistic* personality disorders in men and *borderline* ones in women.

A major reason why people end up with personality disorders is believed to be a very poor development in the foundation of personality during early childhood, as discussed in Stage 5. Genetic and other factors may play a part, and a proportion of those with personality disorders would have underlying impairments or disabilities similar to some individuals with personality problems. Which as elaborated in page 166 might include unrecognized levels of FASD, ADHD, high-functioning or subclinical autism, brain underdevelopment due to high led exposure in childhood, etc.

Nearly all domestic violence perpetrators, emotional time bombs, macho men and certifiable bastards would be medically diagnosable with some kind of personality disorder, if they were properly examined. Estimates of the incidence of all types of personality disorders put together are often quoted as being around 10%. A sizable US study concluded that over 9% of the population met the official criteria for diagnosis, as determined by the American Psychiatric Association in their Diagnostic and Statistical Manual of Mental Disorders.

Certifiable bastards have the lowest risk of killing because they are cold and calculating, rather than overtaken by emotion. When they do kill, it is likely to have been a carefully planned act for the purpose of obtaining financial advantage, revenge, or some other outcome they desire. Around fifteen to twenty years ago from memory, a Sydney wife in a well off couple was shot dead by an intruder while she and her husband were sleeping at home side by side. The husband claimed he had been the intended target, but was convicted for organizing the killing of his wife, and re-convicted on appeal. If he had not been caught out, he would have gotten away with eliminating a wife he no longer wanted without losing her half of the couple's assets in a divorce settlement.

With certifiable bastards higher up in the socioeconomic ladder, it is more common for killing or other acts of bastardry to be done on their behalf by subordinates, associates or hired criminals. Many of the more extreme actions are in third world countries, and inflicted on poor people whose legitimate interests are obstructing the profits of people with power. As a wise old detective in a TV serial said referring to some such people at the top of multinational companies, getting subordinates or associates to "fix problems without themselves knowing how", is for them just another business expense.

Some women can be as cold and calculating as any man, and in rare cases they too have resorted to the most deadly and treacherous form of domestic violence. Two wives who were supposedly happily married for many years had been having an affair their husbands knew nothing about. Their cases were presented on 12 March 2014 in the Australian TV documentary *Lethal Lovers*, by journalists Tom Steintfort, Leila McKinnon, Alicia Loxley and Peter Stefanovic, in the series "Inside Story" on Channel 9.

There was compelling evidence that each wife had planned to kill her husband and manipulated her lover into doing the killing, who was then caught, confessed and testified. In both cases the husbands survived with serious injuries by very good luck. It seems a breakup was not good enough for these women. Obviously they wanted to keep all of the couple's assets and presumably their children, while avoiding the messiness of a divorce.

Both wives and their lovers were convicted of conspiracy to murder and attempted murder. What was uncommon in these women, aside from being very greedy and nasty enough to kill, was that they were unintelligent enough to believe they would get away with it. As their true nature was exposed in the trials, they expressed no remorse. These were extreme cases, but there are many women who pretend to love their husbands, while using lies and subtle or blatant sexual manipulation to exploit them in every way they can.

Among the single feature categories of dangerous men, the riskiest ones to have a relationship with are emotional time bombs, for the reasons elaborated in the heading about them. But by far the highest risk of being killed for a woman arises with a man who has the features of an emotional time bomb plus those of a macho man and domestic violence perpetrator.

With this kind of men even a minor disagreement can easily get out of hand and become very dangerous. When they are not particularly intelligent, most alert women would notice early enough that something is wrong, and keep away. But if educated or successful they may be better at hiding their true nature, especially at the beginning.

The most unsafe time to be physically near these men is during the separation process and the next months, as those are the periods when most killings take place. Women who underestimate the immediate and longer term physical as well as psychological risks of being in a relationship with a man in the "definitely dangerous" category do so at their peril, and I'll give two more examples from TV news to drive further this important message.

In early 2014 a Sydney man claimed his partner had fallen accidentally from the balcony of their fifteenth floor apartment. But was convicted of murder for throwing her off the balcony and jailed for twenty six years. There was video evidence of arguments and physical abuse from indoor corridor cameras. She had also confided to a friend that she feared he would kill her if she left him, and try to make it look like an accident. Later in 2014 another woman who was leaving her partner also fell to her death from another apartment balcony, and he too was convicted of murder.

Over one woman per week is killed in Australia by a partner or former partner, and in the United States that figure is around 21 women per week. We know that if those killed were politicians or the wealthy people who finance the election campaigns for many of them, an effective solution for such state of affairs would be found and financed quick smart.

The reason it doesn't happen is not that the people killed are women, but that too many politicians act as if the men, women and families involved were insignificant and inconsequential. So, why do those of us who respect life, liberty and the pursuit of happiness keep voting for such politicians and re-electing such political parties?

In September 2015 a new and more enlightened Australian Prime Minister referred to the situation as "a national disgrace", and doubled federal funding by allocating a hundred million dollars to the problem. Pressure for action had been gradually mounting, and domestic violence activists and their supporters deserve most of the credit for having built the momentum which enabled it to happen, by making it politically viable.

But the problem remains. We women need to be alert for the seven personality flaws listed under the domestic violence heading, and to give ourselves time to see how any potential partner behaves in a variety of situations, especially before living together. If a man we have tried and rejected does not leave us alone after being asked repeatedly and we feel threatened, it may be sensible to take appropriate safety measures.

For example, we could send him a person to person registered letter without warning, and pay a little extra for a receipt of its delivery to be later stapled to our copy. In it we would say that we feel harassed, and request for the final time that he leaves us alone. As well as inform him that if he attempts to contact us in any way after the delivery date of our registered letter, we will use our copy to request police and Court protection.

The police would hopefully interview him and assist us in obtaining an Apprehended Violence Order (AVO). If we feel seriously frightened this may be one of the less dangerous options, if taken in time. Police and Court intervention have the clout to let him know in no uncertain terms about the precise consequences *to him* if harassment does not stop.

A man came for a consultation after appearing in Court for violating an AVO for a second time, and getting a three month suspended jail sentence. He told me he could not approach his wife or her home under any circumstances, because if caught he would be taken to Long Bay Jail to serve his sentence, and probably lose his job too. He was overemotional and could very easily have become dangerous, but he wasn't stupid.

Getting convictions can be difficult however, and jailing is very costly to taxpayers as well as disadvantageous to victims who depend on a perpetrator's financial and other contributions. Each case is different, but what would be a game changer is for perpetrators to know for sure they will be caught and convicted. It could be achieved by women at risk being legally issued with wireless recording devices, which if in danger they could switch on to call the police and transmit admissible evidence in real time.

This is expensive, and therefore the law needs updating. Judges could be given discretion to make perpetrators pay costs of surveillance systems for the duration of AVOs, to live outside the family home, not go near it, and wear GPS tracking devices. Registers of perpetrators in some Australian States have deterrent value, and should be publicized and extended nationally. AVOs need to be strictly enforced, or victims will remain in preventable danger.

Desirable personality qualities in men (and women)

There are qualities in men which increase the likelihood of lifelong relationship stability and contentment, and it is important that we have those qualities too. To the extent that we don't, it is in our interest to develop them as soon and as much as possible. They are relevant in every relationship and likely to coexist in many potential Mr. Rights, just as various negative features are found together in many Mr. Wrongs.

Every relationship is unique however, involving as it does two personalities (plus sets of circumstances) with different combinations of beliefs, needs, wishes and fears. Therefore it makes sense for every reader to reflect on the qualities named below and consider adding any others which might be relevant, while taking care not to make it into an unrealistic wish list. I have organized the discussion into four groups of related qualities. Active kindness is the most important, and is placed last because its best practice requires a good level of development in the previous ones.

- Tempered honesty, fairness, responsibility
- Awareness, emotional intelligence, communication skills
- Flexibility, tolerance, optimism
- Active kindness

Tempered honesty, fairness, responsibility

We would be hard pressed to think of anyone saintlier than Mother Theresa, yet we suspect that she too had her faults. So it goes with honesty, where there are many gray areas between the need to protect ourselves or others by being sensibly polite at one end, and exploitatively dishonest at the other. Here I discuss four categories of honesty, which I call *tempered, naïve, unburdening* and *deliberately destructive.*

When it comes to searching for a life partner we want a man who will be honest with us, because we feel in our bones that being able to trust each other is essential for a relationship to work. We want a man who can be trusted about fidelity, his feelings for us and other important issues, even if we don't mind the occasional sweet little lie intended to soothe our minor anxieties.

That is why when we are considering a potential partner we need to keep an eye for clues which indicate a strong preference for honesty, as against a lighthearted attitude about dishonesty. The most reliable indicators are those which leak inadvertently out of him. Asking directly would put him on guard, and may produce answers influenced by the impression he wants to create plus whatever he believes is the intention behind our question.

Therefore, such answers would have far less value in terms of revealing his true nature. Any clues or comments which reflect pride in his skill at being able to exploit or deceive others make him suspect. That is so regardless of how he re-labels such actions, and also in cases where the size or security of his income depend on it.

This may be more often the case in certain jobs in business, sales or services, but it can exist anywhere. People with a strong preference for honesty are more likely to avoid such occupations. And if they have them accidentally or out of necessity, they are more likely to lament the need for a degree of dishonesty in order to earn a living, rather than boast about it.

For honesty to be desirable it has to be what I call *tempered honesty*. Honesty may have to be tempered by legitimate considerations, a central one being to avoid damaging others. Sometimes this makes the practice of tempered honesty into a delicate balancing act, where the desire and respect for the truth has to be weighed against an equally justifiable desire to heal human vulnerability. Imagine a woman asking her partner "Does my bum look big in these trousers?" Only 10% may be a question, and 90% a search for reassurance about being considered attractive.

Things are rarely that easy however, which is why tempered honesty takes intelligence and tact. But also assertiveness and the courage to face the consequences of saying what others may not want to hear, when the issue is one that matters. The three other types of honesty which I call *naïve*, *unburdening* and *deliberately destructive* add to the definition of what tempered honesty is, by clarifying further what it is not.

Naïve honesty may be well intentioned, but there is not enough understanding of the possible or likely negative consequences. While seating on a crowded table in a dancing venue I saw a woman say to a man who seemed not to have a relationship, that she found it strange because there were many unattached nice women, including some sitting at the table. And then she proceeded to name two of them as an example.

As it turned out I had never seen that man dancing with one of the two women, and given the way both looked it could well have been because he found her unattractive. The woman in question knew it too, and as I witnessed it all from the sidelines I could see and feel the wave of underlying embarrassment and humiliation in her expression, despite her attempt at appearing unaffected. While the naively honest woman remained totally unaware of the damage she had just inflicted.

An example of *unburdening honesty* is when one partner feels bad about a past infidelity and deals with the discomfort by confessing it to the other.

What is actually happening is that under the guise of honesty, the burden of guilt is being relieved by dumping it on the partner. The burden does not disappear, but is just transformed into a different kind of burden which someone else must then bear. This can have significant negative consequences for the relationship, and they could be permanent.

Being discreet and making up for it in non obvious ways may well be the least damaging option. If any unburdening is still necessary it should happen not with the innocent partner but with a third party, preferably a therapist who does not know the couple socially and is bound by professional confidentiality. A reasonable alternative would be to unburden with a friend we can absolutely trust never to disclose it to anyone, if indeed we are in that fortunate minority who have such a friend.

Finally there is *deliberately destructive honesty*, and sadly I have seen plenty of it during my work with couples. When we allow anger to overrun our sense of responsibility, it is not uncommon to use honesty as a weapon, and a pretty devastating one at that. Women's generally superior emotional intelligence can make us fearsome warriors when we choose to attack with it, and therefore we need to be especially careful not to do so.

Deliberately destructive honesty often takes the form of contemptuous or sarcastic comments, which can cause serious and irreversible damage to the partners' feelings for each other. There is a joke about a bickering couple which illustrates the point rather well: *A man finally arrives home after hours in the pub. His wife hears him stumbling his way inside and snaps at him: "You are drunk again" she exclaims indignantly. "You are old and ugly" he retaliates. "You are drunk!" she repeats in an even louder and more infuriated tone of voice. "Yes", he retorts, "But I'll be sober in the morning".*

Closely related to honesty are the issues of fairness and responsibility. We may need to have a hard look at ourselves in order to ascertain whether we are being fair about meeting our responsibilities for maintaining harmony in the relationship. This issue will be discussed at some length in Stage 8. But for now we are only concerned with finding out whether our man has a sense of fairness and responsibility, because that would make a big difference later, when inevitable relationship pressure points begin to emerge.

A man who first consulted me alone about his marital problems told me: "I would never cheat on my wife because it wouldn't be fair on her". When complaining during therapy in front of her about being dissatisfied with how he felt she was not caring enough about his needs, he still acted respectfully and responsibly, even while she was blaming him for it. We want a man with those attitudes, and it is in our interest to have them ourselves.

Just as with honesty and for the same reasons, we are on the lookout for unintended clues, rather that asking questions to tick him on or off. When he deals with people from whom he has nothing to fear or gain, does he treat them fairly? Do his comments and behavior suggest he sees respecting everybody as the natural and proper thing to do? Does he do what he said he was going to? Is he fair and responsible enough to admit mistakes and apologize if appropriate?

Is he able to talk about such issues or does he avoid them? Does he become defensive or change the subject if we bring it up? The way he treats us is not a reliable indicator of honesty, fairness or responsibility if that is all we have to go by, because at least for now he is doing everything he can to be seen as a very good boy. But it is sensible to assume that once things have settled down and he feels more secure, he will sooner or later begin to treat us the same way he treats others, because that is his nature.

Self-other awareness, emotional intelligence, communication skills

Self-other awareness was discussed at length in Stage 5 as part of a broader elaboration on personality and its components. It is the essential ingredient of emotional intelligence and communication skills, and an important part of what it takes for a man to become our trusted friend. This matters because after the initial phase of overheated sexuality has leveled off, a good friendship is bound to become a substantial part of what it takes to keep a relationship satisfying.

Well developed self-other awareness is a form or knowledge which goes further and deeper than empathy, which is itself a critical component and manifestation of emotional intelligence. Empathy involves understanding how people truly experience whatever is happening at the time. It is as if we put ourselves in their shoes, in order to feel how our actions and reactions and those of others impact on them. That makes it essential in the context of intimate relationships, and its level is a significant factor in determining whether they will succeed or fail.

The importance of empathy becomes still more obvious when we consider what is probably the most damaging consequence of not having it, which is self centeredness. Two extreme examples were mentioned earlier under the heading *Emotional time bombs*, namely Delilah's killer and the Sydney man who stabbed his ex-girlfriend seventeen times. And of course, all categories of "definitely dangerous men" are abnormally self centered.

To the extent that children grow up deprived of enough consistent quality attention and affection, these unmet needs make them more likely to become self centered adults, and in this way "inherit" this feature from their primary care giver and significant others. The consequence of a reduced capacity for empathy can affect women too, although the vast majority are much better at it than most men.

But not always. Years ago I was walking outside a ground floor apartment where the police were standing next to the window in the company of an agitated older woman. A neighbor was to tell me later that the police had brought her in, when her son who was thought to be inside and had broken his parole conditions, was refusing to open the door or acknowledge he was there. And what struck me and kept me there was that she shouted so as to be heard by her son inside "How can you do this to me?"

In such moment of pressure, that came spontaneously out of her heart. It made me think that *her* disappointment and *her* personal sense of being unfairly treated by her son's behavior were foremost in her mind, rather than concern for *his* predicament. This type of personality has always existed in all socioeconomic groups. For example, it is now widely known that Queen Victoria of England was extremely self centered in dealing with her children. That plus her power made their lives a lot harder than would have been, if she had been better balanced in that respect.

Whenever we are getting to know a man with potential, there will be many indications about the extent to which he has a capacity for empathy, plus the self-other awareness which underpins it. His level of understanding of what is happening on and under the surface is bound to show in his ability to manage delicate issues, including being assessed, accepted or rejected by us. And especially, by how he reacts to not getting what he might prefer.

If his self-other awareness is good he will have a better sense of control over his life, and therefore be less prone to stress. The way people deal with stressful situations is a good window into their personality, particularly if they have to do so in the immediacy of the moment when there is little time to think. Our man is going to be at his best behavior in the early stages, but as always, the giveaways are the clues which leak out in all sorts of ways.

Communication becomes easier with a self-other aware man. When we talk about something that matters we will sense the depth in his understanding of whatever or whoever we are talking about, and possibly even learn something from the interaction. Most important of all, we will feel that he understands us and our concerns.

His inner security would make him better able to hold his end of any conversation, including the ones he might prefer not to have. And again, that confidence will make him less likely to become defensive, dismissive or aggressive when under pressure. This means that the differences and tensions which exist in every permanent relationship would be more likely to be managed without undue stress, as his inner calm and balance would have a calming and balancing effect on us too.

Flexibility, tolerance, optimism

Every relationship requires flexibility in order to be satisfying, because even well matched partners are bound to have different preferences at various times over all sorts of issues. In order to be flexible enough to accommodate to our partner's needs and wishes we need to be tolerant, in addition to self-other aware. Tolerant people do not see most things in black or white, and are instead well aware of gray areas. They accept the realities and limitations of human nature plus the necessity of compromising, and can consider and discuss any issues with equanimity.

In contrast, intolerant people are obstinately convinced they are right, and believe therefore that anyone who disagrees must be wrong. They tend to feel threatened or offended by different views, and consequently have a tendency to argue and keep arguing until everyone agrees or pretends to. And sometimes until others are exhausted into refusing to talk anymore, or even forced to physically move themselves out of reach.

Being able to be satisfied and contented with life requires optimism, because people and situations never fit perfectly with what we want or the aspirations of normal human greed. Optimism has to be within the boundaries of reality, otherwise we would be escaping into pleasant fantasies rather than managing the pressures of life in the best possible way.

To put it differently, optimists are usually happy enough despite the pressures and imperfections of life. At the opposite end, pessimists have an entrenched propensity to negativity. Pessimism and the unnecessary stress and unhappiness it brings about are very difficult to overcome unless everything in life is going great, which rarely happens for long. If we pick a pessimist as a life companion, we are walking into a permanent problem.

So, how do we know whether the man we are considering is sufficiently flexible, tolerant and optimistic? Again, we know that initially he is likely to be at his best because he wants us, either temporarily or permanently. Therefore, in order to develop a clearer idea of how he fares on these qualities and even if nothing wrong is showing up, we have to give ourselves time to see how he reacts in a variety of situations.

We need to be alert for the clues which will show up sooner or later in just about all areas of the evolving relationship. And ultimately, how skilled we are and have the potential to become at reading people, is going to depend significantly on our own level of development in the core components of personality and self esteem.

Active kindness: The most important quality

Part of my definition of love in page 135 includes the sentence that it is "everything we do as a way of giving for the purpose of caring". That encapsulates rather well what active kindness is about, as against the passive variety. Passive kindness is easy because all it involves is *feeling* kind. It does not require us to actually *do* anything. And nobody benefits except us, if we can believe that we are good people by just feeling kind.

Active kindness is very different because it involves giving, and expresses itself by benefiting others through the big or small things we do for them. Its manifestations are as varied as the variety of human interaction, and can happen with anyone anywhere. Many forms of active kindness require self-other awareness and emotional intelligence. Without enough of these, some acts intended to be kind may do more harm than good, which is exactly what happened in the example mentioned earlier about naive honesty.

The capacity for active kindness is something we should consider in evaluating any potential Mr. Right. Partly because we all have plenty to be forgiven for, and also because being cared for is such a heartwarming side of being loved. People who are actively kind are more likely to forgive or forget after we behave in less than ideal ways, because their healthier personalities make them unlikely to hang onto resentments.

Unkind people on the other hand, are much more likely to resent and retaliate about any real or imagined misbehavior by their partner. It may well be that what propels their unkindness are significant personality deficits and vulnerabilities originating in childhood through no fault of their own. But irrespective of causes or degree of culpability, living with an unkind person is likely to become increasingly unpleasant with the passage of time.

Although the capacity and desire for active kindness is probably the single most important quality in anyone worth considering as a permanent partner, I mention it last because having it depends largely on the other qualities already discussed. People who do not have enough of those qualities are running on empty. Their capacity to give is heavily depleted by their unmet needs, which can only ever be satisfied by a good enough level of self esteem.

Unless and until such people develop their personality enough towards the healthier end of the continuum, those unmet needs will prevail and often obstruct active kindness and probably also any desire for it. It doesn't matter how much love and support they get from their partner, because their self doubt and underlying fears of inadequacy are just too intense.

However, they tend to be unaware of their condition because they have always been like that. They feel better by believing that everyone else is too, and therefore tend to dismiss or ignore any inkling to the contrary. But when they do understand, accepting it will still be difficult because it would signal that there may be something not entirely right with them, which can feel anywhere from alarming all the way to rather frightening.

Their own emotional wellbeing is so precarious that they find it difficult to care about anyone other than themselves. Again, they have so little to spare that they cannot afford to give much to anyone. They can only take, and any "giving" by them will be little more than a calculated exchange which they consider profitable or eventually likely to become so.

There is a lot at stake in us being or becoming willing and able to be actively kind. Being so will give us the capacity to be a more satisfied and satisfying partner, and increase the chances of finding and being loved by a man who has good personal qualities. In the longer term these become increasingly more important, when compared to features such as attractiveness, money or status.

Genuinely kind men will not lie to a woman about the long term prospects of a relationship, especially in reply to a direct question, even if they know that telling the truth will lose them all those rolls in the hay. If we live with one of them and ask for affection when he is busy or does not want sex, he will give it because we want or need it and because he cares.

For the same reasons he will listen when we want to talk, and make an effort to understand. He is also likely to make a better parent or step parent because good parenting, like good loving, is mostly about having the capacity to understand and the willingness to give.

Further issues in the search for Mr. Right

Do similarities and differences matter?

Normal differences between men and women do not matter. Heterosexual relationships do not fail because of gender differences, or same-sex ones succeed due to gender similarities. After many years of working with couples in an ethnically diverse society, I am also convinced that racial, cultural, religious or linguistic similarities or differences don't matter that much either.

On the other hand common sense suggests that partners who are very similar in attitudes and life expectations are more likely to agree about money, sex, children's upbringing, extended family issues, recreational activities, TV programs to watch and so on, and that this would in all probability reduce the number of potential friction points. While gender, ethnicity or cultural background may play a part in initiating important attitudes and life expectations, many of these are likely to be modified later in life in response to factors such as education, intelligence, occupation and income.

Out of these, formal education, income and intellectual intelligence are less important than emotional intelligence and the level of maturity and wisdom it reflects. In other words, what really matters is the levels of partners' personality health and development. When these are compatible, it enables them to share thoughts and observations plus the myriad of obvious and subtler feelings expressed and released through that sharing. This is why talking is important, and usually the biggest joint activity in most established couples.

The critical issue boils down to whether or not partners are able to have enough big and small conversations which both of them find relevant, interesting or entertaining as against irrelevant, pointless or boring. Much of what matters most in intimate loving relationships is the sharing of information, opinions and emotions, as part of a couple's friendship. When this is functioning well, it becomes possible for many outwardly dissimilar partners to have relationships which remain fulfilling in the longer term.

Good emotional and verbal communication enables partners to strengthen their bonds, irrespective of whether they agree or disagree. Without it there will be boredom, emotional isolation and loneliness, especially for the woman, as discussed under *Men who are much less educated, less intelligent, and/or boring*. But the consequences of insufficient meaningful communication can become just as insufferable for men, as in the next two examples.

A well educated man was divorcing after a five year marriage. He had met a woman with a full-time job, who was better educated than his non working wife and also five years younger. "Is it because she is younger or prettier or financially better off?" I asked. "No", he replied. "It is because with her I can talk about anything". "You would have known your wife's limitations when you decided to marry her, so why did you go for it?" I asked. "I suppose she gave me what I needed at the time" he replied.

He understood his own and his wife's predicament, seemed to have a conscience, and I believed him. He had been in a profession which precluded him from having sexual relationships. On leaving that profession in his later middle age, he suddenly found himself at the deep end of the mature singles market with no experience and in a vulnerable state. Having reestablished a new sense of identity and regained his emotional strength after some years of marriage, being loved was no longer enough.

A rather attractive woman and a much older and less attractive but well educated man formed a relationship, which ended after about six or seven months. I felt sure it was he who left her, despite that for over a year after the breakup I observed him many times looking sad and depressed. And it took around two years for him to no longer seem burdened by it.

I thought that would be a good time to ask if he would mind telling me why he left her, to satisfy my professional curiosity. "After two months it was boring" he told me without hesitation. That was what I had thought too, because I knew her enough to be aware that she was not particularly emotionally intelligent, in addition to poorly educated.

Some of the normal differences between men and women are *externally* complementary, and therefore beneficial to the relationship. For example, most wives tend to become the social secretaries for the couple, due to women's generally greater enjoyment of friendships and superior relating skills. They are usually also more intuitive than their partners, thereby enriching couple functioning intimately as well as socially.

They do so by counterbalancing their men's tendency to rely excessively on what they think, and by assisting with men's generally lesser awareness of what they themselves and other people feel. A smart wife may understand aspects of her husband's needs and personality much better than he understands them himself. What matters here is whether the wiser partner uses that knowledge to help the other and enhance the quality of their relationship, as against using it to exercise power.

Other differences can be beneficial primarily because they are *internally* complementary, although the way this works is more complicated. For example, many men and some women have difficulty being affectionate in non sexual situations, and this can be difficult to change for reasons buried deep within their personality. It may be due to the way they were brought up, the personality of their primary care giver, or to the gender or family inhibitions they grew up with.

But if their partner is naturally and spontaneously expressive of affection, this can be an immensely gratifying experience for them. That is because they can meet their need for emotional connection without having to acknowledge it, let alone put themselves through what *for them* would be the strain of initiating or asking for it. In other words, that need is satisfied without the effort and stress involved in they having to change themselves.

When differences in intellectual intelligence and education are less pronounced, the relationship is more likely to work better when the man is the better educated partner for several reasons. Better education in the man does not clash with traditional roles, which consciously or unconsciously matter to many people. The woman may compensate for her lesser education by being younger or caring. If the man has certain insecurities and his woman is attractive, her lesser education could also make him feel more secure.

A better educated man is more likely to be a better provider, and that matters if she wants to have children. If the woman is financially independent, she may still enjoy the intellectual stimulation and consequently juicier companionship which is more likely to develop with a better educated man, other things being similar. But again and most important of all, women's generally superior emotional intelligence may balance out the effects of lesser education or intellectual intelligence, and so contribute to creating the all important meaningful communication in a relationship of equals-enough.

This kind of satisfying communication and relationship depends on personal qualities as well as on similarities and differences. They function jointly, and I have only pulled them apart for clarity of discussion. Out of them, good personal qualities and the healthier personality they reflect are far more important than most similarities or differences in determining whether a man has the potential to be right for us or we for him.

I finish this heading with a point which applies to us all: On extending our knowledge for the purpose of searching more effectively for a good partner and making any subsequent relationship work nicely, we will also gain significantly in terms of developing all our core components, including self-other awareness. This has the potential to put us on the road towards becoming wiser and happier, whatever happens or doesn't regarding our relationships. And in the final analysis, that is the most important thing we can do for ourselves by reading and understanding this book.

Do significantly older men qualify?

It seems to happen in every society that the later in life people enter into a committed relationship, the larger the age gap tends to be between the usually older man and younger woman. Presumably, many of those women came to the conclusion that it was sensible for them to trade off youth for a more compatible personality, plus perhaps a more attractive man or greater material comfort. And possibly most important of all to many of them, for the greater likelihood of continuing to be loved for life.

Significantly older men would obviously be unsuitable for women with a preference for younger men, and the reasons why such men are a bad bet were discussed earlier under its own heading. Most women willing to consider significantly older men are themselves no longer young, and have to think carefully about the advantages and disadvantages of an older man. A central consideration in evaluating any such potential partner would be how young and healthy he looks, compared to most men of the same age.

In a 2010 offshoot of the landmark "Dunedin Study" (details available in the Internet) 954 people, all 38 years old, were assessed on eighteen medical markers of their biological age. About half showed a biological age close to 38 or a little older. The biological age of the youngest small group was assessed at 30-32, and the oldest similar size group at 56-59. Furthermore, when university students were asked to estimate the subjects age by looking at their photos, those estimates reflected rather closely their *biological* age.

In other words, short of a thorough medical examination, the first and most important clue about people's health and longevity is their appearance. Imagine a scenario where we could see the future of two sixty year old men standing side by side. Both of them are going to die from the usual diseases, one in his seventies and the other in his nineties. The man destined to live twenty years more would probably look healthier and younger. In his case therefore, the same age difference would matter less.

There are many successful marriages with significantly older men. An often cited example is that of the 2008 US republican presidential candidate John McCain and his second wife Cindy, who wouldn't have married him for money because she had her own. One of those often unreliable stories in the Internet included how they came to love each other: Because he found her so irresistibly adorable, he told her he was thirty five although he was actually forty two. And because she liked him too, Cindy pretended to be twenty seven although she was twenty four, in order to encourage him.

According to the Internet story, they only found out their real age when under State law their official announcement of intention to marry had to include their date of birth. They married in 1980, had four children and have been together since. All this reminds me that when I was young and silly I used to think that women liked gossiping too much. Now it seems I have acquired a taste for it myself, as long as it is juicy and harmless. And that could be one of the reasons why for decades now, nearly all my most enjoyable friends have been women.

Many years ago I listened to a talk back radio program where the callers were women married to men who were mostly between ten and twenty years older. All the callers I heard said they were happy with their marriage, and that none of the negative predictions made by some weary friends had come to pass. Even if the callers were a biased sample, perhaps because only women with successful marriages were motivated to call, it still shows that such marriages can work well for a woman.

Several possible reasons come to mind. Because most mature women are more emotionally intelligent than most men of a similar age, many find such men simple to the point of being boring. That is why when they try out an intelligent older man, they may genuinely prefer his company. There are no worries about deepening wrinkles either, because their relative youth gives them a comfortable safety margin.

They feel in their bones the man finds them very attractive, which must be nice. In many cases they can sense that they would be very loved if they became a couple, and that their man would be far less likely to ever be interested in another woman. My own father was much older than my mother, and although he died prematurely from consequences of war injuries, she told me countless times that their marriage had been a very happy one.

These women may outlive their husbands for longer. But considering how hard it is to find an attractive enough nice man who doesn't have too many faults, marrying him can make a lot of sense if they are likely to have twenty or thirty years together. Especially when we know that every big city in the developed world has countless thousands of women reaching their older age alone, after searching for decades for "the right man".

The attractiveness level of a significantly older man matters too. As one woman put it when telling me about the kind of man she might go for: "If he is old he's got to be handsome". But she was also aware of the importance of a good personality. Years earlier she had to divorce an American man who looked "good on paper", as such men were sometimes described in *Sex And The City*. Within a year of a dream marriage ceremony, horse drawn carriage and all, she had to escape back to Australia.

This was the only way she could feel safe, after verbal putdowns and his potential for physical domestic violence became increasingly obvious. Therefore and even with an older man who presents well, is educated, says he loves us and wants to marry, we need to keep an eye for the seven underlying problem indicators listed in page 173 under *Potential domestic violence perpetrators*. Another aspect of why older men may qualify is discussed in Stage 8, under *The gradual turnaround in gender relationship power*.

Financial security and family responsibilities

Issues of financial security and family responsibilities are relevant for evaluating any man. For most people, financial security is about owning their own home and having a regular and secure source of income before and after retirement. It is not so much a matter of having more or less money, but of *feeling* they have enough to afford a reasonably secure and comfortable lifestyle. The opposite is excessive financial stress, and this is one factor affecting some couples who come for counseling.

About one third of divorcees in Australia say the breakup was due to money problems. But I doubt it because, as elaborated in page 52, partners in a good marriage tend to join forces to deal with such problems. This is not in conflict with the fact that economic security removes financial stress, thereby freeing time and energy for better managing marital tensions. And arguably making some of those marriages better, other things being equal enough.

The easiest way for some people to get the security and comforts money can bring, is to marry someone who has it. This is one way of achieving it for women who do not feel financially safe and may not have the time, capacity or desire to earn that security through their own efforts. That is why trading off youth or beauty for money is not uncommon.

But it could be a risky deal too. Many rich men have made their money by using or abusing people, and are not particularly good in the art and skills of getting better at loving. Sooner or later they may conclude that they themselves are being used. And since they are paying for it and just as they do with their cars, is not uncommon for them to upgrade to a newer model when those once young and beautiful women reach their best-before date.

Closely related to the financial security a man can contribute, are his family responsibilities. Supporting his children can take away a substantial part of his time and income. A man's children can sometimes be very unpleasant to the new woman, who may be referred to by their embittered mother as "the whore". I have worked with many such cases, and it is not fun having to care on alternative weekends for children primed by their mother to hate us.

If we do not own our own home and are living in his as a couple, will we inherit it if he dies before us or will he leave it to his children, considering that he can change his will at any time? Even if we inherit it, his children might in some cases be able to legally challenge our ownership of their late father's property. If the home in which we have been accustomed to living is at risk and eventually lost, that could be a disaster.

We could be left having to rent when we are no longer earning an income, to say nothing about the emotional cost of losing our home while trying to cope with the loss of our partner. It would be tactless to question our man about financial security issues in the earlier stages of a relationship, but it is sensible and legitimate to be very clear about it as part of any discussion regarding living together or marriage.

Many women these days have achieved substantial financial security by owning their own home, while some men haven't. It bears repeating that a pre-nuptial *financially binding agreement* is worth considering, for the purpose of protecting our hard earned economic security if the marriage was to end. Because as already mentioned, in Western countries with developed economies roughly around half of all marriages break up, if we count the growing number of de-facto ones which are not included in divorce statistics.

Selecting a man or settling for one?

From time to time we come across articles in women's magazines or discuss with our friends the issue of selecting a man versus settling for one. We are no longer influenced by tradition or necessity, because we are in a very different situation from where our grandmothers found themselves at the same age. They would have happily trotted all the way to the altar with Mr. Good Enough, the specter of spinsterhood looming over their heads.

But we are modern women. Financially and emotionally we stand on our own two feet. No trouble loving and living it up either, and when life delivers its romantic blows we get knocked down but we always bounce back. That is what we say and want to believe, we are prepared to fight it out, and no self respecting woman is going to settle for just any man.

However, the issue of settling for versus selecting is misleading. Every man who is willing and able to love us permanently represents a set of compromises, which we have to accept or reject. If we go after the supposedly closer to perfect men we see around and make it easy for them, they may just enjoy us for a while and then leave. And if they hang around and want us permanently, it could be because they have serious although not immediately noticeable personality or other problems.

In every case that is going to have a chance of working, what we are actually selecting is one particular set of compromises over another, which we hope will fit best with our needs and wishes. Whether or not we choose correctly will depend largely on how well we understand life, love, ourselves and our needs. And this is in turn significantly influenced by how far we have developed our personality and the wisdom which comes with it.

That suggests some questions we may want to think about: How clear are we about the difference between wants and needs? What are our real deeper needs? To what extent is the short term satisfaction of seeking and having younger or more attractive men, making it harder for us to achieve the stable and secure happiness of long term contentment?

Do we understand well enough the processes we have been through during Stages 1 to 4, and have we progressed away from *The Perfect Man Muddle* frame of mind? Is there something preventing us from recognizing the better quality men, or something in us discouraging them away? Have we understood and absorbed the knowledge in Stage 5? That is important, and if we haven't we may wish to go back to it after the first reading.

We are unlikely to find a good man until we stop looking for a Prince. So, have we succeeded in putting ourselves through what it takes to outsmart the trap, by having relationships with less physically appealing men with good personalities in an unplanned way? Or have we done the same thing in the calculated way discussed in Stage 7? Do we now know enough and are our emotional reaction patterns sufficiently disciplined, to search competently and choose wisely?

If we answer "yes" and unless we are very lucky, we will still have to reject many men before finding one who is right for us. We should therefore think about how to reject men in a supportive way if we are not doing so already. This may not always be easy, but it is in our own interest to make the effort for several reasons.

Those of us who consider ourselves decent, would want to treat men fairly in order to minimize the pain our legitimate choices will inflict. This is to safeguard our self respect, and also to prove to ourselves that we have the skills to do so. Furthermore, it would not be prudent to burn our bridges in case we change our mind at a later stage, perhaps with the benefit of hindsight after subsequent sentimental disappointments.

When we have succeeded in developing our personality to a higher and healthier level of functioning, that would have given us enough reserves of inner strength. They and the resilient wellbeing they generate are what gives us the capacity and willingness to respect and spare some kindness towards men who we know for sure would be unsuitable.

Problems and potential of Internet dating and hook-up sites

Hook-up sites such as "Tinder" are based largely-to-exclusively on appearance and easy accessibility. They are more suitable for young adults who have not yet developed a more mature appreciation of factors such as compatibilities in personality, lifestyle or major goals. For fully grown adults of any age who are seriously interested in finding a life partner, one or more of the many dating sites are likely to be a more productive alternative.

For mature people they are even more convenient, because those fewer available potential partners are spread out all over the place, making it extremely unlikely they could meet enough of them through more traditional ways. This means that retired and semi retired people can potentially benefit the most because there are less of them available, and they may not be willing or able to search through activities which involve a lot of travelling, physical effort, or unnecessarily spending their limited income.

The potential of the Internet as a search tool for a life partner is so obvious that dating websites don't bother to include it in their publicity. They emphasize instead their large membership and allegedly good pre-selection methods, which supposedly ensure a wide choice and better chances of success. But the truths left out of the publicity are very different, and often not appreciated until the user has wasted a lot of time, energy and money.

Earlier in the book I commented on the Stage 3 typical conviction that we know the sort of man we want and the do or die determination to find him. Both of these can be intensified for users of Internet dating sites, because they create the impression that there is an almost unlimited supply of candidates. Internet dating operates on the basis of unrestrained wish lists and unverified information, including photos sometimes so unrealistic that the person would be almost unrecognizable in real life.

Despite real time interaction through computer or phone cameras, we are unable to verify the height or get a feel for the totality of someone's appearance. This is what we experience when meeting in person, standing as well as sitting, walking, talking, moving and from all different angles.

It is common for people in Internet dating sites to pretend to be younger, slimmer and taller than they really are, and sometimes single or uninvolved when they are married or involved. There may be exaggerated claims about education or occupation, and any description of their personality may be nothing more than a carefully crafted version of how they want to be seen by the people they wish to attract. Their profile may reflect the personality of someone else who has written it or helped, and not infrequently it may have been partly copied from other profiles.

But probably the biggest problem with Internet dating is that most users are in the *Starry-Eyed Phase* of Stage 3, or in the almost as problematic *Perfect Man Muddle* of Stage 4. Therefore they are not searching with the realism or competence of those who are in Stage 7. When compared with more traditional ways of meeting, Internet relationships make it difficult for the usual checks and balances of reality testing to apply from the start, thereby making it easier for our fantasies to take hold.

There may be also significant delays before meeting in person, which add to the time and emotional investment potential partners have to use up. After all that effort and as soon as there is a live personal meeting, one or both people who seemed promising are likely to turn into yet another flop, from the other's perspective. This may be for reasons other than physical appearance, although that is often the first and obvious disappointment.

Behind the advertising hype of dating websites, the odds are not good to say the least. A lot of time and effort can be wasted, and having to sort out all these men leads to inevitable mistakes. Smart women are just as likely to make them, and intellectual intelligence, formal education or common sense in other areas of life may not be enough to save us.

Exaggerations about the likelihood of finding Mr. Right in dating sites are often aggravated by the nature of journalism. Professional journalists writing such ever popular articles have to work on tight deadlines. With other work piling up on their desk they take the easiest way out, which is to talk with the most willing and available "experts". Not surprisingly these are the spokespeople for the dating sites, and indeed many articles quote them referring to their opinions and claimed statistics.

The majority of clients who actually pay for contacts are men. It is therefore in the interest of dating sites to feed overoptimistic propaganda to all, but especially to women of age brackets in short supply in terms of what the paying male clientele are looking for. Many such articles can be found in women's magazines sold at supermarkets and piled up in doctors' waiting rooms, which is where over the years I got to read some.

One such article I remember was aimed at recruiting mature women, and it mentioned three in their fifties. Just like in the trashiest romantic novels, all three had found a wonderful man around the same age or just a few years older and were living happily ever after. Good publicity for the website, but for how many such women would this be true? There is no doubt many join up after reading such articles, which also include the "information" that they can post their profile and check their "matches" for free.

Television advertising for the sites does the same thing. Therefore, it cannot be overemphasized that users would be well advised to be realistic about their chances, inform themselves about the limitations and risks, and be cautious when corresponding and meeting. Those searching for a more balanced view of what actually happens in Internet dating may be able to get it through a Google search, with the name of a major website plus the word *complaints*, *problems* or comparable words, to tease out the hidden truths.

The one very real and huge advantage of Internet dating is that it can help people meet many others fairly easily on the basis of more or less mutually sought after characteristics, who would have never been able to find one another through traditional ways. Some websites and marriage agencies claim to be using selection formulas based on knowledge of relationship psychology and "mathematical algorithms", so as to imply scientific credibility about their methods for preselecting potential suitable partners.

Such methods can indeed help pair people up by *claimed* and desired features, but have four major unsurmountable problems. The first is that they are based on self reporting by people who may not be self-aware (even if they are actually doing their best to be honest), and many of those with serious personality problems which are obvious to others do not think they have any. The second problem is that it is too easy for self-reporters to present themselves as better than they are by distorting or disguising reality, not only with undated and unrealistic photos, but with various untrue or exaggerated claims.

The third problem is that there are no reliable studies to verify the alleged success rates claimed by websites and marriage agencies, some of whom may be inflating them in order to improve their credibility. The fourth problem is that most of those who think of themselves as matching experts have insufficient knowledge about the deeper personality features which are most relevant for increasing the chances of longer term relationship success.

I have discussed such features in Stage 5 and elsewhere, and summarized them under the heading *The deeper and truer reasons why established relationships succeed or fail*, in pages 151-156. Again, professional matchmakers, websites' matching experts, their spokespersons and most importantly their customers, would all benefit from reading and understanding the lesser known but very relevant issues mentioned throughout this book.

Safer sex issues: Information, criminality and irresponsibility

What follows is intended to increase reader awareness about safer sex. It is not health advice, which should always be obtained from a doctor. Written information on sexually transmissible infections (STI's) and ways of preventing them is widely available in doctors waiting rooms and the Internet. Comprehensive STI tests including for AIDS, hepatitis and now also for herpes virus types 1 and 2 have been free for decades in Australia, with bulk-billing doctors and in specialized sexual health clinics available in major cities.

The only unprotected safe sex is between two monogamous partners who have been thoroughly tested and found to be free of STI's. We know that we have to be careful, but sometimes we haven't been. So far we may have gotten away with it or gotten off lightly. But we should never forget that it only takes one mistake combined with bad luck for things to change drastically and permanently, and some examples further below show why.

What is important to remember is that just asking someone if he or she is free from STI's just before sex is not good enough. In such situations it is tempting to lie, and also to believe people who look clean, healthy and trustworthy. Furthermore they or us may have one or more STI's without symptoms and not know it. In order to be able to make an informed decision about whether what is being said can be trusted and the risk is worth it, we need to understand each other's personality and circumstances well enough.

That may require us to wait for sex, or for sex without condoms. If our potential partner is unwilling to do either, he/she is really not worth the risk. Before putting on a condom we should kill any viruses which may have gotten onto our hands through heavy petting or self touching, by thoroughly washing them with soap. That is because viruses in our fingers may unintentionally go from there to the genitals and the inside or outside of a condom, thereby creating the potential for infection.

Diagnosed chlamydia incidence has skyrocketed in the last fifteen years. Women may be unknowingly infectious because they usually have no symptoms. It is cured easily, but if left untreated for years it may cause infertility. Men's symptoms can be mild, and if unrecognized they too will keep infecting others. Some types of "non-specific urethritis" may also have no symptoms in some men and women, who are therefore unknowingly infectious.

The genital warts virus is incurable. Warts can grow anywhere, often at the edge of the entrance to the vagina or anus, and can be individually removed. They tend to reappear however, although in some cases the immune system finally becomes able to suppress them after many years. They are very contagious, and will become increasingly unsightly and problematic if untreated.

Some people who get hepatitis B overcome the virus and thereafter become immune, while others go on to develop chronic hepatitis without symptoms. They may remain unknowingly infectious for decades, and transmit it through unprotected sex. So, do we really want to risk learning the hard way that we need to be cautious even with men or women who look attractive, honest, educated and absolutely wonderful?

Herpes type 1 virus is extremely common, with around 85% of the population having it by age 25. It is incurable but relatively benign, and most often causes cold sores on the lips of some carriers, with a lot of individual variation in frequency and severity. The main risk when sores appear is that it can lead to herpes in the genitals through oral sex. It might also infect the eyes through kissing, or touching with fingers which have not been thoroughly washed after being in contact with the sores.

The herpes type 2 virus which causes most genital herpes is incurable and problematic. In Australia and the US one in every eight sexually active adults is said to have genital herpes. Furthermore, when we consider that older adults in long term monogamous marriages are likely to have a lower rate of infection, the incidence for older singles is probably higher. Moreover women have it at double the rate of men, probably because it is easier for them to get infected. All in all, **the risk for all STI's combined is very real.**

Some carriers of the herpes type 2 virus may not have genital herpes because the infection did not happen there. A woman was hospitalized as a result of a throat infection her local doctor had been unable to cure, but it was still not going away. Eventually a smart nurse realized what might be happening and told the doctor. She promptly carried out a test, which confirmed the patient's throat had been infected with herpes type 2.

While a first genital herpes infection can be painful and distressing, its management often gets a bit easier overtime. But it is something nasty which may well cause potential partners to reconsider involvement. A few people develop relatively milder symptoms and may not recognize them immediately.

A woman speaking on TV with her face disguised saw her doctor regarding a tiny red dot in the genital area which was not healing. She thought it was an infected hair follicle, and was shocked when told it was genital herpes. Cells with the virus are constantly being shed off by infected people, making them contagious if the virus enters their partner through broken skin, the eyes, or some minute tear caused through normal sexual activity.

There used to be no way of tests differentiating between the extremely common herpes type 1 and the more serious type 2. Therefore standard tests did not include one for herpes because most people would have tested positive. We had to rely on being told, despite knowing that sufferers might be tempted to hide it if they did not have sores and believed were not contagious. But modern tests differentiate between types 1 and 2, and as already mentioned, they are also freely available in Australia.

Some people who know they may be contagious still have unprotected sex without informing their partner. A woman consulting me commented about a friend who had genital herpes. Her friend's attitude was that she got it from men, and that if men happened to catch it back from her that was their problem and they probably deserved it anyway. Such attitude is irresponsible, the behavior is definitely a crime, and it would qualify her into the earlier discussed category of "certifiable bastards".

Even if they know they are infectious, certifiable bastards have no conscience, and some can be very good at hiding their true nature. They act in deliberately dishonest and criminal ways without feeling any guilt, and very few are ever prosecuted and convicted. A case which made to TV national news in Australia was about a woman who years earlier had gone to a European country for a holiday, and spoke publicly as a warning to others.

She fell in love and married a man she thought was very nice, and stayed living there. It was only years later, after she began suffering from AIDS, that she discovered his late wife had died from AIDS and not from cancer as he had told her. She sued him for having unprotected sex without telling her he had HIV. He was prosecuted and imprisoned for years in his own country, which probably saved other women and their later partners from the same fate. People have been jailed for years in Australia for the same offence.

But with more average people too, everyday irresponsibility is in fact quite common. Some drink and drive, risking injury or death to themselves and others. Quite a few are addicted to gambling or alcohol to the point of living in poverty and damaging or ruining their marriages and families. Despite knowing the health risks many people use drugs, smoke, become morbidly obese from too much junk food, or engage in various kinds of dangerous or illegal behaviors. Too often we know, but choose to ignore the implications.

If we happen to meet such a person and there is mutual liking, we are at risk of trusting excessively. It would be very foolish indeed to blind ourselves into believing that those who act carelessly or irresponsibly towards themselves would not carelessly or irresponsibly infect us, especially if having sex depends on not disclosing an STI.

Furthermore, the problem may be with us too because the temptation of sex can be hard to resist for anyone, and being intelligent may not always be enough to save us. The South African president Jacob Zuma admitted publicly to having had unprotected sex with a woman knowing she had HIV, and was very lucky not to get infected.

Most HIV carriers in developed western countries are homosexual men. But it gets into the heterosexual community through bisexual men, intravenous drug users and local or overseas prostitution without condoms. HIV infection may not produce noticeable symptoms for years, and those affected could be unaware.

I have known masculine looking divorced fathers who were living with a male partner, and worked with couples in which I felt sure the man was bisexual or homosexual and the woman was in denial. Many such men stay in denial for many years too, and sometimes for life.

A worried woman told me about a man she had unprotected sex with. Over the course of the night he commented he wasn't particularly fond of breasts, wanted vaginal sex but only from behind her, and kept asking in roundabout ways for reassurances as to whether he was a good lover. He was probably a bisexual in denial.

It bears repeating that being careful is something we owe to ourselves, and to dependent children if we have them. We need enough time to understand the personality and circumstances of any potential partner before deciding on sex. The only responsible thing to do before unprotected sex is for each prospective sexual partner to get *fully* tested (including AIDS, hepatitis and genital herpes) and then give each other the paper copies of the test results.

If we haven't done so and end up infected with something serious, we may have reason to believe our partner deliberately failed to inform us of the risk before unprotected sex. In such case, a lawyer could obtain from Medicare a list of all the doctors our former sex partner has ever used, and then subpoena the date-relevant medical files from any doctor or hospital.

If examination of those files was to reveal that our partner did not inform us of a serious or incurable STI he/she had and knew about, this could well be criminal negligence. It should be discussed with the police for referral to the public prosecutor, and we would also be able to sue for damages. If the perpetrator had to sell his/her home and/or go into debt in order to pay a very big court-ordered compensation, plus ended up getting a jail sentence on top of it, that would surely be thoroughly deserved.

Readers may legally photocopy pages 214-217 for any potential partner, in order to discuss the issues before unprotected sex.

STAGE 7

OUTSMARTING THE TRAP:

Designing and implementing an Action Plan

Men are relationship socialists whose kind heart predisposes them to want to share themselves around. If it weren't a joke, this view would be directly opposite from the equally undeserved irrational blame some of us threw at them during Stages 1 to 4. Feeling angry with men for being as nature made them, makes as much sense as feeling angry with rain for getting our hair wet. Blaming them may temporarily relieve some hurt. But in fact, the most relevant issues in our sentimental disasters have to do with *our* erroneous choices, *our* unrealistic expectations and *our* questionable behaviors.

In due course after the breakup other men may help us heal, explore, learn and enjoy. We reject and get rejected, through it all we and others suffer some more, and now here we are. Reading and understanding this book can help us get our act together. The stronger our grasp of how we and men function, the better we will be able to manage our feelings and actions in delicate situations, by retaining a cool head and a steady heart. Before going into that however, we need to consider the issue of motivation.

Robert and his beloved: A case to motivate us

We know we should not waste any more time if we want to turn our life around, and that the longer we wait the more difficult it is going to get. But just as some people need a diagnosis of cancer to stop smoking or one of diabetes to give up sugary foods, just knowing what we should do may not be enough to motivate us into changing. That is because our usual ways of behaving have an addictive quality, in that we like the comfort and security of the familiar and dislike the discomfort and risk of the new.

When it comes to searching for love, even a succession of sentimental disasters may not be enough to overcome our addiction to the hope of finding an ideal man, for the reasons discussed in Stages 3 and 4. The case of Robert is included next to provide that extra motivational nudge, on the hope it may finally propel us into taking action while there is still time. The case takes the biggest part of an autobiographical narrative by me, quoted next under its title *Time is short*.

TIME IS SHORT:
Life's Turning Points

I had always loved my mother. Born when my brothers were in their mid-late teens and six months before she became a widow, I became her last and loveliest. My father had been able to return from exile, still suffering from the legacy of serious injuries many years after Spain's civil war, following the general amnesty.

It had been granted when the military dictatorship felt securely supported by the United States, all-powerful after their victory in the Second World War. He was much older than my mother but their marriage had been a very happy one, I remember her telling me countless times.

By the time I left my home, her love was in my bones. That was why I no longer needed my mother, or for that matter the rest of my family. I became independent and adventurous, spread my wings rather early, and flew far away. Sometimes, such can be the price of good parenting. Because she thought it was best for me and because it was what I wanted, she never tried to stop me. She had the most to lose, but so deep can be a mother's love.

And by the time I had grown wise enough to understand well people and life, her hair had been white for many years. It was then that I began to like my mother. I became her friend out of friendship and out of love. I told her that I loved her, and how her love for me had given me strength. I kept in touch, helped her financially and sent her presents. When she died I cried. Now, many years later, I remember her with affection and still look at her photo in my bedroom.

But this tale wasn't meant to be about me or my mother. I just want you to know I mean it, when I swear on my mother's memory that what follows is a true story.

We can call him Robert. I only knew him for a few weeks while he was in the psychiatric unit where I was training, with severe reactive depression. I tried to chat with him a few times, but he never said much.

He was still heavily medicated and too stunned by the reality of his suicide attempt, after becoming involved with this woman. Yet, it was important to find out what precisely he had become depressed about, in order to help prevent a perhaps fatal second attempt. Therefore I persevered.

Nobody knew what she had done to him. "She is a lovely girl" was all he would say, "She has a lot of sparkle". He waited eagerly for her evening calls, and during her weekend visits they seemed very happy together. And it was that which was gradually doing the trick, much better than the antidepressants. Evidently despite his condition, Robert had been swept off his feet, was besotted, still seriously in love with her, and she loved him too. So why had he become depressed and suicidal?

I was to find out a little more from Robert in subsequent occasions. Since his parents died he had lived alone, never moving from the family home he then inherited. His younger married brother and sister lived not too far away, he had liked his job, always enjoyed a few drinks with his mates, been a sports follower and keen fisherman.

But he had always been shy and unlucky with women. Then one day he met this girl and fell in love, truly in love for the first time in his life, he assured me. Her family disapproved strongly, but she loved him and wasn't going to give him up. This was heavenly. What he'd been missing all his life. What he should have been having all along. What he so much would have wanted to have.

As he kept talking in subsequent occasions, it became clear that his level of emotional maturity on matters of the heart was more like that of a teenager. This was why, despite his age, he had been overtaken by the overwhelming intensity of adolescent love. He was seventy eight when he had been found by this sixty nine year old widowed grandmother, a few months before he attempted suicide.

To understand Robert I had to hear what he was _not_ saying, what perhaps he would never be able to say. Awareness of the enormity of his loss, of what he now felt as an irretrievably wasted life, had descended upon him too suddenly. It had run him over and mangled his spirit. The silent cry of his anguished desperation was slowly leaking out of him, in all its compelling tragedy: When his life was happening he hadn't lived it as he could have, and now he had nearly run out of time and he knew it.

In his heart of hearts, the intoxicating sweetness of being in love was what married life would have been mostly about. Having lived life without that kind of intimacy was undeniably a major loss, although his unrealistic beliefs about love and marriage had magnified it. However, such finer points didn't interest Robert. To him it was a catastrophe, pure and simple.

He had discovered too late that love is what matters most. With his survival needs always comfortably covered, he had used his spare time and energy in pursuits which diverted his attention from that which he most needed and feared. Until one unexpected day when the reality he had been hiding from finally caught up with him, decapitating his delusions with one fell swoop of its own sweetness.

Robert is probably long dead by now, but each of us faces at least a little bit of our own version of his predicament. Awareness of it often begins to emerge as we enter the Autumn of our life, when a coalescence of factors may propel some of us to reflect over how we have lived, and what we want to do with whatever is left. And it is because aspects of Robert's predicament resonate with us all, that his memory comes back to me every time I hear an old song.

What creates its gripping power is the deep sorrow overflowing from the songwriter's heart. The lyrics convey the poignancy of the underlying feeling by focusing on one point. A point which most of us have got by somewhere along our forties. Or more precisely, it is the point which has gotten us, usually after one or more emotional experiences intense enough to have left us shaken.

The song is a mournful lamentation about the many things the song writer could have done but didn't, when he still had time. And how now, when he finally realizes the value of what he missed on, he has grown too old to do it. We know we are on our way to a time in life when the message of the song will apply to us too, if it doesn't already, and that is why it hits hard. The lyrics are available in the Internet, although the title says it all. The several English versions are called "If I Only Had Time", and it is said to have been first written in French by Pierre Delanoe as early as 1962.

Robert's life stood in sharp contrast against that of his beloved. The limitations of his personality had imposed a high price on him, while she was undoubtedly rather resourceful. Because getting for ourselves that kind of love at sixty nine is no mean feat, even when luck is on our side, if only for the defiance of family and social expectations it entails.

Their relationship was so fulfilling, because there was more to it than the obviously relevant but often overrated physical attraction and cultural similarities. Underneath all these there was the all-important, and in their case well fitting complementarity of inner needs. In other words, they had emotional compatibility at a deep level. This made a big difference for them, because it stabilized and enhanced everything else.

I only knew her from a distance, and by reading between the lines of what Robert was saying. My impression was that in terms of meeting his deeper needs, her major contributions came from well honed emotional intelligence and savoir faire, plus a determination to love and be loved. All of it supported by a foundation of quality self esteem, solid enough to make it convention proof. And fool proof too, when the need arose to stand up to some members of her own family who were obviously less secure internally, and therefore excessively vulnerable to external disapproval. Or perhaps just plain narrow-minded and possibly uncaring about her happiness.

Being fairly uncomplicated, the appeal of his personality to her deeper needs had been more passive, but no less real or potent for her. Robert was a man who despite his age still retained enough vulnerability to be sweet. Genuinely sweet that is, with all the emotional reactions and convictions which went with his appreciation of being truly and deeply loved by such a charming woman.

Their feelings for each other were never diluted or undermined by responsibilities to work and family. They were unhindered by financial difficulties, having enough to live on in a manner they felt comfortable with. And both knew by then that for all sorts of unpredictable reasons, hopes or fears about the future may never materialize. That while it is good to be prepared, we cannot be sure of how long we'll remain alive, let alone healthy. They had learned the hard way that the present is all we ever have. And that at the end of every day, there is one day less left to live.

As far as I could see, these were the factors that had made their love so beautiful. Their story made me reflect on the impact which wisdom and courage can have at critical make or brake points, when a single decision may alter our life trajectory permanently for the better.

They also helped me to realize why I had ended up liking my mother so much, after a carefree childhood and adolescence when I took her and her love for granted and never gave it a second thought, let alone a thanks. She was barely literate and carried her share of foibles. But she could see through petty pretenses, appreciated the shades of gray between the good and evil of human nature, always trusted her judgment, and did what she thought was right despite risk or opposition. She invariably chose to retain her self respect, even when the price was high, and in so doing she was teaching me by example and shaping my own values.

Right up to her old age she was a contented person nearly all the time, surviving with dignity what life had thrown in her path and making the most of what she had. She understood the essence of people, the hidden meanings of what they were not saying, and often didn't know about or couldn't face. She could read people very well, my mother. Many mothers get better at it, motherhood being such a good training ground. More women than men seem able to, and it gives them all a better appreciation of reality as well as more colorful and interesting personalities.

Robert's tragedy had jolted me. For most of us the critical jolt may come from events such as an unexpected brush with our own mortality, the end of an important relationship, or a family tragedy. Our first encounter with such experience can become a turning point. In my case, the impact had pushed certain insights through and indelibly etched them in.

But this kind of knowledge is powerful stuff, and the self questioning was inevitable: As my life was happening and my time in it was ticking away, was I living it the way I wanted? What was it about life, that really *really* mattered? Above all, what was I going to do about it, while there was still time? And as I began getting better at listening to what I had not been saying, something new had been set in motion and life could never be the same again.

Within two or three years I was out of a marriage which could not be mended, and had thrown myself into my second adolescence with all the gusto of a born-again single. Enjoyed the ride despite making most of the mistakes that could be made. Tried to minimize the unavoidable lacerations to myself and others, while remaining convinced that such is the price we must pay in the quest for identity and love.

The nicest among the women who crossed my path allowed me to learn from their wisdom, while our tender moments together left us with the bittersweet taste of an affection destined to become a memory. Life kept beating me into a deepening level of awareness, with every blow bringing me a little closer to my own center.

Closer to the realization that as time keeps getting shorter and the stakes keep getting higher, love can no longer be a game. That no matter how well we play it, more and more it ends with serious heartache or unfulfilling superficiality. It was also becoming clearer that not everyone had the strength to withstand the vulnerability we accept, when we take the risk of loving.

Perhaps most important of all, it was gradually dawning on me that somewhere along the line even the strong begin to need love, rather than just want it. That there comes a time, when nothing else can fill the void.

All that had not quite fallen into place yet, while I was still head on into my born-again singlehood. I simply had not lived or reflected enough, to be wiser. My budding career as a relationship therapist had not matured either, to the point of yielding a richer crop of insights into the human condition.

And it is the layout of that crop of insights into the deeper and often hidden recesses in the minds and hearts of men and women, that these short stories are really about. I look forward to sharing my observations should you turn onto the next page, and continue exploring some obscure but fascinating corners of the male psyche. *(Three more stories as Appendixes A, B and C)*

Considerations before designing an Action Plan

When the mind is pitted against the heart it is the latter which more often wins out, and when both are pointing in the same direction there is only one way to go. Chances are that the unrealistic expectations in our mind were never the only reason for us ending up in the perfect man muddle of Stage 4, and therefore no amount of talking, reading or thinking was by itself ever going to solve the problem. It was also and always the unruly kneejerk visceral reactions of our heart which had to be acknowledged, brought under control, and sufficiently retrained.

In other words, while we need to understand the issues with our mind as a first step for motivating us into the kind of action likely to yield results, the actual reeducation of our heart has to be done through experiential learning. We have to put ourselves under the right kind of pressure accidentally or by design, in order to learn to manage the weight in our heart and the wrenching in our stomach. And do so in a meaningful and productive way until we come out at the other end, not only still alive, but wiser and to that extent relatively "cured".

After too many years in Stage 4 we have had all the adventure we could wish for this lifetime, and now more than ever we want a serious relationship with a man who will love us for life. We know that security about being loved will become increasingly important as we get older and our attractiveness fades away. We know also that most nice men are already taken and kept under lock and key in some living room, pampered and fussed over by watchful women who know the value of what they've got.

We are facing increasingly stiff competition from younger women for the few good men still in circulation, and are fully aware that if we want true love we are going to have to make our relationship skills sharper and smarter. For all these reasons we need an understanding as accurate as possible about the issues that matter, and this book can help us get there.

The most important part deals with personality and self esteem knowledge and development, as elaborated in Stage 5. To the extent we have understood and absorbed it, that will give us a better capacity to read deeper into our and other people's feelings, opinions, actions and reactions, plus the underlying needs, wishes and fears propelling them.

In addition to enriching and strengthening ourselves, this improved capacity will help us recognize features in men likely to become less significant after a while. As against qualities which would meet our immediate desires to an acceptable degree, while becoming increasingly important in the longer term. These considerations suggest certain questions we might like to think about, regarding any possible relationship with realistic potential:

- Is he imperfect and old enough to keep loving me truly, now and for life?
- Are the imperfections he embodies something I can or want to live with?
- Is he nice and attractive enough for me to possibly be able to love him?
- Do his personality and track record suggest he understands what love is?
- Do my personality and track record suggest I understand what love is?
- Would our similarities and differences enable us to be trusting friends?
- Do we both have the personal qualities which would facilitate success?
- Do I have the strength to risk further hurt by us trying out a relationship?

Rationale and components of the Action Plan

What I am about to propose as a way of working our way out of the Stage 4 trap is not an idea plucked out of thin air. It is in fact a universally tested time honored method which I have taken note of as it actually happens, and distilled into a readable form that can then be planned and implemented.

This distillation is based on knowing about many women who have succeeded at it, often without being fully aware of precisely how and why it actually worked. It comes not only from my experiences as a therapist, but also from years as a participant observer, sometimes strolling and occasionally struggling through the fog and quick sands of the mature singles jungle.

The Action Plan is intended as a way for us women to extricate ourselves from the Stage 4 trap, and consists of two parts over and above what has been discussed so far. Part one involves the relatively easy task of recapitulating and writing down three categories of points in three separate pages. The resulting lists can be kept stuck where we can see them often, in order to ensure the issues stay at the forefront of our awareness, and for adding further points at any time they come to mind.

A heading I suggest for the first category is "Problematic Features in Men I Tried Out". These are bound to include some of those discussed under *The relatively less harmful Mr. Wrongs* or *Definitely dangerous men*. The heading for the second category could be "Possible Good Points in the Men I Rejected", which we may have failed to give enough attention to at the time.

That would be especially so, if the rejection was largely on the basis of physical appearance on the borderline of attraction or just below it, income and assets below or age above our preferred limits, and perhaps unverified, superficial or negative beliefs about their personality.

The third category is an "Inventory of Important Personality Qualities". Once compiled, the qualities could be numbered in order of importance. So, we need three separate pages, with the category heading written at the top and the specifics in possibly one-per-line point form, just as a memory aid.

This inventory is about personality qualities representing the kind of lifelong relationship value which would make a man worthy of serious consideration. It should deliberately exclude attractiveness and money, as a temporary counterbalance to the usual wish list inside our head which often overemphasizes those two issues. It is not intended to persuade anyone to ignore them when we have to choose, because they do matter.

If we have problems compiling the second and third categories, we may need to read again *Desirable Personality qualities in men (and women)*. Some of the men we rejected in the past may have had these qualities, regardless of whatever else we felt which at that time made them unsuitable. Other men who come our way in future may have those qualities too. And we are more likely to recognize and appreciate them, after we have already listed and acknowledged their value in order of importance.

Part 2 of the Action Plan is easy to understand but difficult to implement. It involves making ourselves open, and if necessary forcing ourselves, to try out some men who are not one but two notches down in our personal subjective scale of acceptable attractiveness. I say "forcing ourselves" because of the automatic negative visceral rejections towards less physically appealing men, which we have unwittingly trained ourselves to feel over the years.

The purpose is to retrain those first impression heart and gut reactions, and in so doing avoid the counterproductive behaviors which usually follow. Assuming some readers will baulk at the idea, I want to repeat that the Action Plan has been tested and proven countless times. That is because it happens naturally and quite frequently, although usually not intentionally. In most such cases the two participants may not be fully aware of the undercurrents involved, and are certainly not behaving according to a calculated plan.

Imagine for example the following scenario: After one or more significant but unsuccessful relationships, we want someone safe for a change. Someone unlikely to reject us because ... well ... we have had all the rejections we could bear for the rest of our life. We feel exhausted and disheartened, fed up of being fed up, and have been for ages. Deep down we know we are slightly desperate even, and it is hard. We need to be a little bit looked after, because the alternative is to be depressed. We know he hasn't got a chance, but we go along with it for the sake of survival, just for the time being.

We do not want to risk our feelings and our sanity with someone we like too much, because we know that liking him is precisely what makes him dangerous. Instead we prefer someone safe in order to begin to heal. There is no one safer than a man we are not very attracted to, because he would cause little damage even if he rejected us. Such a man provides the kind of company without risk which is needed to survive and try to forget, whether we want him just for dancing, walking, talking and perhaps for dating in what we anticipate will be a limited temporary relationship.

Sometimes it works in the longer term, when such a man happens to have a good personality, genuine feelings and other favorable circumstances. That is because enough time with him allows us to feel and experience his human qualities, plus the security he represents about being truly loved with few conditions and probably permanently. Provided other things apart from his level of attractiveness are acceptable or better, the relationship could unexpectedly become good enough for us.

In fact it often does, and the evidence is all around us. But there is a big difference between it happening naturally and we doing it deliberately. The natural way works best, no question about it, but it has the disadvantage that if it does happen at all it might take years. And years of waiting for something which may never happen is precisely what we don't want. At this point we come up against the difficult part of what it takes to evolve into giving ourselves a better chance of success in the relationship stakes.

So, please forgive me for being firm in what I am about to say. We really do need to force ourselves to swallow the bitter pill of connecting with two notches down men. Why? Well, first of all we wouldn't complaint about bitter pills if they were needed to cure us from breast cancer, would we? So, these ones are needed to protect us from the foolishness of our illusions and consequent bad habits, which so far have failed to deliver the prince and left us at serious risk of never finding permanent love.

The rationale is as follows: By forcing ourselves to date men two notches down our usual attractiveness acceptance level, for as long as necessary and with as many men as it takes, two things will happen. The first is that some lucky men will feel as if they have died and waken up in heaven. As long as we make clear we are not making a commitment and may move on at any time, it is up to them to decide whether they want to enjoy the moment and take their chances, or stay away for fear of getting hurt.

Two essentials are that we safeguard our self respect by not deceiving men, especially those who are emotionally vulnerable, and that we take care of our own security by avoiding any man who shows signs of a problematic personality. Therefore again, I must point out the importance of reading the whole book before implementing anything, with especial attention to the subheadings under *Definitely dangerous men* in Stage 6.

Furthermore, since being with one or several two notches down men for as long as it takes may not be easy, we need to choose someone who has something to make the experience bearable. For example, he could be fun to dance with, cheerful and funny, a good conversationalist, intelligent and insightful, kind and polite, or anything else which we feel gives him enough appeal for us to tolerate it. If he does not have something to compensate for being insufficiently attractive, we will be less likely to withstand it for long enough to achieve the desired effect, and the plan is likely to fail.

A second thing that will happen is that we know the strategy has begun to work when, after having been in the company of two notches down men for long enough, those who previously used to be just one notch down begin to look barely acceptable. So that if their personality is nice and circumstances are compatible, we sense it is within the realm of possibility that we might perhaps be able to love them.

It is only after we have had enough two notches down men to do the trick that we should start to aim for one notch down men, and this will give us the best chance of finding one who is right for us. Right not only in the usual way of liking him plus *hoping* he will like us back and that there will be nothing wrong with him. But right in the sense of having a *reality based expectation* that he too may grow into wanting to love us truly and permanently, plus has the personality which gives him the capacity to do so.

This is not a matter of ending up with a man we don't like just for the sake of having someone safe, because that would definitely not be worth it. The point is to give ourselves the opportunity of coming to genuinely like an imperfect good man. A man of the kind we would have dismissed as a serious candidate mostly on appearance or age grounds, during the Starry-Eyed Phase of Stage 3 and the Perfect Man Muddle of Stage 4.

Unlike knowledge which can be learned by study alone, the implementation of this Plan requires gut level skills development. While knowledge is a prerequisite and motivator for deliberately doing what needs to be done and can be acquired with our mind alone, actual skills development is always something we learn experientially, and that requires repeated practice.

By doing the tasks we will improve the skills we have, and acquire new ones. And as we get better at those skills, the tasks themselves will become gradually easier. It is important to be aware of this before hand, because it is tough medicine to force ourselves close to two notches down men even when it is for our benefit. Of course, anyone who doesn't like it has my sympathy, because I wouldn't either.

That is why most writers of relationship psychology discreetly leave this thorny issue in the too hard basket. They do so by pretending it does not exist, on the hope of producing a more popular book. In so doing, they are effectively colluding with readers in their avoidance or denial of inconvenient truths. It is also clear to me that some writers ignore this matter because they are in denial themselves, or because they don't understand it.

We have all heard about the king who dealt with the bad news by killing the messenger. Similarly, some readers might deal with their dislike of the proposed plan by claiming or wishing to believe that this is a bad book. They may prefer to continue escaping with trashy romantic novels, feel-good movies and TV serials. Or worst of all by consulting psychics, clairvoyants, numerologists or other smooth operators, who will keep predicting whatever their customers want to hear as long as they keep paying.

The problem with all unrealistic options is that they subtly but perniciously encourage us to keep hoping we will find what we want by continuing to look until we get lucky. Worse still, they discourage us from doing our own thinking, thereby obstructing self-other awareness, common sense and every other aspect of personal development. The choice between becoming smarter or hanging onto outdated fantasies is ours, … and so are the consequences.

Other advantages of implementing the Action Plan

In addition to moving us towards finding a man who is right for us, relating with two notches down men will help us develop further our existing relationship management skills. These men are used to seeing us as unattainable, and that makes it more likely we will be genuinely offered something permanent. Depending on the personality of the man it might come with a bunch of red roses, an expensive gift, a heartfelt declaration of love, a promise of lifelong devotion, or other equally terrifying alternatives.

Therefore and first of all we need to be mentally prepared not to panic when it happens, and secondly to say no in an appropriate and supportive way. That would be not only to protect a man whose heart will be in pain, but also to safeguard the integrity of our self respect and sense of control over our relationships. If it is true, we may wish to say that we appreciate his good qualities and have enjoyed his company, but do not feel strongly enough to consider something permanent or necessarily long term.

We will need to remind him that we did say at the beginning that it could be temporary. And if he cannot take it, perhaps conclude that the relationship has reached the point where we regretfully think it has to end. Or we may cruise along with his consent if he has understood, accepted the limits, and can manage his own feelings without overburdening himself or us.

In such case the relationship may eventually change into seeing each other occasionally and without expectations of anything permanent. Or into a plain but trusting friendship if circumstances are appropriate, sometimes after a temporary total break for a while. Having a friend we can trust on the other side of the fence could be interesting and useful because, if he is wise and well balanced, interaction with him may enrich our understanding of people and situations by listening to a male perspective.

Another advantage is that it is comparatively easy for a man to get information about another man as part of a casual conversation, or for a woman about another woman, and that could come in handy. For example I have at times discreetly obtained information from a man about himself, for an interested friend who knew she could trust me, and then organized an "unintentional" introduction.

Developing our skills at being kind towards two notches down men can have other benefits too. We will have learned to appreciate a broader range of male qualities, and feel in our heart in addition to knowing it in our head, that most men aren't bastards or most women saints. We may even have to support a man who cannot hold his tears, which can be unsettling. The experience will make us less likely to have to rely on rules or stereotypes, which suggest an inability to trust our own judgment, and to realize instead the importance of understanding each person as an individual.

Dealing appropriately with the pain of men will bring balance and perspective into those times when we ourselves have been rejected. Hurting will still hurt, but we will become more confident that we can manage and resolve it well enough within a reasonable time. As a result, our fear of getting hurt is likely to diminish. That will make us better able to dare take the risk of loving a man who is worthy, because by now we are sure we can trust our strength to survive in good shape if at some point it has to end.

Unshackling ourselves from excessive fear of getting hurt in relationships is a wonderfully liberating experience. It begins due to the fact that whether a man is trustworthy becomes almost irrelevant. That is because we have developed confidence in our ability to understand men's minds and hearts, as well as ours, more completely and accurately than ever before.

Therefore it doesn't matter anymore whether a man tries to deceive us, or knowing he will grow cooler after some time, because we are likely to see the situation clearly and assess him correctly. We also understand that the cost of a mistake, if we happen to make it, will be compensated by it becoming an additional valuable learning experience. This would add to our reservoir of wisdom, and make us better evaluators the next time around.

Implementing the Action Plan is not as unfair on the man as it sounds, because we could surprise ourselves. Once we have known him for a while and experienced the feeling of being loved, cared for and wanted permanently, his imperfections may not matter that much anymore. Not in the context that we feel increasingly better in his company, despite the fact that it began with us thinking and feeling that he looked no better than barely acceptable.

Chances are that, if he is a good man, the more we get to know him the more we will like him. Especially when remembering what we put ourselves through, struggling to be loved by men who were never going to, or turned out to be wrong for various initially unnoticed or ignored reasons. Who knows whether we might fall for Mr. two notches down, before we have time to drop him in order to try it out with a one notch down man. I have seen it happen, and understood exactly why it worked.

All this serious talk about one or two notches down men reminds me of my own observations about how women in singles venues classify us men, based on something as superficial as appearance. It seems we are seen as belonging to one of four categories: The kissable, the acceptable, the untouchable, and the ones who if they agree to dance with once in a while they are guaranteed to go to Heaven.

Of course, there are some good news and some bad news about what category we all belong to, and they are both the same: Most of us belong to all four categories, which means that for some we are an unattainable dream and for others just a pushover. Yep, observing and gossiping in the mature singles jungle can be fun. And in such a hazy and emotionally destabilizing environment full of hopes and disappointments, humor can help us to survive.

The risks and potential of the Action Plan

Our natural resistance to opening the gate to two notches down men may lead to us pretend that someone fits into that category, when we know he is better than that. On the other hand hopefully, we are determined not to cheat in order to make it work. Therefore we take on the considerable effort of dating men who are two notches down, and in due course just one notch down from what we would have accepted earlier, if only for the sake of seeing if anything good comes out of it.

But we need to be prepared for the possibility that some one notch down man might commit the absurdly foolish and utterly despicable outrage of rejecting wonderful us. This is when the really difficult side of Part 2 needs to kick in. It boils down to making a serious and determined effort to learn the lessons, even if distressing, because doing so is for our benefit.

First of all we need to resist the temptation of indignantly blaming our at least not normal and probably stupid target man, men in general, or some woman or other outside factor. Not blaming opens for us the option of recognizing how we might be contributing to creating such outcomes, and some possibilities were discussed in Stage 4, including most importantly under the heading *Are we giving men negative messages without realizing it?*

If the man is intelligent, it would be worth making the most of it by trying to understand his reasons through a few friendly chats. Asking directly might not work if he is nice, because he could choose not tell in order to protect us. The worst thing we could do is to plaster over our pain with anger and blame, or by having nothing further whatsoever to do with him. Almost as bad is to save face by saying we don't understand. Men use this excuse quite often, by claiming that nobody can understand women and leaving it at that, in order to avoid anxiety arousing self scrutiny.

The way we choose to manage these situations is a critical factor in determining whether or not we learn from experience. If we are able to we will become smarter with every disappointment, and if we don't we remain stuck. In other words, we will in all probability keep repeating the same or comparable mistakes. And just hoping for better luck is not going to get us anywhere, because if that hasn't worked in all these years, it is unlikely it will anytime soon.

It is an unfortunate fact of life that strong emotions tend to overrun common sense and lead us into making errors of judgment, whenever we are hurting from a sentimental disappointment. This is a side of human nature we just have to accept. Therefore it is good to be prepared, in order to minimize the risk of costly mistakes. We can prepare by anticipating various possible outcomes while our head is still cool and our heart steady, so as to work out beforehand how to respond constructively to whatever might happen.

We need to be very careful about these things. Counterproductive behaviors are a tempting escape in the short term, and disastrous in the longer term. This is a central issue, and its importance needs to be emphasized. It is perfectly possible that the man with whom it didn't work could be plain stupid, emotionally unbalanced, an ordinary user, certifiable bastard, alcoholic, or unsuitable in some other way. That would be unquestionably all his responsibility, except for the minor point that we chose him in the first place.

Of course I wasn't serious about such point being "minor", because it is very much *the* major point. Let's us begin by considering the probability that people with a significant personality problem need to be in partial denial at the very least, in order to cope. In addition to that, they would most likely want to hide it by lying. Being only human we may simply not have realized, or perhaps were taken in.

But in the final analysis, it was us alone who failed to notice something we should have. And worse, there may be the alarming realization that he happens to be the last of a number of men we went for who turned out to be inappropriate. Probably in preference to less glowing or appealing men, who might well have been much better husband material. If when it comes to choosing men poorly we recognize a pattern, the question of doing so wisely becomes essential and deserves an elaboration.

We all know there is more to satisfying relationships than looks or money, the problem being that too often we know it in theory rather than in terms of the actual choices we make. We tend to be emotional first and rational second, with the inevitably frequent bad outcomes. So, a different way of understanding the Action Plan is as the manner by which we bring enough reason into the emotional animal inside us.

The reason needed to appreciate that if we sense something might be unsuitable or significantly wrong with the personality or circumstances of the man, we should not brush it aside, because love will not resolve it. And while we have to find his appearance at least acceptable, if he doesn't have enough crumpled edges but wants us, it is likely he will only do so for a limited time or that there is something not entirely right still to come to the surface.

In all probability we will need enough experiences and careful reflection, to work out what are going to be for us the realistic parameters of a productive medium. The need to have experiences and manage them constructively in order to learn, is another reason why risking entering into sensible relationships makes sense. Rather than avoiding them for fear of getting hurt, or of hurting others unless we are fairly sure they are excessively vulnerable.

If we haven't thought these things through, once we are in a relationship and tensions begin to develop, we could become confused and unsettled. In that state of mind it may be difficult to ascertain the difference between serious personality problems and more ordinary peculiarities such as introversion versus extraversion.

The above difference was discussed under the heading *The four categories of inherent higher human needs*, and it may lead for example to the partner who likes to socialize more thinking the other is too much of a homebody, or vice versa. As mentioned there, peculiarities are usually not a good enough reason to dismiss an otherwise potentially good partner, except in the unlikely case that his and ours create tensions significant enough to threaten the viability of the relationship.

When they do, the emotionally uninvolved and possibly more objective perceptions of a competent therapist could be useful to a couple. But when both partners have a reasonably well balanced personality and generosity of spirit, these tensions tend to be negotiated down by the couple alone, to a point where they become quite tolerable.

However, the issue may be one of personality problems. And for the sake of honesty I need to be bold enough to risk offending, by asking whether it might be us who have one. This possibility feels invariably threatening, and it is always difficult to ascertain whether that is the case.

One clue is if several potential or actual relationships could not take off or were ended by the men involved, although they were nice enough and not too handsome. Another is if someone we consider wise and knows us well thinks we are too picky, indecisive, or in other ways fully or partly responsible for what has been happening. One of the biggest difficulties in such situation is that because we have always been as we are, we lack a good internal frame of reference that would allow us to compare different ways of being.

If we were able to though, we would appreciate how we could feel, think and behave differently. But that rarely happens, because it is a bit like trying to understand the concept of color for somebody who is blind from birth. Except that the real blind always wants to see, while nobody is more "blind" than those who are too afraid to look. That could easily be us, if realistically or otherwise we believe that what is going to be found if we examined ourselves deeper and closer feels too alarming to contemplate.

Asking friends if they think we might benefit from personal development is fraught with danger. Because if they do and say so, our knee jerk reaction to what is likely to be felt and thought of as an unfair assessment could include defending our denial. That may well happen if our sense of identity and self esteem are very contingent, because this would make us excessively vulnerable to criticism, which may feel too threatening as well as an unbearable injustice.

If we do ask, some friends would want to be helpful but don't know how. Others will realize the risk to the friendship or the futility of trying, and stay clear. They have learned from experience that attempting to help people with certain kinds of blind spots can be painstakingly lengthy and difficult. The personality features involved are likely to be rather entrenched as well as hard to shift, and smart friends can sense that trying to fix such things is not a job for civilians.

Should we conclude it is possible that we might have some minor but troublesome personality feature, one way of moving towards improvement is by reading this book and understanding it well enough. If we have already done that, keeping a close eye on ourselves when we are in an intimate relationship may help. If we are lucky enough to have a genuinely wise friend who can be trusted, discussing things may be worth a try. Doing it with a good therapist for long enough may well help, if we can find and afford one.

STAGE 8a

ENSURING IT WORKS FOR LIFE:

Some important things to know and to avoid

Some important things to know

If we think about the emotional side of the personalities of most women as having a wide variety of colors, those of most men by comparison are black and white with a few shades of gray. This shows through women's generally superior perceptions about subtler feelings and the skills needed to express them, as elaborated in Stage 5 under *Smaller problems*. That is not a putdown on us men, but merely a statement of fact about gender differences.

However, this needs to be accompanied by an appreciation that each gender has its own strengths and vulnerabilities. They are genetically and hormonally based, although influenced by many factors such as family upbringing, social and personal circumstances, life experiences, education, intelligence, age, work. unexpected events, etc. Such features and experiences enable some men and women to outgrow the limiting propensities of their gender, partly by absorbing or developing many of the strengths of the other, thereby becoming exceptionally well rounded individuals.

Because in general women are more emotionally sophisticated, we are correspondingly more complicated. Therefore so is the workload our man takes on when he commits to loving us permanently, and thereby to doing his bit by contributing in whatever way he can to us being contented and happy. That workload is made more difficult for the average man, because his toolbox for understanding and managing his own and other people's feelings is in most cases significantly smaller than ours.

Even if our man is nice and we love him, he has differences and imperfections to be tolerated. We do it willingly, especially if he compensates with qualities and in ways which are important to us. If we are kind, smart and lucky, he may love us for life. But we know we have our flaws, vulnerabilities and pet peeves which he too has to live with.

Then there are the inevitable differences in preferences about all sorts of things inside and outside the bedroom. They do not require forgiveness because there is nothing to forgive, but still have to be accepted without resentment and accommodated to by both partners. There are also all kinds of life stresses, which put a strain on everyone's patience.

We are getting older too, which will make us gradually less sexually appealing, except possibly in the eyes of a man who loves us because we are very deep in his heart. So, how do we earn and maintain the tolerance and love we like and want from our man? Common sense tells us that if a couple have mutual respect, a good friendship, plus quality physical and emotional intimacy, the relationship is likely to work well enough despite the usual difficulties with money, sex, children, work, in-laws, etc.

However, knowing all the above does not save the approximately half of marriages which divorce (counting also de-facto ones), despite both partners starting with the belief that it wasn't going to happen to them. I discussed in Stage 5 how around three quarters of the population have the contingent kind of personality and self esteem which could benefit significantly from further development, and I have no doubt this is an important reason why hard-to-fix relationship problems are normal and inevitable.

Given all the above realities, increasing the chances of making a relationship work for life has to begin with a recognition that if we have found and married a nice person and are so ourselves, this may still not be enough to ensure the relationship will remain fulfilling. One reason is that if just one of the partners is towards the lower end of the personality and self esteem health continuum, the management of differences in preferences about all sorts of things may become anywhere from challenging to very difficult.

This would be over and above the fact that being towards the lower end of that continuum makes it more likely that expectations will have been unrealistic to begin with. That in itself is bound to result in greater disillusionment, which a better appreciation of reality would have avoided. If on the other hand both partners have sufficiently developed personality and self esteem, they may be able to adapt and manage differences and changes in ways which enable the relationship to survive and thrive.

But for them too, it is important to anticipate (1) *Predictable stress periods and pressure points,* so as to take corrective action in time by adequately managing the risk of inadvertently or otherwise falling into behaviors likely to cause problems. Most women would also strengthen themselves and benefit their relationship by developing a better appreciation about (2) *The role of sex in men's non-sexual needs,* and about the extent and effects of (3) *The gradual turnaround in gender relationship power.*

I discuss those three issues next under their own subheadings. In addition, there are very damaging behaviors we should be especially careful to avoid, which some women (*and men*) can drift into over the years almost unnoticeably slowly, without due consideration about the consequences. These include (4) *Neglect of care and domestic abuse,* (5) *Destructive complaints,* and (6) *Marital sadism.* I discuss these last three further below also in their own subheadings, under the main heading *Some important things to avoid.*

Predictable stress periods and pressure points

Whatever partners understand love to be, it is easy in the early days of mutual discovery and novel sexual attraction. However it often becomes difficult when life changes create pressures, as testified by the rate of divorce and dissatisfaction levels within many surviving marriages. But even if there are no unexpected big changes in circumstances or significant personality problems, most relationships still go through a number of predictable stress periods.

These begin with the adaptations and compromises needed during the first year of living together, when unspoken rules are being established about how the relationship is to function on a day to day basis. If the couple decides to have children, further stress periods will come with pregnancy, the birth of the first child, the youngest one starting school, children's adolescence, and the last child leaving home. Then there is retirement from work and deciding what to do together and apart with all that free time and less money, and finally the physical and sometimes mental decline with advancing age.

In many couples there is also a reactivation of sexual, identity and/or relational needs by at least one partner, when the expression of such needs has been hindered for too long. That may have happened due to the imperatives of parenting or the expectations and limitations of monogamy. Especially if the sexual and friendship sides of the relationship have been less than good, it may lead to sexual or emotional involvement with a third party.

Additional concerns for people in second marriages include children's reactions to a natural parent having a relationship or living with a new partner. And because once bitten twice shy, any issues associated with a previous marriage may become delicate or fraught with tension, unless they have been fully discussed and agreed upon. For example time with our children or his, and financial arrangements.

In addition to predictable stress periods and because partners have different preferences about many things, all relationships are bound to experience other pressure points. There may be also unforeseen events such as an accident, illness or loss of a job. The hardest issue is usually when a partner we care about wants us to change in a way we do not want.

For example, we might be asked to accept our partner's involvement in friendships where we are not expected to participate, and which might lead to or involve an affair. Or to try out a new sexual practice we do not feel comfortable with. When we feel that pressure, good enough core components of personality and self esteem will make it easier for us to at least discuss whatever comes up with equanimity, by retaining our balance even if we feel that our relationship, identity or integrity are under threat.

If the pressure we are under is intense, a healthy personality and self esteem give us flexibility with non aggressive strength. They enable us to regulate anxiety and contain it within, so that our stress will not spill over to degrade the quality of the relationship. That is, they give us the capacity to behave in a calm rather than angry way, and to talk things over without making matters worse despite being in the midst of an emotional storm.

In other words, we are able not to overreact to very stressful situations including someone else's overreactions, thereby avoiding the additional damage which would result from disrespect or emotional distance. We would be able to so regardless of what our partner or anyone else wants us to feel, do, or stop feeling or doing. Being only human, behaving with this level of self discipline can take its toll.

But a healthy personality will enable us to endure the discomfort, because we know that doing so for a good reason is part of what it takes to be a fully functioning human being. If we think about what all that requires us to do, and considering the definitions and discussions on the six core components of personality and self esteem, it is clear that the above interactions involve most or all of them simultaneously or within a short period of time.

For example, a strong conviction of worthiness enables us to remain confident about being a worthy person when we make mistakes or someone points out our imperfections. Self-other acceptance and self-other awareness mean that we will not be shocked or particularly surprised by anything anyone says or does. Our self confidence will give us the security of knowing that on balance we are probably adopting the best among alternative actions or reactions, even if there is little time to think it through.

Self-other respect will stop us from responding in kind to an annoyed or angry partner out of control. Whichever way we choose to deal with it therefore, will probably be measured and for a sensible reason. A solid sense of identity and meaning will contribute to us not feeling unduly unsettled by anything except possibly for a short or limited time, because we have a realistic understanding of who and how we and others are, and also of our place in life and on the larger scheme of things.

The role of sex in men's non-sexual needs

We have heard more times than we can remember that men only want one thing, but we know by now that there is a lot more to it than that. It is often heard in marriage counseling circles that good sex amounts to around 10% of a satisfying relationship, but bad sex can become 90% of the problem. To put it differently, while relationships are about much more than sex, it continues to be very important and has the potential to become the central issue.

That is because in addition to being a physical need, sex facilitates the fulfillment of other needs, especially for men. These include love and emotional support, including most importantly the soothing comfort of regular touching and being touched, all of which generate trust and commitment. And therefore when sex goes bad or is avoided, a lot more than just sex is being lost.

The loss is felt more strongly by men, because apart from the greater sexual urgency which nature has imposed on them, they have to bear the consequences of the prevailing cultural and genetically influenced straightjackets of male upbringing. These make it difficult for them to meet certain natural needs in a non sexual context. One of the most important such needs is to release the pressure created by not feeling able to fully express or admit certain emotional needs and vulnerabilities, to other people and even to themselves.

Much of this pressure is indirectly managed and largely washed away in a good relationship through tenderness and touching during sex with a trusted companion, plus the naturally occurring pillow talk which may follow if either partner needs it. Admitting the longing to give and receive non sexual tenderness and touch, to needing emotional support, or to experiencing fear or any form of weakness or insecurity, are examples of what most men have been brainwashed to suppress in order to see themselves as "proper" men.

Of course, the above and what follows below are generalizations which apply to most people, but in order to understand individuals we need to appreciate their unique personalities and the contexts in which they live. A central feature of a healthy personality is the capacity to know and accept ourselves and others in a deeper way and in all dimensions of our humanity.

As we move up through the continuum of personality and self esteem development, there will be a growing proportion of men who have been able to transcend their culturally and genetically influenced emotional straitjackets. This is bound to make them correspondingly less dependent on sex as a way of meeting important non sexual needs.

But for the vast majority of average men, a nice sexual relationship contributes to them unconsciously maintaining the integrity of what they experience as the manly component of their identity. That is because certain needs and vulnerabilities can continue to be ignored or denied, as long as they are being satisfied and healed in an indirect face saving way, which can then be rationalized as straightjacket-compatible good sex.

Furthermore, good sex means such men can also see themselves as having what it takes to "provide" it, which is another side of their identity they are then able to feel competent about. It is true that men like and want the physical pleasure of sex for its own sake. But if that is all there was to it, they could get it through the good enough alternative of masturbation.

The purely physical side of the inferiority of this alternative would be compensated by sparing themselves from the complexities and difficulties of involvement in a relationship, having more free time for other interests, not having to look their best, getting it whenever they want, and possibly compensating for some of what was missing by loving their dog.

In contrast to such convoluted male needs and vulnerabilities, women have four distinct advantages which enable them to be less dependent on sex with a partner. The first is that with only a small fraction of the testosterone in men, most women feel a lot less sexual urgency. And to that extent, they are generally less physically deprived if relationship sex is not happening.

Second, cultural norms allow women to be vulnerable and express suffering in many visible ways, so releasing internal tensions. Third and in comparison to most men who tend to have less personal connections, most women are more social and relate to a wider circle of family and friends, who become a ready made source of emotional support in times of need.

And fourth, most women have an understanding of their feelings and a corresponding capacity to understand those of others, which is significantly superior to that of most men. And it is precisely those skills which are part of what it takes to manage relationship distress in a better way. Because of all the above, most women get off relatively lightly when relationship sex goes bad or is avoided, while most men feel deprived more intensely and in multiple ways.

This situation provides women with a temptation of easy retaliation and of attempting to control their partner whenever they feel hurt and annoyed with or without a valid reason, by withholding and rationing sex or the sweetness of it. Depending on the personality of the woman and the state of the relationship it can get a lot nastier than that too, and some variations are elaborated further below under the heading *Marital Sadism*.

But for now, the point to know and remember is that when women refuse sex to their partner without a legitimate reason, they can cause serious damage to the stability and eventually viability of the relationship. If such refusals develop into a pattern explained away by something as self centered as not feeling like it, they become a major reason why men feel chronically unloved and uncared for, and this will aggravate tensions.

Every man is likely to experience such situation as a major breach of the marriage "contract", whether or not that has ever been explicitly stated. If such state of affairs becomes an ongoing pattern, even men who once tolerated it may eventually leave never to return.

At the same time, not feeling like sex is different from disliking it. If there is a dislike of sex, this may or may not have anything to do with the man or the relationship, but it is a serious problem. It should be acknowledged and managed properly before it escalates into outright aversion, and finally becomes intractable to the point where divorce is the only way out.

The gradual turnaround in gender relationship power

The balance of gender relationship power changes so gradually that it is unnoticeable from year to year. But if we look at it in ten year periods from twenty to fifty for example, we can see that it undergoes a pronounced turnaround, and the more attractive the woman is the more drastic the change is likely to be. If a woman is unaware or chooses to ignore this power shift, it is probably only a matter of time before she will have a collision against the new reality, often with serious consequences.

That is why I feel duty bound to bring up this uncomfortable issue, on the hope that doing so will assist women in making wiser decisions while there is still time. If we squander that limited time through unwise choices, the compromises needed to find a nice man who will love us for life are likely to become increasingly difficult as we get older. Until finally, making do with our hobbies, friends, grandchildren, cat and pot plants begins to look like a better option, although perhaps a sadder and lonelier one.

At around twenty there is a big imbalance of relationship power in favor of women. Time is on their side, and their sexual needs are much less urgent than those of the testosterone dripping young men they mix with. The latter's unrelenting cravings, frustrations and fantasies are partly expressed through the kind of jokes they like. For example, *Why do women like wearing high heel shoes? Because they are fed up of being kissed in the forehead.*

Attractive women get more dates, propositions and proposals than they know what to do with. Average looking women do quite well too, and smart women who are less fortunate in terms of appearance can also punch above their weight. Such power can very easily be abused at any age, often without a full appreciation of the damage it may cause. This is more likely to happen when we have a problematic personality, a common manifestation of which is an overblown sense of entitlement with concomitant unrealistic expectations about what our chosen man should be, become, or provide.

When he can't or refuses to we may feel resentful and hard done by, and believe it is all his fault. We may ratchet up the pressure in various ways, or just throw our frustration and anger at him because he is an available target over whom we have power. That often includes disregarding our sexual or caring responsibilities, and most women who neglect their partner are able to get away with it for some years, especially in their twenties. Unfortunately trouble looms in the horizon, because even very nice men are likely to run out of patience, eventually out of hope, and finally out of love.

By around thirty the balance of gender relationship power has generally begun to level off, as men's continuing greater need for sex is counterbalanced by women with children or planning them seeking to secure a committed relationship or to avoid the deterioration of an existing one. But when it comes to choosing a partner, the limited maturity and life experience people still have at that age means their understanding of what makes a person "nice" is incomplete, and appearance tends to be what matters most.

Men and women often convince themselves that someone they find attractive who seems to like them back will make a good life partner. And so, they begin living together or tie the knot. Any warning signs are usually brushed aside, on the expectation that problems can be solved or will go away through the magic of mutual love and commitment.

From around forty and except for unattractive uneducated men at the bottom of the socioeconomic ladder and uncommonly attractive women, relationship power is generally beginning to tilt in favor of men for a number of reasons. The first is the common perception that the passage of time is harsher on women, who are by now well aware that their major draw card of physical attractiveness will be decreasing during their forties, and continuing to do so at an increasingly faster rate in their fifties.

Consequently, security about being loved becomes more important and women begin to feel a much stronger need for a man who will keep loving them as they get older, in addition to hopefully being nice and attractive. Many women also become more interested in sex by this time, having gained experience and lost inhibitions, while men of a compatible age are no longer as flooded with testosterone as they were in their twenties. This brings about a lesser disparity in sexual desire, correspondingly reducing further women' sexual power over men, and with it their overall relationship power.

At this age people's personalities are better defined and more women are able to recognize which qualities in a man are likely to make a difference, especially if they left their first husband due to personality problems or limitations. Furthermore, because most women mature faster and become wiser than most men of similar age, they find more emotional compatibility with older men, who by being so have had more time to catch up.

As men grow older and wiser they tend to develop a style of intimate relating closer to that of women, creating additional emotional compatibility. For all the above reasons, a frequent outcome of the search for a suitable man by women in their forties is to choose one who might be quite a bit older. However some are still not self aware enough to understand what their deeper needs are. This is why even those whose attractiveness gives them many options, may not have the wisdom to choose a true companion with whom they could feel genuinely contented and secure.

The biggest danger is to repeat the mistake we made the first times around, which is to allow ourselves to be too influenced by attractiveness plus the hope it will turn out right. Again, this may lead to choosing without enough understanding of what combination of partner features, qualities and imperfections are needed to increase the long term chances of relationship satisfaction and security, given our own characteristics, strengths, limitations, wishes and fears. In other words given who we are and what we really need, as against what we may superficially want or might like to dream about.

By fifty the tables have definitely turned. Every woman without a permanent partner knows that she is at significant risk of missing the boat, and that the risk increases every year. Those who were uncommonly attractive when younger are also aware that their previous advantage does not work as well anymore, and is now dissipating faster than ever.

They can see men who probably would have been deliriously happy to be with them when they were all in their twenties or thirties, who are now looking at and connecting with much younger competitors. Many women who left an unsatisfactory marriage many years earlier never expected to be still unattached at this age. They find themselves a little bewildered at why it is so difficult to find a nice man willing to love them permanently, and at how all those years went by.

The latter may be hard to take, but it is not difficult to understand. The issues have been discussed at some length in Stage 4, but it is worth recapitulating. Every major relationship which does not survive began with a period of searching, followed by one of trying it out, one of deterioration ending in breakup, and then another of recovery. By the time it is all over and we are ready for the next search, it is not uncommon to have used up anywhere between one and several years, and sometimes quite a few years.

Even with less serious "trials" or "adventures" the process can easily take from some months to a year, and it all adds up. In addition, as we accumulate sentimental disappointments our morale decreases, because we become increasingly aware about the difficulty of finding a permanent partner we can be happy with. Consequently every new serious trial risks a greater degree of pain if it doesn't work, plus a longer recovery period. And every new start after that is likely to come with a heavier heart.

When underdeveloped core components or personality problems are not a significant issue in either potential partner, there is one reason which stands out as to why some women keep failing in their search for a satisfying permanent relationship. As they get older, some women's belief about the age difference compromise which may need to be made becomes gradually out of date, when compared to that accepted by most women who actually succeed in finding a good man.

For example, most women in their twenties consider that an acceptable man can be up to around five years older. Thirty years later in their fifties, the reality of what actually happens in most relationships destined to succeed, suggests that a ten to fifteen year difference is almost a necessity. That is the case for most women who want a good probability of being permanently loved, by a man who no longer has to be ideal, but still has to be NUSSC (Not Unattractive, Sane, Solvent and Compatible).

At this point I am prepared to make a possibly oversimplified generalization for the sake of clarity, again without forgetting that generalizations may not apply to individual cases. The difference between none to five years older at twenty and ten to fifteen years at fifty is ten years, which accumulates gradually over a thirty year period. A ten year difference spread over those thirty years gives us an ongoing increase of four months per year, in the age of available NUSSC men who in their heart and mind may consider us permanent relationship material.

I said "in their heart and mind" advisedly, to differentiate them from those less honest NUSSC men closer to our own age, who through lies by omission are willing to collude with our wishful thinking while it suits them. The above figures mean that every three years one extra year is added to the age gap, beginning to count from zero to five years older when we were twenty.

This may be the hypothetical increase in the rate of age difference we have to keep in mind, in order to find a NUSSC man who will love us permanently. It can be seen clearly in Table C (next page), which has been calculated using the above figures. It shows that if we are for example fifty and looking for a NUSSC man who will want us permanently and is no more than five years older or so, our willingness to compromise in terms of age is seriously out of date.

It is worth repeating that Table C is derived from the perspective of what observably happens in many successful relationships, and not from wishful thinking or from what might be politically correct. If we are fifty and want to stick with a five year maximum age difference in a man who also has to be NUSSC, that is absolutely our right. But we are going to need a lot of luck to find a relationship which is both good enough plus likely to last for life.

I know! I know! Love isn't fair for mature unattached women, or at least it feels that way, and this is an unpleasant reality which we are eventually forced to accept. More precisely, the gender power imbalance which favored women in their twenties, especially attractive women, gradually turns around in favor of NUSSC men by the time the same women reach fifty. If these women stick to their age difference expectations from thirty, twenty or even ten years earlier, they could be pricing themselves out of the market.

The age gap suggested in Table C does not apply to women who have been married to the same man for decades, provided their marriage has been at least reasonably nice all along. That is because through all those years a myriad of strong and resilient bonds have been formed through quality tender loving care, friendship and sex. These are part of their shared sense of identity and loyalty to each other, which both partners value.

Neither would want to break that, because they feel their marriage has

Table C

Typical AGE GAPS between women and the NUSSC men they tend to get as permanent partners

(NUSSC: Not Unattractive, Sane, Solvent and Compatible)

Age of woman	Age of NUSSC man	Age gap
20	20-25	0-5
23	24-29	1-6
26	28-33	2-7
29	32-37	3-8
32	36-41	4-9
35	40-45	5-10
38	44-49	6-11
41	48-53	7-12
44	52-57	8-13
47	56-61	9-14
50	60-65	10-15

been good and continues to be. Or as is more often heard, they still love each other and probably always will. Of course there may be joint children and property too. But neither of these is enough to maintain commitment, when there has been something seriously wrong with the central issues regarding caring, friendship and sex.

Nobody knows how the future will turn out, but the radical shift in the balance of gender relationship power between the twenties and fifties is not only predictable but very visible for any woman to look and see. Of course not every woman wants or dares to, and one of the more striking examples of collective denial I have ever witnessed happened in a workshop I attended early in my career, where everyone except me were women.

At some point during the coffee break someone commented about how middle aged men sometimes leave their wives for a younger woman, and other group members quickly joined the conversation. Very soon a consensus emerged that the reason they do it is because younger women, being less mature and more impressionable, can still be admiring of them.

Supposedly, that makes those men feel more competent and secure with a younger woman than they ever did with their wives, with whom they had nowhere to hide because they knew their husbands inside out. This could well be true as a general statement, because most men's personalities may not be particularly well developed and their self esteem is likely to be of the contingent variety, regardless of external symbols of success.

So, there was nothing wrong with what those women were saying. Except that as they commented or nodded in agreement during the general conversation, nobody mentioned that a second and likely reason might be that younger women look prettier because they are younger. And that those husbands are so attracted by the beauty of their youth plus their longing for the secure affection of the man, that some among them choose to leave their wives, especially if their marriage had been chronically unsatisfying.

On observing the whole thing with mounting interest, I was first rather baffled by the fact that none of these women mentioned the second and rather obvious probable reason. But as their conversation progressed, it became increasingly clear to me that all of them could be feeling a little threatened about that reality. By looking the other way they were colluding in a collective exercise of mutual support through jointly reinforced "denial", for the purpose of managing their underlying anxieties. That is, anxieties about the possibility that one day the same thing might happen to them.

As already mentioned, "denial" is a natural and widely used mechanism of psychological defense, which can be healthy and appropriate in the short term reduction of intense anxiety or distress. But depending on denial or its milder more conscious cousin of "avoidance" as an ongoing coping strategy, can weaken our grip on reality. That would damage personality and self esteem health, our ability to search effectively for a good partner, and to keep his love for life if we already have one.

For example, avoidance in the form of disregarding clues about significant differences or problems can cause us to choose the wrong man. Afterwards, denial and avoidance will continue to cause difficulties by increasing the risk of us making further questionable decisions, over the myriad of small issues and some big ones which are part of every marriage.

That is critical, because the cumulative effect of those day to day choices will be a major factor contributing to the ultimate success or failure of a relationship. If dissatisfactions become ongoing they are likely to pile up and combine with the shifting balance of relationship power, in moving the partners towards a greater likelihood of eventual breakup.

Some important things to avoid

Neglect of care and domestic abuse

Living together with an intimate partner is replete with situations which lend themselves to expressions of love and support, but also to neglect of care and domestic abuse. Any woman aspiring to a permanent quality loving relationship needs to be alert about some dangers which she might be primarily responsible for bringing about.

Marital tensions are usually a complex matter and each case needs to be considered individually, but some generalizations can be useful as a starting point. A common example opened to positive or negative consequences arises when our man needs or wants sex more often than we do, because this gives us the power to be sweet and loving or to neglect our care by keeping him sexually frustrated and emotionally dissatisfied.

This does not mean we have a duty to have sex when we don't want to, because we are nobody's property. On the other hand, both partners have entered into a usually implied voluntary agreement to care for each other in whatever ways they are able to, and if either fails to do so frequently or without a good reason, the other will sooner or later begin to resent it.

In addition and just as there are men like that, there are women with a limited capacity to love or unrealistic beliefs about what it actually is and involves. And as mentioned earlier, some such women may use the granting or withholding of sex as a means for exercising power in order to control their partner and the relationship.

The intention behind using sexual power may be to retaliate for anger generated by legitimate dissatisfactions, or by features within their personality but blamed on the partner. It may also be used to satisfy a controlling nature, or as a means of enforcing economic exploitation as in the example below.

A woman may become used to this way of living, and is then taken aback when often after many years of what her husband has experienced as sexual and emotional neglect, he finally has an affair. If he feels loved and cared for by the new woman, the contrast with his wife's treatment will be striking, and he is likely to divorce regardless of promises to change or consequences to their children.

"You have never loved me", one such man about to leave told his wife in front of me. "For you I was only a provider, and never good enough in your opinion". "She is as ugly as a dog", her supportive ten year old told the distraught mum when she and her little brother retuned from their first weekend with dad, who was by then living with the new woman. Her being less attractive than his wife made no difference, and he was gone never to return.

One common example of women's domestic abuse arises from the fact that most of us have a better developed emotional intelligence and are more articulate and skillful than our men when discussing friction points in the relationship. At the healthier and wiser end of the continuum that opens the option of supporting our partner and the relationship, by helping without insulting. While at the worst end, we could deliberately outtalk him into a corner over every big or little dispute.

Some of us may be aware of times when we made him feel like a scolded misbehaving child, or belittled him as an inadequate or stupid adult, although he may actually be nice and smart. And then topped it off by accusing him of refusing to talk about the relationship when he retreated defeated or annoyed into his garage, his television, or the nearest drinking venue. This gave us the additional gratification of giving him a parting kick by having had the last word, which unfortunately made us feel even more self righteous.

There are other situations when repeated respectful talking is not bringing about the changes we want. Unfortunately it is not unusual for a chronically frustrated woman to use the very dangerous strategy of refusing sex as a last ditch alternative to ultimately having to divorce, in order to force her man to change about what she considers her justified dissatisfactions. "As long as I open my legs he is all right", a very annoyed woman told me in front of her husband during their first interview. This is a situation to be avoided if at all possible. But if it is done, there should be definitely no insult added to injury by shouting, sarcasm or contempt.

Men and women who want to be loved by a partner need to take responsibility for avoiding such destructive weapons. It is true that we may have only limited control over how we **feel**, especially in the heat of the moment. However we all have complete control over how we **behave**. Feeling angry is definitely no excuse for the utter stupidity of disrespectfully rising our voice, insulting, or otherwise deliberately belittling the man or woman whose love we want to have … and have to earn.

Claiming that our disrespect or aggressiveness happened because of something the other person did or didn't do is a coward's copout, or a fool's. That remains the case whether we are a man or a woman, and even if the other party is behaving inappropriately. Hopefully it never got that bad with us. But when we feel under pressure or stressed and regardless of who or what the cause may be, it is very easy to fall into the temptation of abusing the power which our partner's love, need or commitment gives us.

And here is something men and women know but sometimes recklessly choose to ignore: In conventional warfare the side who wins more battles wins the war. But if we go to war with our partner, the more battles we win the more likely we are to lose the war. Because after the damage has been inflicted we cannot undo what was done or unsay what was said. We need to be careful, very careful in fact, because there could be many unexpressed dissatisfactions in addition to the ones we know about.

If the friction remains unresolved, many things a partner does or fails to do may be resented and quietly added to a tally of frustrations which will keep getting bigger and increasingly more difficult to bear. By the time we come to realize the full seriousness of the situation it could be too late to remedy it, because the accumulated resentment has become frozen as well as too big, and is therefore extremely difficult to dislodge.

One partner may come to the conclusion that the dissatisfactions will never be resolved due to entrenched personality problems or limitations in the other. He or she may then stop arguing or caring, and begins looking for a way out. This is the point of no return, from where an eventual breakup is almost inevitable. It may well be a desirable outcome when there are sensible reasons for it. But this is not always the case, although it may seem so at the time to the long dissatisfied partner who is about to pull the plug.

"I don't know why I divorced my husband", a woman told me after a number of subsequent relationships over many years had not gone well. She had never really understood how her own personality plus mistaken beliefs and day to day bad choices had contributed to their problems. Her unmet need for love and security plus increasing awareness about getting older had led to her becoming increasingly worried, and re-partnering with a man she felt was nowhere near as nice or attractive as her ex husband.

Another woman told me she divorced "because I didn't love him anymore", but found it difficult to be more specific when I asked. After eight years and many failed relationships she had not yet found a man she could love who also wanted her permanently. And by five years after that, she had become resigned to the likelihood of never finding one. "I haven't had sex for six years", she told me, "and I feel OK about it". Even if that was so about sex with a partner, would it have been true about living without the caring and companionship of a man who loved her?

As a result of their many attempts at trying for the "better" man they had been hoping to be loved by, both the above women had ended up with their hearts beaten to a pulp and couldn't take it anymore. Others are worse off, like the mid fifties woman who consulted me about a year after her divorce. She half told me and half admitted to herself, that she had driven her husband into divorce after decades of arguments and dissatisfaction. Much of the responsibility was hers, she said, for a number of ongoing friction points and quarrels over issues which she now realized were quite unimportant.

His exact words when telling her why he was leaving and never coming back, had been carved forever into her mind by raw pain and regret. I quote them for the sake of accuracy and realism, and as a warning to us all: "Living with you has been like living with a pile of goodies and a pile of shit. The pile of goodies has been too small and the pile of shit too big". I sensed very quickly that her real reason for seeing me was her overwhelming need to express the loneliness and despair which she was drowning in.

All I could do was listen, so that she could get it off her chest. It seemed she had been neglecting and abusing her partner for many years, and getting away with it. The imbalances in her personality had prevented her from realizing she was doing it at her own peril. That reality and its consequences had finally come crashing down on her, and by now she knew only too well that her loss was immense and irreversible.

Destructive complaints

It is desirable and perfectly legitimate within an intimate relationship to request changes we would like, as long as they are something which can be done, within reason. That of course, provided the request is made at the very least respectfully, and hopefully after taking care to have created an intimate context which reassures our partner about being loved even if he or she was not to grant our request.

However, when requests which we consider reasonable are about something important to us and have been repeatedly rejected or ignored, we can begin to feel frustrated. That is when some of us make the mistake of repeating the request in a way or tone of voice which is less than caring and considerate, or oozing annoyance. This is more likely if we fail to realize or accept the reasons why our partner finds it difficult to meet our request, and keeps ignoring or refusing it despite the resulting tension.

When we are unaware of what is going on under the surface, we could mistakenly conclude that our partner doesn't care due to being too self centered, and hence the frustration and escalation of conflict. If the matter is managed badly it could quite easily lead to one or both partners' reactions spiraling into a frame of mind where each feels mistreated. Once this point has been reached, a satisfactory resolution can become increasingly difficult.

Requests may change into increasingly firm demands. These may be resisted with corresponding determination, if the other partner can't meet them or experiences them as threatening or violating some value or conviction important to self respect, sense of identity or to how he/she wants to live life. An escalating pattern of complaint and counter complaint may set in, beginning an accumulating process of unresolved resentment, as illustrated at Diagram 6 in page 130, under the heading *Sum-total problems*.

Such complaints are no less damaging just because they happen to be indirect or denied. The husband in a couple who consulted me felt not only constantly pressured to provide more materially, but also unloved and uncared for. That was because whenever they had any strong disagreement she would withhold affection and sex. The couple owned their home, and he had always worked in jobs on a little under average earnings.

Throughout the marriage the wife had commented about how other couples had a better house, took nicer holidays, went to restaurants or cinemas more often, etc. He had attempted to get a better paying job over the years, but had now given up trying. With their two children being still under ten she decided against his wishes to keep a pregnancy with twins, and money had been tight ever since. Whenever he complained that comments about other people being better off made him feel bad, she justified it on the grounds that she was, she said, "only trying to motivate" him.

When relationships become distressed it is often the case that both partners are contributing to the problem, but not with this couple. There were indications the wife had a considerable propensity for envy due to an excessive concern about comparisons with others, emanating in turn from her very contingent self esteem and the issues underpinning it. She was also failing to accept responsibility for the financial consequences of her decision to have another two children, against his wishes.

Her complaints were destructive because they put more or less ongoing pressure for more material goods on a husband who could not provide them even after having tried his best. And also because she was habitually over controlling and punitive by means of abusing the power resulting from her lesser need for sex plus her husband's commitment to the marriage, whenever they had friction over money or any other issue.

Marital sadism

If the term "marital sadism" makes us shudder, that is because it should. Not only because it is atrocious, but perhaps because we feel unnervingly alarmed by the realization that at times we have inflicted it on our partner. Sadism goes beyond ordinary domestic neglect or abuse, in that it involves obtaining some kind of satisfaction by inflicting or observing suffering. And unfortunately, it is not uncommon.

Let's begin by acknowledging that the vast majority of couples who love each other do not engage in marital sadism. But also that not all partners love each other or not all the time, that some of them occasionally behave as if they hated each other, and that more than just a few actually hate each other. Marital sadism is a form of domestic violence, albeit very different from the indignation-arousing criminality of physical assault or the threat of it as a form of control by intimidation. This kind of sadism may be among the worst, although it does not happen in the vast majority of couples.

One of the most common examples of marital sadism occurs as an escalation of situations such as the one described under the previous subheading about outtalking, humiliating and blaming our partner often in a loud, disrespectful or angry way. It is probably the case that most women who do such things are not initially intending to inflict damage or enjoy their feeling of righteousness at "proving" him wrong.

It is often something unintended which happens in the tit for tat heat of the moment, as a result of accumulated unresolved frustration in both partners. That is an explanation but not a justification, just as more or less similar explanations by male perpetrators do not justify or diminish the criminality of whatever form of domestic violence they mete out.

Women who deliberately inflict such suffering on their husbands and enjoy their "victories", need to acknowledge the reality of what they do. They also need to accept responsibility for it, rather than resort to denial by way of diverting attention towards justificatory or blaming explanations. This kind of denial as an excuse for sadism can eventually result in the destruction of any residual happiness or the hope of it, and may quite easily over the years tilt the marriage towards a breakup.

When men and women realize they have overstepped the line to the point of deliberately harming their partner, many have the insight, sense of fairness, love and personal integrity to sincerely apologize and thereafter change their behavior permanently. That is what the late John Lennon was probably able to do, when as a by then more mature and wiser man he wrote the moving lyrics of the song "Jealous Guy", available in the Internet.

But of course, the personality underpinnings of bad behavior are not easy to change, which is why at times some men and women escalate conflict into undisputable sadism. There are disguised and often denied forms of sadism too, and they come in many forms. A couple who consulted me was atypical in the sense that she wanted sex more often than he did. As a result of that plus his uncaring attitude she was chronically sexually frustrated, as well as deprived of the love and emotional support expressed through nice sex.

One of the wife's complaints was that quite often when they had argued about something during the day her husband, she said, "parades himself at night in the bedroom without his underpants". This was in order to tease her sexually and aggravate her deprivation. He was of course well aware she knew that if she approached him sexually he would reject her, with the excuse he wasn't in the mood due to their earlier argument. She told me all that in his presence, and he did not dispute the events or his motivation.

Clearly he was doing it because he enjoyed seeing her suffer as punishment and retaliation for having argued with him, using the power to reject which her greater desire for sex gave him. I told them my reasons for describing his behavior as a form of marital sadism, and suggested they should consider the likely short and long term consequences of doing something about it versus doing nothing, in addition to looking at the underlying causes of marital distress.

Whenever two people have to agree for sex to happen, the decision whether to do it and how is always under the control of the partner who wants it less, and this gives him/her relationship power. Given that in most marriages husbands want sex more often than their wives, it would be reasonable to assume that for every man who inflicts the above kind of marital sadism, there must be quite a lot of women who do the same.

But outright or subtle sexual teasing for the purpose of aggravating our partner's deprivation and suffering is not the only way it is done. In a sad and funny case I heard about through my apartment window, as indeed would have all the neighbors, an obviously angry woman shouted repeatedly at her partner: "I am available".

A less striking but overtime just as damaging variant is when a woman agrees to sex, but without shouting or being sarcastic deliberately withholds the sweetness of it by making sure her partner knows she is not enjoying it. Or she may agree, but not in the manner or positions she knows her partner likes. Whatever the method and whether acknowledged or denied, both partners know exactly what is happening and how it is being done.

It is very easy for a self centered abuser to fall into the temptation of inflicting suffering for the satisfaction of retaliation, when he/she believes it can be done with impunity. To the extent that it provides some form of control to the perpetrator, it unbalances his/her personality even further.

Marital sadism is recklessly dangerous because it generates accumulating frustration in the victim, and the abuser will probably end up paying a high price sooner *and* later. That is because in addition to the immediate unhappiness and day to day reduction of good will it creates, it makes less likely that the couple will be able to work out a solution while there is still time to save the relationship.

This kind of sadism is the complete opposite of love. As defined in page 135, the first part of it is: "*a combination of mostly pleasant thoughts and feelings plus everything we do as a way of giving for the purpose of caring*". If the love and caring we have been giving is not being reciprocated we have every right to respectfully insist that the situation be remedied, and to ultimately leave the relationship if we are not satisfied.

But feeling unloved or unfairly treated does not give anyone the right or justification to abuse their power by being disrespectful, revengeful or sadistic. Doing so will not resolve anything although it may temporarily relieve some anger. The inevitable consequences are that it will aggravate existing problems, create new ones, destroy the credibility of any lingering claims to self-other respect which male or female perpetrators might wish to believe they have, and increase considerably the likelihood of a divorce.

STAGE 8b

SEX, LOVE AND MONOGAMY:

Needs, wishes, fears, low desire and solutions

The three C's women need in order to be happy, or is it four?

Just as beauty is in the eye of the beholder, what it takes to be happy will always ultimately depend on the needs, wishes and fears of the person seeking happiness. That is why people come up with different ideas about what it is, although most agree that committed quality love is an important part of it. We realize that developing long term commitment depends on more than one thing, but every woman knows that being good in bed is very important in order to strengthen it in her partner.

So, if we want to be good in bed for the man we love, how do we go about it? Some women think that the one track aspect of male sexuality gives them an important advantage. And while that may not be the whole truth, it is certainly part of it. It was a young secondary school teacher who first taught me that lesson, which she began by talking about what men and women needed in order to be happy. I elaborate in the extract below, from an autobiographical narrative I wrote many years ago:

.../... The question of why so many men keep talking about sex while love is tinkering with their heart, could trigger an interesting discussion. It is probably a vulnerability thing, an accepted way of covering up delicate feelings within male subculture. Complicated by the fact that when love is not involved, they still like talking about it.

"Men are simple creatures", this High School teacher told us that very late

Friday night with her disarming candor, after some of us had had more than just a drink or two. "As long as you feed them and bonk them, they are as happy as Larry".

We laughed. And after the heartbreak with Michi some six months earlier in London, laughing was something I needed badly. I was too old by then to have been consoled by my mother, if I had been living with her. Without the friends of my adolescence, with whom I would have joked and drank and sang and tried to forget. Even my cat was on the other side of the world. The one ray of hope in being badly heartbroken at that age, is that the torrent of living soon helps to wash it all away.

I had decided that it would probably be a good idea to date older women only, so that neither of us would fall seriously in love and expose ourselves to all that suffering. Ah!, such hopes! I didn't know yet that love has no respect for common sense, and that nice village boys had no chance against the charm and artifices of smart city women. And so I kept laughing, hoping my youthful embarrassment wasn't making me blush too obviously, as we kept enjoying her Australian lingo.

Another drink seemed to enhance her mood for philosophy. "What women need in order to be happy is the three C's", she went on later. Her girlfriend had already gone home by herself after the two of them came back from the loo. "Talk to you tomorrow darl", she said as they kissed goodbye. "You keep the car, I'll take a taxi. It's not far". There we were, just the two of us, after nearly everyone else had gone home.

The nature of happiness wasn't my forte yet, in my tender twenties. The ancient Greek philosopher Epicurus had done some hard thinking on the subject, and then as well as now his ideas about what mattered in life could well have been right for many. The essence of what people needed in order to be happy, he concluded, was friendship, freedom and philosophy. Or the three F's, as that teacher might have put it. His "freedom" included that from the unnatural treadmill which mindless materialism forces us onto. And in contemporary terms, what he meant by "philosophy" would incorporate personal development in its broadest sense.

But at that time I had never heard of Epicurus. What I had heard though, was someone on television taking about the three R's. And my English was good enough by then to have picked up that it had something to do with educating children, which was right up her alley. But the three C's? "What are the three C's?" I asked. "Caring, companionship and cock" she told me softly, without the slightest hint of discomfort.

Gosh! Unaccustomed to liberated women I couldn't help but to admire her daring. Although with hindsight I probably looked very non threatening, which would have helped. As we kept laughing and chatting ever closer and softer she happened to touch my hand, just for a moment and kind of casually, as part of the conversation.

She was doing me gently, and I was beginning to feel cozy. I needed a cuddle, and she had one. Very much later that morning, she was to tell me I was the sweetest and cutest and most smoochable boy she'd ever met. I took a bus home after breakfast, as happy as Larry. And ever since I've had a soft spot for nice High School teachers .../...

So, it is that easy to keep younger men happy. With some properly grown up men it can be a bit the way it is with us women, in that the more their personality has evolved the more complicated it becomes to do our part to keep them happy. But the good thing is that even they are not very different from younger men in terms of some of the important things they need and want in order to love their woman.

There is a slightly questionable joke about men's marital bliss fantasies, which is revealing because its oversimplification lays bare men's hopes and disappointments in a striking manner. One version of it is: *Men dream about having a wife who is an economist in the kitchen, a lady in the living room and a slut in the bedroom. But many end up with one who becomes a lady in the kitchen, a slut in the living room, and an economist in the bedroom.*

These days of two income couples, husbands who cook, microwave dinners and cheap takeaways, few people care about what happens in the kitchen. But the bedroom and living room are a different matter. "She gives him just enough to keep him around", told me a woman who knew what she was talking about, when commenting on an unhappy couple.

Regardless of the reasons and as already mentioned, being an economist in the bedroom will not resolve anything for a woman with a lower desire for sex, except in the immediacy of the moment and at the cost of damaging the relationship. And whether the slut in the living room is the man or the woman, it is not only a mark of disrespect for our partner but also an indication of insufficient self respect.

So, it is never just a matter of getting the three C's, but of keeping them too. That makes it not three C's, but actually four of them. The fourth one is Commitment, manifested through the giving and receiving of all the necessary verbal, emotional and behavioral reassurances about being truly loved. In order to retain it, both partners have to be mindful of the need to look after the first three C's. But that is only likely to happen if our personality is healthy enough, plus we were wise or lucky in choosing our partner.

Managing properly the central relationship issues of caring, friendship, sex and commitment is essential for those of us who want to love and be loved for life. The joke about men's marital bliss fantasies brings us back to the issue of what being good in bed and in the living room is about, and how to get better at it. Some of what that takes has already been discussed in Stages 5 and 6, and I elaborate further over the next headings.

Bedroom competence begins with knowing who and how we are

Those who understand well people and life realize the importance of self-other awareness, and that appreciating the deeper sides of ourselves is a big part of what it takes to be able to know others better. And the latter, in turn, keeps improving our self knowledge further. That is because, as discussed in Stage 5 under the heading *Self-other awareness*, others are like a mirror which gives us different but comparable reflections of how we are.

Certain things about us are easier to notice in others, as we do not normally observe ourselves from the outside and therefore lack that perspective. In addition most of us need to protect our self image to some extent, which usually happens by distorting inconvenient truths whenever we try to self examine. Only that minority among us whose fortunate upbringing plus subsequent personal development has resulted in *secure high* self esteem, are able to significantly bypass this inbuilt automatic defense mechanism.

But for the majority, knowing ourselves and others well enough is not easy. The less developed our core components of personality and self esteem are, the more difficult it is to understand situations accurately and to calculate and measure our behavior in order to achieve just the effect we want it to have. Both of these depend on and reflect the level of our self-other awareness, and are one indicator of where we stand in the continuum between very high personality health at one end, and a personality disorder at the other.

A woman who had recently started a new relationship called her man a few hours after he had left her home earlier in the morning. In what that man described as a surprisingly agitated way and obviously trying to contain her anger, she half asked and half accused him of having wiped off the mirror above the hand basin in her bathroom hours earlier, when he brushed his teeth after breakfast.

The tone and content of her call made clear very quickly that she believed his wiping off the mirror was because he thought it was not clean enough, and that she felt this reflected a negative judgment about her cleanliness. He realized that at that moment, when she was noticeably quite emotional, it would have been counterproductive to say that such an unimportant matter was not worth all the fuss.

Instead he kept that point to himself and said that he did not specifically remember having wiped the mirror. But he might have done it automatically, just as he did occasionally in his own home when a particle of saliva accidentally sprang onto the mirror during flossing. That explanation saved the moment, but made him reflect on what her excessive emotional reaction suggested about the imbalances in her personality.

This incident reminded him that the previous night when they were naked and about to make love he had asked if she could dim the ceiling light in her bedroom or switch on a side light, and that she appeared unexpectedly resistant. As a result of her demeanor and insistence on he giving her a reason, he had the impression that she might have though his reason could be he had found something about her body not entirely to his liking, and wanted less light in order to see less of her imperfections.

Therefore he was more or less forced to explain that his own bedroom had indirect adjustable lighting, and that laying in bed with the full brightness of the ceiling light on his eyes was uncomfortably glary. He concluded that the two incidents were a red flag about her personality, and this influenced his perception about the viability of an ongoing relationship.

It is likely that this woman had an underdeveloped conviction of worthiness. Being the foundation of personality and self esteem, it had affected at least several of the core components which are subsequently built upon it. The most obvious was underdeveloped self acceptance regarding body image and other aspects of herself, which made her excessively vulnerable to any real or imagined criticism.

She also seemed to have less than good self-other awareness, manifested by her overreaction concerning his possible motives and her likely miscalculation about the effect which telling him in the manner she did was going to have. In addition she had proven unable to control herself, because at least to some extent she must have realized that her emotional call over the mirror issue could have negative consequences.

The vulnerabilities in her personality were bound to remain unresolved, as long as the way of managing her inner tensions continued to be based on protecting herself from threatening feelings by becoming angry and ascribing blame to somebody else. People with this problem do not think they overreact, because for them this is the way life is and the only experience of reality they have ever known.

There is one critical issue about what is going on under the surface: The realization that there is a different and better way of being is a bit beyond the reach of what they are able to comprehend, or dare to. This a hard problem to fix, even with help from a good therapist. Any well meaning friend or partner who innocently suggests that their reaction may be excessive would be unwittingly aggravating the already triggered intense anxiety, by pulling towards the surface of awareness the very fears such people want to push down and keep buried as deeply as they possibly can.

That jump in anxiety feels so threatening that it has to be defended against at almost any cost. Refusal to condone the person's unconscious cover up by way of anyone with a different viewpoint holding their ground, may trigger escalating arguments. And ultimately intense anger and blaming, with the likely outcome being the end of the friendship or relationship.

Unfortunately most sufferers never overcome these erroneous and counterproductive patterns of thinking and reacting, which end up being seen by others as permanent problematic features of their personality. They become no go areas for those who know them well, or the kind of territory where one steps onto very carefully and at our own peril.

It is clear that the woman in this example was unlikely to ever be much good in the bedroom or living room unless she developed her personality and self esteem. Or alternatively, unless she got a partner with whom she felt unquestionably accepted, with a safety margin big enough for her to feel secure. Otherwise her out of control anxieties were likely to propel her sooner or later into throwing another bucket of cold water, over any attempts by her and her partner to be sexually and emotionally nice to each other.

Her bucket of cold water had taken the form of a rapid and major mood swing over something which most people would consider insignificant, and she was totally convinced that it was all her lover's fault. Her oversensitivity and underlying fear of inadequacy had lead her to a barely contained aggressive accusation and blaming, as her dysfunctional defensive structure did its short term anxiety relief work.

Such defensiveness is very counterproductive in the longer term, because it automatically filters out of awareness anything which is too uncomfortable to contemplate about the way we are or behave. Consequently we fail to see certain things which are strikingly clear to impartial observers, and may remain totally oblivious to it. In other words, the perceptual skills side of personality is distorted by a few or many big and small blind spots.

Some of us may be alarmed by a realization in the privacy of our mind that we have a pattern of overreacting in such ways too often, and of then failing to see our contributions to the subsequent consequences. The intensity of these overreactions stands out in contrast with the more common, milder and less frequent reactions which most people have, over being touched in the odd sensitive raw nerve.

When we have had this problematic pattern for decades, we can expect our mind and heart to fight strenuously against recognizing it. That is because developing this kind of awareness would increase anxiety, in addition to requiring the kind of knowledge which takes time and work to develop. By comparison and apart from being easy, blaming others is addictive because it immediately makes us feel less bad.

If we are like that, what may be needed if there is ever to be a chance of correcting the situation is for us to develop enough capacity to see ourselves from the outside, as we come across to others. The knowledge embodied in this book is intended to facilitate such difficult but important task. If we cannot do it alone, another possibility is for someone wiser to take the risk of telling us what we are doing and the effect it is having, combined with our determination to resist the intense knee jerk urge to argue or escape.

Not fighting against awareness of certain threatening truths could require a lot of courage in some of us, plus an almost bloody minded determination to get to the bottom of it in order to improve our life. The fear of facing reality may be overwhelming and irrational, based as it often is on issues which go back all the way to early childhood. At that time, negative ways of relating by one or more significant others would have carved certain protective reaction pathways in the mind, which the child needed in order to cope.

The ultimate and almost inevitable consequence for the personality is blind spots and underdevelopment in its core components, leading towards hard to dislodge dysfunctional behavior patterns within any ongoing sexually intimate relationship. Depending on a multitude of factors, the person may become oversensitive, jealous, self centered, resentful, emotionally less intelligent, exploitative, depressive, aggressive, domineering, prone to excessive and poorly controlled anger, or develop other problematic tendencies.

Any minor incident with the slightest negative connotation can be blown out of proportion, ignited and fueled up by the mostly unconscious reservoir of unresolved fear and anger which began to be created in childhood. That reservoir has probably grown bigger since, as a result of the very way such people mismanage their relationships. This propensity can make their emotional reactions unstable, unpredictable and/or excessive, with serious enough cases meriting a diagnosis of some kind of "personality disorder".

In conclusion, a realistic view about how we are is very important for bedroom competence and indeed in every aspect of life. If we suspect we may have a pattern of overreacting and blaming our partner, and especially if it has happened with several men who were nice enough, we could give ourselves a chance of improvement by reading and making sure we understand properly the elaborations on personality and self esteem in Stage 5, followed by the material in Stage 6 and in this Stage 8.

Sometimes that may not be sufficient, and we could continue to have significant problems in managing our emotions and behavior within intimate relationships. If that is so and we can afford it, we might wish to consider the possibility of therapy, keeping in mind my comments about the trustworthiness of therapists in the *Should-read-first introduction* and elsewhere.

Why a man's personality makes a big difference in the bedroom

Many of the ways in which an underdeveloped personality can affect relationships have already been discussed in Stage 5. But even if there is nothing problematic enough about our man to be really worried about, the difference which his having a healthy personality makes (as against having an average one) can be significant, in terms of how good or otherwise sex becomes.

If the core components of his personality and self esteem are well developed he is likely to be more tolerant and forgiving about everything. He will be more secure and relaxed within himself, and these qualities will relax us too, both in the living room and the bedroom. We will not need or wish to fake pleasure we don't feel just to reassure him, because we know his masculinity is not threatened if we don't come or just go along mostly in order to please him.

His approach to sex will be more natural, and that will help bring out the natural woman in us. We will be more likely to be able to ask for what we want to do to him and have him do to us, because he has the qualities needed for the relationship to have become very trusting. And also because we can feel he wants to please us in addition to pleasing himself, and nothing we suggest is going to unsettle him or diminish his love for us.

In contrast, an average or below average level of development in our man's core components can make a difference for the worse. He is likely to be less secure as a person, and therefore less accepting of his and our physical or emotional imperfections. We will feel his uneasiness, which may in turn make us less relaxed and trusting about everything in bed, and this would narrow down our sexual repertoire making it more repetitive.

Instead of encouraging our sexual naturalness, the discomfort we sense in him may influence us into "performing" in a manner we believe he likes or at least thinks is acceptable, in order to protect both of us and the relationship. He is also more likely to withdraw or overreact when displeased or stressed for any reason. As a result, things which should be talked about are not or only rarely and incompletely, as his uneasiness aggravates ours and both of us opt for the safety of silence.

Therefore, instead of relaxing and enjoying the beautiful sexual sensations, we can never totally relax. One consequence is that rather than evolving for the better as would happen spontaneously in a trusting relationship, we remain sexually and emotionally stuck within the narrower limits of whatever doesn't unduly unsettle either partner.

Unlike men's desire and capacity for pleasure, ours are much more influenced by the quality of the relationship. That may significantly affect whether or not we can bring ourselves to orgasm or just let it come to us, and so we may deprive ourselves and him of the pleasure, plus the deeply satisfying emotional warmth and closeness which comes naturally after it. Furthermore, if the feelings aren't right sex can quite easily begin to feel like a job after a while, rather than something we look forward to.

The result is that instead of becoming a couple who enjoys sex throughout life, we are more likely to end up going through the motions with decreasing frequency and satisfaction due to sexual and emotional boredom. That is why in the longer term, his personality is more important for us enjoying sex and becoming good in bed than most of us realize, when we are in the heady stages of searching for a good man.

Remembering the above is critical, when we are deciding which man to check out further. When we find ourselves at the cutting edge of the mating game, where the choice of rejecting or exploring a man has to be made, it is very easy to be excessively influenced by the pull of physical attraction or other easily noticeable features. That is how evolution designed us to function, and therefore it feels natural. By comparison, thinking about the longer term relationship consequences of his personality is a slower process, requiring from us a deeper understanding and careful consideration.

We may have to go through a few relationships which started on the basis of attraction but did not survive, for us to learn the lessons. As mentioned in Stage 6, choosing a partner with a poorer personality because of his attractiveness, increases the longer term likelihood of an unhappy relationship or of us having to leave him. And if his personality was to evolve and become healthier, the more attractive he is the younger and more attractive our future competitors are likely to be. And therefore the less comparatively sexually appealing he may find us, especially as we get older.

Nature has designed men to be very drawn to youth and beauty. Therefore those are bound to be major factors when he thinks about making a relationship truly permanent, as against being seriously tempted to leave months or years later. Of course women are attracted by youth and beauty too. But because we are generally emotionally savvier and more sophisticated, most of us are at least a little bit better able to give due consideration to good qualities in the personality of any man being evaluated.

The most important are probably those discussed in Stage 6 under the heading *Desirable personal qualities in men (and women)*. But we may only be able to recognize and appreciate their true value, if we have enough of them ourselves. When that is so and we have chosen wisely, we are likely to increase our capacity to be good in bed and enjoy his enjoyment and ours, plus the stability and security which this brings to the relationship.

The consequences of childhood sexual abuse

Some women and comparatively fewer men were sexually abused as children to varying degrees, and the damage to their capacity to function well in relationships ranges from very serious and lifelong to none at all. At the same time, a perfectly possible positive outcome of someone having to work hard at overcoming any problematic consequences, could be that his/her personality becomes healthier and wiser than average. All that makes child sexual abuse an important issue which merits some elaboration.

This woman told me how as a child she was lured several times on her way home from primary school by a man who took her to his home. Once there he would give her a lollipop and they would play a "game", which involved he masturbating while they sat very close in front of each other and he wanting her to caress his genitals. As a mature woman, she still felt very uncomfortable if her husband or any other man after her divorce asked her to masturbate him, and found very difficult to hold a man's penis near her face.

Another woman related how as a young adolescent she had been raped quite a few times doggy style by a family member. Now as a married woman with a loving husband, she still had great difficulty in relaxing whenever he requested sex in that manner, despite the fact that she loved him too and wanted to please. Unlike the woman in the previous example, she had no problem masturbating her partner or giving him oral sex.

A successful professional woman told me how she had been repeatedly sexually fondled by a close family member during early adolescence, when he would take her on horseback to distant parts of the farm where he had to work, and they slept overnight in a tent. Later as an adult, when she was in a relationship and the man she wanted to be loved by began to initiate sex, she would freeze because she couldn't help it.

She would close her eyes overwhelmed by the distress she was trying not to feel, and just let it happen as if she wasn't there. Several men had realized there was something sexually wrong and left her. She had never succeeded in keeping a relationship despite her desire to love and be loved, and had been too ashamed to ever seek help until she finally came to see me. This and the previous two problems may be resolvable with a properly designed therapeutic intervention, especially if the woman has a caring partner.

Someone I had a relationship with long ago, confided how as a young child she had been repeatedly sexually fondled by a family member, until he was caught out by her mother and it stopped. She expressed her concern that it could still be affecting her, and knowing I was a relationship therapist asked me if I had noticed anything wrong with her sexuality.

Contrary to what was being heard on TV at the time, not every woman who has been sexually abused as a child is significantly affected by it, and many are not affected at all. Having been with enough women to know the difference, I was able to reassure her she came across as nice and relaxed in bed. It seemed to me that she enjoyed the experience as much as I did. She had no sexual problem aftereffects from the abuse at all, and absolutely nothing to worry about.

Claims that one in every three female children had been sexually abused and damaged by it were being publicly made by the feminist movement, and vigorously defended without credible evidence. The odd activist who dared to say she had been sexually abused as a child but not damaged by it, was often given a hard time by other activists for contradicting the accepted view.

In a case which became publicly known after being discussed on TV, a woman had accused her father of sexually abusing her as a child, which he strenuously denied. As it turned out after all the protracted private and public trauma, the daughter finally said that the abuse had actually happened in a previous life. There was at the time a lot of discussion about whether overzealous counselors were unintentionally triggering "false memories" in the minds of suggestible women, who could sense what the counselors were after and were eager to please and enjoy the attention.

Later in the 1980's an alleged new variety of child abuse involving babies and known as "ritual abuse" gained notoriety, following awareness of the issue emerging from the United States. Books had been written on the subject, and for a time its veracity was so widely accepted that courses were run to educate workers in women's refuges and women's health centers.

Eventually witnesses came out saying that ritual abuse was not only sexual, but that babies had actually been murdered during the abuse, and they had seen their blood dropping on the ground as they were being killed. After thorough investigations which included laboratory analysis of ground samples for blood residues at the alleged locations, a police chief speaking on television said that there was no evidence and they were treating the matter as a "medical problem".

In other words, some women with fragile mental health had yet again developed "false memories", following all the fuss about the issue and the resulting questions by well meaning counselors. Acceptance about the veracity of ritual abuse had become so widespread, that even in the later 1990's some workers interviewed for certain counseling jobs were still being asked what they thought about it, just in case they continued to believe it.

Ritual abuse came and went, but there are always people who strive for attention in a big way. Like those who falsely claimed to have fought in Vietnam, escaped from the collapsed Twin Towers, or been abducted by aliens. Attention seeking is nothing new and a historical example is the florid sworn testimonies in the courts of the Middle Ages, about witches having been seen flying in their broomsticks to their Sabbath midnight meetings with the Devil, during which babies were said to be eaten raw while still alive.

Pain during intercourse, genuine, misdiagnosed and fake

Much of the discomfort many women experience during intercourse is due to penetration before the woman is sufficiently aroused. Emotional issues affecting the relationship have already been discussed and are absolutely critical. When the state of the relationship or unacknowledged anxieties about sex are not the cause, the solution may be as simple as delaying penetration while continuing foreplay until she is ready, or using personal lubricant.

Pain during intercourse is often due to medical causes, and a doctor should always be consulted. A common reason is endometriosis, in which benign growths in the reproductive organs keep expanding and develop adhesions until the area becomes filled in and tight. Penetration may push on that tightness or adhesions, triggering pain. A "retroverted" uterus can also cause pain during intercourse, and sufferers may never recognize the cause.

Even doctors don't always get it right. The wife in a couple who consulted me said she had suffered from pain during intercourse for many years. Her doctor found nothing, but referred her to a gynecologist just in case. The gynecologist did not find anything physical which could be causing the pain. Therefore he concluded it could be psychological and suggested they might like to see a sex therapist.

The sex therapist said that for various reasons some women have involuntary contractions of the entrance to the vagina when penetration begins, which make it painful. This could be due to some kind of sexual anxiety, in which case it may be resolved by "systematic desensitization". This procedure involves relaxation while inserting progressively thicker objects, from the size of a pencil to that of a penis. She tried it but it didn't fix the pain, and the couple eventually became resigned to living with it.

When later they decided to have a family she was having problems conceiving, and was told it could be because her uterus was at an atypical angle. She had surgery to correct it, and afterwards she never again had pain during intercourse. She didn't need to tell me any of this, because they hadn't come to consult me about sex. But did so, she said, because I might be able to use that information to help other women with the same problem.

A couple with significant marital tensions were having sex infrequently because the woman said she had pain during intercourse. She would like to have sex more often, but if it was painful she found it difficult to go along with it, and her husband certainly did not want to hurt her. The woman had problematic personality issues going back all the way to early childhood, when she had felt rather neglected by her parents, and had come to see me alone a number of times to discuss those matters.

She told me that the most important person for giving love to her and her little brother was neither of her parents, but an elderly lady next door who used to invite them home and give them sweets. Her husband seemed rather nice, I told her while alone with me, when compared to many other husbands I had known during counseling and socially. My concern was that if their problems were not resolved or at least improved, there was a short term possibility and a longer term probability that he might be tempted away by someone else and she might lose him permanently.

At some point she said that it didn't actually hurt "that much". It seemed to me and she later admitted that she had been using alleged pain to avoid sex. This was a variation of the proverbial headache, which some wives claim to have when their partner wants sex and they don't feel like it. One of the reasons why I sensed what might be happening was that it would have been consistent with other aspects of the relationship, where she appeared not to be taking enough care of her responsibilities.

I saw the main underlying issue as one of excessive self absorption, and consequent insufficient care in looking after her husband's needs. This was caused by underdeveloped core components in her personality, which were underpinning her beliefs, feelings and behaviors. Her personality had become as it was through no fault of her own, because she had not chosen her parents. But it was up to her to decide if she wanted to do something about it while there was still time, or live with the problem plus the ultimate potential consequence of losing her husband.

A woman told me that during her marriage they had sex about once a month or less, because every time her husband had an orgasm he got a nasty headache afterwards. In another rare condition, some men are allergic to their own semen and become ill for one or two days after ejaculation, but for some this can be fixed by taking a niacin supplement some hours before sex.

Pain in intercourse is far less common in men, and usually due to physical reasons. For example by a too narrow opening in the foreskin, which is therefore overstretched during penetration, and circumcision or still more minor surgery can fix the problem. And of course, men and women can have pain or discomfort during intercourse due to various health problems. The usual ones among otherwise healthy younger people, are undiagnosed or untreated sexually transmissible infections.

Dealing with normal differences in sexual desire

The most common significant sexual difference couples have after the early phase of an established relationship is in desire for frequency. Many husbands want sex more often than their wives, especially among younger couples, and many wives would like to desire it more often but find it difficult for any number of reasons. Men's craving for sex is designed by nature to be ongoing however, and if a man feels chronically frustrated the relationship is unlikely to remain happy or even survive in the longer term.

Women know it, and often go along in order to please their man. But if they are too dry due to insufficient arousal when penetration begins and it is done without lubricant, it can be uncomfortable. This reduces the enjoyment a woman might otherwise have, and the memory of such repeated experiences can begin to gradually erode further her desire thereafter. When pressures like parenthood, work, financial issues and possibly a few personality based friction points are added to the mix, loving feelings may begin to erode.

Unlike women's libido which is strongly influenced by circumstances and the overall temperature of the relationship, that of men remains regardless.

As a result couples could find themselves with a problem caused by a combination of factors, but manifested most strongly in the bedroom. If the situation remains unresolved it may deteriorate into some variation of an approach-rejection struggle most nights, and the resulting stress and dissatisfaction affects them during the day.

Hard to resolve differences in desire often become more acute after the birth of the first child. It is reasonable to assume that any woman with a first baby is in shock at the massive change in lifestyle. Every mother knew what was coming, but probably mostly in her mind. Now she is right in the middle of the effort of living with it hour after hour and day after day.

This can be exciting, enjoyable, time consuming to the exclusion of other activities, etc. in varying proportions for different women. At one end of the continuum they absolutely love it, while at the other some get overwhelmed and depressed. The latter may be due to a number of reasons including aggravation of preexisting personality vulnerabilities by stress, insufficient support, and brain chemistry imbalances thought occur in "post partum depression".

In any case, some of these women may then feel guilty because they believe incorrectly that they should love it all the time without any negative feelings, and that they are bad mothers if they don't. Regardless of how motherhood is affecting them, a frequent wish and often imperative need of just about all mothers with a newborn baby is to be able to sleep till dawn, and making love till dawn is for now just a nice memory.

As an experienced father of four told me once, "For the first six months the father's job is to mother the mother, so as to give her the support she needs in order to be able to care for the baby". It has to be like that now, although it used to be different when parents lived in extended families with grandmothers, aunties or sisters around.

Men still need sex but it is OK for tired mothers and indeed for any woman if she doesn't feel like it, to do it out of love and not come if she has no need. It will be nicer to do it in a position which is restful such as laying on her side with the man behind, and to use lubricant. Both partners need to understand that this is OK and totally normal. We men need not feel uncomfortable if our woman is not quite fully into it every time, and appreciate instead her caring and cooperation.

Women with young children can have some of the same pressures as new mothers, and it is well known among family therapists that mothers with three children under the age of ten are more likely to be overstressed or depressed, even if they have a supportive husband. Having less energy for sex may also happen to many super-mums who need or want to have an outside full time job in addition to the one at home.

The desire to please their man may lead some women to fake orgasm sometimes, so that he will not feel bad by not having fully aroused her, ... and so that they can both finally go to sleep. Faking an orgasm is always a bad idea, and not only because it involves lying to our intimate partner. The biggest problem is that as soon as we have done it once we are under pressure to do it again to keep reassuring him, and the more we do it the more difficult it will be to come out with the truth.

But if we hide the truth from the person we most need to trust, this will create an increasingly heavy burden in our heart, because we have to be on our toes in order to keep up the lie and suppress any comments which might lead to its discovery. A much better option than faking is to acknowledge our enjoyment of his sexual arousal and the pleasure we give him, and of the sharing of love and tenderness through sex.

Just as bad is being in the habit of refusing sex simply because we do not feel like it. This is a neglect of responsibility, which eventually is bound to damage his feelings for us. Similarly, making our "granting" of sex conditional on having our way in other aspects of the relationship will say loud and clear that we do not love him. Worse still, that we do not have the capacity for giving which is the essence of loving, and are using sex as a tool of power to manipulate him and control the relationship for our own ends.

If we are unhappy about the sharing of housework, childcare, income earning responsibilities or anything else, it needs to be negotiated. If we mismanage the situation by bedroom retaliation, we are gradually dissolving much of the caring-friendship-sex glue that creates and maintains commitment. It is never a good idea to have such discussion in the bedroom, which should be a place for trust, tenderness, comfort, pleasure and sleep. However if nothing is changing by negotiation and the issue is very important to us, it may be appropriate to talk about the viability of the relationship.

In the final analysis, managing differences in desire and whether or not we have sex at any one time has to rely on love, part of my definition of which in page 135 was "everything we do as a way of giving for the purpose of caring". Doing, giving and caring should never be a matter of counting either, or of mechanically each taking turns at deciding what to do or not do about sex whenever there is a difference in desire.

The question about sex I put to women is this: How much effort will take us to let him have it while we are in a restful position, when compared to how much deprivation he will have to endure if we don't? And here is a parallel consideration for men: When we know it would make her genuinely uncomfortable, letting our woman have her "no" without guilt is an expression of love. That is because we don't love by just sexually desiring her, but also by caring about how she feels. In such situations, masturbating alone or with her friendly collaboration could be a sensible option.

Loving relationships function best when they operate on what is often referred to as the central principle of communism, namely "From each according to his ability to each according to his need". On that basis, the expression and sharing of physical affection and sexuality would ideally happen whenever either partner wants it. This is not about mercy affection or sex when we don't need it ourselves, but about genuinely caring for the partner we love.

Other sexual tensions in established couples

Most sexual tensions in couples are caused by non sexual issues and therefore "sex therapy" is not indicated, if that is taken to mean therapy about sex. Information and advice may be beneficial for managing sexual tensions, but it is important to think about whether those giving it deserve to be trusted. Furthermore again, and for reasons already elaborated on, many professional counselors are not very competent, and relying on their advice could be risky in addition to expensive.

Some governments, religions and religious individuals believe they are entitled to tell others what they should and shouldn't do regarding sex. They use whatever power they are able to muster to enforce it if they can, which effectively involves undermining the right of consenting adults to be who they truly are. Some feminist ideologues like to preach about what women should and shouldn't do to enhance their attractiveness or please their partner. These people may mean well, but their views are often unscientific or overemotional, and that makes anything they say rather questionable.

For all the above reasons, it makes sense for a couple struggling with sexual tensions to first try to resolve them through relevant education, by for example reading and discussing parts of this book in the manner suggested in the *Should-read-first introduction*. If that was not enough and the marriage is reaching a crisis point, it might be worth consulting a reputable therapist if the couple can find and afford one. That is because the cost of a divorce and the life consequences thereafter could be quite significant.

When both partners are sexually reasonably well informed and relaxed, and as long as the emotional side of the relationship is at least acceptable, the quality of sex tends to become good. Even if they had a shaky start due to initial discomforts or insufficient knowledge and technique, they will soon develop them by noticing what their partner likes and giving it before it is asked, and by requesting what they want.

On the other hand, if at least one partner is and remains poorly informed and uncomfortable or anxious about sex, that side of their relationship is unlikely to become good no matter what they do with their bodies. That is why the kind of education relevant for better communication is likely to be part of what has to be done, in order to better manage sexual tensions.

While each couple and person needs to be considered individually, some generalizations are appropriate. The fact is all of us are imperfect, and therefore the sexual side of many relationships has room for improvement. Doing so can be useful not only for its own sake, but because enjoying each other helps partners tolerate and forgive differences, imperfections and mistakes. This is how better sex can contribute to better love, and that is undoubtedly the most valuable thing they can have for each other.

For many people the biggest barriers to sexual desire and enjoyment are the emotional blockages they carry from their past life. Understanding those barriers in order to remove or reduce them is the obvious first step in enhancing sexuality. Some barriers have already been discussed, for instance regarding consequences of child sexual abuse. There are further examples below, and more will be discussed later under the heading *Safe and risky sexual fantasies, alternatives to "yes" or "no", and the importance of understanding and caring*.

The most common psychological barriers to sexual desire and enjoyment women experience, which are non-relationship and non-physical in origin, are anxiety and guilt. These can be implanted and reinforced early in life, through the way parents react to children's natural curiosity and exploration of their genitals. Parents influenced by cultural or religious associations of sex with shame or sin are likely to transmit their anxiety to the child, by for example expressing disapproval and just telling the child not to do it.

Even with a proper explanation however, children are limited in what they can understand intellectually. But they are very good at picking up the mood of the parents, including their anxieties. As a result, whenever their nature propels them to explore by touching themselves, they may feel bad because they know that doing so would incur parental disapproval. Later in life, cultural and religious influences can strengthen the parentally induced associations of sex with sin, shame, anxiety and/or guilt.

This problem tends to become worse for girls. Their genitals cannot be held in their hand and easily looked at, which in boys removes much of the mystery about them. As they grow into adolescence, they do not experience the intense surge in libido boys do. The force of it usually overcomes inhibitions by frequent masturbation, which is accepted as being what adolescent boys do. The repeated pleasure of it keeps further removing shame and guilt, as they grow towards adulthood.

When it comes to girls and at least in Christianity, the virginity of the Virgin Mary was traditionally held as an example for them and influenced parental attitudes. "Good girls" weren't supposed to masturbate, let alone engage in sex, and their lower libido than adolescent boys certainly helped. As a result, the normal way of gradually eroding sexual guilt and anxiety by masturbation in boys, is far less common in girls.

The same beliefs and values operate in many non Christian traditional societies. They originated and made sense when sex was likely to result in unwanted pregnancies, with all the economic costs and social distress associated with it for the mother and her family. Therefore traditional parents believed that their daughters should not explore sex too much or at all until they got married, in the belief that this would make them more desirable to any future husband as well as better and happier wives.

All those factors can add up to a significant suppression of natural instincts, and the accumulation of a lot of sexual anxieties due to ignorance, shame and guilt. To the extent these have been hammered further in through the formative years, they become even more entrenched and operate partly unconsciously. That makes them harder to dislodge, and their existence diminishes considerably the woman's capacity to enjoy sex.

In contrast to the effects of outdated cultural and religious beliefs, parents who are tolerant and relaxed about their own sexuality may simply explain to their children that self touching is something to be done in private, just like going to the toilet. Through the mood and manner in which the explanation is delivered and parents talk and act about these issues, children absorb the message that sex is nothing to be anxious about and instead something to be enjoyed, in private or with a partner.

In addition to the above common barriers, there may be minor discomforts about physical appearance, and acceptance is not always the best or easiest way of dealing with it. For example, a dermatologist can remove most spider veins, moles or other minor imperfections from our face or body, if we want it done. That may be one more way of taking care of ourselves and him, by staying as attractive as possible within reason.

Some women dislike their inner vaginal lips protruding from their outer vulva in what they consider an excessive manner. An increasing minority among them choose to trim them flush by a cosmetic surgery procedure which is relatively safe and simple, keeping in mind that all surgery carries some risk and some doctors are better than others. The result is sometimes referred to as a "designer vagina", which in its natural form occurs more frequently among East Asians than in Caucasians or African Americans.

The dissipation of anxieties about appearance often happens spontaneously, just by being loved. One of my favorite university lecturers made a comment about it, which I have never forgotten. On one occasion I had seen her husband picking her up in his car, and something in his demeanor gave me the impression that he was a caring man who loved her. She was average looking and had a very minor but noticeable facial abnormality, which would have been difficult to correct by surgery.

And her comment left an impression on me, because I sensed immediately she was talking about herself and it was coming from her heart. The lecture included body image issues, and she said: "We can never completely accept ourselves, until we feel completely accepted by the person we love". I think that for many men and women this is indeed the case, and it is a point worth remembering when deciding who to choose as a life partner.

Apart from the critical roles of sex education, personality, self esteem, love and trust in enhancing mutual sexual pleasure, there may be physiological reasons playing a part. For example, men and women have a natural variability in desire for sex. In terms of anatomical differences, sex therapists are aware that women whose clitoris is one inch or less from the upper side of the entrance to the vagina, tend to orgasm more easily through penetration alone that those in whom that distance is over one inch.

But that is no big deal either way, and in any case it is sensible for loving couples to talk about whatever positions or practices they fancy to enhance their enjoyment. Men are easy: If we caress their genitals, nature will probably do the rest. It is pleasurable for the man if we hold his erect penis fairly tight at the base and shaft, but we need to be gentle with the head. It is not a carpet ripping tool, it's a little baby of a thing to be handled with care, and even the upper side of the tongue can feel a bit rough on it.

There is no hard and fast formula however, and just as they do with us we have to play by ear and learn his preferences by trial and error. Asking how he likes to be masturbated is also important, and one more nice thing we can do for him as foreplay. Because we have the time and opportunity, we can learn to do it better than any other woman he ever had, and he is bound to appreciate it. It would also be helpful those times of the month when it may be inconvenient for tender loving care to be followed by penetration.

Most women like their man to caress their clitoris with fingers and tongue. But many men don't know how to do it the way their woman likes, and so they fumble about while trying their best. We men need to ask for feedback in order to train ourselves, until we learn to do it just the way our woman likes and until she says or otherwise indicates she is had enough. And because we love her and are eager to please we may ask, tactfully and without insisting, if there is anything else she might like.

Many women have battery operated vibrators, said to work very well. They give nice effortless stimulation, and are often suggested by sex therapists as a way of making it easier for some women to reach orgasm, alone or during penetration with their partner. Women who don't have a vibrator but think they might like it, may wish to consider buying one through the Internet, or together with their partner at some discreetly located adult shop.

In addition to the physicality of it, sex in loving relationships is a very emotional issue. Therefore again, the most important side of enhancing mutual sexual pleasure is not about what to do with our bodies or parts of it, but what we feel about ourselves and our partner. We often hear that the biggest sex organ is the brain, and this is true in the sense that it is within it that we experience our desire for sex and the preconditions for it. This brings me to the six major factors influencing sexual desire and enjoyment.

The six major factors influencing sexual desire and enjoyment

Some or all of these six factors may combine in all sorts of ways, to influence sexual desire and enjoyment differently in each person and couple. The first factor is **circumstances**, including age, attitudes to sex, state of the relationship, financial situation and other stresses of life. Much of this has already been commented on, and a lot of it can be managed by using common sense. The second is **medical issues**. For example normal and abnormal hormonal changes, physical and mental health, sexually transmissible infections, and side effects of medications. If we suspect a problem we need to see a doctor.

The third is **libido**, which is the biological craving for sexual gratification. It can be greatly affected by circumstances, medical issues, natural variability, and the availability plus quality of a loving relationship. The issues impinging on how to get and keep a good relationship are discussed at various points throughout the book. The fourth is **romantic love**, as in infatuation with one particular person. It is natural and wonderful, but unsustainable after a period. The length of it will be shorter if partners live together and longer if they don't, and an example is included as Appendix B.

The fifth is **attachment**, a stable bond between partners, forged form being together for years in a mutually satisfying relationship. One of its positive consequences is the creation of a strong collaborative alliance for emotional support, affection and sexuality. Whenever any of these is needed by either partner while the other doesn't, the latter will willingly provide it or collaborate out of genuine caring, rather than out of duty or mercy.

The sixth and least understood factor is the **level of personality and self esteem development.** The higher that level the more confident those who have it will be, and the less affected by the inevitable pressures of life, as greater inner security means less energy is needed for coping with stress or self protection. That extra energy plus better emotional intelligence enables such people to become better at developing and taking care of the healthy attitudes and emotions, which significantly influence our desire for sex and the quality of it.

A wife in a couple who consulted me had difficulties with desire and orgasm. Her discomfort about sex had always prevented her from masturbating without anxiety, and she never did it during sex with her partner. That had always obstructed her ability to reach orgasm when she was very aroused and with her partner inside, but needed a little extra stimulation to get over the line, which is normal and indeed very common.

Apart from recommending they tried using a vibrator during sex, I lent them an education video to be watched together at home, designed for teaching women how to masturbate, with an actress who looked like an average woman in an ordinary household. After they watched it, she began practicing the exercises on her own, as shown in the video and discussed and agreed by the three of us during the previous consultation. It was working well, and she reported feeling increasingly comfortable about it.

But two consultations later, she told me in front of her husband that her progress was seriously set back after he made what she felt was an unflattering comment about her body. That is because the way our partner sees us and treats us, can have a major effect on our capacity to be sexually relaxed and to experience desire and enjoyment in his/her company.

This woman had significant uneasiness about sex due to her cultural and family upbringing. Like most people, she also had self esteem of the contingent variety. As a result she was vulnerable to negative comments from others, but especially by her partner. She had been improving in their opinion and mine, but her progress was brought to a screeching halt by what she experienced as a prickly putdown.

As a second example about the importance of personality and self esteem for sex to become good, a woman consulted me after being horrified into inability to talk about what her husband had requested. The major underlying issues were similar to those in the previous example, and the case is elaborated extensively further below under the heading *The man who asked his woman how she would feel about trying bottom sex.*

Therapy with both women included education through exposure to written and/or audiovisual material. And also by learning new and better ways of feeling and talking about sexual issues through interaction with me as their therapist, which included modeling on how I was doing it.

Safe and risky sexual fantasies, consequences of mismanaging them, alternatives to "yes" or "no", and the importance of understanding and caring

When people form a permanent monogamous relationship they bring to it sexual needs, which can be manifested as either wishes or fears. Some of these will be in the form of spoken and unspoken expectations which are similar for both, while others will be somewhat different, and at least a few are likely to be very different. When both partners have well developed personality and self esteem, these incorporate the skills and attitudes needed to resolve those differences and become nice in bed for each other.

For them it happens spontaneously due to their own wish for variety, and also through wanting to please by accommodating to their partner's preferences. As the initial sexually overheated phase of a relationship settles down, this brings it into line with partners' natural needs within an established relationship. This is a normal and inevitable decrease in desire. But there can also be an avoidable significant-to-major decrease, and some issues influencing it are illustrated in Diagram 7 and discussed next.

In order to desire sex, most of us want and like physical-emotional comfort and intimacy with a man we trust, because in order to enjoy it we need to feel good in his company. But as mentioned earlier, if those emotions include associations of sex with shame, sin or guilt this can cause problems. If both partners are like that, the couple will be even less daring about trying anything different, and their sexual repertoire will be limited to the narrower confines of what both think of as "normal" and therefore acceptable.

By doing always the same thing sex can become monotonous, and this is one more way in which excessive vulnerability to disapproval adds to the

Diagram 7

Safe and risky SEXUAL FANTASIES, consequences of mismanaging them, alternatives to "yes" or "no", and the importance of understanding and caring

Partner 1	Partner 2	Short term consequences	Longer term consequences
Do what both consider as "normal" sex	Do what both consider as "normal" sex	Less variety may cause boredom and/or avoidable reduced desire	Growing sexual frustration and boredom. Less capacity to deal with all sorts of differences well enough. Lower satisfaction in both and higher risk to stability of relationship, making a break up more likely.
Wants to try some safe fantasy	Refuses due to inhibitions. Off-limits sex because of it	Fantasy avoided, reduces anxiety. Boredom raises, frustration grows	
Wants to try some risky fantasy	May threaten identity and relationship. Bodily injury?	Fantasy causes anguish, conflict. Boredom raises, frustration grows	

Examples of safe to risky sex fantasies

1. The woman who asked to watch her man urinating, and its unexpected bonus
2. The woman who dared to request having her man tied up and blindfolded
3. Two female fantasies about rape: Tied up while having sex and home intruder
4. The man who asked his woman how she would feel about trying bottom sex
5. The man who asked his woman to consider swinging with safety precautions
6. The grass is greener elsewhere: The most common and dangerous fantasy

cost of being faithful, which includes not acting on the attraction we feel towards other people. As the weight of monogamy's limitations increases overtime, sexual fantasies in one or both partners may increase as a natural compensatory mechanism. Many couples manage the issue by watching erotic material together, as an outlet to the need for variety which avoids the dangers of involvement with a third party.

Fantasies are a normal part of sexual functioning within satisfying relationships, and everybody has different ones. They often result in one partner wanting to try something new. But if this is outside the range of what the other considers acceptable, it can trigger anxiety and at times even emotional and physical recoil.

Such reaction may aggravate existing inhibitions in the partner who perhaps just barely dared to suggest a fantasy or started to act it out. He or she may then stop in order to spare the other from experiencing that anxiety, or the anxious partner may refuse to go along or even talk about it. The desire for it in the partner who wanted it remains however, and this is likely to affect her/his level of satisfaction with the relationship.

Sometimes one partner wants to try a riskier fantasy which represents a threat to the security of the relationship, or a challenge to the other's body image or sense of identity. Whatever the nature of the fantasies, they are part of human sexuality and will not disappear just because we or our partner want to. Therefore the only sensible thing is to manage them constructively.

That includes considering how safe a fantasy is. It is safe when it can be satisfied within the couple without danger of injury, and risky if it involves other people or the possibility of injury. The most important thing to begin with is to have or develop enough trust and a non judgmental attitude. This enables anything and everything to be discussed and understood in a caring and supportive manner, rather than avoided or dismissed out of hand.

A common dilemma arises when our partner wants something we feel uncomfortable about, but we don't want to say "no" out of love and also to keep the relationship in good shape. If what is being asked is a safe fantasy, a well functioning couple should be able to meet most requests. If not fully, perhaps one quarter of the way, half way and so on, with appropriate safeguards if necessary. And then seeing how it goes and how they feel.

If our partner requests or initiates something we dislike, it would be a bad idea to say something as inflexible and final as "never", because he or she may have been fantasizing about it for quite some time. A drastic refusal could hit hard, especially if accompanied by negative comments. In contrast, our agreeing to fully or partly satisfy safe or low risk fantasies can make for a bigger and better sexual repertoire. This could reduce the natural craving for partner variety, strengthen commitment, and contribute to us being considered as the best and sweetest lover our partner ever had.

Many among the things people like may seem strange to others, who had never associated them with sex. One example is the first of the fantasies listed below about watching a man urinating. It might have started by something as simple and innocent as the woman unintentionally seeing some man urinating from a distance, at a time when her own sexuality was awakening in adolescence. And because the penis is also used for sex, the experience triggered some pleasant sexual thoughts and sensations.

Such thoughts and sensations may be re-experienced whenever the person remembers what happened, until the original non sexual act of a man urinating becomes a trigger for sexual excitement in its own right. Once such association has been created, that individual may typically fantasize about it while thinking about sex, probably as an arousal enhancement during masturbation. And the more it happens the stronger that sexual excitement becomes, until it ends up as part of the person's established fantasy repertoire.

This is a process known in psychological terminology as "classical conditioning". It is a usually unconscious way of sexual programming and reprogramming, which is part of normal healthy sexual functioning. Another example of this is added as Appendix C, which is an extract from an autobiographical narrative by me entitled *Prescription glasses can be sexy: The formation and reshaping of sexual preferences*. It looks at how and why sexual attraction preferences in men and women may come about and evolve.

The six fantasies listed in Diagram 6 are examples from ordinary couples, and they are discussed next under their own headings. Regarding my respect for the rights to privacy and confidentiality of the people involved, I refer readers to my explanatory "Note" at the bottom of page 019. Understanding what went on in these cases could come in handy, if we ever have to manage comparable issues within us or by our partner in a loving relationship.

The woman who asked to watch her man urinating, and its unexpected bonus

This was a totally safe fantasy, and it might have originated in the manner discussed above. She got not only full satisfaction, but an unexpected little extra too. It happened a long time ago and is part of an autobiographical narrative by me, quoted next, which in addition to the actual events includes some of my thoughts and feelings about it.

"…/… We had been resting for quite a while, completely relaxed. "Well", I told her, "I feel wonderful just laying down here with you, but I have to get up or my bladder will explode". And as I was about to enter the loo, her voice came from behind: "Can I ask you something?" I turned around. "Of course, what?" "Would you mind if I look while you do it?" she asked, with an expression of contained uncertainty. It came as a total surprise. "Bit weird" I thought.

It is in fact most people's understandable first reaction, to anything sexual outside their range of fantasy or personal experience. The reason being that we tend not to disclose our most private sexual longings, except possibly to a person we really trust. Therefore we remain largely ignorant about how common and ordinary most of these things really are.

Fortunately, I had by then heard all sorts of closely guarded bedroom secrets, in the context of professional confidentiality during my relationship therapy work. And perhaps partly for that reason, I felt almost immediately that it was simply incorrect and unfair to think of her request as weird, given that like everybody else I had my own very private sexual fantasies. Besides, no self-respecting man can afford to see himself as a prude, and I had always fancied myself as sexually open minded.

All that had gone through my mind in a flash, and just as fast I knew I wanted to please her. However, I was not entirely comfortable. "No, of course I don't mind if you want to, but … you know, … it will smell a little". "It doesn't matter, it doesn't matter" she assured me eagerly, "I've always wanted to watch but never dared to ask". I could almost touch the excitement and anticipation in her expression and voice.

"Well, OK then" I said, taking the opportunity to prove myself. "Slightly atypical though" I thought again as she got up, having already moderated myself into a non-judgmental mode in order to accommodate to her wishes. "But if it is going to give her that much pleasure and it doesn't hurt, why not?". I would never have guessed, but my body was about to surprise me.

Perhaps I should have realized it could happen. But no. Not to me. Things like that only happened to women, I had naively concluded while doing Psychology 101. It was this lecturer who explained why what people say, even if they genuinely believe it, may not be the whole story when it comes to sex. Or when it comes to anything else, for that matter. In this experiment he told us about, first year male and female psychology students had volunteered to watch blue movies and note down their 0 to 5 level of enjoyment in a questionnaire, at regular intervals.

That, after having their genitals wired up, to simultaneously obtain objective measurements of their physical reactions. In the case of female students, the degree of wetness triggered by sexual excitement inside their wired up vaginas increased the level of electrical conductivity. This was recorded by the experimenters' electronic apparatus, and seen as an objective measure of physical arousal. The "soft" blue movies had a built in love story and no genital close-ups. The questionnaires of female students noted their physical arousal, which was corroborated by the objective measurements.

When it came to the triple X-rated videos in the second day of the experiment, with no love story and lots of genital close-ups, something else happened. Most female students recorded they weren't enjoying it, while at the same time there were significant increases in the level of wetness in their vaginas, as per the objective measurements of electrical conductivity. The researchers concluded that they had been acculturated to believe they ought not to enjoy such images, and had therefore managed to convince themselves they weren't. While their bodies were telling a different story.

But as I said, such things could never happen to me, I thought. Like most men I had no problem admitting I enjoyed sex, triple X-rated or not. As far as I was concerned, either I liked something or didn't, and that was that. So, we went to the loo. And as I saw her avid eyes watching my hand beginning to take my penis out from the side of my underpants, it became rather stiff all of a sudden, and therefore I couldn't wee.

And no matter how hard I tried to push it down on the hope it would acquiesce, it kept asserting its independence and refusing to budge. "It's just a fluke erection", I told her and myself. "Let's go and lay for a while, while it calms itself down". After it had we went again. And, you guessed, it raised up as stubbornly as the first time.

"Well, I never knew *he* was going to enjoy it" I said, still resisting reality by pretending that he wasn't me, "But it seems he is telling me otherwise". Despite the strong urge to empty my bladder, it took another break and a third attempt to do it. And even then, only after I had grabbed it by its neck early enough to prevent another uprising, and struggled to hold it down. Eventually I managed to half do it, in a battle of wills. She had obviously enjoyed the entire show, while I continued to be utterly baffled by my own arousal.

With hindsight, what had done it for me was watching her sexual excitement. And if the relationship had become permanent, having a wee while she was around might have never been the same, because repeated exposure within a loving relationship could have kicked in the "classical conditioning" effect (page 281). That is, her sexual enjoyment could have ended up reprogramming me into liking it. Or to be more technical for anyone interested in that sort of thing, the plasticity of the neural circuitry underlying my emotions could have resulted in additional connections among the brain cells involved, leading to me enjoying it with her rather than just doing it in order to please.

This happens frequently in sex, as loving partners try their best to accommodate to each other's fancies. But if I had never quite grown to like it or perhaps never been open minded enough to admit it, I would have no doubt become a willing participant whenever she wanted, for the very sensible and absolutely commendable purpose of giving my partner sexual pleasure.

And here comes the point I have been getting at all along: Becoming a bit more sexually open minded for the sake of accommodating to our partner, may require in us the minor effort of being non judgmental and a little more tolerant.

But when we do it, and especially if we let ourselves enjoy the pleasure we are giving, the fulfillment it generates can become a powerful force for trust, acceptance and commitment within a marriage. It can also ease any pressure points which monogamy might impose on it, and compensate for our real or imagined shortcomings. .../..."

The woman who dared to request having her man tied up and blindfolded

It is usually the case that couples who come for marital therapy do so in a state of crisis. Typically they are at a point where the fear of a breakup has become greater than that of confronting and exposing their vulnerabilities and imperfections. This is why it is important, especially at the beginning, to get the partners to relax a bit by reducing their concerns about being judged and ease them into talking about their problem.

A common technique for doing so is for the therapist to ask partners to remember something they did together which they particularly enjoyed when things were going well, preferably in the aspect of the relationship which is now causing problems. The presenting problem from the viewpoint of husbands is often about sex, usually not happening enough or their wife not being interested when it does happen, although the underlying issues are typically about something else.

Husbands are often the partner who has to do most of the changing for the relationship to improve, and deep down many of them know it by the time they come. Furthermore, it is common for reluctant husbands to be dragged into therapy kicking and screaming, with their arm twisted by a wife's threat of divorce. That can be very real, as reflected by statistics that about six out of every ten divorces in Australia are initiated by women, two by men, and the other two more or less jointly.

Sometimes therefore it is important to give these usually straight faced but internally distressed men enough support, especially at the beginning, and the above mentioned technique is one way of doing so in an indirect way unlikely to be rejected. That is how over the years I got to ask many husbands to remember something nice they did together when the relationship was going well, and the stories I heard include the one which follows.

One evening the couple had come home from a dinner party where both had drank a bit, and she was feeling happy. She initiated sex and at some point was on her knees and on top, with him outstretched on the bed with his eyes closed. When it was over and they were relaxing and feeling good she disclosed that sometimes she had fantasized about having sex with a man who was tied up to the bed, outstretched and blindfolded. Without even stopping to think, he said it might be nice.

Wanting to please his wife, he bought some rope form the hardware store the following weekend. He felt comfortable about being blindfolded, but not about being tied up. So he prepared four lengths of rope to be attached to the bedposts at one end, and with a loop at the other so that he could put his hands and feet into the loops. That was a good enough pretense, he could "untie" himself if he wanted, and his wife was happy with that.

By doing it without asking questions which she might have experienced as awkward, he had made it easier for her to do whatever she fancied. Furthermore, she could do it without the uneasiness of being watched in some positions she might not want to be seen, or with an expression of unrestrained lust in her face that she might not have felt entirely comfortable with. This was a totally safe fantasy in which he gave her virtually all she had asked for, and they both agreed it had enriched their sexuality and enhanced their feelings for each other.

Two female fantasies about rape: Tied up while having sex, and home intruder

Women who fantasize about being raped are perfectly normal. They would be as disgusted by this abhorrent crime as women who never have such fantasies, and would fear it just as much if the possibility of it happening to them were to arise. Rape fantasies come about and remain rewarding through the "classical conditioning" process described earlier. Some of these women may not dare to tell a partner about it because they believe the fantasy could be seen as improper, or out of fear their man might feel he is not good enough to satisfy them.

A traditional explanation from psychoanalysis is that by having it "forced" on her, the woman relieves herself of responsibility and guilt while getting exactly what she wishes, if not in real life at least in fantasy. When we feel our man loves us and can be really trusted, we are more likely to be comfortable enough with asking for what we want because we know he cares about us and wants to do whatever he can to keep us happy and contented.

A woman who consulted me had not been so lucky, and despite having been married for many years all she had ever dared to do was give her husband a hint. That was in the form of a comment about having read in a magazine that among European women, Italians were the ones who most often reported liking being tied up when they had sex. She then waited for his reaction. With some trepidation she told me that what she really would have liked to tell him was that she wanted to be tied up.

But she had been too embarrassed to actually say it and also uncertain about how her husband would feel about it because, she said, he could be unpredictable. Their relationship had never been very good, her husband was either unwilling or unable or to pick up the hint and put two and two together, and her fantasy was never fulfilled. I said this was rather sad, because doing it would have contributed to making their relationship nicer.

She told me the story about three years after her divorce, when she came to see me regarding a new relationship, and related her unhappiness in her previous marriage. I sensed that without wanting to ask directly she was looking for reassurance that she was "normal", from someone who was supposed to know and could be trusted to keep a secret. I felt she was also looking for some kind of permission to try it out with her new man, because she seemed still uncomfortable about it and unsure whether it was "proper".

I showed her my copy of a well known book about the sexual fantasies of women, and photocopied for her the Table of Contents. I then suggested she might like to borrow it through her local library, so that she could read for herself how normal and ordinary such fantasies are, and perhaps show the book to her new man to see how he reacted and what he thought about it.

As a passing comment somewhere along the line, I added that those Italian women probably felt very safe as long as they were with a man who could be trusted. All that was intended to give her the reassurance and permission I believed she was seeking. This plus the feeling of support and approval she felt from me would have been more than enough to do the trick, while respecting her choice not to be direct about what I thought she really wanted, which might have been a bit too embarrassing for her to admit.

The second fantasy is about a home intruder and I am sure it happens for real, although this is a clinical example I read somewhere. In it, a man who has broken into a house with a nylon stocking over his face forces himself on a woman he finds there, and rapes her despite her vigorous resistance. After it is all over he takes the stocking off, she embraces and kisses him, and then goes to sleep satisfied and contented with her pretend rapist partner, who she had obviously trained to do exactly what she fancied.

The man who asked his woman how she would feel about trying bottom sex

Most heterosexual couples do not practice bottom sex because both partners prefer it the usual way. Other times the partner who wishes it may feel uneasy about it, and doesn't ask or insist. There are still strong prejudices about it in some people, and few women ever initiate it. But more men than in previous generations request it nowadays, partly due to more liberal sexual attitudes and possibly after having seen explicit pictures in the Internet.

What often happens next is that their female partner dislikes the idea and refuses. The man's desire is unlikely to go away however, and the impasse can cause significant tension in quite a few couples. Doing or not doing it is one thing, while being or not being able to talk about it is an altogether different matter. If one partner recoils at the thought of talking about it or engages in a tirade of irrational or uninformed prejudice, he/she would have the most to gain by obtaining further education about it.

"My husband wants us to do something disgusting", told me a visibly distressed woman within the first few minutes of the consultation, while almost looking down to the floor with embarrassment. "Even talking about it feels a bit uncomfortable, doesn't it?" I replied, stating the obvious in order to acknowledge her distress and facilitate further discussion.

Her reply and what followed convinced me that I would have to move no faster than she was able to cope with. That education was going to have to be a big part of what needed to be done. And that this case was going to take some time and effort before meaningful progress could be made. During the rest of the session I encouraged her to talk about it, and at the end I gave her some material to read before the next appointment.

It was an article from an ordinary women's magazine of the kind sold in supermarkets, which I had borrowed from my doctors' waiting room and photocopied years earlier in case I ever needed it as a giveaway handout. The article had been written by some agony aunt advising young women on how to go about having bottom sex if they and their partner had agreed, in a manner intended to minimize the risk of harm or embarrassment.

In addition to plenty of lubricant in both partners, the suggestions included having at hand a dark colored towel. If the woman wanted to be unnecessarily fussy about it, she could self administer a small enema earlier that day in order to clean her lower colon. The risk of uncomfortable smells could be minimized by avoiding foods known to cause gas or by taking a couple of gas absorbing capsules after meals on the day they were going to do it.

If done carelessly and roughly bottom sex carries a risk of damaging the woman's pelvic floor, leading to other complications. And of tearing the anal skin, which in extreme cases may require stitches. But if done with care and lubricant it is unlikely to cause a problem, at worst a minute tear in the skin of the anus known medically as a "fissure", which can cause a stinging sensation on defecation until it heals. If fissures have happened repeatedly in the past for any reason, it might be worth consulting a doctor.

The risk can be greatly reduced by doing it slowly and gently when the woman is aroused or relaxed, to reduce inhibitions and any physical discomfort. On trying for the first time, it is generally safer if only the woman moves while she is positioned on top and on her knees, while he is on his back, so that she has complete control and can stop at any time if she thinks it might hurt. If she decides to try just a little bit to see how it feels, any loving man would agree to not move at all while they do it. Sex should be about enjoying together, and never about using or abusing our partner.

There is also a risk of passing normal colon bacteria into the vagina where it might cause an infection. Therefore the woman should be careful to always wipe from front to back, and both partners should wash with soap before further penis-vagina contact. For some couples, doing it without full penetration might be an acceptable compromise by which each partner cares for the other. Discussing it in a supportive way includes not pressuring a woman who is unsure. If the couple agree to do it in a limited and careful way, that will give the man an opportunity to prove that he can be trusted.

A porn actress who had done it many times said in a documentary that for a short time afterwards until sensation in the area returns completely back to normal, it is better to use the bathroom if the woman feels like passing wind, to preempt any embarrassment by accidentally passing something else.

The above raises the question of whether frequent bottom sex might eventually cause problems with incontinence, perhaps later in life. I have asked experts from two different Sexual Health Clinics, to make sure. The categorical answer by both is that it doesn't if done gently and with enough lubricant, not even in the case of gay men who do it only that way. If we were to consult our doctor to make absolutely sure, we might wish to request an assurance before discussing the issue, that it will not be recorded in our medical file.

We can make that request easier for our doctor to agree, if we go with another health issue so that something else can be written in the file to justify the Medicare charge. It we don't want our doctor to know, one place to get trustworthy information which is free of charge and <u>we</u> can make sure will be forever confidential is at a Sexual Health Clinic. There are several in Sydney and other big cities.

Their services are free, they do not require the person to show a Medicare Card or provide any identification, and no address has to be given apart from a postcode. Sexual Health Clinics are required to request patients' name and date of birth, for authorities to monitor the use of the service and justify the expense, and for the Clinic to identify the file if patients return for further consultations. But we could give a false name and date of birth without saying so, in order to protect the Clinic from involvement in anything which might possibly be misconstrued as not strictly above board.

An appointment can be made with any name, and we should write it down somewhere safe together with the given date of birth, so as not to forget it in case we ever want to go back. If we have some medical problem in the area and want an examination to find out if bottom sex could aggravate it, we could request an appointment with a doctor. Otherwise a nurse or counselor would be fine, and we can ask for a female if we prefer.

The woman consulting me was perfectly entitled to think that bottom sex or even the mention of it was disgusting, although obviously her husband had though it might be nice. Somewhere in between are the majority of women and men, who may feel apprehensive about it but would probably consider it if requested by a loving partner in a committed relationship.

What I said in the first consultation and later as needed, is that there was nothing morally right or wrong with what either of them thought or felt about bottom sex, or with her rejecting or accepting his request partly or completely. What couples like or dislike and do or don't do in the privacy of their bedroom is entirely personal, and for them alone to decide.

Many women in good trusting relationships actually end up liking it or some half way variation. A woman I heard in a talkback radio program said her partner liked to insert his finger in her bottom, when she was very aroused through vaginal sex and getting close to coming. She had grown to enjoy it, she said, and now found difficult to reach orgasm through penetration unless he did that. This may happen because the area has a lot of sensitive nerve endings, and being touched there in such manner can enhance sensations during vaginal sex, masturbation or orgasm.

Some women end up liking bottom sex due to their own arousal at seeing the expression of uncontrollable pleasure in their partner's face, and as one more way of strengthening the relationship by pleasing their partner. Those who don't like any kind of sexual variation outside their comfort zone should not assume that their man's request is because of Internet pornography, or only because of it. In the case of bottom sex, it is as old as humanity.

The Bible mentions it in the story about Sodom and Gomorrah, hence the name "sodomy". Among some Japanese Samurai communes, homosexuality did not have the negative connotations it has in Judaism, Christianity or Islam, and was seen as morally neutral and a matter of personal preference. It was also accepted in classical Greece, where some men with families had openly a male lover. The Greek king known as Alexander The Great took along his male partner during his military campaigns.

Heterosexual bottom sex was the usual contraception method of the Greek peasantry for centuries during the Middle Ages, which is why "Greek sex" is a common euphemism by female sex workers who provide this service. Some years ago and in reference to a Middle East country, a woman who obviously knew very well what was going on, commented on TV about some sex workers as well as some ordinary women who had premarital sex as part of trying out a relationship. She said they practiced the bottom variety only, in order to be able to "lose their virginity" with their future husbands.

The common expression "silly bugger" is often used in a joking way, implying that at worst such men are seen as sick puppies rather than deserving of any hostility. This friendliness and tolerance are features of the Australian character. Although as always there are some antiquated people, religious fanatics and recalcitrant homophobes propelled into obnoxiousness by ignorance. And not infrequently, by the conscious and unconscious defensive strategies associated with poor self esteem, as elaborated in Stage 5.

Despite all the above, many people would be surprised to know that most bottom sex happens within ordinary heterosexual partners. This makes sense because they comprise the majority of couples, and even if only a minor proportion do it the overall numbers would be higher than in the much smaller male homosexual population. But it is generally a closely guarded bedroom secret, for reasons of privacy and as protection against social disapproval.

It has been widely known since at least the 1970's, when anonymous research with thousands of men was published in books intended for the general public, that fantasizing about or practicing bottom sex with their female partners is no indication of homosexual tendencies in men. Checking that out is now easier than ever, just Google "anal sex", and probably all the photos will be about heterosexual bottom sex.

Some men's desire for bottom sex may have to do with their responsiveness to the beauty and sexiness of female bottoms, the thrill of the forbidden, and the tighter physical sensation which they may fantasize as being pleasurable. Although as one of the men quoted in the 1970's research pointed out, once it is inside, the sensation is not that different from vaginal sex.

Books for the general public based on anonymous research with thousands of women, were also published in the 1970's. These women described their private thoughts and feelings about their sexual practices and fantasies, including what they liked and didn't, the importance of clitoral stimulation during sex with a partner and for masturbating alone, how orgasm felt to them, etc.

Given this woman' situation, one of our agreed goals was to make it easier for her to discuss the subject with her husband, in a manner which would at least not damage their relationship and preferably improve communication and trust. We also agreed that further knowledge would help, hence my giving her a lot of reading homework between consultations.

This included selected parts of the above books on male and female sexuality and fantasies. She could borrow the books direct from her public library, and if not in their collection, the library could borrow from elsewhere in order to lend them to her. That is still the case, and we may find titles, summaries and tables of contents in online bookstores. Interested readers could Google for "female sexual fantasies books" or something similar.

In addition, some readers might wish to get additional insights on the subject by hiring the French film entitled in English *A Pornographic Affair*. It was written by Philippe Blasband, directed by Frederic Fonteyne, and has been shown in Australia at SBS TV with English subtitles. It is about a recently divorced woman who advertises for a man with body hair to practice bottom sex with, in order to fulfill her own fantasies. This happens in a manner which is unambiguously clear, but never seen or explicitly discussed.

My client and her marriage had something to gain by she broadening her sexual horizons, whatever they decided to do or not do about the issue at hand. Her discussing it with me provided the sanction of professional respectability, and indirectly with it, the permission she needed to further educate herself without feeling that doing so was immoral or improper.

Through exposure to additional knowledge, she became better informed and a little more relaxed about sex in general. By doing so she grew out of feeling horrified into inability to talk about less common aspects of it, even with her own husband. Our conversations enabled her to develop a new and better style of discussing what she had initially experienced as very awkward issues, by modeling on how I was doing it.

She was able to practice her developing capacity to discuss such issues within the safe context and confidentiality of therapy, and to gradually get better at it with my encouragement and feedback. The ultimate goal was not only to increase her sexual knowledge and competence through further education, but by doing so and also as means to it, to improve relevant core components of her personality and self esteem.

These included better acceptance about her own sexuality by increasing her awareness about the wide variety of sexual preferences different to her own, thereby strengthening her general self confidence and specifically sexual confidence. They were in turn bound to increase her conviction of worthiness, to the very small extent this was possible in the circumstances and limited duration of therapy. All the above would have the effect of shifting her contingent self esteem a little bit towards the secure variety.

Achieving it involved my giving occasional nudges in the right direction, as required. This was done by using the opportunities which opened up during our conversation, in order to improve her sexual confidence and body image. Or to say the same thing in counseling terminology, I was helping her "reframe" for the better certain feelings and opinions, using as leverage my "unconditional positive regard" and professional credibility.

But no form of human interaction is ever a one way process, and any honest therapist will acknowledge that we learn from our clients just as they learn from us. Unfortunately and inevitably, this means that part of what it takes to acquire expertise is to have made mistakes with people who consulted us earlier in our career. Hopefully as a result we learned to teach trainees better, so that they might minimize similar mistakes with their own clients.

She saw me for about eight or nine consultations spread over about four months, initially weekly and later fortnightly. I had indicated from the beginning that it is usually more effective to see couples together. But she felt more comfortable discussing these issues without her husband being present, and in this case it worked to her satisfaction.

The man who asked his woman to consider swinging with safety precautions

In the years before AIDS became a well known public health issue there was an increase in the practice of partner swapping, or "swinging" as is commonly called. The classic Australian film "Don's Party", written by David Williamson and directed by Bruce Beresford, includes a clumsy attempt to initiate it by two middle class husbands. Such attempts reflect a sexual dissatisfaction which is common in established marriages, and a need for better self-other awareness and communication skills especially in men. Swinging contacts are now easier than ever, through the Internet.

Couples contemplating swinging would be well advised to consider carefully the pros and cons as well as safer alternatives. The possibility of sexually transmitted infections may be reduced with proper precautions, but never completely eliminated. The main risk however, is about aggravating existing dissatisfaction within the relationship.

The area of Sydney where I once worked for the Department of Health was reputed to have many swingers. As I overheard one of our secretaries commenting in a surprisingly matter of fact way, all the young couples in that particular street were mortgaged to the hilt. And swinging with one another was, she said, "the only entertainment they can afford". But it is never that simple, and this was why over the years I worked with quite a few cases in which the issue had currently or in the past caused serious marital tensions.

A couple came to see me because the husband wanted them to swing with safety precautions, he said, while his wife was reluctant but felt pressured to agree. As he kept trying to persuade her and she continued to resist, they had reached a worsening impasse which was damaging the relationship. This is a not uncommon scenario when couples are struggling with whether or not to do it, because what one partner wants may violate the other's values, sense of identity or need for security in a fundamental way.

I told them that a decision about swinging could only be made by them, because if I gave an opinion that would reflect my beliefs and values and not theirs. They would make their own decision, they replied, but wanted an informed and impartial person who could be trusted to keep the matter confidential, and were insistent that I give them my honest opinion. That was what they wanted and had come for, so I agreed.

The husband had repeatedly reassured his wife that he loved her and was only interested in swinging to add variety to their sex life. Other than that and in addition to using condoms, the safety precaution he believed would work was that if either of them did not like something about the other couple for any reason, they would not swing and instead keep searching until they found a suitable couple.

And the difficulty with such argument is that the emotions which are at the center of loving relationships do not necessarily or frequently respond primarily to reason, although they can be influenced by it. Some of these emotions may be subtle, unrecognized or not clearly delineated, but still operating under the surface. The idea of swinging may come about because the sexual side of the relationship is not as good as it could be and probably hasn't been for a long time, at least for the partner who fantasizes about it.

Swinging is unlikely to improve the issues which may be the real causes of dissatisfaction however, and if unresolved they will continue to create friction. It may move partners closer towards a break up, by getting to know intimately someone who they can see and feel might be better suited as a partner than their current one, and wants them permanently. If that never happens, it may still give one partner a taste for what intimacy with a better suited person feels like, and on doing so increase discontent. Swinging may also aggravate preexisting insecurities in at least one partner.

That is because in the final analysis we all want to be loved, and need to feel secure about the commitment of our partner and the stability of the relationship. Any of the above factors can increase underlying unhappiness, even if it is temporarily contained or not entirely expressed. For anyone or several of the above reasons, a proportion of couples who start swinging end up divorcing, and a few divorcees then remarry one of their former swinging partners. However, it would be equally true to say that in some of these cases the divorce was likely to happen, with or without swinging.

I have also worked with couples where swinging had, according to the partner who prompted it and with somewhat less conviction according to the initially reluctant partner, stabilized their marriage with an outcome which was better than the alternatives. In one case, not only did they say it probably prevented the breakup of their de-facto relationship of many years, but resulted in both increasing their commitment and formalizing it by marriage.

In cases where both partners though it had worked for them, neither appeared to have noticeable personality imbalances and they had a fairly good marriage of some years to begin with. Furthermore, they were strongly committed to each other and had no major financial or family problems. So, swinging seems to work well enough for a minority, usually because some important circumstances and personality features are favorable, including both having the kind of personality which can handle jealousy.

My view still is that for the vast majority of couples who want to remain together, there are alternatives far safer than swinging which are generally good enough for addressing tensions due to the sexual limitations of monogamy. The first thing is to work out exactly what the causes of dissatisfaction are, and often they include personality issues in one or both partners. These may be causing problems most visibly on the sexual side but also in other areas of the relationship, and obstructing their good enough management.

The grass is greener elsewhere: The most common and dangerous fantasy

When two people choose committed monogamy, they enter into a usually implied voluntary "contract" which includes three major expectations. The first is about not getting involved with a third party to satisfy the natural craving for sexual variety. Both genders experience this craving, although more men than women struggle with it. The second is that they will care for each other in every way they can, and become each other's most trusted friend. And the third is that the relationship will be permanent.

The combination of caring, friendship, sexuality and commitment which monogamy is best at providing, is essential for permanent relationships to remain satisfying. When one or more of these four C's (as that "three C's" teacher would have called them) has not been going well for too long, all four may be damaged because they are interconnected and influence one another.

Insufficient understanding, personality problems or limitations, poor communication, financial pressures and any number of other unfavorable circumstances can make matters worse. Eventually, the resulting chronic frustration may lead one or both partners to wonder whether life would be better alone or with someone else.

In these situations the more dissatisfied partner often begins to think other couples appear to be happier, and ponder why they can't. If attempts at remedying the problems have repeatedly failed, such partners may begin paying more attention to people who have given signals of being sexually interested in them. Or they could begin secretly looking at dating sites in the Internet, and feel tempted to make contact. The possibility of some adventure behind their partner's back is no longer dismissed out of hand.

Whether they are aware of it or not, their chronic relationship dissatisfaction has primed them for an affair. However, it is important to appreciate that some people's dissatisfaction with their relationship could in fact have nothing to do with it or their partner. They may believe it does, but might actually be dissatisfied within themselves for reasons having to do with their own personality, circumstances and/or stage of life.

Being unaware or unwilling to accept the true reasons, they tend to over focus on whether what their partner is or isn't and does or doesn't is in line with what they would prefer, and before long they could be openly or silently blaming the other for how they feel. Their resentment leads to some sort of neglect or mistreatment towards their spouse. If that becomes ongoing it can trigger relationship conflict, and a vicious cycle of deterioration may quite easily be set in motion and keep feeding on itself.

Once this high risk situation has been created, the temptation for an affair can come suddenly and unexpectedly. For example, women in long established marriages may go out with married, single and divorced girlfriends to celebrate a birthday. They end up in some dancing venue where men approach them. The temptation to accept is strong, and they want to believe there is nothing wrong with just dancing with a man, especially if their girlfriends are doing so too and they have all had a drink or two.

For a woman dissatisfied with her marriage who has been immersed in the roles wife and mother for years and years, suddenly dancing with a man she finds very attractive can be an intensely erotic experience. As the situation makes it easy to get physically close, she surrenders to temptation.

The closer she dances, the desire to get even closer can be very hard to resist. And as she gradually gives in, the experience can blow her off her feet. The man feels it and propositions. She typically refuses but has been touched deep, and thereafter may begin to fantasize about it.

If her marriage has been deficient in any of the four essentials of caring, friendship, sexuality or commitment, and especially when this is being aggravated by a vicious cycle of deterioration, the temptation to have a secret adventure will be stronger. If she does, there could be a striking contrast between those now reawakened beautifully erotic feelings and sensations with a new man, and the routine sex with a husband she has not been happy with for a long time. It is very difficult to improve such marriage while one partner has an outside sexual liaison, whether or not the other knows about it.

In usually different circumstances, the above unrealistic distortions can happen just as easily in a man. Men' sexuality is very visual, there is a never ending stream of attractive women younger than his wife looking for a nice man, and the temptations for appealing NUSSC men can be considerable. For both genders, perceptions could easily become distorted towards undervaluing their marriage and partner, and overvaluing the implied promises which the possibility of a new relationship brings about.

Many married men and women fantasize with having an outside sexual liaison. Over the years I have worked with countless couples who came to see me after an affair had been discovered and triggered a marital crisis, both of which are likely to happen if it becomes ongoing. And the big horrible problem with affairs is that they destroy trust, which is then difficult or impossible to rebuild.

Retaining a solid grip on reality is vital in order to avoid a potentially catastrophic life changing decision. "Leaving my wife was the biggest mistake of my life" told me a man whose ex wife had rejected his attempt at reconciliation, years after his subsequent de-facto and other relationships had failed. Comparable mistakes by women have already been discussed. Advice from a wise trusted friend, family member or therapist could be timely and beneficial. It may help us bring our head down from the clouds, and get our feet back on the ground.

A woman consulted me after becoming alarmed and guilt ridden by her own overpowering emotions. Around ten years earlier she was in a brief relationship with a man she found very attractive. She had seen him again for the first time after all those years, accompanied by a woman and young child who were probably his family. Although now married with two children, she told me, "If he had approached and asked me to go with him, I would have abandoned my husband and children".

There is a risk of unwise decisions at the opposite end too. By staying in a bad relationship which has no chance of improvement due to entrenched serious personality problems or limitations in our partner, we set ourselves up for a life of avoidable unhappiness. In these cases a divorce may be the least damaging option for the partner who chooses to leave, and sometimes a very sensible and beneficial one. If there are children involved, their distress is likely to be reduced if it is done carefully and cooperatively.

So, what can we do to minimize the risk of us or our partner being tempted into an affair, and then suffering longer term unhappiness plus risking relationship breakup? Or to put the question in a more positive and productive way, what can we do while it is still not too late, to maintain and enhance the health and quality of our relationship? This has already been discussed at various points, but a brief recapitulation is appropriate.

First of all, nothing we do is likely to work if one of us has a significant personality problem and keeps pretending that it does not exist. If our partner has such problem and he/she doesn't want to change or has tried and failed repeatedly, we can bear with it, see a therapist or drift towards divorce. If we suspect we are the one with the problem and want to change plus are prepared to do what it takes, understanding the knowledge embodied in this book and especially in Stage 5 is our first step.

The second step would be to develop the qualities listed under the heading *Desirable personality qualities in men (and women)* elaborated in Stage 6. Having a partner with such qualities would be very helpful in acquiring or maintaining them ourselves. But even if we were smart or lucky enough to have found someone like that, our attempt at personal development will only work if we are willing to grow in terms of practicing those qualities with people in general, and are able to make the effort which implementing the necessary changes would undoubtedly bring about.

If we have a good man, we still need to understand his needs and cater to them to the extent that is possible, within reason. We need to be lovingly assertive about him doing the same for us, without ever forgetting that nobody is entitled to anything and we all have to earn our partner's desire to care for us out of love. This raises the question of how to get ourselves dearly loved, despite our imperfections and limitations.

How to get dearly loved, as well as forgiven for our favorite faults

In order to make full and proper sense of what is recapitulated here, it is important to have read and understood the rest of the book. Assuming this is the case, let us begin with what could be done if the reader happens to be a man, and then I'll make some comments for female readers.

Stage 5 began by clarifying how "second order" understandings go beyond trying to work out what is happening by using the typical limited and limiting intellectual-emotional tools we have and are used to. It focused on sharpening those tools and creating new ones in order to improve our equipment. This consists of knowledge plus emotional balance, and their enhancement results in a higher level of relationship-relevant skills.

A good enough emotional balance is critical for the purpose of acquiring "second order" understandings, because a higher or lower level can help or hinder the development of relationship knowledge and skills. The combination of knowledge and emotional balance will give us an improved capacity to appreciate more accurately the issues affecting any relationship. And therefore, a better chance of managing it as constructively and effectively as the situation allows.

Therapy offers the opportunity for sharing insights about the emotions being experienced and expressed. That makes it an individually tailored effective method of developing the kind of awareness that matters, when done between a good therapist and a person or couple genuinely wanting to extend their understanding as a means for improving their relationship.

But good therapists can be expensive and hard to find. While this book is cheap, not difficult to read, and might just be enough to learn what is needed in order to understand ourselves and others better. Discussing any issues arising from it with the woman we love, could help us expand our existing emotional knowledge and skills. And doing so is definitely an excellent way of becoming more articulate about the subtleties of relationships.

The above would be a sensible investment, because women like talking about the ins and outs of feelings and meanings, at least until they've got their fill. Doing our best to cater for such needs is a mutually rewarding way of men improving our skills as intimate communicators and lovers, and both things go hand in hand. But there is a further benefit from getting better at picking up subtler feelings and nuances of meaning.

We would become better able to obtain more enjoyment out of everything to do with people including family, friends, work relationships, social observation and harmless gossip. This is what most women are able to do, using their genetically supported superior understanding of emotions. For us men, that is a little bit like when we walk our dog and know it is having satisfactions we don't, in the sense that it is getting a huge amount of very interesting smell information. We know it is there, but our nose can't detect it.

Men have huge potential for emotional development, but it is not easy for us to reach women's level in those skills. While some of us become gradually better as we get older, knowledge and practice can speed up the process. Empathy is an especially important skill, and a method for men who want to improve it was discussed in the Stage 5 subheading *Smaller problems*, within the main heading *Communication: Bigger, smaller and sum-total problems*. An example of good emotional intelligence in a man, is the male central character in the film (and novel) *Lady Chatterley's Lover*.

Being loved may be easier for women, **if** they chose or were lucky to get a man with a good balance of qualities and imperfections. It requires mostly catering for his sexual-emotional longings and soothing his vulnerabilities. If we are intellectually sophisticated, it would help if he can communicate at that level too, and this should be considered when seeking a life partner. But every couple is unique, and intellectually dissimilar partners can create a satisfying relationship if they are equal enough in emotional intelligence.

In terms of how women want to be loved, there is one thing most mature women want to know and feel sure about. Namely, that our man will still love us as we get older and our sex appeal declines, because not being loved at such time of life would in all probability be rather difficult to remedy. This is why it makes increasingly more sense for many mature women to go for a man who is emotionally intelligent, a better communicator, has a good heart and can be trusted, even if he is poorer, older or less attractive at first sight.

And why continuing to choose men primarily on the basis of physical attraction, status or money is likely to become an increasingly costly error of judgment. If our choice of man has been wise and our own personality is OK, the rest is fairly easy. The first thing a woman needs to do sexually involves noticing what he likes and offering it by showing willingness. Or by taking the initiative whenever we sense he wants it, without having to be asked.

If the non sexual sides of the relationship are good enough and we love him, caring and giving will be easier in those occasions when what he likes or the timing would not be our first preference. Our own enjoyment is also important however, but in order to get it we have to risk being daring enough to ask for what we want. Again, good personal qualities in our man make it easier to trust him enough to ask for whatever we fancy, just for our own pleasure and without being judged. This benefits him too, because enjoying sex is a very nice way of being "good in bed".

Most of the second part of what it takes to be dearly loved by our man is understanding and soothing his vulnerabilities. That is not a particularly difficult task for women, because most of us are quite smart and can sense those vulnerabilities even if he doesn't talk about it or denies them if asked. We also tend to be savvy and diplomatic enough to know what to do or not do and say or not say, on the basis of what would be constructive given how he is and what he can take on board at any point in time.

It would be very satisfying to be able to talk about these things with him on the same level of understanding. But if he is not quite there yet or is never going to be, the situation can still be managed in unspoken subtle ways. And it should be, because the point is not to be equal in everything but to love and to be loved. While it would be a problem if differences were so big as to become unbridgeable, not being equal means that we have to be comfortable with being superior in some ways, and resist the temptation to brag about it or throw it on his face in a moment of anger.

That would be marital sadism as well as a grossly stupid thing to do, because being superior carries some responsibilities. For example, if we have to lift and move the fridge for some distance we would expect him to take the heavier bottom side because he is stronger. And by the same token, if we happen to be emotionally better developed (as women often are), it is only fair that we take on more than half the weight in caring for the relationship.

Because our carrying seventy per cent of the responsibility, for example, could take no more effort from us than the one he has to make to support the thirty per cent he may be able to understand or take on. In other words, equal contributions are not always fair, whether it is about carrying a heavy load or caring for the relationship. In any case, over focusing on counting reflects an excessive interest in not being taken advantage of, and that is a sure fire indicator that there is a lot which is not well with us or the relationship.

Whether we are a man or a woman, doing our part in caring for the relationship means that when our partner touches a raw nerve and it hurts us, we are able to take responsibility for calming ourselves instead of just reacting.

It means we retain our equanimity and stay in control of our behavior, even in the middle of a storm which is unsettling our emotions. In other words, we refuse to be helpless puppets of a destructive compulsion to be loudly confrontational or alternatively passive-aggressive, just because we feel annoyed justifiably or otherwise.

Caring for the relationship includes our being able to be generous when our partner feels cornered because he/she knows we have a valid reason to be dissatisfied, and probably therefore needs our tolerance more than at other times. Within the overall context of a relationship which is satisfying or has the potential to be, caring and loving means we are able to let our partner win unfairly without resentment when he or she needs it.

At the very least we need to let our partner not lose, especially when we sense that it is important for safeguarding core values and self respect, or to avoid feeling humiliated. Doing so means we have developed the wisdom, the capacity and the stamina to give ourselves a choice. The choice, that is, of not adding fuel to those inevitable fires igniting every now and then from our human imperfections.

Rather than withdrawing, sulking, arguing or "forgetting" about something we dislike, we could give ourselves a cooling off period. After that, we should set a time to search cooperatively for a solution to significant unresolved issues, while letting go of small matters. That requires agreeing on a time for talking, reassuring our partner we will do it in a respectful manner, and doing so whether or not he/she does likewise.

When we have made our personality healthier, none of the above requires us to stop being lovingly assertive about our needs. If we decided to end the relationship it would probably be for valid sensible reasons, rather than as a result of badly handled escalations and accumulations of mistakes and counter mistakes. This is often what has been happening when the situation has reached the point of becoming irretrievably bad, and is no longer worth the effort of trying to improve it.

But irrespective of whether we stay or leave, the really important point is that as we advance through personal development into higher levels of inner strength and wisdom, we become more lovable than we ever were. And therefore better able to create and enhance love around us, and to retain it permanently as part of a happy and secure relationship.

By becoming good at giving love the way our partner likes or needs, by learning to caress the mind and heart as well as the body, we make ourselves much more likely to be dearly loved. As well as forgiven without resentment for our imperfections, limitations, occasional silliness and favorite faults.

302 Recapitulation about influences from the relationship knowledge environment, and barriers to improvement

One way of visualizing what the above heading covers is as in Diagram 8, which can be used for considering where we were within it, where we are now, plus where we want to be and why.

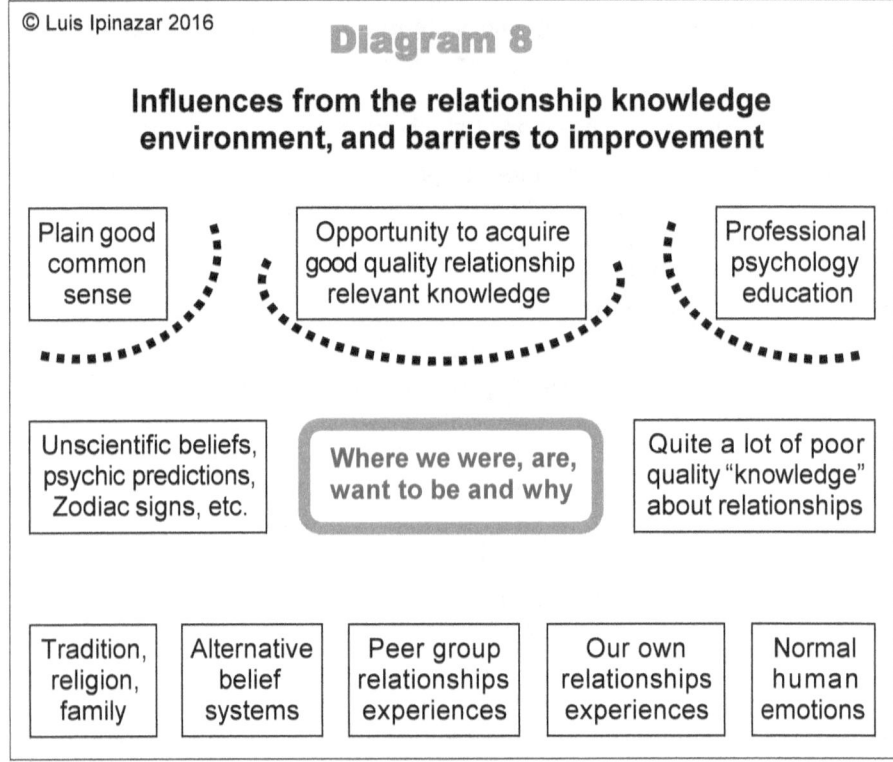

The outer rectangles represent common factors influencing the relationship knowledge environment we live in. The barriers represented by the dotted lines obstruct us from improving on the knowledge we already have. Crossing them in order to acquire more of it may be difficult for a number of reasons. But doing so is important for ourselves, our relationships, and ultimately for achieving better emotional security, stability and contentment.

By far the most important rectangle is "plain good common sense", but the hardwiring of normal human emotions predisposes them to override it, thereby creating a barrier. For example we like someone a lot, and therefore blind ourselves into not giving due consideration to clues about likely problems.

Other times, unruly emotions may cause us to blunder away from what could have been a relationship with potential. To the extent that normal emotional hardwiring has been distorted by an unlucky childhood or other adversities, the smooth operation of common sense will have been further eroded. Its causes, manifestations, consequences, potential for improvement and ways of doing so were discussed in Stage 5.

The main barrier to professional psychology education is that it takes four years. Apart from that, undergraduate and nearly all postgraduate degrees do not provide enough relationship relevant knowledge. And unless students had it beforehand, neither such degrees nor their professional practice guarantee that they will acquire the all-important healthy personality, which is needed for balanced emotional reaction patterns and reliable common sense.

Despite an ever expanding mountain of books providing relationship advice, the vast majority of them are mediocre or bad for the reasons elaborated in the Introduction. Ascertaining their worth can be difficult, especially for individuals influenced by unscientific beliefs, which are unfortunately quite common. These are subscribed to by those who have no better way of alleviating the void created by their unfulfilled need to understand the complexities of relationships, and of their own and other people's personalities.

Bad books and unscientific beliefs often create faith in fake knowledge. This hinders the acquisition of real knowledge, by crowding it out and confusing those who cannot distinguish one from the other. True knowledge can be scary too, when it cuts close to the bone. Therefore some will avoid it, and so remain less able to act wisely when important decisions have to be made.

Tradition, religion, family, alternative belief systems and experiences by us and friends may provide valuable insights. What matters here is to separate the wheat from the chaff and to be aware of how and why they may sometimes, subtly or directly, obstruct the acquisition of the kind of knowledge which could be really helpful. Much of this was discussed in Stage 4.

As a concluding comment, this book provides professional quality education on relationships by discussing critical issues affecting them, in a manner which is comprehensive enough plus not too difficult to understand and remember. It focuses on increasing the kind of knowledge, skills and wisdom which can make a difference at making our life better. That is no easy task, and readers will be the ultimate judges of my efforts at helping them do so.

Appendix A

THE DOORS OF HEAVEN:
Boyhood rites of passage before the days of sex education

Our fight for survival begins with conception and ends with death. And it is usually not until later in life that we can look with a smile to the struggles and tribulations of our adolescence, and share an affectionate pat on the back with the child we once were. But it was serious while it was happening. And most of us needed all the resourcefulness we could muster in order to defend our turf within the peer group, and so ensure emotional wellbeing. That was not always easy.

"Get out of here!" they said, "This conversation is only for those who've entered the doors of Heaven". They had told me off before and this time I wasn't going to let them get away with it. "I've been there" I said defiantly. "Bullshit", the bully boy retorted. "When did you do it?" "The last time I went to buy clothes" I replied. "That's a lie", he insisted aggressively, "Who saw you?"

"Nobody, I don't buy clothes with my mother" I retorted, trying obliquely to reassert my adulthood while refusing to surrender, but sensing it wasn't going to be enough to pull it off. "And I already have enough money to do it again". The money bit was true, as we had all started working and those of us determined enough could manage to save it. They doubted.

Looking younger than your age can be a pain, when you are only fifteen. I was fed up of always being the one hassled at the door when we went to see a movie for over-fourteens, and then teased about it. And that was one reason why stratagems for acting older were important. The deal I had agreed on with my mother, because it sounded reasonably fair, was that nobody was old enough to smoke until they were old enough to work. But being working, I could now show off. And carrying a cylinder between the top of my ear and the side of the head was a cool way of doing it.

The older schoolboys had started the joke after the teacher had accidentally farted standing with his back to the class, while writing on the blackboard during a geometry lesson. It was them who began laughing their heads off as they smoked behind their parents' backs, while trying to be creative at imitating the funny noise every time their one shared cigarette came round for another puff. Cigarettes happen to be cylindrical, you see, and the teacher had been explaining how to calculate the volume of a cylinder.

It was to become his most successful class ever. Every man of drinking age learned that you could do it by multiplying its height by the surface area of the base. They just kept learning and learning, during their after Sunday Mass mooring rounds of the half a dozen or so village pubs, as they joined the fun trying to forget about life. The name was an instant hit with us, coming so soon after we ourselves had finally escaped from school discipline. And we kept enjoying the joke long after most people had forgotten about it.

So I picked the cylinder off the top of my ear, put it in my mouth, and took a loose match out of my pocket. And then casually bent my left leg up at the knee as far as it would go and lit it, with an irreverent rub on the shoe leather sole. Without even looking, of course, just as I'd seen some actor do in some film.

There were no safety matches yet, and earlier ones would light up by being rubbed against just about anything. I had been secretly practicing, until I could do the whole bit with all the panache of a Clint Eastwood re-lighting his half smoked cigar in his best spaghetti westerns.

"Want a cylinder?" I asked them as I lifted the pack from my shirt pocket while exhaling the puff, offering the first one to the bully boy. We laughed, someone pretended to fart, and we laughed again. The tension of the challenge had dissipated and I was still there, holding my ground.

I knew I was under probation, hanging by the skin of my teeth. And that the next time they went I would have no choice but to join in, unless I was demonstrably half dead. If I failed to do so I would be utterly discredited, and put back right down with the uninitiated where I would then belong. However, that was a fight for another day, and for the time being I had just pushed myself over the line.

The deeply ingrained conviction of being worthy which my mother's love had given me, was to come in handy when the pressure came crashing down during the daunting but exciting initiation of going through the doors of Heaven. A rite of passage which allowed aspiring boys to join the upper ranks and thereby enjoy full rights of participation in the juiciest street corner conversations, whilst earning them the privilege of looking down on those who hadn't done it.

My sex education had started around five years earlier. It was this boy about one year older, who persuaded us to go with him claiming to know the location of the hiding holes under the rock boulders, where trout could be caught. Catching trout by hand in the one mile or so stretch of river around the village was a traditional pastime for adolescent boys, and the knowledge of the right holes and techniques was passed on from generation to generation. We were catching small fry here and there, but that was all.

The trick was to dive in, and get an arm into the deep hole while blocking the other exit with the other hand. And while there, grab the trout by sticking the thumb and forefinger into its gills, the only non-slippery part other than its teeth. So that it could be pulled out securely with just that one hand, before our lungs run out of air. We did manage to reach the odd trout's tail, but had no chance of pulling it out.

The truth was our arms were too short and we weren't skilled enough. That didn't count however. As far as we were concerned his credibility wasn't looking very good, and we were letting him known about it. He was feeling increasingly cornered, but still had one bullet left. "Do you know what fucking means?" he asked us, knowing we'd want to know.

We listened, eyes wide opened and jaws dropped. "You put your wily inside her pussy and take it out", he explained. We were dazzled with fascination and wonder. "How many times do you do that?" I asked. "Three times", he added without hesitation. "And what do you do when it is inside?" He looked a bit uncertain. "Anything you want", he said, regaining control of the situation. "Can you wee?" someone asked. He doubted for a moment. "If you want to" he added, looking well informed. That was his story and he was sticking to it. His honor had been saved.

It would have been a few months later that I saw this boy running at top speed down the street in my direction. And just as he was about to pass me by, he suddenly veered towards me and stopped, still puffing from the run. "Do you know what the word fuck means?" he asked between breaths, with excitement jumping off his face.

I looked at him over my shoulder, which wasn't difficult because he was a bit younger and smaller. "Of course" I exclaimed, "I've known it for years!" Letting him known by the tone of my voice that I was slightly indignant the question needed to be asked. And then swaggered away without looking back, refusing to discuss such matters with youngsters and feeling awfully good about myself.

That's when I saw this cat, enjoying the leftover warmth from the fading sun on the surface of a rusty metal barrel. It suddenly pricked its ears and then turned ready to pounce, with its gaze fixed on a crack in an old wooden fence, where a fearful lizard had just hidden. As I approached from behind I saw an empty can of paint laying temptingly ahead of me, just where I would be able to kick it.

It flew straight against the side of the barrel and made an almighty racket. The poor cat jumped into the air, and then onto the top of the fence. Where it looked back for a second while it recovered from the fright, its hair puffed up and standing on end, before jumping away to the other side. I enjoyed every drop of my belly laugh, with the utterly guiltless conscience of a ten year old. Life was good, and I was riding on it.

The big day came, and that Sunday we were going to the city to take a trip through the doors of Heaven. "We are going to the city to see the soccer match", I told my mother. She knew from experience that resistance was futile, having been thoroughly trained by my two brothers fifteen years earlier. "Take care darling. When will you be back?" I gave her my usual answer: "Don't know, in time to catch the bus to work tomorrow morning at the latest" I said, as I walked out.

Times were safer those days, but mothers were still mothers and that reply was the less cruel option. If she didn't expect me back till breakfast time on Monday, I knew she wouldn't be as worried if I happened to get home a few hours later than anticipated. I had to do what I had to do, but I still cared about my mother. Without ever having thought it through, I understood instinctively that sometimes parents just had to be accepted and outsmarted. It was her fault of course, for having been such a devoted parent that she'd made me into the resourceful-enough-to-survive boy I had become.

There were no drugs or too many really serious dangers out there, and cultural norms allowed quite a bit of freedom to boys who were already working. There was the risk of venereal disease, but in the infrequent occasion it happened it tended to be of the kind that is easily remedied. And when it did, older adolescents would often let it be known with a pretense of discreetness intended to mask the underlying boastfulness, as uncontestable proof that they were doing it. There was a general perception that for a single man it would be nothing more than an acceptable temporary nuisance, if one happened to be unlucky enough to catch it.

We saved the ticket money and watched the match on television, in a cheap bar near the red light district. And as soon as it was over we raced there, hours ahead of anyone who had actually been inside the stadium, to ensure nobody from the village would see us there if they happened to go. The moment of truth had arrived.

The bully boy went in first, and was back within fifteen minutes. "How was it?" we asked. "Shit, I didn't come", he blurted out. "What happened?" we said. "Don't know, I think I enjoyed it more while I was touching her tits". "But you came the last time you did it, didn't you?" Supposedly, he too had done it before. "What?" he retorted. That was enough for whatever he said next to be accepted without question, and for the subject to be dropped. He was big enough to thump anyone who dared step a toe out of line. Having lots of muscle and a nasty disposition, he didn't need to be smart.

This woman took me a few doors away and we began climbing the stairs. Being seen to be dragging my feet wouldn't have looked good, and I had armed myself with valor and done the deal without delay. It was dark and scary when I looked up the first flight of stairs, as I walked behind her. My heart began pounding heavily against my chest cavity, and I felt like running away. I looked downstairs, but my friends had followed us there and were looking from the door. I gave them a thumbs up sign and they returned it. There was no escape.

"They go to Mass every day at five o'clock in the morning", this old man had told me once, "To confess all the sins they've committed the night before". He worked in the factory with me, and had once lived in a dilapidated area of the city near the red light district. He needed a steady pulse in order to do his welding, and an uncomplicated nature to avoid going nuts with the monotony of his work. "And they still want to have a boyfriend", he added with a laugh in a tone of amused puzzlement. "As if they weren't getting enough of it already". He was a good welder.

The power of the Catholic Church had become pervasive after they had allied themselves with the military, the aristocracy, the landed gentry and the industrialists. They had won the war against the democratically elected government with help from Hitler and Mussolini, active collaboration from America and England, and passive collusion from France and other nations.

And with the Catholic Church in charge of public morals ever since, the much crowed about virginity of the Virgin Mary had become quite harmful to unmarried mothers. Because obviously they had committed the mayor sin of losing it out of church-sanctified wedlock, and were therefore social outcasts. If in addition they happened to work as prostitutes, as some had to do in order to survive in those difficult times, they were seen and made to feel as the lowest of the low.

That was why even in that brief encounter, the woman had explained she was a mother. And was going to do whatever it took to ensure a good education for her daughter, so that she would never have to experience what life had put her through. She needed to justify herself, to a boy who looked no older than fourteen. And many of her fellow sex workers lived in chronic fear of being judged too, feeling they needed forgiveness from God as they went to pray in their early morning Mass.

"If it hadn't been because your grandfather was able to work till a very old age", I remember my mother telling me once, "I would have had to work as a prostitute". "Because", she added, "There is nothing worse than seeing your children hungry and asking for food, and having nothing to give them". She had lived as a single mother with my two very young brothers through the so called "years of hunger" after the Spanish Civil War, while Europe plunged into the Second World War and she tried to survive without my father.

He had managed to escape to France in the nick of time, and was eking a living while being in constant danger of being deported by the pro-Nazi regime, back to certain death in Spain. Where the Generalissimo had executed two hundred thousand after winning the war, as Western ruling elites looked the other way because he wasn't a communist.

So, I could never have been disrespectful to prostitutes. And obviously neither did the priest, who got up so early every morning to offer support in the only way he could, during the Mass he had arranged to fit in with the end of their night shift. It is difficult for any half-decent person to demonize or dislike a whole class of people, when we get to know individuals at a personal level. If only, because we all share our common humanity.

The lyrics of the song "Russians" by the British pop singer Sting were making that very point: "I hope the Russians love their children too", he sang, in an effort to counteract the official promotion of insanity during the later Cold War years. It could equally have applied to prostitutes, religious fanatics, the filthy rich, the amoral middle class, or any other negatively stereotyped category of people.

With hindsight, the woman was being a little motherly towards me, I had the distinct impression. That wasn't surprising, as she was a mother herself, I really did look a bit too young for that sort of thing, and she had to have noticed the underlying terror behind the bravado. Given her doubtless previous similar experiences, one look at me and my friends would have been enough for her to work out the whole story.

She wasn't a bad girl and gave me a fair go. But she was in a tough occupation with very early compulsory retirement, and had to make the most of it while she could. "Look, how about if we do it a bit longer, and if you still can't come perhaps we should leave it at that". That was fine by me, as long as I could get out of there alive. "Don't worry", she told me gently as she was getting dressed. "Sex is easy, once you learn to relax". "It is love that is difficult", she added with a sigh a moment later, as she grabbed her handbag and made for the door.

And by the time the assistant pimp had come in with a fresh towel and warm water pan and I was beginning to put my pants on, she was back in the street. Where I had to go next and face the music. Alone and full of unease in that room, I took a look through the curtain down towards the pavement below, looking wearily for my friends. The bully boy could get away with not having come, but not me. If I told them what had happened they would no longer believe I had done it before. They could tease me for weeks, and would certainly be watching the next time we went.

As I prepared to meet my fate, I knew it wasn't going to be easy. My mind kept racing, struggling in that drowning urgency, searching unsuccessfully for a believable way out. There was a narrow alley just a few feet to the left of the entrance. Perhaps I could sneak there unseen, and pretend to have lost them. They would never have believed it, but at that moment of intense pressure I toyed with the idea that it might perhaps work. And if that wasn't possible, I'd better put on a convincing show. The ordeal wasn't over yet.

I walked downstairs just out of the door and slyly shifted my eyes towards the left where the alley was, to see if the coast was clear, without moving my head in order not to give away my intentions. And then to the right to check whether I had been noticed, still considering a disappearing act. But they had seen the girl come out, and were almost right there waiting for me. "How was it?" they asked smiling from ear to ear. It was time for plan B. And the problem was I didn't have one. Catastrophe stared me in the eyes.

"Great!" I exclaimed in a fit of despair, flying by the seat of my pants. Smiling from ear to ear too, lifting my arms effusively into the air with my fists clenched. "Ohhhhh! ...., it was good!" "But the last one was even better". "Mmmm ..." I smacked my lips still savoring the experience, "I think I'll be trying a different one next time". Once the following few minutes of overexcited all round cock and bull storytelling were over, and the conversation drifted towards who was going to go next, it was clear that I had made it. I had been seen to have entered the doors of Heaven, and was now and for the rest of eternity a fully fledged member of the club.

We arrived back in the village well before midnight. And headed straight for our favorite hangout, behind the back wall of the old cemetery, to have the last cylinder of the day and let off some more excitement before going to sleep. As we made our way there we began singing one of our favorite tunes. And to enjoy in anticipation the frowning disapproval of the good God-fearing folk, who could hear us through their open windows in that warm summer night.

It was a catchy tune that half-rhymed in Spanish, which is why I still find myself humming it occasionally and internally smiling at the lyrics. Which together with the comically naughty-sounding name of the canary, conveyed a connotation of secondary school street-smartness. Reinforced as soon as the sexual undertone clicks in, a few seconds after it is heard for the first time. I include the original version, for the benefit of those who speak Spanish.

My girlfriend has a canary,
whose name is Quisquillete,
and underneath her apron,
she has a cage where he gets in.

Mi novia tiene un canario,
que se llama Quisquillete,
y debajo del delantal,
tiene una jaula y se mete.

Appendix B

THE JAPANESE CONNECTION:
Men's fascination with women's bottoms

Asking oneself what the London transport system could possibly have to do with my beginning to become rather partial to women's bottoms, would be a reasonable question. Well, it wasn't because of all the perving I was doing, while the enjoyably long mechanical stairs in the London underground placed them oh!-so-invitingly right in front of my eyes, on the way up.

Although it could have been and undoubtedly is for many, as this is one view we men are likely to become increasingly fond of with the passage of time. That of course, because we can keep endlessly appreciating its beauty and savoring the good feelings with minimal risk of offending sensitive souls, for obvious reasons.

But no, not in my case. Like every decent dirty young man about the place, I was very proper. Enjoyed the sightseeing discreetly, and went about my business without giving it another thought. OK, may be just the odd delightful thought or two, on exceptional occasions. We can't help ourselves from noticing and admiring. We confess, reluctantly, because we care about the feelings of the woman we love. We like it but we couldn't possibly love it, just as we couldn't love those erotic pictures our eyes are irresistibly drawn to.

Every savvy woman knows the male eye is always on duty. She knows it regardless of the well intentioned denials triggered by her questioning, which is not always warranted. And although even a savvy woman would prefer things to be different, she manages to accept that reality non-judgmentally, knowing full well it is the genetic inheritance of *men*kind.

Or more precisely, she manages to manage it, most of the time. Provided of course, that she knows her man loves her and is as discreet and tactful as *she* feels the situation requires, particularly in her company. And of course, no self respecting man would want it any other way.

No, it wasn't the perving that got me hooked. It was Michiko's beautiful bum. She was my Japanese girlfriend, who spoke about as little English as I did and attended the same classes. In central London everybody was from everywhere, and that language school was full of exotic possibilities.

Despite slaving all day as a waiter and kitchen hand, studying English most nights, and laying in bed exhausted the rest of the time, the pull of love was too strong. And unlike the women I would just look at, I had developed feelings for Michi. Her gentle oriental charm had touched me deep and brought to bloom all the sweetness in my heart, which had been previously suppressed by the straitjackets of traditional male upbringing.

We used to travel by underground to the room I rented. And late at night back to her place, where as an au-pair girl she minded the frequently empty house of a childless jet-set business couple. The husband preferred their au-pairs to be Japanese, because he found them so lovely and polite. It seemed his wife didn't feel threatened enough to object, and wanted to please him.

Michi's presence ensured burglars knew the house was occupied during their frequent absences. Other than that, her duties were looking after the cat and that formidable South American parrot, plus making sure they got along in reasonable terms. I found out about them the first time she took me there, when the owners were away. As she invited me towards the living room and I approached its entrance first, I was greeted by this amazingly powerful meow. "Wow!" I exclaimed. "Where is that tiger?"

Cats and I had always understood each other. It was during the worst of winter, while the village was snowed under and the puddles were frozen solid, that our growing kitten first began to find his way onto my bed. It wasn't long before I was encouraging him to settle in the coziest spot, between my belly and curled up knees, and there we would enjoy each other's cuddles and warmth.

"You haven't let the cat inside the bed, have you? I would hear my mother asking from her bedroom, ready to take matters into her own hands if I had. "No", I would reply trying to sound convincing, and then hold my breath listening for her reaction, to see whether it had worked.

We were good chums, my cat and I. Just like me, he recognized what my mother's tone of voice meant and kept still and silent too, knowing what was good for him. If the worst came to the worst there would be mostly noise, and he was likely to outrun the storm by escaping through a hole on a rotten board. Into the safety of his domain under the floor of the house, where he was lord and no mouse dared to tread. But it rarely came to that, and most times we got away with it. We knew our boss was a softie, and the risk was well worth it.

Michi's cat didn't strike me as a tiger when I saw him, licking its paw and minding his own catty business, while waiting for dinner to be served. On his own cozy soft blanket, in his own imported hand made cane basket near the electric fireplace. Which, of course, was permanently switched on during cold days for his majesty's comfort.

And while I stroked him and he purred, there came the same ear-bursting meow again, right behind me from the other side of the room. I turned around startled, as Michi burst into laughter. "Everybody falls for it", she told me as she kept laughing. Her laughter always filled my heart with joy, and we embraced tenderly.

It was the parrot who meowed the loudest, she explained. And according to the owners, who never missed an opportunity to tell the story to everyone they could, he had learned it while teasing the cat into a really bad mood. After all the poor parrot felt justifiably possessive, having done nothing wrong to deserve this kitten-come-lately usurping the attentions of his favorite lady. And between kisses and cuddles and bites of cake, and more kisses and cuddles and sips of coffee, we amused each other with the adventures of various pets and other stories, as we laughed and dreamt our evening away.

But let me come back to this underground thing. When we used to go down through the mechanical stairs I made sure Michi rode in the step above mine. For easier eye contact and out of good manners, of course, as she was a little shorter. And as we gazed adoringly into each other's eyes and the rest of the world faded away, I would embrace her comfortably and naturally from her bottom, which on her higher step was around the height of my waist.

We ended up liking it so much that sometimes when we got down I would smile nodding towards the stairs: "How about it?" And then we would retake the stairs all the way up, with her always riding the higher step, just to enjoy it all over again. It takes so little to be happy, when the feelings are right. Yes, I believe it was the sheer joy and magic of those loving bottom embraces that got me hooked. Or was it her beautiful eyes which did it, as our hearts melted while I just happened to be embracing her on her bottom? I am not sure and it doesn't matter. The point is that ever since I've never stopped being a bit partial to women's bottoms.

I had told her I'd been approved to come to Australia. But because our English was so poor, she thought I meant Austria. And assumed that whenever I happened to go, I would soon be back in London. When my departure time began to get closer and I brought up the subject again, she finally understood. Her pain added to mine, and then mine to hers. She was only nineteen, and Japanese culture at that time had not evolved yet to allow girls of that age to act independently. Her parents were most insistent that she returned to Tokyo, and were even talking about coming to London to pick her up.

I was a younger looking and very immature twenty two with little education or life experience, having left school on turning fifteen to start working as a child laborer, and except for the time as an army conscript lived my life within a poor village family. I had no idea of what Australia had in store for me or what I wanted to do with my life. She didn't have a visa to enter Australia. The whole prospect felt much too daunting.

Between the two of us, we weren't yet strong enough to win against the world. That last time we traveled from my room to her home, where we would share our final embrace, all of a sudden she begun crying uncontrollably. My boys-don't-cry façade couldn't hold for long. Soon my tears crashed through too, and we kept embracing and crying, kissing and crying, unable to stop. It didn't hurt any less, just because of our youth.

We must have been a sad sorrowful sight, so young, and so heartbroken. In that almost empty underground carriage I caught a glimpse of two ladies some seats away. The look in their faces said they understood, as their eyes quickly looked away respecting our pain and not wanting to intrude. And as I found myself travelling back, now completely alone in the carriage of that late train, I still couldn't stop crying.

I had kissed my darling Michi for the last time. I cried and cried, and then cried out loud. And squeezed my head between my hands as I pressed my eyelids hard, trying to push away the overpowering heartache. But the train kept taking me away from her, in the final journey to my room. That cheap rented room with shared facilities, where we had been so happy.

My alarm clock kept ticking during that sleepless night, indifferent to our grief, and the next morning I was on a plane bound for Sydney. We had come from very different worlds, and our lives were still too uncertain. Deep down we both knew we were too young, and that love alone wouldn't have been enough to make it work.

But that realization wasn't making it any easier, as my heart held out in a tight knot while the tears wanted to flow. "Are you all right? Can I get you something?" I looked to the flight attendant and felt that she was kind. "No, thank you", I said trying to put on a smile and look composed, "Don't worry, it is only heartache". But I knew it was more than that. I was heartbroken like I had never been during my adolescence, and it was hurting badly.

And as the cotton wool clouds and the big blue sea drifted below, I couldn't stop thinking about Michi. I knew she was hurting too, probably crying alone in her bed, while the image of her inconsolable tears in that train carriage kept replaying itself in my mind. We never thought about whether we were right for each other, while we shared our tender loving embraces. It was pure unadulterated young love. We loved just because we fell into it, without games or calculations. It was that simple, and it was that beautiful.

Michi and I were each other's first love to involve full sexual intimacy. It lasted many months and left a strong imprint. Although life separated us then, the sweetness and happiness we had shared were to warm my heart forever. Not as a fantasy ghost interfering with later relationships or erecting unreachable standards. But rather, as a cherished memory belonging to a very nice and more innocent stage of life.

The intense fulfillment of love accompanied by sexual intimacy and the subsequent heartbreak had been invaluable experiences. They are a part of growing up for most of us, and an important preparation to enter adulthood proper. .../...

Appendix C

PRESCRIPTION GLASSES CAN BE SEXY:
The formation and reshaping of sexual preferences

.../... There are strong natural selection influences in what men and women like, of course. But the "classical conditioning" effect (page 281) is also certain to be a significant player, in the formation and reshaping of sexual preferences. The classical conditioning effect does not kick in only in relation to body parts or sexy attire. And I know for a fact that all sorts of things may end up triggering sexual interest because it once happened to me, strange as it may sound, with prescription glasses.

When I was fifteen, you see, I met this most adorable girl with rather thick prescription glasses. It was during an open dance in a nearby village square, when the annual Patron Saint festivities were on. She treated me very kindly, and we danced lovingly all night long. While all the time groups of two or three miracle-loving elderly ladies watched from the sidelines, as they patrolled up and down never missing a beat.

They liked to burden themselves with the duty of keeping an eye on the morality of youth, while stubbornly refusing to let themselves enjoy their vicarious pleasures in order to smooth out their way to Heaven. "The young should have healthy joy" they believed, as the priest loved to remind his flock during the Sunday sermons, gorging himself in his own righteousness. While unconsciously feeding the catholic clergy's favorite obsession, forever fuelled by the unnatural suppression of their guilt ridden sexual urges.

We must have believed the priest too, because we kept dancing in the sort of manner which made us feel healthy and joyful. Overflowing with tenderness and sexual arousal, out of this world for all those wonderful hours which we wished would never end. With God squarely on their side however, the saintly dears must have thought of it as so scandalously immoral that they couldn't keep their eyes off us, no matter how hard we tried to hide right in the middle of the surrounding dancers.

We both knew she was going to be in trouble at home the following day. But she was feeling good too, and didn't care. And as I looked into her beautiful eyes through her thick glasses and felt the pull of intense attraction hitting me deep, I didn't care either if her imperfect eyesight had anything to do with that much beauty being so close to my heart.

It so happened that the newly married electrician from the factory where I worked had seen us too, while he looked on with his wife. "It was too much", he told me the following Monday in a tone of moral disapproval, as he kept swinging his head sideways "It was too much". Only the rebellious hint of a smile he couldn't quite suppress gave a clue about his other feelings. They were different times, those days. Young love was always a sin, and innocence was no extenuating circumstance.

By coincidence, the next girl who treated me very kindly while we danced a few months later also happened to be wearing prescription glasses. And for no reason at all, thereafter I began catching myself noticing that whenever there was a girl I fancied, I began thinking how much prettier she'd look if she was wearing prescription glasses. And when one of them did, I couldn't help feeling how good they made her look.

Prescription glasses were what I was hooked on, apart from all the other usual things. I remember it well because it lasted for years, although I thought at the time it was rather odd and didn't tell anybody. And strangely enough, it just didn't feel the same if they happened to be sunglasses. Even now when I see a woman I find attractive, sometimes certain prescription glasses can enhance rather than diminish her sex appeal.

Whatever it is that tickles us during the hormonal upsurge of adolescence and early adulthood, tends to leave a strong imprint. It is probably part of our genetic inheritance, for that previously blank area of our psyche to be programmed in this way. It may help shape sexual likes and dislikes for a long time, or for life. And in cases of gender preference gray areas, it could contribute towards tilting them to either side, or to both.

But when we are exposed to different and significant sexual experiences at any age, the classical conditioning effect may create new associations and reprogram us to like other things too. This can contribute to making us wiser and more relaxed about sex. And therefore better able to accept those aspects of our own and other people' sexuality which we might not have felt completely comfortable with, at younger and less well informed stages of life.
…/…

===================================

Qualifications and References

THE UNIVERSITY OF NEW SOUTH WALES
P.O. Box 1, KENGSINGTON, NSW, 2033 Australia.

19 October 1983   Ref: KPS: EK: B992/7

This is to certify that LUIS IPINAZAR attended the University in the years indicated

Year	Code	Subject	Grade
1978	15.701	Economic History 1A	DISTINCTION
	52.103	Introduction to Philosophy A	DISTINCTION
	53.103	Introduction to Contemporary Industrial Society	CREDIT
1979	53.104	Introduction to Social theory	HIGH DISTINCTION
	12.001	Psychology 1	HIGH DISTINCTION
	15.511	History 1B	DISTINCTION
	63.123	Australian Social Organization	HIGH DISTINCTION
1980	63.251	Social Welfare 1	DISTINCTION
	63.242	Social Philosophy 1	DISTINCTION
	63.272	Social Work Practice 1B	SATISFACTORY
	63.203	Human Behaviour 1	DISTINCTION
	63.213	Social and Behavioural Science	DISTINCTION
	63.263	Social Work Practice 1A	DISTINCTION
1981	63.341	Social Philosophy 2	CREDIT
	63.371	Social Work Practice 2B	SATISFACTORY
	63.332	Research Methods 1	DISTINCTION
	63.303	Human Behaviour 2	CREDIT
	63.353	Social Welfare 2	HIGH DISTINCTION
	63.363	Social Work Practice 2A	DISTINCTION
1982	63.431	Research Methods 2	DISTINCTION
	63.453	Social Welfare 3	DISTINCTION
	63.463	Social Work Practice 3A	HIGH DISTINCTION
	63.473	Social Work Practice 3B	SATISFACTORY
	63.483	The Social Work Profession	DISTINCTION

Admitted to the Degree of Bachelor of Social Work with Honours Class 1 on 6 May 1983

Subjects are graded: High Distinction - Outstanding performance (introduced 1964)
                     Distinction   - Superior performance
                     Credit   - Good performance
                     Pass   - Acceptable level of performance
                     Satisfactory   - Satisfactory completion of a subject for which graded passes are not available

(original signed by)

I.R. Way
REGISTRAR

THE UNIVERSITY OF NEW SOUTH WALES
P.O. BOX 1 • KENSINGTON • NEW SOUTH WALES • AUSTRALIA • 2033

Ph. 662.3711

Ref:KPS:EK:8992/7

This is to certify that

LUIS IPINAZAR

attended the University in the years indicated

1978	ARTS B.A.		
	FIRST SESSION		
	15.701	ECONOMIC HISTORY 1A - EUROPEAN ECONOMY AND SOCIETY TO 1800	DISTINCTION
	52.103	INTRODUCTORY PHILOSOPHY A	DISTINCTION
	53.103	INTRODUCTION TO CONTEMPORARY INDUSTRIAL SOCIETY	CREDIT
1979	SOCIAL WORK B.S.W.		
	SECOND SESSION		
	53.104	INTRODUCTION TO SOCIAL THEORY	HIGH DISTINCTION
	BOTH SESSIONS		
	12.001	PSYCHOLOGY 1	HIGH DISTINCTION
	51.511	HISTORY 1B - THE EMERGENCE OF MODERN EUROPE, 1500-C.1850	DISTINCTION
	63.123	AUSTRALIAN SOCIAL ORGANIZATION	HIGH DISTINCTION
1980	FIRST SESSION		
	63.251	SOCIAL WELFARE 1	DISTINCTION
	SECOND SESSION		
	63.242	SOCIAL PHILOSOPHY 1	DISTINCTION
	63.272	SOCIAL WORK PRACTICE 1B	SATISFACTORY
	BOTH SESSIONS		
	63.203	HUMAN BEHAVIOUR 1	DISTINCTION
	63.213	SOCIAL AND BEHAVIOURAL SCIENCE	DISTINCTION
	63.263	SOCIAL WORK PRACTICE 1A	DISTINCTION
1981	FIRST SESSION		
	63.341	SOCIAL PHILOSOPHY 2	CREDIT
	63.371	SOCIAL WORK PRACTICE 2B	SATISFACTORY
	SECOND SESSION		
	63.332	RESEARCH METHODS 1	DISTINCTION
	BOTH SESSIONS		
	63.303	HUMAN BEHAVIOUR 2	CREDIT
	63.353	SOCIAL WELFARE 2	HIGH DISTINCTION
	63.363	SOCIAL WORK PRACTICE 2A	DISTINCTION
1982	FIRST SESSION		
	63.431	RESEARCH METHODS 2	DISTINCTION
	BOTH SESSIONS		
	63.453	SOCIAL WELFARE 3	DISTINCTION
	63.463	SOCIAL WORK PRACTICE 3A	HIGH DISTINCTION
	63.473	SOCIAL WORK PRACTICE 3B	SATISFACTORY
	63.483	THE SOCIAL WORK PROFESSION	DISTINCTION

ADMITTED TO THE DEGREE OF BACHELOR OF SOCIAL WORK WITH HONOURS CLASS I ON 6 MAY 1983

No alterations or erasures

Dated: 19 October 1983

Subjects are graded:
High Distinction - Outstanding performance (introduced 1964)
Distinction - Superior performance
Credit - Good performance
Pass - Acceptable level of performance
Satisfactory - Satisfactory completion of a subject for which graded passes are not available

I.R. WAY
REGISTRAR

Industrial Program Service

SYDNEY
209 Castlereagh Street
2nd Floor (cnr. Bathurst St)
Sydney NSW 2000

6 November 1990

TO WHOM IT MAY CONCERN

I have known Luis Ipinazar since 1984 when he took up his present position at Caringbah Community Clinic. At the time I worked there as a Senior Clinical Psychologist and Team Leader with the Child and Family Team.

During 1984-85 Luis was a participant in the regular clinical skills/dynamics training sessions which I provided for my own team and for some workers from other centres. During this time I observed Luis' work with couples directly through a one-way screen, on occasions I was joined by other members of the Child and Family Team as part of the supervision process. These observed sessions took place at Luis' own request, for the purpose of improving his own clinical skills and getting feedback from the observers. In 1988, while I was Clinic Director, Luis made a presentation to all clinic staff on marital counselling.

In my opinion Luis is a highly skilled clinician in general, with particular expertise in work with couples. His clinical style is practical but reflects a good understanding of underlying dynamics. In his presentation he has the ability to combine clinical examples and theoretical concepts in a manner which is clear and convincing.

Yours sincerely

(original signed by)

Ray Miletic
Senior Clinical Psychologist   (Former Caringbah Clinic Director)
Counselling Services Manager

Ref: 2202

Employee Assistance Programs endorsed by the CAI, ACTU and ADFA.

Industrial Program Service

SYDNEY
209 Castlereagh Street
2nd Floor (cnr. Bathurst St.)
Sydney NSW 2000
Mail: Box A645
Sydney South
NSW 2000
☎ (02) 264 7488
Fax (02) 264 9046

WOLLONGONG
5th Floor AMP Centre
90 Crown Street
Wollongong NSW 2500
☎ (042) 24 5417
Fax (042) 24 5444

NEWCASTLE
2nd Floor
169-179 King Street
Newcastle NSW 2300
☎ (049) 26 4393

PARRAMATTA
Level 4
69 Phillip Street
Parramatta NSW 2150
☎ (02) 264 7488

6 November 1990

TO WHOM IT MAY CONCERN

I have known Luis Ipinazar since 1984 when he took up his present position at Caringbah Community Clinic. At the time I worked there as a Senior Clinical Psychologist and Team Leader with the Child and Family Team.

During 1984-85 Luis was a participant in the regular clinical skills/dynamics training sessions which I provided for my own team and for some workers from other centres. During this time I observed Luis' work with couples directly through a one-way screen, on occasions I was joined by other members of the Child and Family Team as part of the supervision process. These observed sessions took place at Luis' own request, for the purpose of improving his own clinical skills and getting feedback from the observers. In 1988, while I was Clinic Director, Luis made a presentation to all clinic staff on marital counselling.

In my opinion Luis is a highly skilled clinician in general, with particular expertise in work with couples. His clinical style is practical but reflects a good understanding of underlying dynamics. In his presentation he has the ability to combine clinical examples and theoretical concepts in a manner which is clear and convincing.

Yours sincerely

Ray Miletic
Senior Clinical Psychologist   (Former Caringbah Clinic Director)
Counselling Services Manager

Ref:2202

Employee Assistance Programs Endorsed by the CAI, ACTU & ADFA.

THE UNIVERSITY OF WOLLONGONG
Department of Psychology

23rd May, 1990

TO WHOM IT MAY CONCERN
Re: Luis Ipinazar

I have known Luis as a member of the Adult Mental Health Team at the Caringbah Community Clinic where I was a Senior Clinical Psychologist from August '85 to February '88. During this time I was the Clinical Supervisor to the Adult Team and the Drug and Alcohol Methadone Unit at Sutherland. Luis continues to be a member of this team at present. He participated in the clinical presentation at both these centres as part of my supervision sessions and made several useful contributions. He also formally presented cases and led discussion topics with enthusiasm. These were always appreciated by all the members of the group.

In my opinion, Luis has developed considerable clinical skills particularly in his chosen area of interest, namely, marital relationships. He presents cohesive arguments that reflect good background reading in the area and supports it well with case illustrations.

More recently, I understand he has had discussions with members of the Department of Social Work at the Universities of N.S.W. and Sydney with a view to introducing more clinical material in their undergraduate and postgraduate courses. These would be presented by senior clinicians from the field. Luis certainly shows a keen interest in improving professional standards which is to be commended.

As you can see, I feel that Luis has wide clinical and teaching skills which would be reflected in his professional role.

(original signed by)

Saroja Srinivasan
M.A., D.A.P. (Clin.), PhD., M.A.P.S., A.F.B.P.S.
Lecturer, Department of Psychology.

P.O. Box 1144 (Northfields Avenue), Wollongong, N.S.W. 2500, Australia.

THE UNIVERSITY OF WOLLONGONG
DEPARTMENT OF PSYCHOLOGY

23rd May, 1990

TO WHOM IT MAY CONCERN

Re: Luis Ipinazar

I have known Luis as a member of the Adult Mental Health Team at the Carringbah Community Clinic where I was a Senior Clinical Psychologist from August '85 to February '88. During this time I was the Clinical Supervisor to the Adult Team and the Drug and Alcohol Methadone Unit at Sutherland. Luis continues to be a member of this team at present. He participated in the clinical presentation at both these centres as part of my supervision sessions and made several useful contributions. He also formally presented cases and led discussion topics with enthusiasm. These were always appreciated by all the members of the group.

In my opinion, Luis has developed considerable clinical skills particularly in his chosen area of interest, namely, marital relationships. He presents cohesive arguments that reflect good background reading in the area and supports it well with case illustrations.

More recently, I understand he has had discussions with members of the Department of Social Work at the Universities of N.S.W. and Sydney with a view to introducing more clinical material in their undergraduate and postgraduate courses. These would be presented by senior clinicians from the field. Luis certainly shows a keen interest in improving professional standards which is to be commended.

As you can see, I feel that Luis has wide clinical and teaching skills which would be reflected in his professional role.

Saroja Srinivasan
M.A., D.A.P.(Clin.), Ph.D.,
M.A.P.S., AF.B.P.S.,
Lecturer,
Department of Psychology.

THE SUTHERLAND HOSPITAL CARINGBAH AND COMMUNITY HEALTH SERVICE
SOUTHERN SYDNEY AREA HEALTH SERVICE

Caringbah Community Clinic
126 Kareena Rd, Miranda NSW 2228

12th September, 1990

TO WHOM IT MAY CONCERN

Re: Luis Ipinazar

I have worked as a psychiatrist in the Health Commission of N.S.W. since November 1967, in community health since 1970, and in my present position with the Adult Mental Health Team at Caringbah Community Clinic for approximately the last twelve years. Luis joined this team in 1984 and since them we have often shared cases, had clinical discussions and observed each other's clinical presentations.

Luis' clinical work has always impressed me as particularly sound and his approach to it has been realistic and pragmatic, reflecting a solid and eclectic theoretical background. Of special value has been his contribution to, and availability as a consultant for problems in marriage and family, separation and sexuality, which are his areas of specialization.

It is also clear to me that Luis has read extensively in his own field, and that makes him valuable as a resource person. He has always been willing to locate and provide references and written material, whether it be of a technical nature or suitable for reading by our own clients.

(original signed by)

I. F. Godstein
M.B.BS., D.P.M., M.R.A.N.ZC.P.
PSYCHIATRIST

THE SUTHERLAND HOSPITAL CARINGBAH AND COMMUNITY HEALTH SERVICE
SOUTHERN SYDNEY AREA HEALTH SERVICE

Telephone: 525 6055

Caringbah Community Clinic
126 Kareena Road
Miranda NSW 2228

12th September, 1990

TO WHOM IT MAY CONCERN

Re: Luis Ipinazar

I have worked as a psychiatrist in the Health Commission of N.S.W. since November 1967, in community health since 1970, and in my present position with the Adult Mental Health Team at Caringbah Community Clinic for approximately the last twelve years. Luis joined this team in 1984 and since then we have often shared cases, had clinical discussions and observed each other's clinical presentations.

Luis' clinical work has always impressed me as particularly sound and his approach to it has been realistic and pragmatic, reflecting a solid and eclectic theoretical background. Of special value has been his contribution to, and availability as a consultant for problems in marriage and family, separation and sexuality, which are his areas of specialization.

It is also clear to me that Luis has read extensively in his own field, and that makes him valuable as a resource person. He has always been willing to locate and provide references and written material, whether it be of a technical nature or suitable for reading by our own clients.

I.F. GOLDSTEIN,
M.B.B.S., D.P.M., M.R.A.N.Z.C.P.
PSYCHIATRIST

THE SUTHERLAND HOSPITAL CARINGBAH AND COMMUNITY HEALTH SERVICE
SOUTHERN SYDNEY AREA HEALTH SERVICE

Caringbah Community Clinic
126 Kareena Rd, Miranda NSW 2228

*(undated, but written
in September 1990)*

TO WHOM IT MAY CONCERN

Luis Ipinazar has been known to me since he commenced employment as a Social Worker with the Adult Mental Health Team at Caringbah Community Health Centre in 1994.

My position on this team is Psychiatric Nurse/Welfare Officer, with over twenty five years experience in this field and thirteen and a half years in the team of which Luis is a member.

Over the years I have seen Luis become more specialized in marital and family work. He is considered by the team to be the expert in this area, and has built a reputation in Health and Welfare Agencies, as well as in the community, as having special expertise in relationship counselling.

Team members use Luis as a valued consultant with his knowledge and professionalism. He also acts as an educator to the team and other staff members by interesting and informative presentations.

Luis is a respected and well liked member of the team.

(original signed by)

Esther Penrose
PSYCHIATRIC NURSE
ADULT MENTAL HEALTH TEAM

THE SUTHERLAND HOSPITAL CARINGBAH
AND COMMUNITY HEALTH SERVICE
SOUTHERN SYDNEY AREA HEALTH SERVICE

Telephone: 525 6055

Caringbah Community Clinic
126 Kareena Road
Miranda NSW 2228

TO WHOM IT MAY CONCERN

Luis Ipinazar has been known to me since he commenced employment as a Social Worker with the Adult Mental Health Team at Caringbah Community Health Centre in 1984.

My position on this team is Psychiatric Nurse/Welfare Officer, with over 25 years experience in this field and thirteen and a half years in the team of which Luis is a member.

Over the years, I have seen Luis become more specialized in marital and family work. He is considered by the team to be the expert in this area, and has built a reputation in Health & Welfare Agencies, as well as the community, as having special expertise in relationship counselling.

Team members use Luis as a valued consultant with his knowledge and professionalism. He also acts as educator to the team and other staff members by interesting and informative presentations.

Luis is a respected and well liked member of the team.

Yours sincerely,

Esther E Penrose

Esther Penrose
PSYCHIATRIC NURSE
ADULT MENTAL HEALTH TEAM

SOUTHERN SYDNEY AREA HEALTH SERVICE COMPRISES THE PUBLIC HOSPITALS OF CANTERBURY, ST. GEORGE AND SUTHERLAND, ASSOCIATED COMMUNITY HEALTH SERVICES AND THE THIRD SCHEDULE HOSPITALS OF CALVARY AND GARRAWARRA

Max Cornwell B.A, B. Soc. Stud. (Hons.), Q.
Therapy with individuals, couples and families
Consultation, Teaching and Supervision

91 Pittwater Road
Boronia Park NSW 2111

9 May 1995

Dear Sir/Madam,

Mr Ipinazar was a student of mine at the school of Social Work, University of NSW in 1982 when he undertook the casework speciality in the final year Social Work Practice. He was intellectually outstanding and extremely conscientious. He was fluent in at least four languages. He was respected by other students and took a leadership role among his peers in a special project of mine at that time, which was the development of a teaching video tape on the use of interpreters in casework. This tape has since been well-received in a number of countries and, while I take full responsibility for the arguments it conveys, Mr Ipinazar was undoubtedly a significant contributor to its execution.

Mr Ipinazar had comfortably overcome the difficulties of being an overseas-born student and had a very high level of verbal and written skills that would have easily, along with his intellect, equipped him to complete successfully a Masters or Doctoral program. However, as is common with new graduates, he elected to immerse himself in professional practice in a service complex enough to offer him broad experience initially and then to develop areas of particular expertise. I have every reason to believe that he has been successful in achieving both those goals.

Recently I have read a substantial professional document of his which impresses with its high level of intellectual achievement and his capacity to mount and sustain complex argument and analyse a major area of contemporary Social Work Practice. The document offers a critique of present-day understandings in the area of domestic violence and offers constructive suggestions about how such practice may be improved.

Mr Ipinazar is a man capable of showing great commitment and determination. He is able to invest intense amounts of hard work and tenacity in achieving desired outcomes, not only in his work but in a range of personal interests.

(original signed by)

Max Cornwell
(Psychologist and Social Worker)
(Editor, ANZ Journal of Family Therapy)

Max Cornwell B.A., B.Soc.Stud.(Hons.).Q.
Therapy with individuals, couples and families
Consultation, Teaching and Supervision

P.O. Box B 98
Boronia Park NSW 2111

91 Pittwater Road
Boronia Park NSW 2111
(02) 879 6144

9 May 1995

Department of Defence
Naval Headquarters
Command Personnel Services

Dear Sir/Madam,

Mr Ipinazar was a student of mine at the School of Social Work, University of NSW in 1982 when he undertook the casework speciality in final year Social Work practice. He was intellectually outstanding and extremely conscientious. He was fluent in at least 4 languages. He was respected by other students and took a leadership role among his peers in a special project of mine at that time, which was the development of a teaching video tape on the use of interpreters in casework. This tape has since been well-received in a number of countries and, while I take full responsibility for the arguments it conveys, Mr Ipinazar was undoubtedly a significant contributor in its execution.

Mr Ipinazar had comfortably overcome the difficulties of being an overseas-born student and had a very high level of verbal and written skills that would have easily, along with his intellect, equipped him to complete successfully a Masters or Doctoral program. However, as is common among new graduates, he elected to immerse himself in professional practice in a service complex enough to offer him broad experience initially and then to develop areas of particular expertise. I have every reason to believe that he has been successful in achieving both these goals.

Recently I have read a substantial professional document of his which impresses with its high level of intellectual achievement and his capacity to mount and sustain complex argument and analyse a major area of contemporary Social Work practice. The document offers a critique of present-day understandings in the area of domestic violence and offers constructive suggestions about how such practice may be improved.

Mr Ipinazar is a man capable of showing great commitment and determination. He is able to invest intense amounts of hard work and tenacity in achieving desired outcomes, not only in his work but in a range of personal interests.

Max Cornwell
(Psychologist and Social Worker)
(Editor, ANZ Journal of Family Therapy)

THE UNIVERSITY OF NEW SOUTH WALES
P.O. Box 1, KENGSINGTON, NSW, 2033 Australia.

15 June 1993

TO WHOM IT MAY CONCERN

RE: LUIS IPINAZAR

On 18.2.93 Mr Ipinazar presented a one-day workshop named Communication in Adult Intimate Relationships, as part of the 1993 Summer Studies Program. This program was developed and is run jointly by the School of Social Work from the University of New South Wales and the Department of Social Work from the University of Sydney, with the cooperation of the Australian Association of Social Workers. The first half of the workshop dealt with average and difficult couples. The second half dealt with very difficult couples where one or both partners have clinical levels of "narcissistic vulnerability", more commonly referred to in psychiatric terminology under the general category of "borderline personality disorders".

There were sixteen participants, all of them professional counsellors. Each participant filled the standard anonymous evaluation form plus a second anonymous evaluation form supplied by Mr Ipinazar, and all the forms were collected by me at the end of the workshop. Nearly all the participants described the presentation as "very interesting", the actual material as "very useful" and the workshop as a whole as "one of the best they've ever attended". Many participants added side comments indicating they found the presenter enthusiastic and able to maintain their attention throughout the six face-to-face hours, and that the workshop would be better if extended into a two-day one. A sample of each evaluation form is attached.

Yours faithfully

(original signed by)

Peter Miller-Robinson
Program Coordinator, 1993 Summer Studies Program
School of Social Work, University of New South Wales

THE UNIVERSITY OF NEW SOUTH WALES

P.O. BOX 1 • KENSINGTON • NEW SOUTH WALES 2033 • AUSTRALIA
TELEX AA26054 • FACSIMILE (02) 662 8991 • TELEPHONE (02) 697 2222
EXTN 4745

PLEASE QUOTE

SCHOOL OF SOCIAL WORK

15 June 1993

TO WHOM IT MAY CONCERN

RE: LUIS IPINAZAR

On 18.2.93 Mr Ipinazar presented a one-day workshop named Communication in Adult Intimate Relationships, as part of the 1993 Summer Studies Program. This program was developed and is run jointly by the School of Social Work from the University of new South Wales and the Department of Social Works from the University of Sydney, with the cooperation of the Australian Association of Social Workers. The first half of the workshop dealt with average and difficult couples. The second half dealt with very difficult couples where one or both partners have clinical levels of "narcissistic vulnerability", more commonly referred to in psychiatric terminology under the general category of "borderline personality disorders".

There were sixteen participants, all of them professional counsellors. Each participant filled the standard anonymous evaluation form plus a second anonymous evaluation from supplied by Mr Ipinazar, and all the forms were collected by me at the end of the workshop. Nearly all the participants described the presentation as "very interesting", the actual material as "very useful" and the workshop as a whole as "one of the best they've ever attended". Many participants added side comments indicating that they found the presenter enthusiastic and able to maintain their attention throughout the six face-to-face hours, and that the workshop would be better if extended into a two-day one. A sample of each evaluation form is attached.

Yours faithfully

Peter Miller-Robinson
Program Coordinator
1993 Summer Studies Program
School of Social Work
University of New South Wales

THE SUTHERLAND HOSPITAL CARINGBAH AND COMMUNITY HEALTH SERVICE
SOUTHERN SYDNEY AREA HEALTH SERVICE

Caringbah Community Clinic
126 Kareena Rd, Miranda NSW 2228

19 May 1992

EVALUATION OF THE IMPLEMENTATION AND OUTCOMES OF THE MARITAL COMMUNICATION COURSE DEVELOPED AND RUN BY LUIS IPINAZAR, SOCIAL WORKER, IN 1991-1992.

In mid 1991 Luis organized a meeting attended by the social worker running the Domestic Violence Group, another senior social worker, myself as Team Leader and himself. The purpose was to discuss the appropriateness of the course he was developing and to ensure it followed guidelines by the National Committee on Violence Against Women. I understand Luis also had a substantial discussion on the same subject with the local Senior Health Promotion Officer, Natalie Baig, to keep the course in accordance with Health Promotion Planning Guidelines.

The course was run in three sessions, on 20.11.91, 27.11.91 and 4.12 91. A sample of each session's anonymous evaluation form is attached and they are included in a Group file. These forms were filled at the end of the sessions, which were also attended by two workers from the team, at Luis' request for the purpose of providing feedback. Their feedback to Luis and myself was that the course was very good and clients found it very useful. Nearly all the client evaluation forms described Luis' presentation style as "good" or "excellent" and the material in the sessions as "very useful" or "extremely useful".

There was also a four month follow up anonymous client evaluation survey, a sample of which is attached. Nearly all the respondents said they found the course "very useful" or "extremely useful", and all of them said they would recommend the course to a friend and would now feel comfortable seeking counselling if their marriage was in trouble. All twelve clients signed for attendance in every session, and the record is included in a group file.

(original signed by)

VAL GILMORE
TEAM LEADER
ADULT AND FAMILY MENTAL HEALTH TEAM

SUTHERLAND HOSPITAL CARINGBAH AND COMMUNITY HEALTH SERVICE
SOUTHERN SYDNEY AREA HEALTH SERVICE

Telephone: 525 6055

Caringbah Community Health Centre
126 Kareena Road
Miranda NSW 2228

19 May 1992

EVALUATION OF THE IMPLEMENTATION AND OUTCOMES OF THE MARITAL COMMUNICATION COURSE DEVELOPED AND RUN BY LUIS IPINAZAR, SOCIAL WORKER, IN 1991-1992.

In mid 1991 Luis organised a meeting attended by the social worker running the Domestic Violence Group, another senior social worker, myself as Team Leader and himself. The purpose was to discuss the appropriateness of the course he was developing and to ensure that it followed guidelines by the National Committee on Violence Against Women. I understand Luis also had a substantial discussion on the same subject with the local Senior Health Promotion Officer, Natalie Baig, to keep the course in accordance with Health Promotion Planning Guidelines.

The course was run in three sessions, on 20.11.91, 27.11.91 and 4.12 91. A sample of each session's anonymous client evaluation form is attached and they are included in a Group File. These forms were filled at the end of the sessions, which were also attended by two workers from the team, at Luis' request for the purpose of providing feedback. Their feedback to Luis and myself was that the course was very good and clients found it very useful. Nearly all the client evaluation forms described Luis' presentation style as "good" or "excellent" and the material in the sessions as "very useful" or "extremely useful".

There was also a four month follow up anonymous client evaluation survey, a sample of which is attached. Nearly all the respondents said they found the course "very useful" or "extremely useful", and all of them said they would recommend the course to a friend and would now feel comfortable seeking counselling if their marriage was in trouble. All twelve clients signed for attendance in every session, and the record is included in a Group File.

V. Gilmore

VAL GILMORE
TEAM LEADER
ADULT AND FAMILY MENTAL HEALTH TEAM

LEICHHARDT WOMEN'S COMMUNITY HEALTH CENTRE
55 THORNLEIGH STREET, LEICHHARDT NSW 2040

26 of February, 1991.

TO WHOM IT MAY CONCERN

This is to certify that Luis Ipinazar has acted as consultant to me in the course of my work as the Spanish Community Health Worker at the Leichhardt Women's Community Health Centre.

As the Spanish speaking worker I see, either in counselling, groups or through my contact with other Spanish speaking workers or agencies a fair amount of Spanish clients. When issues of marriage or problems in couple relationships arise I often consult Luis to discuss the cases with him. Also when a woman expresses her need or willingness to undertake marriage counselling, if appropriate because of language or area, I would refer to him.

I have maintained professional contact with Luis since 1984, when I took my position at Leichhardt Women's Community Health Centre, and he has demonstrated his willingness to collaborate with and support our Centre when his assistance was requested.

I consider Luis' experience and knowledge in the relationship field an invaluable asset which I may resource when necessary.

Yours faithfully,

(original signed by)

Silvia Olona
Spanish Health Worker

26 of February, 1991.

TO WHOM IT MAY CONCERN

This is to certify that Luis Ipanazar has acted as consultant to me in the course of my work as the Spanish Community Health Worker at the Leichhardt Women's Community Health Centre.

As the Spanish speaking worker I see, either in counselling, groups or through my contact with other spanish speaking workers or agencies a fair amount of spanish clients. When issues of marriage or problems in couple relationships arise I often consut Luis to discuss the cases with him. Also when a woman expresses her need or willingness to undertake marriage counselling, if appropriate either because of language or area, I would refer to him.

I have maintained professional contact with Luis since 1984, when I took my position at Leichhardt Women's Community Health Centre, and he has demonstrated his willingness to collaborate with and support our Centre when his assistance was requested.

I considerer Luis' experience and knowledge in the relationship field an invaluable asset which I may resource when necessary.

Yours faithfully,

Silvia Olona
Spanish Health Worker

Lucy's Out West Single Women's Refuge
P.O. Box 438, Mt Druitt, 2770.

22nd, February 1991.

TO WHOM IT MAY CONCERN

This letter is to certify that I have known Luis Ipinazar for the last three years, while I have been working at Lucy's Women's Refuge as a Spanish speaking worker.

Most of the women who come here are escaping from domestic violence situations and we provide them with a secure place during the crisis. Sometimes these women want to go back to their husbands, but they also want advice on how to deal with some of the problems they have with them.

It is in these cases that I have found very useful to be able to consult with Mr. Ipinazar, whom I know has been working in the field for many years and whose advice I have found useful and to the point. Through my discussions with Mr. Ipinazar I have developed some of my knowledge on these matters and I still find very helpful to know he is available for consultation when I need it, which is something he has always done willingly.

(original signed by)

MIRIAM MARQUEZ
Spanish Speaking Refuge Worker

Lucy's Out West Single P's Refuge.

P.O. BOX 438, MT DRUITT, 2770.

PHONE: 6751657

22nd, February 1991.

TO WHOM IT MAY CONCERN

This letter is to certify that I have known LUIS IPINAZAR for the last three years, while I have been working at Lucy's Women's Refuge as a Spanish speaking worker.

Most of the women who come here are escaping from domestic violence situations and we provide them with a secure place during the crisis. Sometimes these women want to go back to their husbands, but they also want advice on how to deal with some of the problems they have with them.

It is in these cases that I have found very useful to be able to consult with Mr. Ipinazar, whom I know has been working in the field for many years and whose advice I have found useful and to the point. Through my discussions with Mr. Ipinazar I have developed some of my knowledge on these matters and I still find very helpful to know he is available for consultation when I need it, which is something he has always done willingly.

MIRIAM MARQUEZ
Spanish Speaking Refuge Worker.

www.ingramcontent.com/pod-product-compliance
Lightning Source LLC
Chambersburg PA
CBHW032303300426
44110CB00033B/279